Mussolini's Children

Mussolini's Children

Race and
Elementary
Education in
Fascist Italy

Eden K. McLean

University of Nebraska Press

Lincoln & London

Portions of the introduction and chapters 1 and 2 have
previously appeared in "The Rhetoric of Race in Fascist
Elementary Education," in *New Perspectives in Italian Cultural
Studies*, vol. 2, *The Arts and History*, ed. Graziella Parati
(Madison and Teaneck NJ: Fairleigh Dickinson University
Press, 2013), 265–84. Used with permission.

Library of Congress Cataloging-in-Publication Data
Names: McLean, Eden K., author.
Title: Mussolini's children: race and elementary education in
Fascist Italy / Eden K. McLean.
Description: Lincoln: University of Nebraska Press, 2018. |
Includes bibliographical references and index.
Identifiers: LCCN 2017043090
ISBN 9781496206428 (cloth: alk. paper)
ISBN 9781496207203 (epub)
ISBN 9781496207210 (mobi)
ISBN 9781496207227 (pdf)
Subjects: LCSH: Fascism and education—Italy. | Fascism—
Italy—History—20th century. | Fascism and youth—Italy—
History—20th century. | Italy—Race relations.
Classification: LCC LA791.8 .M35 2018 | DDC 372.94509/041—dc23
LC record available at https://lccn.loc.gov/2017043090

Set in Sabon Next LT by Mikala R Kolander.

For Malcolm

CONTENTS

ILLUSTRATIONS

Following page 154

ACKNOWLEDGMENTS

I only realized the complexity of my research ambition during a dinner with an Italian politician of impeccable anti-Fascist pedigree. I had recently arrived in Rome for a year of dissertation research and hoped my idealism and curiosity made up for a distinct lack of archival experience. When the gentleman in his three-piece suit asked me for the focus of my research, I simply and guilelessly stated, "Fascist racism." He pondered this information for a moment and then responded, "Well, that is interesting, because the Fascists were not racist." I made some early attempts to explain my approach, but it was soon clear that we had very different views of race and racism. My host explained, "Italians cannot be racist, because there is not just one race in Italy." When I then suggested that his assertion indicated a belief in the existence of races, he looked at me blankly. "*Come no?* Of course races exist." I tried to articulate the problem behind any biological notion of race, and he soon conceded, "Okay, maybe there are no biologically pure races, but certainly there are races based on history, culture, and language." And with that explanation, I saw both the challenge and the necessity of a project on Italian ideas of race during the Fascist years.

I dreamed of writing a book based on sources no one had ever seen, on documents that automatically changed the way I and everyone else understood the power and limitations of Italian Fascism. Instead, I wrote a book that relies on evidence accessible to and read by millions of people and that tackles what most readers will agree is a contentious topic. The distance between there and here has been long and hardly linear.

What did not change over the course of that decade-long journey were my entwined convictions that we must not ignore the power of ideas and that racism played a fundamental role in Italian Fascism. Along the way, I have relied on innumerable people to help me navigate the difficulties of exploring a delicate subject from a new perspective and develop the skills, questions, and friendships necessary to enjoy the adventure. I know I cannot take full credit for whatever strengths this book might have. All its faults, however, are entirely my own.

As with any project that starts in the mind of a naïve graduate student and eventually turns into a book, I could not have completed *Mussolini's Children* without the patient and persistent work of many graduate mentors and colleagues. I must first thank Frank Snowden for the guidance and friendship he has shown me since I arrived in Yale's Department of History over a decade ago. During my time in New Haven, he often anticipated my needs before I knew they existed: he pushed me to explore ideas or avenues when I felt I went far enough; he suggested sources, contacts, or opportunities before I had a chance to ask for them; he expressed concerns when I focused too narrowly or too broadly on a subject; and he always had advice for how to improve. Even still, half a continent (or farther) away and with a very full schedule, Frank is never too busy to read a draft or lend an ear. I owe so much of my growth as a scholar and a teacher to Frank and hope he knows how dear he is to me.

I also owe many thanks to my other generous graduate-school mentors. Both Tim Snyder and Mark Choate read numerous drafts from out of state and country, and I very much appreciate their continued support. John Merriman and Adam Tooze also read various chapters and gave invaluable suggestions for further reading and clarification. Penny Marcus, too, offered her endless enthusiasm for the project, and Ute Frevert generously shared friendship, knowledge, and martinis with her neighbor. I also had the distinct pleasure of sharing my work with two writing groups in New Haven. Julia Irwin, Grace Leslie-Waksman, and Alison Greene, as well as Sarah Cameron, Lisa Pinley Covert, and Yedida Kanfer, offered their detailed readings and broad knowledge to expand and clarify my writing and thinking. Of course, there were many other graduate-school friends who offered food, dog care, and other forms of support while we worked to figure out the strange world of academia. Kirsten Weld, Steve Prince, Jason Ward, Marco Duranti, Sam and Dana Schaffer, Megan and Sylvan Long, and the Sacks-Huether family—I am forever grateful to and for you all.

The end of graduate school can sometimes leave a young scholar feeling a little unmoored, but I have been fortunate enough to find warm and supportive communities within my departments at Western Connecticut State University and Auburn University, and at a variety of conferences and archives. Since arriving at Auburn in 2012, I have felt the encouragement and confidence of all my colleagues and am constantly impressed by how thoughtful and smart they are. Ralph Kingston read early (atrocious) new chapter drafts and provided me with profoundly helpful feedback. Christopher Ferguson, too, has read a variety of rough-hewn pieces and, just as importantly, has served as an intellectual coach and cheerleader. The members of the "cul-de-sac"—Sarah Hamilton, Kate Craig, Alan Meyer, Kelly Kennington, and Melissa Blair—have sustained me with their humor, kindness, and deep supply of word suggestions. Ken Noe and Donna Bohanan, despite their busy schedules, have consistently been sources of wisdom and support for me. And then there's David Carter, who has been an irreplaceable mentor, editor, ally, therapist, babysitter, and colleague to me. I was so grateful to find family here in Auburn. I have also benefited from the generosity and intellects of Joshua Arthurs, Alessandro Pes, Valeria Deplano, Tommaso Dell'Era, and Erica Moretti, each of whom has provided vital feedback and encouragement for this project. I so appreciate all your help.

I scoured many libraries, archives, personal collections, and flea markets for the sources included in the following pages. In Rome, the staffs at the Archivio centrale dello stato and Fondazione Giovanni Gentile were extremely helpful in my months of research, as were the librarians at the Biblioteca della storia moderna e contemporanea, Biblioteca Giustino Fortunato, Biblioteca nazionale, Ministero dell'istruzione, dell'Università e della ricerca, and the American Academy. The archivists in the library at the Museo della storia della didattica were especially accommodating, sharing with me books and documents from their personal libraries. In Florence, the librarians in the rare-book room at the Biblioteca nazionale were thoughtful and pleasant, as were the librarians at the Biblioteca Marciana in Venice. In the United States, the staffs at the Hoover Institution at Stanford University and the archives at the University of Wisconsin–Madison made my brief stays fruitful and enjoyable.

A special word of appreciation is due to the Wolfsonian Museum in Miami Beach, Florida. With one of its generous grants, I spent five weeks at the Wolfsonian during the summer of 2009. Containing the largest collection of Italian Fascist artifacts and books outside of Italy, the resources and expertise of the library and museum were essential to my project. The kind help of Jon Mogul, Amy Silverman, Nicholas Blaga, and Frank Luca made for an especially productive month of research.

Financial support from numerous other institutions was also critical to the completion of this project. Fellowships from the U.S.-Italy Fulbright Commission, Yale University's MacMillan Center, John M. Olin Foundation, Smith Richardson Foundation, and George Frederick Jewett Foundation, as well as the Ganzfried Fellowship and the Birgit Baldwin Scholarship, all made it possible to conduct research in Italy over three summers and the 2007–8 academic year, as well as to spend a year exclusively writing my dissertation. Subsequent grants from Western Connecticut State University and Auburn University's College of Liberal Arts allowed me to conduct additional research for the book in the summers of 2011 and 2013.

Finally, I am forever indebted to my family for its unconditional love and support. Whether reading proposals and chapters, listening to preliminary ideas, driving hours to see lectures and talks, taking on the bulk of childcare, or offering much needed perspective, I owe so much to Karin Knudsen, the Bellons, and the McLeans. Malcolm, you especially have made this book possible. Your patience and incisive analytical skills consistently buoyed the project. Anticipating family dance parties and three-course meals at the end of the day hastened its completion. You, Sofie, and Ronan are in every page of this book.

ANIMI   Associazione nazionale per gli interessi del mezzogiorno d'Italia (National Association for the Interests of Southern Italy)

CRIG   Croce rossa italiana giovanile (Junior Italian Red Cross)

ENEF   Ente nazionale per l'educazione fisica (National Organization for Physical Education)

ERR   Ente radio rurale (Rural Radio Corporation)

GIL   Gioventù italiana del littorio (Italian Youth of the Lictor)

MEN   Ministero dell'educazione nazionale (Ministry of National Education)

MPI   Ministero della pubblica istruzione (Ministry of Public Instruction)

ONB   Opera nazionale balilla (National Balilla Organization)

ONMI   Opera nazionale della maternità e dell'infanzia (National Organization for the Protection of Mothers and Children)

PNF   Partito nazionale fascista (National Fascist Party)

Mussolini's Children

Introduction

According to Benito Mussolini's Fascist hagiography, his mother, Rosa, served as an elementary school teacher—"the most noble calling then available to women"—in the small village of Dovia, Emilia Romagna.[1] The boy's father, Alessandro, was the local blacksmith.[2] Seeing great intelligence in their eldest child, the story continues, Rosa and Alessandro urged Benito to become a teacher. And as a good son, he listened to his parents, trained for the profession, and spent his first year out of school (1901–2) as an elementary teacher in the small town of Gualticri, about one hundred miles from his family. The ambitious new teacher aimed to mold "the men of tomorrow" through his work in the school and community.[3] He understood the "nobility of the work he had undertaken—even if it was humble, unappreciated, and undervalued—and determined to carry it out as honorably as possible."[4] And yet by springtime of that year, Mussolini was restless, knowing that his lessons were meant to reach far more than the youth of Gualtieri. He did "not want, nor have the right, to stop his journey"; no, he had "the obligation to follow his path to the very end without hesitation."[5] Such determination would benefit the future Duce, and clearly he felt that it was one of the most important qualities he could instill in his young wards. His parting words to them—as he relayed in his so-called autobiography—would become a common refrain for the Fascist leader: "You arrive by persevering."[6]

We do not know how effective Mussolini was in his brief career as a teacher, but it is certain that his identification as the son of a schoolmistress and as a professional educator served a valuable purpose for the coming Fascist Revolution.[7] The Duce and his supporters frequently used his connections to the classroom and the concept of the teacher to characterize Mussolini's role within the nation and Fascism. Just as young Mussolini had dreamed of using the tools of the classroom to develop the morals and intellect of Gualtieri's "men of tomorrow," the Duce determined to undertake a project of *bonifica umana* (human reclamation) to save Italians from the corrupting forces of their past and forge their race into its ideal form— the New Italians of a New Italy.[8] Employing the infrastructure of elementary education and the language of racial superiority, Mussolini and his Fascist state aimed to educate new, stronger generations of Italians who could resurrect an empire for Rome.[9]

This mission to rejuvenate the Italian race depended on the simultaneous beliefs that the Italian population did indeed constitute a distinct race and that certain aspects of its moral and physical makeup could be influenced during childhood. In turn, the Fascist state believed that a campaign of bonifica umana targeting children would ultimately protect and strengthen the race as a whole. Consequently, from its earliest days in power, Mussolini's regime developed an increasingly totalitarian education system that worked in tandem with— and lay at the heart of—a comprehensive and ever more exclusionary racial campaign. In order for Italians to best fulfill their racial potential, they needed to be informed of their collective superiority, political and economic entitlement, and essential ability to strengthen their innate characteristics of *italianità* (Italianness). And while all Italians needed to embody the Fascist racial ideal, elementary school students were to serve as the transmitters of these lessons to the adult population. Mussolini's children held the keys to the future of the Italian race.

This book uses modern understandings of race and biopolitics and the lens of state-mandated youth culture—elementary education and the auxiliary organizations designed to mold the minds and bodies of Italy's children between the ages of five and eleven—to explore and understand the evolution of official Fascist racism.[10] Evidence collected from elementary textbooks, pedagogical journals, state policies, and other educational materials proves that racism was always a central tenet of the Fascist project to create New Italians. As a result, this study explains how the most infamous period of Fascist racism, which began in the summer of 1938 with the publication of the Manifesto of Race, while absolutely not inevitable, played a critical part in a more general and longer-term Fascist racial program. More profoundly, this book's concrete examples from one of the twentieth century's most influential political experiments reveal the intricate layers of definition and identification that compose the ideas of race and racism.

Considering the ease with which Westerners use the terms race and racism, one might assume that their definitions were firm and universal; certainly there are aspects of each that come to most minds when asked to elaborate on meaning, which is why these same words do emerge in myriad national contexts, languages, and historical periods. And yet their substance ultimately proves to be quite malleable, somewhat reflecting the particularities of those specific contexts, languages, and periods but also revealing the complexities of the terms themselves. So before diving into the specific nature of Fascist racism, it is critical to discuss definitions of race and racism that embrace their history as well as their current uses. Only then can we appreciate the power of Fascist racism and, more generally, the full implications of the words in the development of modern national and ethnic identities across the globe.[11]

The debate over when the concepts of race and racism first developed remains an active one. The word *race* has been detected in languages for millennia, but a majority of scholars argue that its popular understanding as a category of identification based on biological attributes is quite modern.[12] Undoubtedly many premodern instances of the term *race* had the more fluid meaning of "a group of people" with dubious claims to common biological decent. Additionally, numerous historians have argued that the premise for ancient and medieval instances of collective persecution that might resemble racism was more consistently defined by religious or cultural differences and certainly did not carry the moral baggage of modern racism.[13] However, more-recent attempts to understand the historical nature

of race and racism have found more than superficial commonalities among premodern and modern attempts to create hierarchies of peoples—and to discriminate actively according to
such hierarchies—based on physical and cultural characteristics that were generally considered immutable.[14]

It is the idea of the inheritability—and general inalterabili-
ty—of certain human characteristics on which modern Western
racial studies have pivoted. The study of the systematic categorization of population groups based on supposedly inherited characteristics blossomed within the greater context of the
Enlightenment and its *philosophes'* desire to classify and explain
the natural world through scientific principles. Eighteenth-
century scholars ostensibly sought objective explanations for
physical variances among human societies.[15] Thus, the Enlightenment concept of race—what is generally considered the foundation of modern racial theory—was couched in the supposedly
impartial, scientific language of biology in order to rationalize
the differences among human groups and ultimately articulate why human societies exhibited divergent patterns of set-
tlement and thinking.[16]

Yet as scholars over the last half century have pointed out,
Enlightenment racial science was motivated by moral evalua-
tion as much as by observation and description; from the start,
scientific measurements made in the pursuit of racial theory
were laden with cultural and political meaning, especially in
consideration of Europe's increasing interaction with peoples
around the globe.[17] George L. Mosse explained that the "observations, measurements, and comparisons that were basic to the
new eighteenth-century sciences were combined with value
judgments following aesthetic criteria derived from ancient
Greece. Whatever the physical measurements or comparisons
made, in the last resort the resemblance to ancient beauty and
proportions determined the value of man."[18] In practical terms,
this collaboration meant that the closer a population mirrored
the aesthetic and cultural attributes of what most Europeans
considered the founders of Western civilization, the more "developed" scientists determined them to be. That is, this classification of peoples was not merely for scientific purposes but

was rather used to create a hierarchy of peoples based on the assumed superiority of those who most closely echoed the values of ancient Greek (and Roman) civilization.

What also resulted from this confusion of science and values was not a clarification of the origins of human difference, as had been anticipated, but an increasingly complex conversation about the extent to which the human character and form was inherited. Despite the plethora of anthropological, biological, and philosophical studies grappling with this question, historically there has been little consensus.[19] Still, a vast majority of racial theorists in the eighteenth, nineteenth, and early twentieth centuries argued for a broad definition of inherited attributes (either from the dawn or time or over generations of environmental evolution) that blurred the lines between culture and biology. This broader understanding of inheritance would become essential to Fascist rhetoric about the Italian race.

Further muddying the waters were the political and cultural demands of nationalism as it developed in the eighteenth and nineteenth centuries. As nationalists from across Europe struggled to define nations based on the supposedly common cultural, linguistic, and historical characteristics of their members, they often employed the language of contemporary racial thought.[20] To declare biological the features that unified a nation of people—including appearance but also language, behavior, and history—was to further legitimize claims to political unity and collective superiority. In turn, individuals and groups who did not personify this newly determined collective identity of the national community increasingly became objects of discrimination, particularly as European imperialism entered a new era in the nineteenth century.[21] This statement does not mean to imply that all forms of nationalism are forms of racism, but the influence of nationalism on the evolution of modern racism is undeniable and would become readily apparent in the case of Fascist racism.[22]

Ultimately, then, the notion of race, and its corollary of racism, has evolved over the modern period to adapt to scientific, political, and cultural demands; any presumed scientific foundation of modern racial theory collapses under close scrutiny, as is especially clear when considering the development of racial anti-Semitism in the late nineteenth century. Rarely before then were Jews ever attributed with specific physical character-istics; instead, their claimed differences were largely composed of behavior and language.[23] In other words, supposedly biolog-ical characteristics largely reduce to social, political, and cul-tural factors.[24] As the scholar David Theo Goldberg has argued, "racism is found to be a function of the fashions of racial for-mation in given socio-temporal conditions."[25] In other words, the definitions of racial categories most dominantly reflect their historical moment and cultural context. Thus, a broader but more nuanced understanding of race is required to illumi-nate its full significance. Drawing on the language of the his-torian Matthew Frye Jacobson, the most useful explanation of race—one that works with the multitude of historical and cul-tural permutations—articulates it as an invented category char-acterized by allegedly heritable attributes "coined for the sake of separating peoples along lines of presumed difference."[26] In turn, racism could be expressed as the privileging of one cate-gory of people—defined by presumed inherited differences—over other categories of peoples, resulting in the discrimination against and persecution of those unprivileged categories. Armed with these definitions, a look at Fascist rhetoric clearly shows how the regime described (and worked to improve) the Ital-ian population as a group favored by an apparently biological, cultural, and historical inheritance—italianità—which gave legitimacy to a set of increasingly aggressive and discrimina-tory policies and actions against its enemies.

As a study of this interwar racial ideology, *Mussolini's Chil-dren* must take into account a well-established historiography that wrestles with Italy's relationship to the Holocaust and the ideas that helped perpetuate it. A majority of the related schol-arship has focused on anti-Semitism during the Fascist years, and in particular the period between 1938 and 1943.[27] This atten-tion clearly responds to the essential role anti-Semitism played in the racism of Nazi Germany and of interwar Europe more generally. It is also a reaction to the stark contrast between the participation and support of a number of Jewish Italians in the

Fascist movement and party starting in 1919—something that never took place in Germany's Nazi movement and party— and the passage of strict anti-Semitic legislation after the summer of 1938.[28] A significant shift in Fascist racial policy certainly did take place in 1938, and the racial laws after that date remain the most obvious manifestation of Mussolini's racism. Still, the overwhelming focus of the historiography on the post-1938 period is built on the problematic convictions that anti-Semitism previously had little value in Mussolini's Italy and, more generally, that racism was quite foreign to the modern Italian nation-state.[29] And while there were significant differences between Nazi and Fascist racism, this book follows in the footsteps of research conducted in the last two decades that shows how anti-Semitism was in fact quite present in the worldviews of Mussolini and many of his followers throughout the regime's twenty-one-year tenure; Fascist anti-Semitism did not appear out of thin air in 1938, even if it did not play the same role as it did for the Nazi regime.[30] Moreover, David Kertzer has convincingly argued that the long history of Catholic anti-Judaism and anti-Semitism necessarily left its mark on modern Italy and the Fascist regime, illustrating that Fascist anti-Semitism absolutely did not arise in a vacuum.[31]

Furthermore, while legal anti-Semitism was the most notorious outcome of the 1938 legislation, it was applied under much broader declarations of Italian racial discrimination, indicating that this anti-Semitism was part of a much larger network of ideas, policies, and actions regarding the Italian race and nation-state. Accordingly, some historians have justly argued that any discussion of Fascist racism must contend with Italy's colonial experience. A portion of these scholars has accepted Mussolini's own explanation that the post-1938 domestic racial laws were a direct reflection of colonial race laws enacted in Italian East Africa after 1936.[32] Since the mid-1990s, however, more scholars of Italian colonialism have worked to expose the violent racism that characterized Fascist imperialism since the 1920s, and Liberal Italy's colonial rule before that, just like in all other colonial regimes of the time.[33] These latter studies support the dual contentions of this book that racism was just as much an inspiration for Fascist imperialism as it was a result of Italian colonial relationships, and an analysis of Italian racism must look at its domestic roots as well as its colonial implementation.

The extensive scholarship on Italian national identity exposes some of the roots of Fascist racism, as it underscores a general preoccupation of Italian politicians and scholars with the definition of Italian collective identity at least since the nineteenth-century Risorgimento. At the heart of this literature, and the history it seeks to illuminate, rest two essential questions: What does it mean to be Italian? And has the Italian nation ever truly unified?[34] The most obvious obstacle to answering these questions has consistently been the cultural and linguistic plurality of the peninsula and islands. At the time of unification in 1861, a majority of public schooling, media, local business, and daily activities were conducted in regional languages that incorporated influences as diverse as Arabic, ancient Greek, Latin, Catalan, French, and German.[35] In fact, the Italian linguist Tullio De Mauro has posited that, at the time, only about 2.5 percent of Italians comfortably spoke the official national language. This proportion of the population was just slightly larger than that which official statistics had determined spoke "nonnative" languages, such as German or French.[36] Many of the larger cities in the center and north of Italy also contained members of the ancient, if small, Italian Jewish population, most of whom were working hard—since the opening of the ghettoes at unification—to assimilate more fully into their respective regional and national communities.[37] Furthermore, if we are to accept Benedict Anderson's claim that a lively print culture is essential to the development of a national community, it bears noting that the 1861 census identified approximately 78 percent of the Italian population as illiterate, suggesting the great difficulty the state might face in their efforts to unify the population.[38] In 1921 almost 30 percent of the population was still illiterate.[39] Thus, if Italian identity connotes sharing a common language and culture, Massimo d'Azeglio's legendary remark in response to the declaration of a unified Italy—"We have made Italy, now we must make Italians"—contained more than a bit of truth.[40] As such, the political efforts to develop citizens who viewed themselves as Italians—as opposed to Neapolitans, Venetians, or Tuscans—became a principal objective of the young Italian state.

Despite the great efforts of Italy's constitutional monarchy to prove the historical and organic connections among the diverse collection of communities, languages, economic systems, political traditions, and social structures in its kingdom, a common sentiment persisted through the late nineteenth and early twentieth centuries that there were (at least) "two Italies"—one legal, the other experienced; one urban, the other rural; and, perhaps more than anything else, one of the North and the other of the South.[41] The northerners who formed the backbone of Italy's first national governments, particularly between the 1860s and 1890s, had naïvely supposed that the bonds that had held the Roman Empire together more than a millennium previously would remain inherent in its descendants throughout the peninsula and that therefore political and economic policies good for the North would hold similar benefits for the South.[42]

The subsequent failure of many of these policies led to questions about the causes of the cultural, political, and economic differences within the kingdom—especially between the North and the South—and, subsequently, the employment of racial explanations.[43] Perhaps most famous were the studies that the Veronese physician Cesare Lombroso (1835–1909) conducted on southerners in the 1860s and 1870s. Lombroso's pioneering anthropometric and ethnographic work explained southern Italy's "inferiority" by way of ethnocultural and biological disadvantages.[44] Building on Lombroso's explanations for southern "criminality," Alfredo Niceforo (1876–1960) later famously argued that much of the South was delinquent because members of lower social classes (which most southerners were) were inherently inferior to those belonging to upper classes, both psychically and morally.[45] Echoing these racial rationalizations, outsiders who toured the southern regions after the Risorgimento often wrote home with words of amazement about how foreign much of southern society was to them. It was not uncommon for northern or central Italians to describe southern languages as "African" or to attribute the South's poor economic conditions to its population's innate laziness or stupidity.[46]

Of course, these were not the only explanations for the differences between the North and the South; nor were they the only racial theories at play in the kingdom. Some racial anthropologists at the turn of the century argued that race actually connected all Italians rather than caused economic, cultural, and political factionalism. The Sicilian and internationally renowned anthropologist Giuseppe Sergi (1841–1936) used the cranial measurements that were very much en vogue at the time to determine that the entirety of the Italian peninsula shared the skeletal similarities indicative of racial commonality.[47] In fact, he proclaimed that all peoples of the Mediterranean came from the same racial lineage.[48]

Regardless of their conclusions, these numerous racial inquiries indicate that nineteenth- and early twentieth-century Italian elites were deeply involved with the scientific, cultural, political, and philosophical conversations about identity and race consuming intellectual circles throughout Europe. While the idea of a shared history was perhaps the central argument for Italian nationalists of all stripes—Benedetto Croce argued that history *is* a people's identity—there was clearly a vociferous segment that focused its unification efforts on defining italianità in terms of what it was *not* as well as what it was.[49] These late nineteenth- and early twentieth-century nationalists established italianità through the exclusion of others, as the other was identified by supposedly inherited behavioral, cultural, and physical—racial—difference; the contributions of the Fascist period were not aberrations from a longer narrative of Italian or European history.[50]

Two popular Italian terms illustrate the concept of race as it manifested in the particular context of Fascist Italy from its earliest days.[51] The first, *stirpe*, is a word still used in Italy to denote family heritage. Then, as now, the word carries with it a sense of personal connection to all those who came before, through a process of spiritual birthright. As one fifth-grade textbook proclaimed in 1929, "And the stirpe was one: the stirpe of Rome!"[52] Under Fascism the term was used to denote the his-

torical lineage of the Italian people: a common spiritual identity that ran through the entire population. The stirpe was not
necessarily, and certainly not primarily, determined by the physical attributes with which one was born; more important were
the historical, moral, and spiritual characteristics of the people.
Nevertheless, Fascists understood these qualities to be inherited.
They might additionally be strengthened through moral and
healthy lifestyles, but these traits were born within all members of the stirpe, making them just as racial in nature as the
pseudoscientific cranial measurements that Giuseppe Sergi and
subsequent Nazi racial scientists employed. And while Fascist
officials gradually cultivated a more "scientific" veneer for their
ideas of the Italian race over the course of the 1930s and early
1940s—developing according to political and cultural needs—
these spiritual, moral, and cultural characteristics were consistently the most valued of the Italian people.

The second term deserving special attention, *razza*, is most
often translated into the English word *race* but is more accurately
described as breed or stock. Razza can be somewhat difficult to
distinguish from the idea of stirpe. The main difference—which
became ever more nominal as the Duce's tenure progressed—was
the idea that stirpe implied a diachronic relationship between
individuals (or having a common historical heritage), whereas
razza primarily identified a relationship among individuals syn-
chronically (having a contemporary similitude). In a 1929 source
using both terms, the author argues that an imperial consciousness would reaffirm the youth of Italian Fascism. Expanding
Italy's colonial holdings would illustrate how "the new Italic
razza has kept the glorious destiny of bringing the stirpe back
to the height of its historic origins."[53] In this statement, the word
razza indicates a group in which an awareness of its inherent
greatness had been reawakened in order to perpetuate the glory
that had been passed down through the stirpe.

The term *razza* was certainly present in early Fascist rhetoric.
If it was originally intended to indicate breeds of animals—a
kind of cow or dog—it became a term used to differentiate
ethnic populations. Particularly as the campaign to develop
an imperial consciousness intensified in the 1930s, the term

razza became more prominent. But again, this idea of race did not focus as much on physical traits as on moral and spiritual characteristics. As Mussolini proclaimed in the mid-1930s, "The razza for us is not as much blood as it is spirit, it is not so much the quantity of physical things as the ideality of spiritual values that are handed down from generation to generation in a constantly increasing number of citizens."[54] And yet as this quote indicates, the fundamental traits of the Italian razza were inherited, connecting the present to the past and clearly demarcating it as racial.

In part, Fascist ideas of the Italian race could not focus on defining a national physical form because of the dramatic variety of physical types on the peninsula and the islands; the nation-state contained such disparate images as the six-foot, fair-skinned German speaker from Venezia Tridentina and the five-foot-two, swarthy Calabrese speaking a language combining remnants of Greek, Arabic, Spanish, and Italian. Of course, the relative flexibility in determining the somatic attributes of the Italian race did not completely negate the importance of physical difference in Fascist racism; Fascists did not hesitate to differentiate between dark-skinned Africans and Italians, for example. Nevertheless, given the rather vague physical composition of the Italian razza and the even less clear definition of stirpe, the Fascist campaign to strengthen the Italian race and nation-state logically turned to more historical, moral, and spiritual characteristics that defined the Italian inheritance. This tendency clearly differentiated it from Nazi rhetoric about the German race. Still, both concepts of collective identification were defined by invented categories of people characterized by supposedly inherited traits, which is the essence of race.

In the most pragmatic terms, the anxiety that Fascists—and Liberals before them—exhibited regarding the biological, cultural, and moral health of Italians reflected modern ideas about power more than about collective identification; the government increasingly institutionalized concern for the racial health of the kingdom's population in order to secure the greatest economic and political capital from its members. By the turn of the twentieth century, politicians and academics throughout the West widely accepted the correlation of a nation's political, economic, and demographic fortunes.[55] They developed this theory in two different but related directions: on a practical level, they contended that the more numerous a national population, the more space that population would occupy and the more territory the nation could control; on a "scientific" level, they argued that those peoples with larger populations were naturally more fertile and therefore biologically superior, giving them an inherent claim to more territory and control over "inferior" peoples.[56] Therefore, in the wake of World War I and its destruction of large portions of the European population, reduced birthrates appeared to be an alarming menace to the social and political preeminence of western Europe in the world.[57] For its part, Italy's birthrates did not actually look to be falling in the 1920s, which was a great source of pride and proof of Italian entitlement to a more significant role in the world.[58] Nevertheless, numerous politicians and social scientists, including Mussolini, warned that Italians were becoming too isolated and materialistic—obvious threats to this privileged position as a nation with great economic and political potential.[59]

Michel Foucault's concept of biopolitics is particularly helpful when considering the belief that Italy's political and economic strength could be ascertained by the quality and quantity of its population. Since the population was a source of power, the state needed to find ways to harness it: "It was essential that the state know what was happening with its citizens' sex, and the use they made of it, but also that each individual be capable of controlling the use he made of it."[60] What resulted from the struggle for command of this "biopower" was the formation of discourses of control, such as those found in laws regarding sex but also in social sciences such as demographics, in the fields of public health, eugenics, and pedagogy, and even in popular media.[61]

And though Foucault emphasized that the power relationship inherent in his theory of biopolitics is far more diffuse and dynamic than a simplistic government-governed binary, state institutions and mechanisms provide crucial sources of the biopolitical discourses that frequently underlay all others.[62] In other words, while biopolitics permeated all aspects of modern life in Liberal and Fascist Italy, an analysis of the formal attempts to institutionalize a particular set of discourses allows us to explore its content as well as the ways the state attempted to manipulate it and the population.[63] A study of the Fascist regime's extensive efforts to exert control over the bodies and minds of Italians as a fundamental component of its racial campaign is an excellent case in point. The expanding network of institutions, mechanisms, and practices that aimed to transform Fascist rhetoric into reality worked to produce the skills and materials required of Fascist society and, just as importantly, reproduce Italians' "submission to the rules of the established order."[64] It is important to recognize that it was not enough to obtain this popular submission to the power of the state through force; the regime needed to engender, in Antonio Gramsci's words, "the spontaneous consent" of the masses to the Fascist project in order to hope for any lasting success in any of its campaigns.[65] One of the central ambitions of the Fascist state apparatus, therefore, was to present the Italian population with a new political, cultural, and social order to which there was no alternative. Examining even a portion of Fascism's totalitarian experiment reveals a racism that underpinned the official discourses and practices of gender, politics, health, and education at the heart of this new order.

The Fascist educational process was a fundamental component of this apparatus and its quest for spontaneous consent, and it provides crucial insight into the regime and the role of race in its goals.[66] Western society had significantly revised its concepts of youth and education over the course of the nineteenth century, and the resulting development of organizations and culture for the social and cultural category of "children" illustrated the growing importance of this population in the evolution of modern nation-states.[67] The school, as the core of this network of institutions, took on the increasingly involved job of preparing model citizens of the nation-state, and debates over the appropriate approach and reach of such an education duly followed.[68] These were, it bears remembering, lessons meant to last a lifetime and to build a framework of cultural hegemony for the state. In the case of interwar Italy, Mussolini and his regime worked to "reclaim" a generation of Italians who would embody the ideals of Fascism—and therefore the Italian race—and resurrect the Roman Empire. Central to this racial campaign was the belief that the grandeur of ancient Rome rested within a unique, inherited italianità. Centuries of misrule, infighting, and barbarian invasions had weakened the character of the Italian people, but Mussolini fervently argued that even all these disasters could not erase the traits that were embedded in the body and soul of every Italian. Combined with the power and modernity of Fascism, a reeducation in the essential elements of italianità was meant to arm young Italians for the conquest of a Fascist empire that could surpass its ancient Roman predecessor in power and glory.

In addition to the school system run by the Ministry of Public Instruction (MPI) until 1932 and thereafter by the Ministry of National Education (MEN), two auxiliary institutions became especially important to the educational and racial missions under Mussolini's rule. The regime founded the National Organization for the Protection of Mothers and Children (ONMI) in 1925 to address demographic concerns, including public health and health education. Then, in 1926, the National Fascist Party (PNF) established the National Balilla Organization (ONB)—which expanded to become the Fascist Italian Youth (GIL) in 1937—to attend to the physical and military education of young Italians. The royal decrees announcing the establishment of these organizations explained that the goal of each organization was not simply to entertain but to educate and engage the Italian spirit. Education was to take place at all times, with excursions, competitions, lessons, and other collective activities that would encourage children to work harder and become stronger individuals so that they could better serve the nation. Both institutions initially followed in the footsteps of Western trends, but their increasingly totalitarian measures served as useful models for and comparisons to like-minded organizations in the interwar regimes of the Soviet Union and Nazi Germany.[69]

Of special concern to these Fascist organizations was the education of two populations the Italian state had long considered in need of greater attention: rural Italians and girls. The education campaigns among these populations had begun as private enterprises in the late nineteenth and early twentieth centuries, but the expansion of the Fascist state eventually incorporated most of the independent and pre-Fascist organizations into the Education Ministry, ONMI, or ONB. Fascists deemed both groups essential to bonifica umana: girls were to be the mothers of Mussolini's children, while peasants embodied the purest form of italianità. Urban boys benefitted most from the state's education efforts—they were the most accessible and important to the future of the regime's military—but ensuring the rejuvenation of the Italian race required the education of all demographics. And while many of the regime's elementary lessons were universal, the chapters of this book also note the special efforts and lessons prescribed for these two specific demographics.

Developing child-rearing courses and mobile pediatric clinics, building record numbers of schools in rural areas, creating extensive children's radio programming, establishing state-sponsored and state-financed summer camps, and instituting a vast system of extracurricular activities and community resources, the Fascist government and its network of educational organizations worked to incorporate its concern for the healthy development of the Italian race into each and every part of the population, in every part of life. This project to establish a presence in all aspects of public and private life—indeed, to eliminate the distinction between public and private life—lay at the heart of Fascism's totalitarian project. The state would never attain total control over the lives of Italy's children, but the consistent and ever-expanding efforts to do so—the totalitarian *intent* of the Fascist state—remains essential to understanding the Fascist ideology. As the political scientist Juan Linz commented, the practice of "totalitarianism cannot be understood without the study of ideologies."[70] The regime believed that through its integrated education system, all children would learn to connect with the Italian nation and identify the extensive corpus of characteristics that made its people superior to those of all other nations and races. Only with this understanding of italianità and full participation could Italians possibly fulfill the destiny of the nation with the creation of a new Roman Empire. Of course, the popular interaction with and reception of these lessons varied dramatically throughout Italy.[71] And yet regardless of how successful the regime was in instilling its vision for the Italian race and nation-state within its children, *Mussolini's Children* shows that this aspect of Fascism's ideological framework played a fundamental role in shaping many of the state's most prominent policies and practices over the course of more than eighteen years in power.

To tell the story of the Fascist campaign to educate new generations of a strengthened Italian race, this study relies on material from pedagogical and popular journals, teaching manuals, textbooks, student notebooks, and ministerial publications collected from a variety of libraries, archives, museums, private collections, and flea markets. Additional evidence has come from the archives of the Fascist state, though there is a remarkable paucity of relevant resources at the Central Archive in Rome. The archives of the Ministry of Public Instruction retain very few documents from the Fascist era—mostly from the mid-1920s and late 1930s—apart from the official ministry bulletins. The documents regarding the ONB (and its successor, the GIL) are largely missing. Furthermore, the Italian government destroyed most of the ONMI records at some point in the last forty years. Smaller collections, such as the papers of Giovanni Gentile, Pietro Fedele, and Renato Ricci, yield interesting documents, but the image of Fascist elementary education painted in the following pages springs primarily from the sources that were available to contemporary students and teachers. This work attempts to view the Fascist efforts to form an ideal Italian race through the eyes of their anticipated—and most impressionable—targets.

The narrative of Fascist racism that these varied sources yield is one of constant evolution over eighteen years. In part, this projection of a steady evolution of Fascist understandings of race and Italian identity was a byproduct of the need for pedagogical resources to rise above the factional variations and personal opinions that accompanied government documents, academic journals, or even official public statements. The textbooks published for Italian elementary students emphasized the most basic and confident of Fascist beliefs. Scholars of Fascist Italy have all recognized the collection of virulent individual racists, and particularly anti-Semites, within the Fascist Party who held fierce debates with other members of the PNF.[72] These conflicts only intensified with the mounting aggression of the racial campaign in the 1930s. In other words, the picture of Fascist racial politics is a complicated and contentious one, and one can easily become lost in the contradictions among individual personalities and policies. And while this study will highlight a few individuals who played exceptionally formative roles in the growth of the Fascist elementary education system, such as Giovanni Gentile and Giuseppe Bottai, this book's primary goal is to identify the most-basic messages the state wanted to impart to its followers. These are the messages that withstood the battering of individual opinions and party factions. These are the messages the state found most urgent to articulate to Italians; thus, the literature associated with elementary education comprises important sources that help identify an official Fascist stance on Italian racial identity. These texts presented a relatively unified voice that was prescribed by the state and accessible to a mass Italian audience. More than that, educational texts imparted an image of the Italian people that the state wanted to perpetuate in its youngest members. So educational texts give readers a sense of not only the beliefs that Fascist officials held but also the way in which they hoped to shape Italy's future. Thus, the narrative evolution of Fascist schoolbooks nicely illustrates an important facet of the state's efforts to obtain the popular consent that Gramsci argued was such an essential part of any regime's aspiration for hegemony. It elucidates the core of the Fascist project as Fascists themselves conceived it.

The struggle for the creation of Fascism, its New Italy, and the New Italians who would represent them was hardly uniform or linear; and despite the regime's image as the handiwork of one man and one vision, Fascism did not entail a swift, revolutionary takeover. Instead, both the state and doctrine that became known as Fascist were constantly evolving, gradually sharpening their contours, drawing on the strengths of a great number of individuals, institutions, philosophies, and pragmatic concerns. The racial discourse that emerged was nuanced, and certain elements changed over the course of Mussolini's reign. Nevertheless, the Fascist process of developing the ideas of a New Italy and the New Italians who would populate it was primarily one of accretion. Even at the height of the regime's political and legal racial campaign after 1938, school texts largely relied on the powerful and familiar narrative of inherited Italian cultural and historical superiority that had permeated the educational rhetoric since the earliest days of Fascist rule. Though less violent in their words than the legislation affecting many Italians and non-Italians at the time, these ideas were no less steeped in racial ideology and, in fact, reflected the foundation on which all other Fascist racial policies were based.

The organization of *Mussolini's Children* reflects this evolutionary process. The eight chapters at the heart of the book are arranged in four chronological sections that correspond with four general stages in the development of Fascist racism between 1922 and 1940. The first section looks at the infrastructural and pedagogical framework for racial education that the regime developed between 1922 and 1929 as Fascism itself established control over the Italian state. Part 2 focuses on the changes— and continuities—in the years between 1929 and 1934, when the state intensified its project to make Italy's educational system totalitarian and "Fascistized" through a more centralized infrastructure and curriculum. Part 3 explores the Fascist imperial project and its relationship to the domestic racial campaign as it took center stage between the years 1934 and 1938 (and, unlike the other sections, further divides the period into 1934–36 and 1936–38). Finally, part 4 analyzes the development of Fascist racism between 1938 and 1940 as an ideological continuation of the Fascist racial campaign that had evolved since 1922. *Mussolini's Children* ends with Italy's declaration of war on June 10, 1940, not because Fascist, or Italian, racism ended with Italy's involvement in the war, but because the focus of the regime—and its elementary education—changed so radically thereafter. Indeed, the Fascist racial campaign would continue throughout the war, and many of the core tenets of Fascist racism continued well after Mussolini's ignominious death in 1945.

A little more than twenty years and several professions passed between when Mussolini taught the elementary students of Gualtieri and when he arrived in Rome to begin his post at the head of the Italian government. Nevertheless, that dictum that the young and inexperienced teacher had proclaimed to his students in the spring of 1902 appeared to mirror a constant theme in his professional efforts and prescriptions for the Italian nation and race: "You arrive by persevering." With this short and rather-vague aphorism, Mussolini emphasized what would become long-standing appeals to strive for greatness; to surmount apparent obstacles; and above all, to act.

One

Defining Fascist Power and Identity, 1922–29

Designing a Fascist Elementary Education

Youth, both the notion and the demographic, was a central theme of Fascism. Its associations with beginnings, strength, energy, virility, and optimism were fundamentally useful to a movement and regime founded in the aftermath of World War I that pledged to fight against anything "weakening" the Italian nation-state or race. Fascism was portrayed as a "magnificent adolescent" who heralded the resurrection of Italy's innate strength and dominance in the world.[1] Moreover, as one 1928 book dedicated to describing the importance of children to the Fascist Revolution stated, "it is the youth, the pure, the restorers, 'the host of the fatherland,' who will endure everything to fulfill their destiny and continuously raise up Italy."[2] It was Italy's children who were primarily tasked with carrying out the long-term Fascist mission to reawaken the "stirpe that has slept for centuries in ignorance of its true power."[3] The negative influences of foreign powers, inept Italian leaders, and material decadence had submerged much of the evidence of Italians' racial superiority; under the guidance of the Fascist state, however, children would have the capacity to harness the "twenty centuries" of history within their hearts and become the greatest representatives of the Italian race.[4] The urgent question for the nascent Fascist regime then became, How could it transform these children physically, mentally, and spiritually into the New Italians who needed to create a New Italy and restore Italian glory?

The answer came in the development of a complex network of institutions designed to educate a new generation of Italians to embody italianità and take the lessons of Fascism to the broader realms of family and community. School and its ancillary organizations were primary tools the Fascist state used to establish and impart discourses of racial identity and bio-power, and it is significant that the reformation of the education system was one of Benito Mussolini's first priorities after becoming prime minister in 1922. At the same time, the development of a Fascist educational system in many ways resembled the Fascist "seizure" of power over all other aspects of the Italian bureaucracy, economy, and culture: Fascist leaders initially appeared to maintain continuity in educational policies and personnel but increasingly centralized and politicized the system. In other words, it took years for the regime to articulate and enact the changes they believed necessary for the system that was meant to transform Italy's society and race; of course, this process was neither linear nor simple.

An important element in the first stage of this institutional and pedagogical evolution was the regime's reliance on educationalists and welfare advocates who did not necessarily consider themselves Fascist but who considered Fascism to be a malleable project that could be made to fit their own visions of New Italians and a New Italy. A significant portion of the pedagogues in Mussolini's first administration at the MPI were supporters of broader Western trends in education and health, and they seized the regime's early calls for reform as an opportunity to restructure an educational system they considered stagnant and unproductive. Under the leadership of Minister Giovanni Gentile and his sweeping 1923 Gentile Reform, they argued that increased education of all kinds—humanistic and vocational, spiritual and physical—among all children would result in a stronger and healthier population as well as a more advanced and productive economy. Liberal Italy had generally supported such calls to action, but inadequate resources and other strains on the state largely limited education and health reforms in the kingdom to those carried out by independent or semiautonomous organizations.[5] Though not without its own financial and infrastructural challenges, the Fascist regime, by contrast, prioritized the implementation of mandatory primary education and the centralization of the institutions tasked with accomplishing it. And yet the many educationalists who took advantage of this opportunity to pursue their own pedagogical ambitions would be forced to reevaluate their commitment to Fascism by the mid-1920s, especially in the aftermath of the 1924 Matteotti Crisis. Some, like the director general of elementary education, Giuseppe Lombardo Radice, chose to abandon the MPI and its increasingly unpalatable political project. Others, including Giovanni Gentile, became ever more convinced of the urgency of Fascism's goals and ever more eager participants in the Fascist regime.

The Fascist education system of the 1920s unquestionably reflected more-general Western educational trends, but its ultimate objective reflected particularly Fascist aims. The system expected to create Italians who were not simply "fit" citizens but models of the Italian race who could fulfill the demands of the Fascist state. While there were numerous opinions about how such an objective could best be achieved, ministry pedagogues between 1922 and 1929 shared the belief that the ultimate beneficiary of education was to be the collective, not the individual. Likewise, the key architects of elementary-education reform in the 1920s, Gentile and Lombardo Radice, might not have personally espoused racial theories, but their collectivist language and pedagogical principles, firmly espoused in the 1923 Gentile Reform, would prove valuable frameworks within which Mussolini's racial project could develop and thrive. Moreover, the founding of the ONMI in 1925 and the ONB in 1926 furthered the state's pedagogical and political emphases on collective discipline, health, and physical strength. These characteristics of the expanded educational infrastructure, above all else, separated early Fascist education from contemporary pedagogical trends in Western Europe and the United States.

The Architects of a Fascist Education System

The primary administrator tasked with formulating a Fascist approach to the education of the Italian youth was the philosopher, pedagogue, and Mazzinian nationalist Giovanni Gentile (1875–1944). Serving as Mussolini's minister of public instruction from 1922 to 1924, he grew up in the small village of Castelveltrano on the west coast of Sicily and only traveled to the Italian peninsula for the first time at the age of eighteen to begin his studies at the elite university Scuola normale superiore in Pisa. At the turn of the twentieth century, the Scuola normale was known as the most prestigious place in the Italian Kingdom to train as a teacher of the humanities and sciences, and Gentile had been one of four selected in 1893 to study under its renowned humanities faculty. His new environment, professors, and peers highlighted the stark distinctions between the provincial education of his childhood and the cosmopolitan pedagogy of Europe's leading institutions.[6] Consequently, Gentile's experiences at the Scuola normale helped cultivate the young intellectual's desire to reform the nation's educational system in order to create a modern and united kingdom throughout all its regions. It was also in his first years in Pisa that Gentile began corresponding with the emerging philosopher and historian Benedetto Croce, who would become a significant influence in Gentile's personal and professional life for the next three decades.[7]

Gentile used this period of intense collaboration with Croce to delineate the core of the philosophy he termed actual idealism (*idealismo attuale*). Actual idealism, also known as actualism, followed in the footsteps of early nineteenth-century German philosophical idealism that argued for a unifying explanation of the human experience. More specifically, Gentile built on Georg Wilhelm Friedrich Hegel's theory that all constituent parts and experiences of the universe are integrated in the single concept of *Geist* (spirit).[8] The Italian philosopher and subsequent actualists argued that there were "no 'objective' truths, if 'objective' was understood to mean that human senses and will had nothing to do with its determination."[9] However, actualism posited that reality was not an individual construction but rather a form of collective consciousness.[10] This assertion offered a significant critique of Karl Marx's interpretation of Hegelian idealism, particularly of his insistence that history was grounded entirely in a materialist dialectic. Gentile believed that nineteenth-century emphases on materialism and positivism had played a central role in the decline of European—and particularly Italian—society. Gentile's philosophy therefore emphasized the values of voluntarism and sacrifice of the individual to the collective. The will of the individual lay at the heart of all action, but identification with a group or community—relational and collective experiences—was fundamental to that individual's choices and, therefore, to the development of engaged members of society.[11] As such, he argued, a strong national education system was critical to molding desired individual and group identities.[12]

Gentile's view of the importance of education in modern society reflected the opinion of a growing number of Italians, like the philosopher and popular children's author Ernesto Codignola (1885–1965), who believed that education was the "most powerful instrument of civilization" that formed "the spirit and mind of a people." He further explained, "If school lies at the center of education, the national government must focus its most loving and assiduous efforts on liberating [the school] from the complex of impediments that have deformed it and made it inhuman."[13] This call for educational reform in Italy had first found a considerable following at the turn of the century, echoing the movements in other western European countries and the United States. Children were no longer viewed simply as small adults; medical professionals, teachers, and welfare activists determined that children had different ways of thinking, learning, and developing from those of adults.[14] This perspective gave rise to a new orthodoxy about how educators should approach their relationship with young children: progressive educationalists (also known as educational idealists) viewed the traditional reliance on repetition and memorization as inadequate and conducted numerous studies showing the positive impact of experiential learning—lessons incorporating the skills of observation and creative thinking. Such an emphasis on connecting students to the environment and people immediately around them would be crucial to Gentile's pedagogy under Fascism and, while not necessarily racial in intent, was fitting for a Fascist regime that wished to forge unbreakable bonds between Italy's children and their so-called racial community.

The expansion of public health initiatives throughout western Europe in the second half of the nineteenth century also influenced the early Fascist reformers and the regime's evolving biopolitical discourse. The twin realizations that educating the public about personal hygiene could reduce the spread of disease and that exposing the body to exercise and fresh air would strengthen the individual and lessen the likelihood of some infections drove public officials to promote outdoor learning, physical education, and "active" lessons in public schools. Educators, too, argued that students should develop their intellect not simply with facts and figures but also with an intimate understanding of physical fitness and discipline. Early twentieth-century doctors and educators resurrected the ancient Roman belief in *mens sana in corpore sano*—a healthy mind in a healthy body—and the aspiration to mold physically healthy young citizens fed directly into the more general goal of these educationalists to produce "fit" members of the larger society.[15]

Scholars have written much on the growth of educational and health movements in Germany, Great Britain, France, and the United States at the start of the twentieth century; seldom do these studies mention the Italian case.[16] However, Italy was no exception to the international trends, and numerous Italian pedagogues contributed significantly to the broader Western movements.[17] Furthermore, Gentile's early work to transform the educational system to adhere to Fascist ambitions did not change the nation's participation in the international discussion about pedagogy.[18] Italian representatives continued to play an active role in conferences and symposia on education and child rearing, and many of the projects and proposals started under the Liberal government as far back as the late nineteenth century continued to find support after 1922.[19] According to historian Adrian Lyttelton, Mussolini's decision to appoint Gentile as his first minister of public instruction was largely influenced by the philosopher's international renown and therefore potential to increase support for Fascism abroad through his redevelopment of the educational system based on popular Western pedagogical trends.[20]

Gentile's contributions to the development of a Fascist educational framework were not limited to his reputation as a respected Western pedagogue and philosopher, however. Gentile's theories on the social nature of humans and the formation of their collective identity meshed nicely with Fascism's emphasis on the collective over the individual.[21] Additionally, the weakened position of the Italian nation-state after the Great War further convinced Gentile of the need for change through the implementation of a new, "ethical state."[22] Such an ethical state—as the political manifestation of the nation—would have an obligation *not* to be objective or "agnostic"; rather, its primary responsibility would lie in training Italy's citizens to realize their own strength and, through it, the strength of the nation.[23] This concept would be particularly helpful in Mussolini's campaign to strengthen the race, even if Gentile's primary concern was a *national* community not necessarily tethered to a racial identity.[24] Likewise, Mussolini's invitation to design the future of Italian education provided Gentile with the opportunity to enact some of the changes to Italian society he had advocated since the turn of the century. Still, by the second half of the 1920s Gentile had thoroughly wedded himself to the Fascist regime and its supposed continuation of the Risorgimento. With the 1929 publication of his *Origins and Doctrine of Fascism*, Gentile did his part to define the goals of the Fascist project and argue for the historic necessity of Mussolini's regime.[25] Gentile might have begun his career in the MPI as an independent pedagogue, but by the end of the decade, he was Fascism's ideological spokesperson.

In his capacity as minister of public instruction, Gentile was in charge of all levels of public education, but he agreed with the Duce that mandatory primary education was one of the most effective means with which the ethical state could implant communal values and beliefs.[26] Because of the impressionable age of the pupils and the powerful role of primary school teachers as surrogate parents, Gentile and other pedagogues held that "teachers truly are the most noble, patient, and effective propagandists of our civilization."[27] The editor-in-chief of the *Annals of Elementary Education* (*Annali dell'istruzione elementare*), Emilio Bodrero, expressed such a conviction in the journal's 1928 inaugural edition, writing that "almost six million children are entrusted to the care of teachers who must create in them the religious, civil, and national consciousness that will make them knowledgeable citizens and modern Italians." The editor continued, "In primary school, in fact, the citizen receives his first training, which, in order to stay with him for his entire life, must be so effective that nothing would be worth erasing it."[28] In short, the primary-education experience was to imbue Italian youth with the values and characteristics that would lead Italy to a glorious, united future.[29] Early education was the perfect venue, and the elementary school teacher was the best purveyor of Fascist ideals, racial and otherwise. Many of the changes to the primary-education system and curriculum of the 1920s were made in order to develop a stronger impression of these ideals on the minds of the youngest Italians.

To head up the reforms specific to elementary education, Gentile appointed his longtime friend and intellectual partner Giuseppe Lombardo Radice (1879–1938) to the new position of director general of primary education.[30] While Gentile focused the majority of his attention on the reform of secondary and university education, Lombardo Radice played a leading role in the formation of Fascist elementary pedagogy between 1922 and 1924.[31] This first director general of primary education was another Sicilian-born educational idealist of the time who, like Gentile, made his first journey north at the age of eighteen to study at the Scuola normale. Enrolling in 1896, Lombardo Radice's time at the institution overlapped briefly with Gentile and initiated a friendship that would last more than three decades.[32] Together the two intellectuals—along with Croce, Codignola, and others—formed an intellectual circle that engaged in numerous discussions and debates over the state of Italian education and culture in the early twentieth century. Lombardo Radice shared much of Gentile's interpretation of Hegelian dialectics and, perhaps even more than Gentile, argued against the predominance of positivist curricula in Italian schools; he most notably promoted the didactic importance of local culture and personal experience in elementary education.[33] As their mutual friend and colleague Armando Carlini would later write, "[Lombardo Radice] was not a pedagogical philosopher as Gentile was: he was a pedagogical *educator*, and the greatest one that we had in Italy during his time."[34]

Lombardo Radice's work primarily focused on integrating "spiritual" education and genuine enthusiasm for learning into nursery and elementary education, as will be evident in the reforms delineated in the following pages.[35] And despite his initial trepidation regarding the Fascist ascension to power, Lombardo Radice was eventually convinced to join the initial Fascist educational regime in what he liked to consider a didactic, rather than political, position.[36]

Together, Gentile and Lombardo Radice and other educational reformers embraced the challenge to create an educational system to reform the Italian mind and spirit. The reforms that resulted, known popularly as the 1923 Gentile Reform, provided a framework forged in Western educational idealism but quite adaptable to the evolving rhetoric and needs of Mussolini's racial ideology.

The Bureaucracy of Elementary Education after the 1923 Gentile Reform

In bureaucratic terms, Gentile's 1923 reforms attempted to restructure the MPI, which most Italian pedagogues and politicians agreed was in a state of institutional crisis. The bureaucracy was largely corrupt, its finances lay in ruins, and the school infrastructure was in desperate need of repair. The High Council for Public Instruction (Consiglio superiore della istruzione pubblica), which consisted of thirty-six academics chosen through a combination of ministerial appointment and election, rarely represented the significant diversity of regional needs. Shackled by limited resources and rampant corruption, the MPI had largely resisted reform since its mid-nineteenth-century inception. Gentile's modifications to this system began by placing the authority to appoint delegates to this high council exclusively with the king. This change helped ensure that bureaucrats whose loyalty and priorities were defined first and foremost by the Fascist government dominated the ministerial decision-making process.[37]

More than that, the 1923 Gentile Reform required all children to attend school between the ages of six and fourteen—raising the mandatory school age by two years—and enforced the greater standardization of the curricula in both public and private schools.[38] To do so, new laws organized the public schools by region rather than province, allowing greater state control over the network.[39] They also increased the scope of elementary schools from three grades to five, dividing the extended age range into two phases: grades 1 through 3 (*grado inferiore*), for children approximately six to nine years old, and grades 4 and 5 (*grado superiore*), for students approximately nine to eleven years old.[40] At the end of each school year, students were required to take a state exam in order to advance to the next class. These two stages of primary education generally catered to children between the ages of six and eleven, but since students advanced to the next grade or remained another year in the same grade depending on their annual performance, it was not unusual to have twelve-, thirteen-, or even fourteen-year-olds in a fifth-grade class.[41]

After fifth grade, each student could continue a classical education in the liberal arts and sciences if he or she passed the mandated state exam. If he or she did not pass that exam, the student was to attend one of any number of vocational schools for professional training or a junior high school that would serve as the end of the individual's education. Such options allowed students who did not advance to a classical middle school to gain a practical education in a future trade.[42] Despite Gentile's aims and efforts, however, historian Elena D'Ambrosio has pointed out that in the 1920s three out of four Italian students finished their formal education at the elementary level, again highlighting the immense importance of primary education in the Fascist project to strengthen the Italian race.[43]

This standardized educational infrastructure did not mean that the new administration abandoned specialized policies and curricula for discrete demographics, and Gentile's ministry was particularly aware of the distinct needs of Italy's rural communities.[44] An Italian rural education movement had already begun in earnest in the early 1900s, particularly with Alessandro Marcucci's 1905 founding of the Schools for the Peasants of the Agro Romano and the Pontine Swamps (Le scuole per i contadini dell'Agro Romano e delle Paludi Pontine). This organization worked for the "cultural reclamation" (*bonifica cultur-*

ale umana) of the people who lived in the countryside of Lazio just outside Rome, and it would continue to do so during the first years of Fascist rule.[45] Marcucci's project illustrated Italy's long tradition of the promotion of rural education through private or government-associated (*parastatale*) organizations. Such a variegated system required fewer financial commitments from a relatively poor state but also resulted in both an irregular establishment of schools throughout the nation and limited oversight of the schools that the MPI did not directly run.[46]

The rural education campaign took on a sense of urgency under Gentile's leadership of the MPI and with Mussolini's determination to enact bonifica umana throughout the nation. The combination of an increased concern for maintaining "demographic strength"—that is, increasing the national birthrates through an active pronatalist campaign—and evidence that the Italian rural populations produced considerably more children than their urban counterparts meant that the rural populations were to be exalted and protected portions of the Italian race.[47] At the same time, a sizeable proportion of Italy's peasant population was still illiterate in 1919—something public officials saw as a mark of national (but not racial) inferiority.[48] According to D'Ambrosio, even in 1921, 25 percent of Italy's male population and 31 percent of its female population between the ages of twenty-one and twenty-nine could not read.[49] Rural schools, above all, needed to teach their communities basic skills, because, as one government report stated, "illiteracy should not and cannot exist in a civilized nation, particularly with the directives and lofty goals indicated by the Fascist Revolution."[50] More importantly, rural education was an essential component of the spread of Fascist ideals for the Italian race: "The rural school represents the future generation that will know how to materialize all our hopes. Guided by the Duce, this generation will know how to reach the goals dreamed by those who fought and bled, crowned by glory and victory, in the trenches, seas, and skies."[51]

Consequently, despite the eagerness of the new government to increase agricultural production—something that discouraged school attendance—the Fascist regime further invigorated and expanded the rural education movement with a number of institutional developments. First and foremost, the state took increasing control over the administration of the rural school system and placed all organizations working in rural education under the regulation of the state (*consiglio di stato*). It also combined classes in so-called unclassified elementary schools, increasing the number of establishments similar to the American one-room schoolhouse, where age diversity was a central component of the curriculum and methodology. Often there was one class for grades 1 through 3 and another class for grades 4 and 5, though many other rural schools only maintained the first three grades, after which children were expected to attend vocational schools for the remainder of their primary education. Students rarely made that transition, however, because they needed to help support the family but also because the vocational schools in many communities were never built.[52]

In tandem with the need for a dedicated rural education program, the MPI was markedly aware of the need for an appropriately gendered education system.[53] Certainly the belief that girls needed an education that catered to their "unique" role in Italian society was not new; handbooks articulating the specifics of "girls' education" were prevalent in the kingdom since unification. The obvious corollary to such a discourse was that the standard pedagogy was essentially designed for boys. Girls were the exception to the norm. It was the "standard" side of this constructed gender dichotomy that received increased attention after Mussolini came to power. Masculinizing the male population—and the concepts of nation and race—had been central to Fascist political rhetoric since the beginning of Mussolini's movement, and pedagogical discussions of the 1920s mirrored such a campaign.[54] In particular, fear that the public education system did not contain enough male teachers as role models for the male student population became a growing preoccupation for officials, pedagogues, and even parents.[55] The situation was complicated by the fact that mothers were largely the ones who began and then continued their children's education at home. Fathers were rarely available to oversee this portion of their children's education and often participated only in what one article on child rearing considered "the most serious cases."[56] This arrangement did not diminish the father's importance in Italian home life, but the Fascist administration had to grapple with the implications of having women at the forefront of early education.

Fascist officials further exacerbated the gender imbalance among elementary teachers with a law passed in December 1925 allowing for the forced retirement of any public officials who did not express Fascist sympathies. This measure led to a significant purging of educational administrators and elementary teachers in the kingdom in order to replace them with more faithful followers and transmitters of Fascist pedagogy, much as the Nazi regime would do shortly after coming to power in 1933.[57] Since Mussolini subsequently had to decrease the pay for elementary teachers in order to afford the increase in school personnel that the expanded school system required, it was especially difficult to find men willing to enter the profession. Instead, more women—both single and married—came to fill the positions.[58] Clearly, then, the initial Fascist adaptations to the educational infrastructure made for less than the regime's ideal primary school system, but they would prove to be the launchpad for the expanding scope and reach of the Fascist state in the lives of Mussolini's children.

The Pedagogical Principles of the 1923 Gentile Reform

More than establishing a new bureaucratic architecture, Gentile's 1923 educational reforms defined the philosophy of Fascist education that would help mold new generations of the Italian race. Many of his most dramatic reform efforts concerned secondary, postsecondary, and professional education; still, the measures put forth for the improvement of primary education were significant and indicative of the role Fascists envisioned for the Italian youth in their campaign for bonifica umana.

On the one hand, the minister's conception of education reform was rather egalitarian: he believed all students—regardless of background or ability—should have a standard, introductory education in the humanities, including art and literature, so that each child could access all parts of his or her "spirit."[59] Few children would ever have a chance to continue these studies after elementary school, and even fewer would find any practical use for such knowledge in their professional or home lives. Nevertheless, the educational idealist believed that such studies would help develop the richest parts of italianità, giving children the tools to realize their fullest potential as Italians at home and in society.

With similar purpose, Gentile announced that lessons in religion would become mandatory for all elementary school children. This reform was one of Gentile's most striking and controversial changes to primary education for a number of reasons. Religious education had been stipulated in the 1859 Casati Law, the legal foundation of the modern Italian school system until the Gentile Reform.[60] Implementation was hardly uniform, however, and the contentious political relationship between the Vatican and the unified Italian state had strained many of the cultural ties between the Catholic Church and the national government. By the end of the Great War, most religious education was limited to parochial schools and other church organizations. Gentile's decision to integrate religious instruction into public education was also unexpected because he had been an adamant supporter of the separation of church and state, and Mussolini had been outwardly hostile toward religion until his rise to power.[61] Not everyone embraced this decision, either; many educational idealists believed the inclusion of parochial instruction in any national education system was antithetical to the modern idea of public education for all.

In other ways, this aspect of his reforms signaled important characteristics of Gentile's educational philosophy and Fascism's political and cultural outlook. The minister of public instruction believed that understanding the principles of religion was a prerequisite for anyone to engage with philosophy; religion was, in his estimation, popular philosophy.[62] In turn, to engage in life philosophically was the best method with which each individual could realize his or her personality to the fullest. Politically, this initiative can be seen as an essential building block in the long negotiations that ended in the 1929 Lateran Pacts.[63] Most important to Fascist racial education, however, were the cultural reasons behind Gentile's reform. The philosopher recognized the critical role the Catholic Church played within Italian culture and believed that students would be able to access and develop the most valuable traits of italianità in part by retrieving those found within Catholic culture. An Italian's religious identity could not be separated from his or her national identity, Gentile argued: "Even our speech, our religion itself, which do indeed live in the human mind, may yet be considered as natural facts similar to the geographical accidents which give boundaries and elevation to the land of a people."[64] Beyond the specific tenets of Catholicism, instruction in religious observance taught Italians the principles of filial piety and, more generally, obedience to a higher power.[65] These traits were essential to developing a Fascist conception of italianità—the subject of the next chapter—and Mussolini often took advantage of Catholic traditions to establish himself as the leader of a secular religion.[66] The frequent public parades, songs, prayers, and other ceremonies gave Fascism a religious atmosphere that was both familiar and extremely appealing.[67]

The promotion of religion in primary education was illustrative of the overarching philosophy driving the reforms; it also highlighted the first of two pedagogical pillars essential to the framework of Fascist education, which this study terms organic learning. Fascist educators were encouraged to base their lesson plans on material with which their students were already familiar—the local environment, family traditions, community customs, and languages. This type of organic learning capitalized on the idea that students would be better able to connect with familiar concepts and to build on a preexisting knowledge base.[68] As a result, early Fascist educational manuals presented curricular requirements as indicative rather than prescriptive; while the MPI wanted to keep the principal concepts uniform throughout the various regions, its leadership also encouraged teachers to use the conditions of their posts, their own experiences, and their own personalities to improve their lesson plans, especially in rural settings.[69] As Ernesto Codignola—the turn-of-the-century children's author and Gentile's close philosophical colleague—explained in his

1925 book, *The Difficulty of National Education in Italy*, such a methodology relied on the belief that there should be no distance between the educator and the student. Instead, within education, "the teacher can appeal to himself, his intuition, his intelligence, his psychological effects: there are no presumptions, no norms, no laws."[70] Ultimately, this quote reflected the fact that during his time as minister of public instruction, Gentile was far more interested in training teachers in the essence of italianità than in pure dogma.[71] In other words, students were to learn *how* to read, observe, think, and act like Italians and Fascists but not *what* those observations, thoughts, or actions should be in each moment of their lives. Certainly this philosophy exposed the changeable nature of Fascism, but it also led to one of the most significant effects of Gentile's reforms: to elevate the role of the teacher in the lives of both the students and the nation-state.[72] Furthermore, it urged the development of intense bonds between students and their community, a key component of the Fascist campaign to promote racial awareness among young Italians.

The second pedagogical pillar of the Gentile Reform, the principle of action over ideas, conformed largely to Liberal-era and Western educational trends but was presented as unique to Fascist doctrine (much like the phenomenon of Fascism itself). Italian pedagogues of the 1920s pushed the importance of observation and active learning so that students would become men and women of action. The language of the Gentile Reform encouraged students not to be passive observers of their own education but to develop their senses of spontaneity and creativity.[73] Despite the aggressive, authoritarian nature of the Fascist movement, Gentile and his educational-idealist colleagues in the MPI did not want to inhibit the impulse to explore; the true educational goal in Gentile's reforms was to create a new mentality in young students with which to carry forth their own investigations.[74]

As a whole, then, Gentile and Lombardo Radice envisioned this pedagogy as transforming the Italian youth into thoughtful, ambitious, proactive, and disciplined individuals who were tightly connected to the spiritual and social community around them. Such an aspiration, while not in and of itself racial, provided an approach with which the regime could promote the biopolitical discourses geared to elevate the racial identity of Italy's children.

Carrying Out the Pedagogical Principles of the Gentile Reform

As the pedagogical principles of organic and active learning make clear, the new educational system relied on a holistic notion of education that embraced the mind, body, and spirit. A central piece of the implementation of this pedagogy, then, was to mandate the improvement of physical education programs throughout the national school system.[75] In 1923 Gentile organized the National Organization for Physical Education (ENEF) to help train teachers to emphasize the importance of discipline and physical health through exercise (though it would be shut down four years later).[76] The ENEF also established playgrounds and playing fields and collaborated with community athletic clubs to popularize physical fitness.[77] A subsequent series of laws in 1924 then made physical education mandatory in all state schools for both boys and girls.

These initiatives took great inspiration from early twentieth-century trends in other European countries; likewise, the MPI was similarly motivated to expand its physical education reforms beyond the walls of public schools.[78] Fascist officials and pedagogues were deeply concerned about the limitations of the classroom in terms of assuring the intellectual, physical, and moral education of Italy's youngest members. One journalist of the period articulated these fears particularly well: "After school and in addition to school, the student continues his life as an evolving little being. But how will he live that life? The family is not always in the position to provide for his gradual and rational development; often it lacks the competency and even more often the means. It is here where the subsidiary and auxiliary scholastic institutions intervene, all of which, in a certain sense, are substitutes for the family to fill the gaps that elementary school necessarily leaves in the physical and spiritual education of the student."[79] In line with this position, the new Fascist government promoted a number of policies, programs, and organizations in the 1920s that would more directly control the extramural activities of their impressionable children.

Of greatest note in this campaign was the establishment of the ONB in April 1926.[80] As with a growing number of extracurricular organizations throughout the West, such as the Boy and Girl Scouts of the United States and, later, the Hitler Youth in Germany, the ONB focused on developing "the physical and moral health of the Italian youth" between the ages of eight and eighteen with the goal of "preparing them for the new Italian way of life."[81] The regime named the ONB in honor of a Genovese boy, Giovan Battista Perasso, whose nickname, Balilla (originally a Ligurian term that referred to a lively boy), played a central role in Italian nationalist mythology.[82] As a young patriot in 1746, the legend held, Balilla stood up against occupying Austrian Hapsburg troops in an attempt to start a revolution to free his city, Genoa, from foreign oppression. As a textbook later related, "Balilla, for however young he was, hated the domineering enemies of his fatherland, and one day in Genoa, many years ago ... he threw a rock at those terrible foreign soldiers. So everyone followed his example and the citizens picked up their arms and threw the Austrians out of the city. The gesture of that young Genovese hero demonstrates that even kids can love and serve the fatherland."[83] The strength of both Balilla's body and character had allowed him to stand against the foreign invaders and protect the honor of his fatherland. Such a story was to serve as a model for all Italians; it illustrated the ideal spiritual and physical aspects of the Fascist youth organization's members and the Italian race more generally.[84]

A significant factor in the development of the ONB as a foundational institution in Fascist youth education was its leadership. Of course, as an organization of the national government, its ultimate leaders were King Vittorio Emanuele III and the Duce himself. However, Mussolini found an indispensable partner in Renato Ricci (1896–1956), who headed the organization until 1937. Like the other foundational members of the Fascist educational system, Ricci's personal narrative elucidates certain characteristics of the Fascist project. Born in Carrara, a small coastal town in Tuscany known for its marble, Ricci became an early member of Gabriele D'Annunzio's legionaries in 1919 and followed the original duce later that year in his quest to take Fiume for Italy.[85] After the fall of D'Annunzio's short-lived Italian Regency of Carnaro in late 1920, Ricci settled in as the Fascist leader of his hometown, where he gained a reputation as an enthusiastic and brutal *ras* during the days of the Fascist squads. In many ways, Ricci was a representative figure of the early Fascist movement: youthful, strong, and impulsive; Ricci was much more concerned with showing power through strength and force than through words and negotiation.[86] Though these characteristics of Fascism had to be tempered once Mussolini came to power, they would remain inseparable from the image of the movement and regime. In this sense, the not overly bright but immensely ambitious young Ricci appeared to be the perfect spokesman for an organization designed to augment the physical and premilitary education of Italy's children.[87]

While the physical education of Italy's future soldiers was of immense value to the organization, the ONB became equally dedicated to the physical development of Italy's female population. Indeed, the organization was intricately involved in the regime's call for the "assistance and physical education for women in light of the fundamental need to prevent the decay of the razza and to strengthen it at the source."[88] In 1929 under the guidance of Angiola Moretti, the ONB founded the Piccole Italiane (ages eight to fourteen) and Giovani Italiane (ages fourteen to eighteen), which became the female equivalent of the boys' Balilla and the Avanguardisti.[89] As with the boys' sections, the Piccole and Giovani Italiane created the extracurricular environment in which girls strengthened their bodies, established friendships, and learned the racial ideals of the new Fascist society; as the Balilla were trained to become the future soldiers of the fatherland, the Piccole Italiane were taught to be the future wives and mothers of the race. In other words, the creation of the Piccole Italiane aimed to carry out "the miracle of having a great number of women marching toward a common destination of improvement and well-being."[90]

As was the case with most Fascist organizations at the outset, membership in the ONB was voluntary, though students were increasingly pressured to join as the years progressed, with the regime strengthening its hold on Italian society and more employers, schools, and government departments giving preference to its members. Because of the ONB's ever-growing importance, its instructors went through a rigorous selection process. Only the most upstanding moral role models could participate in its leadership, and they were required to report to the central command of the organization twice a month for updated directives so that they could effectively carry out the mission of the Fascist Revolution.[91] Beginning in 1927 the ONB held the annual Fascist "calling to the colors," or *leva fascista*, on April 21, which the party considered the most important measuring stick of its progress toward rejuvenating the Italian race. At this highly orchestrated and pseudoreligious gathering that resembled Catholic confirmation, regiments of ONB members exhibited their strength and skills to local officials and community members in gymnastic competitions and parades. After these demonstrations, children matriculated to the next level of responsibility and honor: at the age of fourteen, boys who had been Balilla became the young men who formed the Avanguardisti, and girls who had composed the Piccole Italiane graduated to become Giovani Italiane. The ultimate promotion occurred at the age of eighteen when the organization's eldest members, the Avanguardisti and Giovani Italiane, gained the privilege of membership in the PNF. Like its counterparts in Nazi Germany and the Soviet Union, the ONB would be the source of the party's most devoted members.[92] This ceremony, sometimes referred to as "the surety of the future," symbolized the increasing maturity and responsibility of the Italian youth and presented an image of the strength, virility, and fertility of the Italian race under Fascist leadership.[93]

Gentile believed that the concepts of organic and active learning were the best tools to enhance the Italian spirit, but he was highly aware that hygiene and health education could not be ignored in this expansive campaign for the physical, intellectual, and moral development of Italy's children. The Italian public health movement had grown considerably around the turn of the century, but the rise of Fascism ensured its importance in the political and social infrastructure of the nation as a

fundamental piece of its racial project. The regime institutionalized the idea of *bonifica igenica* (health reclamation), again giving words to the biopolitical trope of needing to "reclaim" the
health of the Italian race. Already in 1922 the government illustrated the importance of public health education among children by giving the Junior Italian Red Cross (CRIG)—founded
by the American Red Cross in the aftermath of World War I—a
much more prominent position in the public school system.[94]
The purpose of the organization was, according to one journalist, to "discipline and coordinate the healthy impulses of the
members to the greatest advantage of school and nation."[95] In
these first years of the Fascist regime, membership numbers
increased steadily, as the government encouraged entire classes
to sign up. Group leaders trained students in basic hygiene and
first aid and encouraged them to share the skills with friends
and family. The organization produced a wide variety of materials with basic information on hygiene and health, including
workbooks, posters, and pamphlets to distribute within schools.

The widespread establishment of open-air schools (*scuole
aperte*) represented another aspect of the public health and
physical education movements that contributed to the expanding racial campaign of the 1920s. The belief in the importance
of frequent interaction with nature—extending the ideas of
organic education and a return to the nation's rural roots—led
to the founding of numerous outdoor schools throughout Italy
during the early Fascist period. Public health officials deemed
these institutions particularly important to childhood development and racial purification: "The outdoor schools are one
of the most effective prophylaxes against alcoholism, smoking,
and immorality, since there is no tavern, no mud on the roads,
and no foul language to corrupt in the countryside. . . . In the
open air one begins to be a man, adapted to work hard, and to
become strong so that he can honorably defend the nation if
enemies threaten."[96] According to school officials, the lack of
sunlight and air circulation often found in traditional classrooms had the potential to cause innumerable illnesses and
contribute to others, including tuberculosis, alcoholism, and
malnutrition.[97] In response, the open-air schools were useful in

"removing the children from the enclosed environment of the classroom and letting them breathe in the sunshine; this benefits not only those who are predisposed to hereditary and serious illnesses, but all the students, for whom fresh air and light cannot but help in their development."[98] In the mid-1920s most of Italy's more populous communities rushed to establish outdoor classrooms for at least part of the year; and in many cases, the finest pedagogues were hired to develop the programs.[99]

Climate colonies (*colonie climatiche*) shared the goals of the open-air schools and were also first founded by the American Red Cross in 1919 but expanded considerably in the 1920s.[100] Like all Fascist public health initiatives, these camps—established at beaches, in the mountains, and along rivers—were critical sites for bonifica umana, and officials saw the opportunity to attend one of these camps as essential to a child's physical and moral (racial) education.[101] Giuseppe Fanelli, a prominent children's author of the time, wrote that "the advantages children derive from the camps and the colonies are not only physical, but also moral, since the communal life of the camps teaches them discipline, develops the sense of solidarity, and unites Italians from different regions. They [the children] can therefore better understand, engage themselves with, and love their shared nation."[102] While these camps targeted the "physical regeneration of the children who are less favored by nature," they were generally open and free to those children from urban Italy who could not otherwise afford to go to the beach or the mountains.[103] Oversight organizations hired doctors who were largely responsible for choosing who was accepted into these camps. They based their decision on several formal criteria that supposedly "transcended political or religious influences" but that primarily responded to subjective analyses.[104] Over the course of the 1920s the number of children who attended such camps grew appreciably. In 1922 there were only 150 colonies in Italy, but by the summer of 1927 there were 1,200, with approximately 170,000 children attending them.[105] The regime clearly saw these camps as an essential part of its campaign to create young Italians who could see to the success of the Fascist Revolution and the rejuvenation of the Italian race.

The number of public health institutions continued to expand over the course of the 1920s, the most critical of which was the 1925 launch of the ONMI under the control of the Ministry of Health and with Italy's Queen Elena named honorary president.[106] One 1924 government document articulated particularly well the urgency of founding such an organization: "The protection of mothers and children represents one of the highest and most urgent priorities of our national life, an essential element of its defense, conservation, and progress. Youth truly constitutes our future society, and every action taken toward protecting their integrity and promoting physical, moral, and intellectual development is generally directed toward preserving the new generations from the influences of degenerative factors and preparing the progressive forms of social life."[107]

The Fascist concentration on the collective, as opposed to the individual, contributed to the idea that the state should not improve the healthy population at the expense of any unhealthy members of society.[108] Consequently, the goal of the ONMI was to strengthen the demographics of the nation both quantitatively and qualitatively, and to redeem the most vital elements of the entire Italian race. Though this early position—that the state needed to reclaim the health of *all* Italians—was in stark contrast to the Nazi concept of racial health in the next decade, the ONMI similarly argued that its measures were essential for "the health and physical improvement of the razza, and therefore one of the elements of strength and power of the State."[109] The programs that the ONMI organized and oversaw extended into many areas of Fascist life, but the majority of them addressed issues of education and child rearing. The program for a conference organized by the National Congress of Italian Women (CNDI) in 1923 explained that because the family was the first educator of the Fascist child, the regime was obligated to train men and women in Fascist values so that they could pass them on to their children from the very first days of life.[110] The ONMI played a leading role in organizing nursery schools, climate colonies, and medical conferences. In addition, it instituted a system of rural ambulatory clinics, whose mission mirrored that of the organization at large: to teach peasants about childcare, health, and hygiene; to administer medication; and to help with prenatal care.[111] These clinics helped to cut down on mortality rates, and in 1929 officials established programs in twelve national universities to train doctors and medical assistants in the requisite skills to establish and run increasing numbers of them.[112] All the services that provided for the health of women and children were—in the words of Attilio Lo Monaco-Aprile, the ONMI's first president—"necessary elements of, and therefore inseparable from, the unified and totalitarian project that has, as its ultimate goal, the defense and physical and moral improvement of the razza."[113]

Developing a Written Curriculum

Notwithstanding the pedagogical emphasis on organic and active learning and the logistical variations between rural and urban schools, the effort to create generic textbooks played an essential role in developing a national Fascist elementary curriculum. But while the 1923 Gentile Reform articulated the new institutional and pedagogical foundations of the Italian elementary education, teachers in these early years continued to use many textbooks from the pre-Fascist period.[114] This reality certainly pointed to the limitations of Fascist efforts to transform the education system quickly and fully, but it also performed a valuable service for the new administration. The majority of the material in these textbooks came in the form of passages and quotations from famous Italian heroes and authors, which bolstered Lombardo Radice's strong support for providing students with lessons from the most respected Italians of the past and present. Such specialists and celebrities could inspire in young students the passion and curiosity for subjects that were essential to Lombardo Radice's conception of education. Moreover, this format lent legitimacy to the nascent Fascist project: national experts and historical texts could provide clear evidence that Fascist ideals were inherently Italian ideals.

Nevertheless, the new administration was certain that pre-Fascist texts could be improved to further define and strengthen italianità. Under the Gentile Reform, and through the initiatives of Lombardo Radice, the MPI instituted a semiannual commission to review all existing public school textbooks and select those that were acceptable for the coming year.[115] The primary school committee, chosen by the minister of public instruction, read through hundreds of texts submitted by authors from all over the nation. In 1926, for example, out of 1,326 entries, the committee approved 949 texts for classrooms and 100 more for school and town libraries, denying state approval to 277 books.[116] The assignment was presented to Italian children's authors as a competition, requiring the publishers to submit several copies of the texts along with a fee. The committee then published their selections in the summer editions of the ministry's *Official Bulletin* (*Bolletino ufficiale*), and in 1925 the committee started printing small explanations of why they chose each book, in the hopes that such descriptions would guide authors in the right direction for upcoming years.[117]

The requirements for selection grew more restrictive as a result of the government's clearer understanding of its own mission, and the MPI began complaining about the difficulty of finding appropriate elementary textbooks. The commission argued that this difficulty resulted in large part from the substantial time involved in reviewing all the submitted texts.[118] Such a task needed to be handled with patience and care, Arrigo Solmi, a contemporary historian and Fascist official, explained, because the educational and cultural worth of elementary school largely depended on the quality of the textbooks, and the undertaking was made infinitely more challenging with such a great number of submissions. He believed that many of the proposals were written out of more commercial interest than educational concern—selection was certainly critical to the livelihood of these publishers—leading to a sizeable number of them being inappropriate for the new system and the elevated purpose of elementary education. Solmi concluded that the government needed to play a more significant role in designing the texts, and the content of the books needed to reflect the ideals of the New Italy, which were coming more clearly into focus.[119]

Partly as a result of such critiques, a royal decree on March 18, 1928, stated, "History, geography, literature, economics and law textbooks for elementary schools and for vocational schools must respond, in the spirit of the current curricula, to the historical, political, legal, and economic demands established from October 28 [1922] on."[120] This vague proclamation encouraged the ministry to become increasingly stringent in its textual requirements but gave authors few specific guidelines to inspire their writing. Authors submitted a dramatically larger number of new publications in 1927, 1928, and 1929; correspondingly, the commission approved fewer and fewer books.[121] This fact pointed less to the lack of Fascist sentiment among some children's authors—though that may well have been the case— than to the persistent imprecision of the ideals of the New Italy. The criteria of what made a textbook properly Fascist appeared to be much like the U.S. Supreme Court's Justice Potter Steward's 1964 definition of pornography: the commission would know it when it saw it.

The approved texts of the late 1920s did contain more overtly nationalistic and Fascist rhetoric.[122] Nevertheless, later in 1928 the commission published a report that explained that less than half of the books presented to them had been appropriate for Fascist schools; it also included a list of texts that authors or editors needed to reexamine or amend.[123] Then, in 1929, the MPI began to deny the approval of texts by foreign authors, because students were supposedly not graduating from school with enough of a "Fascist spirit."[124] The Fascist state believed in the tremendous importance of textbooks in the formation of a more uniform, widespread sense of italianità among the youngest Italians and sought to define those racial ideas ever more clearly over the course of the 1920s. The debate over textbooks seemingly ended in the 1928 demand for nationalized textbooks to begin production in 1930.

The Legacy of the 1923 Gentile Reform

The Fascist government of the 1920s presented the 1923 Gentile Reform as illustrative of the goals of the state and the mission of the education system. Pietro Fedele, the minister of public instruction from 1925 to 1928, explained that "Fascism was and is, in all respects, a conscious, documented reevaluation ... of the essential virtues of the Italian stirpe: and the Gentile Reform

is eminently Fascist because, inserted in this work of rehabil-
itation, it proposes to the Italian youth ... the goals of education and culture that are identified in our thousand-year-old
and eternal civilization."[125] The authors of the 1923 reforms—
Giovanni Gentile as well as Giuseppe Lombardo Radice, Ernesto
Codignola, and others—conceived of education as a means to
form the spirit of the Italian youth.[126] This characterization of
the reforms relied heavily on the vague and mutable meaning of
Fascism at this early date, illustrating the struggles the government faced in formulating its own identity during these years.
Ultimately, however, they created the institutional and pedagogical framework that would train Italian children according
to a distinctly Fascist elaboration of the Italian race.

Gentile's policies almost immediately elicited harsh criti-
cism from both sides of the political spectrum. On the one
hand, some of Gentile's closest colleagues balked at the philosopher's increasingly close relationship with Mussolini and
his vision for the nation-state; many of those philosophers and
pedagogues who had seen the rise of Fascism as an opportunity
to shape the new educational system in their own image abandoned the ministry, especially in the wake of the 1924 Matteotti
Crisis. Croce, who would become one of the most famous anti-
Fascist intellectuals, quickly distanced himself from his former
partner after Gentile's rise to political prominence. Additionally, by the end of 1924, Lombardo Radice, who had never hid-
den his concerns about the new political environment from his
good friend Gentile, left the realm of national education policy
amid debates about the role of politics in elementary education
and the future of democratic politics in Italy.[127] While he and
Gentile would maintain a cordial relationship, their collaboration and friendship appear never to have resumed the same
intimacy. Just as Mussolini abandoned—or lost—the support
of more-moderate political reformers as he gained confidence
in his New Italy, Gentile, too, would choose to support the
more uncompromising position of the regime at the expense
of many intellectual friendships.[128]

At the same time, Mussolini's more precise vision of his
mission, as well as pressure from more-intransigent Fascists

who believed that Gentile's pedagogy was not nearly political enough in intent or content, ultimately overwhelmed many of the reforms' original intentions. By the end of the 1920s Gentile himself would be long gone from the offices of the MPI, as the alterations to the 1923 reforms multiplied and the party and regime became clearer in their purpose and more confident in their power. The more authoritarian members of the regime could not and did not immediately dismiss the principles of Gentile's reforms, however. His reforms contributed significantly to the centralization of the school system, and the institutions founded in the 1920s would remain critical for the regime's efforts to rejuvenate the Italian race throughout the 1930s. Furthermore, Gentile and his colleagues had instituted the methodological approach to elementary education that would remain central to Italian pedagogy well into the next decade and, in many ways, beyond the Fascist period.[129] Ultimately, the early efforts of Gentile, Lombardo Radice, Ricci, and others would prove an essential foundation from which to prepare the race for its supposedly predestined role as ruler of a renewed Roman Empire.

2

"Reawakening the Spirit"

In 1927 the prolific author Armando Esposito published a series of books for elementary students on summer vacation. These texts aimed to synthesize and review the most important lessons of the previous academic year in order to keep them fresh in students' minds; officials believed that without such resources children might forget the fundamentals teachers had so assiduously imparted during the school year. Published roughly five years after Benito Mussolini's March on Rome, a majority of the collection's readers began their elementary school experience after Giovanni Gentile and Giuseppe Lombardo Radice had settled into their offices at the MPI. By exploring Esposito's exercises, one begins to ascertain the definition of italianità as the new Fascist regime presented it to a new generation of students. One exercise—designed to help rising fourth-graders distinguish between the active and passive voices—illustrated especially well the types of values the state expected educators to emphasize in their daily lessons: "Romolo founded Rome. The Romans conquered the world. Italy was plundered by barbarians. The fatherland is loved by its children. Martyrs face death for the fatherland. The summer produces the most beautiful fruit. The peasant works the land. The sea is crossed by speedy steamers, just as the sky is sliced by fast airplanes. Vices destroy men. Work strengthens and enriches citizens."[1]

This interplay of messages about ancient Rome, Italian martyrdom, rural life, modern technologies, and discipline—interspersed among versions of popular lullabies, fables, and fairy tales—was a crucial feature of the Fascist effort to create a holistic concept of italianità. Indeed, it characterized elementary lessons between 1922 and 1929, but it also permeated primary education for the duration of Mussolini's rule.[2] In particular, the themes of language, geography, history, discipline, and obedience were key subjects for Fascist officials and educators as they demarcated the boundaries of the Italian race within the notion of italianità. Of course, like the regime's education system and pedagogy at large, Fascist italianità was not crafted out of whole cloth or overnight; many of the ideas analyzed here were longtime leitmotifs of Italian identity in pre-Fascist Italy. Liberal and Fascist italianità shared the assumption that Italians were the descendants of the mighty Romans, connected by blood and soil. Essential characteristics of the Italian stirpe therefore included the mythic attributes of the Romans, such as great strength, wisdom, and morality. In addition, Fascists increasingly emphasized the "inherently Italian" values of obedience, faith—both religious and national—discipline, and will to action; and officials believed that an intensive campaign of bonifica umana could prepare Italians to reawaken their elemental selves and emerge as *New* Italians who could use their collective superiority to reestablish a Roman Empire.[3]

This racial conception of the Italian character was intrinsically linked to the Fascist understanding of Italian national identity. In fact, during the 1920s, Fascist ideas regarding Italian racial and national identity were frequently interchangeable, as the boundaries between the two were quite porous at this stage. In part, Fascist language about race and nation was interchangeable because of the contemporary notion of nationhood. Certainly the most basic understanding of nation was the organization of a group of people under a single, autonomous government. But what was more important to the modern notion of nationhood—as it manifested among Italians as well as many other Western populations—was the idea that a nation was an entity separate from its government.[4] In Ernst Renan's famous 1882 speech, "What Is a Nation?," the French philosopher concluded that "a nation is a spiritual principle, the outcome of the profound complications of history; it is a spiritual family, not a group determined by the shape of the earth."[5] In other words, at the heart of a modern nation was the idea that bonds more powerful than shared government—such as history, culture, language, geography, religion, economies, and race—naturally united groups of people; ultimately, the political entity of a nation-state should reflect these politically transcendent commonalities.[6] In the case of interwar Italy, the notion of nation relied on an ethnocultural definition.[7] As the political scientist and sociologist Liah Greenfeld has explained, "in ethnic nationalisms, 'nationality' became a synonym of 'ethnicity', and national identity is often perceived as a reflection or awareness of possession of 'primordial' or inherited group characteristics, components of 'ethnicity', such as language, customs, territorial affiliation, and physical type."[8] Italian nationalism and ethnicity—which, in our case, was synonymous with race—formed a dialogical relationship. The Fascist construction of an Italian national identity—which, the sociologist and philosopher Ernest Gellner has argued, "sometimes takes preexisting cultures and turns them into nations, sometimes invents them, and often obliterates pre-existing cultures"—was also the construction of a shared Italian racial identity; both consisted of a set of characteristics that was inherited not just by politics but also by lineage.[9] The Italian national community was the Italian racial community.

Nationalists and politicians in the Kingdom of Italy had worked to inform its subjects about their shared national identity since unification. A fundamental difficulty in this campaign under the Liberal government had been the limited reach of a state bureaucracy and infrastructure that could unify the popular experience of an Italian identity.[10] Therefore, the first step for the new Fascist regime to was to establish an expansive official presence that could educate the population about italianità, and the administrators at the MPI spent much of the 1920s doing just that through the development of the bureaucracy and institutions discussed in the previous chapter. The next step was to instill an italianità that incorporated Italy's multitude of distinct communities, that transcended physical and linguistic differences, and that emphasized the inherited nature of Italian grandeur.

The elementary curriculum of the 1920s supported this mission by clearly establishing each student's connection to the larger community, highlighting the role language, geography, history, obedience, and discipline played in the foundation of the Italian nation and race. Teachers were to apply Gentile's principles of organic and active learning to the education of what Italy was; what it meant to be Italian; and ultimately, how each student could personally embody the ideals of italianità. At the core of elementary education, therefore, lay two parallel and mutually dependent projects: spiritual instruction (for the minds of the students) and physical training (for the bodies of the students). The lessons became more uniform as Fascism itself gained clarity and confidence in the 1930s, but 1920s educational materials highlight critical concepts—frequently appropriated from pre-Fascist rhetoric and rebranded as Fascist—that helped define the Fascist understandings of race and nation for the entirety of Mussolini's regime.

Defining the Italian Racial Community through the Concept of Patria

One of the key terms Fascism used to portray Italy's national and racial community simultaneously was *patria*, or "fatherland." The very translation of the word indicates both the political and racial meaning of the term; *patria* referred to the Kingdom of Italy as the political manifestation of the Italian community but also suggested the shared parentage of all Italians. As Armando Esposito explained to rising fifth-graders, "Without a fatherland you would have no name ... or feel any brotherhood with its peoples."[11] The educational idealist Pietro Romano attempted to capture the rich meaning of patria when he wrote that the "fatherland is not only a physical place, but a complex of traditions, customs, institutions, laws, language, and also religion, all of which distinguish one people from another."[12] Perhaps the best way to access these numerous layers of the word, however, is to explore a passage from another one of Esposito's many textbooks, this time geared toward students about to enter the second grade:

Child, learn from a young age to love your fatherland, the great and beautiful Italy. It is the country that gathers many families like your own who speak like you; it has high mountains, wide rivers, and rich cities; it contains forests, waterfalls, gardens, lakes, and magnificent fields that you will become acquainted with when you are more involved in your studies. Imagine that, at one point not long ago, this Italian land was prey to evil men who did not speak our language, who came from other, faraway lands and stole our treasures. In order to be free, the Italians had to go to war, and they fought numerous enemies: it cost many young men and cities; the struggle caused many fires and created many ruins, all so that we could finally gain the freedom to live peacefully in our homes. For that reason, love your fatherland that has cost so many sacrifices; honor its symbol, the tricolor flag, and think that you, too, so young, working and studying in school, will make it stronger and more powerful.[13]

In this paragraph, Esposito touched on four aspects of patria that were particularly important to the Fascist ideology and pedagogy in these first years of the regime and remained central to the evolving ideas of racial identity throughout its reign: language, geography, history, and obedience.

"It Is the Country That Gathers Many Families like Your Own Who Speak like You"

Of the four themes Esposito introduced, he gave pride of place to the linguistic characteristics of the fatherland. Of course, identifying language as a critical component of national identity was nothing new. For example, Edmondo De Amicis (1846–1908) was a prominent Italian author of children's literature in the late nineteenth century who often discussed the importance of language to the definition of the nation. His writing, most notably his classic 1886 children's book, *Cuore*, was frequently excerpted in early Fascist textbooks. In one such example, De Amicis argued that language was "the strongest link in the unity of our people, the echo of our past, the voice of our future," and the essence of the fatherland.[14] Reflecting such sentiments, Giovanni Gentile and his 1923 reforms mandated that classes throughout the kingdom were to be taught in the language of the state; instilling a single, vernacular language would be essential to the creation of a national community, both practically, through interregional communication, and spiritually, through a broader feeling of cultural solidarity.[15] Furthermore, Gentile's reforms required elementary students to be versed not only in standard Italian grammar and vocabulary but also in famous passages and speeches from Italian history and literature to teach them about the Italian language and prominent figures in Italian history, as well as the shared literary tradition that united all Italians.[16]

This promotion of the Italian national language directly confronted—and conflicted with—the predominance of regional languages in Italian daily life, and Gentile and his colleagues were well aware that they could not redefine Italy's linguistic landscape overnight. Indeed, other stipulations of the reforms, and particularly many of Lombardo Radice's initiatives, acknowledged this challenge by embracing the prevalence of regional languages. The idealists believed that highlighting local culture would ultimately strengthen pride in the national culture; instead of underscoring the divisions of the nation, an appreciation of local cultures would feed into a deeper cultural understanding of the fatherland.[17] Accordingly, the peninsula and islands' many local experiences—historical, cultural, and linguistic—became an important feature of the 1920s elementary curriculum.[18] One writer, reflecting on the goals of Gentile's reforms in the state-sponsored journal *Annals of Elementary Instruction (Annali dell'istruzione elementare)*, explained that the Gentile Reform "rehabilitated the idea of tradition, in its innumerable aspects, recognizing its supreme importance in the spiritual formation of children; and not just the noble and learned, or national, tradition, but also popular, or regional, tradition, that varies from place to place, like folklore and dialect."[19] This movement to embrace local heritage coincided nicely with the pedagogical principle of organic learning. Honoring the diversity of regional cultures, "still distinct and at times contrasting," would enable students to better understand them; and "fused together, they would give new energy, almost a new youth, a virgin and pure blood, to the Italian school."[20] The ideal, then, was to embrace linguistic and cultural diversity as long as students recognized that national (and racial) unity necessitated the use of the national language.[21] The author of one fourth-grade text-book shared his vision of an Italy unified by its linguistic rich-ness: "Soldiers from all regions of Italy march together, speaking various dialects, but still understanding one another because they all learned the beautiful Italian language in school. They joke among themselves on marches through the mountains or on the plains, chatting, laughing, or teaching each other songs from Trieste or Naples."[22] In other words, Italians would main-tain connections to their individual histories while understand-ing that they existed within a greater racial community.

This archetype appeared not to work quite as well in the newly acquired territories of Venezia Tridentina and Venezia Giulia in northern and northeastern Italy, where inhabitants pre-dominantly spoke Germanic and Slavic languages—languages of populations that actively participated in the conception of their own spiritually conceived nations and races.[23] The Fascist priority, then, was to emphasize the spiritual belonging of these "historically Italian" regions to the kingdom; and since it was difficult to argue convincingly that their languages were histor-ically Italic—that is, having at least partial roots in ancient lan-guages found on the peninsula—the regime had to be wary of their inclusion in daily lessons. The curriculum in these terri-tories was taught in standardized Italian, as it was in all public schools. But while local languages in most other regions were treated as essential components of lessons in the national Ital-ian language and culture, the Germanic and Slavic languages of the "redeemed" regions could only be taught as secondary languages.[24] Alto Adige (known to German speakers as Süd Tirol) was a particularly salient example of these Fascist mea-sures. As early as May 29, 1923, all Austrian place names were Italianized; and by early August 1923, it was forbidden to use the terms *Tirolo, Sud Tirolo,* or anything related therein.[25] Addi-tionally, and more telling of the racial concerns in these terri-tories, by the second half of the 1920s the national government began to recruit teachers from other, more "Italian" regions and offered prizes to those who initiated activities and propaganda that promoted italianità.[26] The MPI emphasized the importance of linguistic richness in a nation with disparate traditions; however, where regional languages threatened to undermine rather than enhance national and racial unity, the regime insisted on uniformity over diversity.

"It Contains Forests, Waterfalls, Gardens, Lakes, and Magnificent Fields"

The second layer of meaning in Esposito's passage concerned the geographical aspects of patria. Historians and geographers have recently devoted much attention to the strong links nineteenth- and twentieth-century nationalists identified between ideas of nation and landscape. Illustrations of supposedly characteristic landscapes created, as the geographer Joshua Hagen has argued, an image of the nation for its members as well as for outsiders. Landscapes gave literal shape to the ideas of shared histories, cultures, and morals that nationalists championed among members of their communities.[27] Italian educators, too, urged young students to learn about the land on which they lived; children needed to love its wide rivers and undulating hills protected by the expanse of the Mediterranean Sea and the heights of the Alps. Such a landscape was the physical embodiment of their fatherland and the literal progenitor of the people: "The land is our mother; she gives us bread, oil, fruit, colorful flowers and grass; then, when we are dead, she welcomes us into her arms and holds us there forever, as children, all equal and all at peace."[28] According to the curriculum, then, being a true Italian required understanding one's connections and debts to the land that sustained the race. Many educational texts integrated imagery of Italian landscapes, and field trips to the countryside drew on Gentile's principles of organic and active learning to establish stronger bonds between students and their homeland.[29]

It is important to note, however, that though textbooks often described a number of regional landscapes, the imagery was frequently limited to an idealized depiction of central Italian geography: tended fields of green and yellow, a single farmhouse framed by tall Cypress trees, sunflowers following the daily path of the sun. Educators spoke of the importance of local landscapes and personal connections to the land, but illustrations aimed to create, as historian John Agnew has described, "a bounded national space with a considerable degree of internal cultural homogeneity."[30] Like the establishment of a single national language, a common vision of the Italian land helped consolidate the vast array of diverse cultural, linguistic, economic, and social experiences of the Italian population and reassert the unity of the racial community.

"In Order to Be Free, the Italians Had to Go
to War, and They Fought Numerous Enemies"

The third facet of Esposito's description of patria was the history that all Italians inherited. According to Mussolini himself, "the nation is, above all, spiritual and not only territorial. There are states that have had immense territories and have not left a trace on human history. . . . A nation is great only when it can translate its power into the strength of its spirit."[31] Intrinsic to this indistinct idea of an Italian national spirit—the spirit of the Italian race—was the belief that every child should have an active knowledge of Italian history. History lessons explained that even if other societies were theoretically capable of becoming civilized, or if other peoples had at one point developed impressive societies, most of them eventually declined and died out. By contrast, Italy was a civilization that had experienced *periods* of difficulty and regression but would always return to the pinnacle of civilization.[32] Rome was the past, present, and future center of world civilization: "Of course victory will be for Rome, which always was the dominator and teacher of peoples throughout the centuries, and which, therefore, represents [the definition of] civilization."[33] Furthermore, Italians were the only *true* descendants of ancient Rome. As one fourth-grade textbook exclaimed, "We are proud to be Italians and to be a part of this people that has thirty centuries of civilization, and that was big when others were not yet born!"[34] The Italian race and nation were founded on the great achievements of Italy's past, and administrators urged teachers to revitalize its essence that was inherited by each and every Italian.

Elementary history lessons tended to avoid an explanation of human origins and, instead, plunged right into the power of and respect for the peninsula's ancient Etruscan, Greek, and Roman past. Many of the 1920s textbooks started with the legendary birth of Romulus and Remus, and the Roman society the two brothers helped create. In addition to these lessons, Mussolini initiated a national archeological campaign to substantiate the greatness of the Roman past—and connect it to the present— thereby confirming its role in Italy's future.[35] These physical examples of Roman grandeur surrounded Italians young and old with clear evidence of their racial obligation to ascend once again to the greatest heights of global power.[36]

Though the Roman Empire represented the height of the Italian race's past glory, elementary lessons in Italy's rich heritage did not stop at its downfall. The history curriculum picked up again with the monumental contributions of the Renaissance and then the dramatic events of Italy's nineteenth-century Risorgimento. This latter subject represented a bit of a departure from pre-Fascist lessons, and newer texts aimed to portray this period as one involving Italians from all classes and regions in the seamless creation of the Italian Kingdom. As soon as Pietro Fedele, himself a trained historian, took the reins as minister of public instruction in 1926, he declared that the Risorgimento was to be taught with the highest sense of italianità—that is, with the greatest emphasis on the themes of unity, sacrifice, and faith in the greater mission of the race.[37] Educators and Fascists believed that the heroic acts of its participants—some of whom were still living—would rejuvenate the race and instill pride within Italy's children.

Greater delicacy was needed when approaching the subject of Italy's most recent war, which had destroyed so many lives and ended with such an unsatisfying peace treaty. The war experiences of parents and older siblings were not far from children's minds, and the state needed to present the broadly unpopular war and disorganized military as a story of national unity and stoicism. At the same time, Mussolini could not deny his people the pain of their memories. In sum, portrayals of World War I had to focus on the importance of the great sacrifices that Italian soldiers and civilians made in that bloody struggle.[38] One vignette in a child's 1926–27 almanac accomplished such a task by avoiding descriptions of the military battles and instead relaying a 1917 clash between a proud Italian woman, Oliva Teso, and a member of the invading Austrian force. When the Austrian soldier tried to prevent Teso from displaying an Italian flag, she cried, "I will still display it! And if you want to shoot, here is my flesh. At least I will die wrapped in my flag, the flag of Italy!"[39]

The historian Michel Ostenc aptly described this predominant vision of the last war as "instilling in the child the conviction that the great periods of his national history are those in which the people knew self-sacrifice."[40] In line with this approach, the Fascist writer and teacher Nicolò Giurlanda wrote to his students, "I saw and knew the indescribable joy of liberation after having known the terrible pain of seeing our land profaned by the enemy . . . the land has been rendered sacred by the blood of the dead."[41] Textbooks and educators primarily approached the Great War as a war of national liberation from foreign influence—a step toward the completion of the Risorgimento to some—and it was not until the late 1930s that Italian textbooks began in earnest to remark on the embarrassment of the Versailles Treaty and the necessity of vindication.[42]

Overall, these lessons stressed the importance of teaching Italians that the nation was bigger than the self—that Italian history stretched far behind and ahead of the lives of individual Italians and that their primary role in the world was to contribute, sacrificially if needed, to that great history of the Italian race.[43] The history lessons that took place in the classroom were combined with the new practices of daily salutes to the Italian flag, pilgrimages to historic sites, and the establishment of memorial parks, all of which incorporated the memory of Italy's past into the everyday life of the students. Of great significance in this regard was the Italian Tomb of the Unknown Soldier. Its innovation and importance in the postwar period lay, as John Gillis has explained, in "remembering everyone by remembering no one in particular."[44] Nations all over Europe erected such monuments, and the Italian government established its memorial on the steps of the National Monument of Vittorio Emanuele II—a sizable tribute to the first monarch and "father" of united Italy—placed in the center of ancient and modern Rome, the heart of the Italian nation and, to Fascists, the birthplace of the Italian race.[45] Designed and constructed in the final days of Italy's Liberal regime, the monument played a crucial role in the Fascist commemoration of the Great War and became the site of innumerable other ceremonies, pilgrimages, and speeches.[46]

The focus on the heroic history of the fatherland—ancient Rome as well as the Renaissance and Risorgimento—served the essential purpose of justifying the national and racial claims to political and cultural superiority, but it was not enough to say that Italians were superior because they had been superior in the past. Elementary lessons required a delicate balance of honoring the greatness of Italians' past and illustrating their shortcomings. They needed to create a collective bond to the immortal Italian race but also to prove the need for the Fascist regime. Textbooks made clear that young Italians could not be satisfied with past laurels. Rather, as the Duce was quoted in one textbook, "We will be great only when the past is simply a platform from which to launch into the future!"[47] The regime, with the help of its youngest followers, was working to restore and strengthen the grandeur of the fatherland, and that project necessitated much work from all Italians: "Rome, the city of the empire, the holy city of our religion, cradle of our people and glory of our stirpe, is reawakening to a new life. But to allow it to reconquer the triumphal place that is its right requires great effort and unrelenting work for many years."[48]

Beyond simply creating a strong sense of national and racial pride in the Italian youth, such messages echoed the regime's calls for irredentism and colonialism to fulfill the needs of the race and nation-state. Educators were to stress the need for international respect and power that was their racial birthright: "No other nation can boast of a history such as ours; no other people has faced such adversity, or has overcome that adversity so masculinely [*virilmente*] as ours. . . . We are aware of this greatness, just as we are aware of the need to expand beyond our natural boundaries."[49] In these early years of the regime, the ostensibly logical conclusion that the historic greatness of the Italian race obliged the modern nation-state to redefine its borders primarily manifested itself in irredentist claims. Fascists called for the return of all "rightfully Italian lands" and people along the Aegean that had not been granted to the kingdom in the Treaty of Versailles.[50]

Still, by the mid-1920s, the regime began to lay the groundwork for more-extensive colonialism abroad. Mussolini's declaration of the Battle for Wheat (Battaglia del Grano) in mid-1925 initiated his measures to wean the Italian nation from dependence on the importation of wheat (and subsequently other products) and to become a self-sufficient society.[51] The next year, in 1926, Minister Fedele announced that April 21—recently declared Rome's official birthday—would also be a day to celebrate Italy's colonial holdings in order to "promote the formation of a colonial consciousness within the Italian population." The notice in the official MPI bulletin continued, "This event should demonstrate the maturity our country has achieved in the realms of conquest and colonization as well as be an act of faith in our future as a colonial nation."[52] The ministry required all teachers to prepare their students for this day of celebration by having talks and lectures on both the utility and necessity of Italian colonial expansion. So despite Mussolini's personal history of protests against Italian imperialism, it was clear that part of his plan to reclaim Italy's greatness would demand overseas conquests.[53]

Textbooks illustrated three primary reasons for the Fascist need to increase Italian territories: first, to regain the ancient title of being the most inspiring, powerful civilization in the world; second, to reclaim the historically Italian lands and people that foreign invaders had taken from Italy; and third, to become a global model of self-sufficiency, shedding dependence on inferior, foreign nations and providing lands for the constantly increasing Italian race.[54] In 1928 the minister of corporations—later to be minister of education—Giuseppe Bottai wrote that once the nation had truly re-created an Italian empire, "we will find faster and easier resolutions to our demographic and alimentary problems as well as our difficulties with access to resources and wealth."[55] The rationale underlying all these motives, however, was that the Italian race, with the necessary guidance of the Fascist Party, was politically, culturally, and spiritually superior to others and—according to theories of social Darwinism— had a right to subjugate other populations that the government deemed inferior. Certainly such an argument was nationalist in intent. But just as importantly, it was racist—Italians were *born* inherently superior to certain populations and therefore were entitled to subjugate those populations.

Most textbooks presented students with the concept of Italian colonialism as one of great benevolence and mutual benefit—a clear result of Italians' racial superiority. Felice Casale, in one of his 1929 third-grade textbooks, articulated a predominant attitude regarding the Italian efforts in northern and eastern Africa:

> Our colonies are vast African lands that at one time were uncultivated and unhealthy because their inhabitants were semisavages. Italy sent its soldiers to occupy those lands, to civilize those peoples. . . .
>
> Today the Italians in Africa are at home; they rendered the land fertile, constructed railroads, factories, churches, buildings, schools, and they continue to work. Italy needed colonies to be able to give work and well-being to all its children, who are many, and our peninsula is not sufficient.[56]

Because Italy was more powerful—evinced in part by its growth in population and wealth—the regime argued for its need to expand to meet mounting needs and to spread its superior civilization. In another educational text of the same year, Casale made his argument even clearer when he stated that Italian colonies helped form "the new Italic razza, which has kept the glorious destiny of bringing the stirpe back to the height of its historic origins."[57] The official view held that inherent racial superiority entitled the kingdom to maintain colonies but also that those colonies would increase the moral, economic, and political strength of the Italian race.

All these lessons in the legacy of Rome and the unchanging, innate characteristics of italianità worked to establish the trajectory of a coherent Italian past. Such a past obliged the nation's members, as Fascists, to march steadily toward the inevitable renewal of Italian glory in the kingdom and the creation of a new Italian empire.

"Love Your Fatherland That Has Cost So Many Sacrifices"

Therefore, it was not enough just to identify the language, geography, and history of the fatherland; as Esposito directed his readers, Italians needed to express their loyalty to the fatherland—as the homeland of the race—through the values of obedience and discipline. If the school system was to become "the lifeblood, the intellect and the heart, the meat and the muscles of the new youth," then one of its prime missions was to teach its students to be conscious of their individual obligations to the fatherland.[58] Only by accepting these requirements of membership to the race would students truly be able to partake in the great national project.

The priority of elementary education was not necessarily to endorse intelligence or specific skills—though those byproducts could certainly be useful—but to encourage hard work and discipline as representative values of the race.[59] Many textbook parables illustrated the terrible consequences of disobedience, laziness, and greed. Esposito appealed to his young first graders on vacation to "try to do something useful every day ... laziness is the father of vices and a lazy child quickly becomes bad, unreliable, and hateful."[60] To reject these moral weaknesses and embrace the responsibilities inherent in belonging to the patria meant to understand the essential attributes of the perfect Italian and Fascist. Though the texts of the 1920s made few direct references to Fascism or Mussolini, authors and officials utilized and augmented pre-Fascist educational materials to address the broad racial goals of Fascism. A critical exception to this tendency was the primary example illustrating Fascism's principle of "strength through unity"—the *fascio littorio*. The image of a bundle of sticks lashed to the handle of an ax brought the ancient Roman symbol of power to the present, and it served to remind Italians that they could always harness greater strength by working together—by supporting the center—than by working alone.[61]

Strength through unity required great discipline; therefore, an emphasis on the need for obedience was central to the education of a fundamentally Italian and Fascist student. In a textbook designed specifically for the moral education of the New Italian, the author explained, "He who is used to obeying from a young age will obey when he is grown up: life must be taken seriously when he is a child, and when he is a man."[62] It was imperative to train Italians from a young age to put their utmost faith in the authority of the fatherland and to recognize obedience as a core attribute of a young Fascist Italian. Authors of many first- and second-grade textbooks included a classic Italian piece titled "Obey!":

> A wise man was asked, "What should be a child's first virtue?"
> He responded, "Obedience."
> "And the second?"
> "Obedience."
> "And the third?"
> "Obedience."[63]

Gentile's keen interest in developing children's senses of freedom and spontaneity—that is, students' instinctive responses to the world around them—through organic and active learning ostensibly pushed against the Fascist need for obedience and collective action.[64] However, the philosopher believed that exposing students to the idea of personal freedom ultimately enhanced their dedication to authority. Teaching young students to trust their intuition and to develop their emotional intelligence meant building more passionate and thoughtful individuals but also fostering more-organic bonds with the patria and its community. He called for "an education that is not intellectual or rationalist, but rather one that is lively because it directs everything to nurture and develop sentiment; that is an education that is not abstractly humane, but personal, and for that reason it is national and patriotic. For us, it is an Italian education."[65] As they grew to understand their connections to the nation through personal engagement with their surroundings, children—and later adults—would naturally develop a sense of filial responsibility to the fatherland and the race. In short, encouraging personal freedom would not lead to anarchy but instead help Italians see that their interests coincided with—and were subsumed by—the interests of the larger community.[66]

Gentile's integration of mandatory religious education in primary education illustrated his approach to this cognitive process. Religion, as the historian Oreste Sagramola has explained, injected an "objective absolute moment," in which each individual recognized him- or herself as the unique product of a creator—or in other words, a small part of a much larger whole.[67] Gentile believed that such an existential lesson encouraged students to focus their creativity and efforts toward the success of the greater community.[68] Therefore, texts made it clear that "the perfect Fascist is a believer."[69] This pedagogical tactic also supported a more pragmatic consideration Mussolini and his regime had to accept when trying to define Fascist italianità: the success of the Fascist project ultimately hinged on establishing popular support. Consequently, Mussolini had to acknowledge the importance of the Catholic Church in Italian life. Furthermore, the overwhelming adherence of the Italian population to the Catholic faith provided the state with an identity that transcended language, geography, and class. The Duce accepted the emphasis on religion in elementary education because he envisioned it "as a tool of national unification" and "a source of moral and civic elevation" for the race.[70]

Moreover, Mussolini and his regime relied on the values and lessons of Catholicism to segue into lessons on the morals and values of Fascist faith in much the same way that the MPI used pre-Fascist resources to initiate early Fascist educational reforms.[71] The concepts of faith, humility, and selflessness were familiar to Italian Catholics, so Fascist calls to develop these characteristics did not present new material—they simply came from a new authority. By appropriating the values that already existed in Italian society, the state was gradually able to adapt and mold them to the evolving needs of the regime.

Employing the traditional institution of family became equally valuable to Fascist lessons in obedience and its role in italianità. Popular concepts of the ideal Italian family relied on clearly defined roles for each of the parents and the children.

According to this schema, fathers were to be the head of the family as strong, virile providers, while mothers were to be the moral role models in the realm of the home.[72] Children, above all else, were to obey their parents. Preparing students to become good children meant instilling the more general Fascist ideals of order, hierarchy, and loyalty. One can see this interaction of Fascist ideals in Alfredo Chiarini's proclamation: "Children must love their parents tenderly and with infinite respect, and help them when they need it; they should maintain healthy and strong bodies and balanced minds, and thereby they can reach not only the ideal of being happy, but maintaining the health of the family, which is the most important contribution to making the fatherland great, powerful, and feared!"[73]

Additionally, children needed to recognize the responsibilities that would be required of them in adulthood as husbands and wives, fathers and mothers. Since the household was the first school for the Italian child, the regime had to train boys and girls in the values of the race so that they could pass them on to their own children.[74] Thus one of the principal goals of the ONMI—as well as of the CRIG and other public health institutions—was to teach all young Italians, both male and female, the skills needed to maintain healthy and happy homes so that they could serve as the birthplace of the expanded and stronger Italian race.

It was in this realm of the curriculum that lessons became particularly gendered. Of primary concern was, as one text explained, to teach the Italian girl that she was to be an "affectionate daughter and loving sister, but we especially want her to be a mother; from the physical side, of perfect health and in full possession of hygienic norms. . . . But also a mother from the moral and spiritual side, because she must teach those who are the hope and the new blossoms of the stirpe patriotic, religious, and Fascist education from the earliest years of childhood."[75] Particularly in the rural areas of the kingdom, elementary education was an important source of information on the upkeep of the house and the family. One journalist emphasized the importance of such training, when he explained that "the house is the building block of the nation, and the nation is a complex organism that is much more noble than the cells that compose it. The propaganda created to form good house-wives, excellent mothers, and lovely homes is among the most valuable and effective."[76] In rural schools, young peasant girls, but not peasant boys, were required to take courses in *lavori donneschi*—domestic (women's) skills—which would teach girls the basics of rural homelife: "The subject is not professional material, but an element of the spiritual formation of the female student, and cannot be absent from any girls' elementary school."[77] As another journalist wrote, such gendered education was essential to the "civic and hygienic formation of the people," and teachers needed to establish and practice the skills at school so that they could be used in the home—"the foundational organism of the nation."[78]

As the education system trained Italy's girls to become dutiful wives and prolific mothers, boys were introduced to their future responsibilities as husbands and fathers. Because of their overwhelming obligation to protect those who depended on them, once the foundational value of obedience had been instilled in students, teachers and texts needed to cultivate the asset of courage: "Courage to conquer your ego and become charitable; courage to conquer your laziness and persevere honorably in all your studies; courage to defend the nation and to protect your peers in every encounter; courage to ignore illnesses and hardships of every kind; courage to resist bad examples and unjust derision; courage to yearn for perfection."[79] According to Fascist racial rhetoric, courage was the foundation of virility, which, in turn, was the foundation of the New Italian man.[80]

By stressing one's obligations to and roles within the family, the regime was able to prepare students for their duties to and connections with the greater racial community. Piero Domenichelli wrote to his third-grade readers, "Do you feel united by bonds of blood to your family both in life and in death? It is the same for the industrious and united nation, for the nation in which there are pure and sacred bonds of blood that unite us all together."[81] As in the case of religious education, using the familiar model of the family enabled Fascist educators to convey the importance of the blood bonds children also had with the race and nation. The regime was able to co-opt the language of the family, and its inherent hierarchy, to define the nation as a family, at whose head sat the father of all Italians: Benito Mussolini. In such a way, Fascist rhetoric further blurred the line between nation and race—as well as public and private life—and in the end, these bonds were ultimately meant to raise the Italian race above all others to create a superior New Italian and New Italy.

The courage needed in the everyday life of a faithful Italian and Fascist, in turn, required great discipline, both attributes clearly exemplified in Fascism's martial culture. Thus, the military became a third exemplar for teachers and texts educating the young male population about the critical importance of obedience, loyalty, courage, discipline, and strength to the patria and, through it, the race. While the Fascist exaltation of the military did not fully permeate the educational system until the 1930s, it was impossible to form a Fascist pedagogy without insisting on the importance of the military. In addition to praising the accomplishments of the Italian armed forces, texts often romanticized the life of the soldier and what it signified for the life of the nation. Soldiers were "the heroic defenders of the fatherland" and conducted "military exercises, hard and exhausting, to prepare themselves for war and to save the fatherland."[82] It was imperative to prepare the male population for their participation in the life of the race as protectors, but all Italians needed to respect the troops, who would fight and die for the glory of Italy.[83] By the end of the 1920s, authors and educators had begun to use military language to describe everyday activities, to promote the military lifestyle and its values. To go to school was to engage in a battle against ignorance; children learning to read were "soldiers of the alphabet"; miners were "soldiers of the abyss"; and peasants were "soldiers of the earth."[84]

The 1926 establishment of the ONB helped advance the militaristic aspects of Italy's education in italianità. The organization taught children about the spirit of sacrifice, responsibility, and pride.[85] The potential of the Italian race was captured in the image of these young Fascists, and textbooks described them as the embodiment of the Italian character. A Balilla was "swift, active, agile, disciplined"; he knew "how to fulfill his duty to school, to love his fatherland and to respect his religion in his daily activities"; and he was able "to distinguish himself in all competitions and, at the same time, to be always ready to stand at attention, to respond with 'yes, sir' when a command is directed at him, and proudly to demonstrate the Roman salute."[86] Shortly after the Senate approved the founding of the ONB, the organization's head, Renato Ricci, promised, "We will teach the youth the purest ideals, we will prepare them in the practice of all social virtues, so that we will have men prepared for the most painful and difficult sacrifices, men capable of the most generous derring-do."[87]

The primary objective of the ONB was to prepare boys to embrace their responsibilities and obligations as soldiers of the fatherland. As Leonida Fazi, a member of the ONB in the 1920s, would later explain, "The youth organizations offered adolescents the amazing opportunity to experience officially the game dear to every male: the uniform, the rifle, the tools, the camping; then they indulged in my exuberance, my desire to do and to be an active part of a the whole.... I always had with me the image of the handsome youth, always dynamic, smiling, full of enthusiasm."[88] Likewise, Elio Gizzi, who joined the ONB in its inaugural year of 1926, would recall, "To us boys ... it gave a sense of discipline, collectivity, participation, and, subsequently ... the pride of being a part of a nation-state and regime that were making history and constituted an original example, an object of study—and often admiration—in other parts of the world."[89]

These examples of the intended "masculine" response to the ONB are not meant to imply that the ONB neglected its female members; young girls who partook in the Piccole Italiane also learned to embrace martial order, hierarchy, and discipline. One textbook of the period explained to its readers that Piccole Italiane "always come to school on time, they never forget their promises, they never neglect their duties, they are obedient and respectful, and they love each other."[90] In addition to the self-restraint and conformity inherent in the military practices of the ONB, such a culture encouraged the familial bonding that so characterized military life and reinforced the patriotism that was essential to the meaning of patria and, ultimately, the Italian race.

For both boys and girls, a pillar of the ONB's project was to advance the physical education mandated in elementary school. Mussolini echoed the opinion of many public health officials in and outside Italy when he stated that to educate the body meant to educate the spirit and refine moral virtues. He cited numerous international and national studies indicating the significant links between physical and mental health.[91] As the author of one physical education text explained, "I will have done some good for our country if my modest work demonstrates to our youth the ever growing need to turn oneself to physical exercise. It is indispensable, especially in young students, to rebalance the intellectual forces which tend to weaken without it."[92] Children had a responsibility to become healthy and strong, not only for the good of their family, but also for the good of their neighbors and the good of the race.[93] Physical education, the administration argued, would perpetuate the passion and discipline that historically had imbued the Italian race and that would animate the New Italian.[94] Therefore, as the journalist Manlio Morgagni pointed out in 1928, the national regulation of physical education would inevitably "give the razza the opportunity to realize all its desired conquests."[95] Whereas the promotion of physical education was on the rise throughout western Europe and the United States, the spokespeople of the Fascist Revolution promoted not only its institution but also its centralization and, ultimately, its politicization for the good of the Italian race.

Through the 1920s, physical education in elementary schools was largely unisex.[96] As Esposito exhorted all his young readers, "Take many walks in the open air, in the sun that gives you strength and color; go swimming every day, as it makes you clean and your skin healthy and awakens your blood and appetite."[97] At the same time, many pedagogical articles of the 1920s characterized physical education as "virile" education (*educazione virile*)—even going so far as to establish a journal on the topic titled *L'educazione virile*—which would establish the masculine order necessary for the new generations of Italian men.[98] Nevertheless, Italian scholars referred to U.S. studies showing that physical education was quite helpful for the moral education of girls—preparing them for their roles within the family— but warned that educators had to consider different factors in the physical fitness of young Italian girls.[99] As the regime increasingly delineated the characteristics of the New Italian and demarcated gender roles in Italian society, girls' physical education changed to reflect the Fascist views of the sensitivities of the female sex: girls were trained physically through exercises emphasizing grace, coordination, and teamwork, rather than strength, aggression, and competition.[100] Such precautions would ensure their physical fitness while simultaneously maintaining their femininity.

The various outdoor schools, summer camps, and climate colonies that the ONB and ONMI organized also played a critical part in the efforts to inculcate a culture of exercise and vigor among all Italian children.[101] They were, in general, geared toward instructing children in what Fascist officials and doctors considered a healthy lifestyle. Like the ONB and Esposito's vacation-time textbooks, the regime hoped these extracurricular opportunities would further implant the principles of a Fascist existence while at the same time encouraging camaraderie and genuine enjoyment. The author of a 1927 article in the *Illustrated Journal of the Popolo d'Italia* (*La rivista illustrata del Popolo d'Italia*) asserted that "schools, gymnasiums, libraries, and social and book clubs are not enough: it is also necessary to offer oases of beauty and purity to our children, where they may restore their minds and rejuvenate their bodies."[102] The journalist Morgagni further explained that with these resources, "Fascism rebuilds the nation . . . in its human material, which is the greatest of the divine creations and, for Italy, constitutes the rich reserve of the stirpe."[103] Physical strength would allow the greatest characteristics of the Italian race to come to the fore once again. Thus, participants spent their days engaged in a variety of outdoor activities that depended on the time of year and location. Swimming, skiing, hiking, painting outdoors, playing soccer, and team-building exercises (such as using their bodies to form messages to the Duce on the ground) combined with sunbathing, napping, reading, and singing songs about the nation and the Fascist Revolution, to strengthen the body, create a sense of solidarity, and tighten the bonds between the Italian youth and the patria. One vignette in Felice Casale's 1929 textbook for fourth graders described the scene of children heading off for a month at state-sponsored summer camps: "When the train started moving, I heard the first notes of the hymn 'Giovinezza.' It was a thanksgiving to the fatherland, to Fascist Italy who loves his children and wants them healthy and strong, and will not stop at anything for their physical and spiritual education."[104] Such an image, which ended the textbook and sent its readers off on summer vacation, aimed to illustrate the generosity and joy associated with being loyal and enthusiastic Fascists.

There was an interesting juxtaposition of the lessons that glorified military life with others that encouraged a life of peace in these early years of the regime.[105] It seems that the state struggled to reconcile the militaristic core of the movement—as well as the sense of idealized masculinity inherent in military culture—with the deep desire of most Italians to avoid war at all cost. Authors and educators especially praised the life of the farmer and the ideals that rural life represented to Fascists. One passage in a textbook for fourth graders attempted to combine the ideal lifestyles of soldier and peasant: "After victory, the veterans of the last war joyfully returned to cultivate their fields and orchards, to plant wheat and corn, rice and hemp, to tend the valuable soil of the fatherland! With love they returned to the work that provides bread, the life, the true and noble wealth, for the nation!"[106] In many textbooks, the Italian peasant was the true national hero: he worked hard at "the healthy work of the fields" to provide sustenance for the nation and—at least in the eyes of Fascist propagandists—was content with a simple family life in the countryside.[107] Through examples of this type of Italian, authors also taught peasant children to appreciate the sparseness of their lives and not to envy those who lived more extravagantly. Luxury, writers claimed, most often brought unhappiness; the children of the countryside supposedly had a purity of spirit that those of the wealthy and urban lacked.[108]

As in many other European nations at the time, Italian politicians and academics were concerned about the negative effects of urbanization on the health of the population and nation at large.[109] On a basic level, they argued that cities were unhealthy for children because there were few open spaces for them to run and breathe fresh air.[110] Alternatively, returning to the agricultural roots of the Italian people would strengthen the race in body and spirit; connecting one's life to the outdoors would provide the hygienic benefits of exercise, sunshine, and fresh air, as well as the spiritual benefit of connecting with the historical and cultural roots of the Italian race. One writer for the ONMI journal *Motherhood and Childhood* (*Maternità ed infanzia*) wrote, "Ruralization, according to the Duce's concept of Fascism, as everyone knows, is the return to a love of the fields and to rural life, the return to the legendary virtues of the razza that was born of the earth and from the earth, enriched by its labor."[111] Public education was the primary weapon with which to fight for ruralization, and the ideal of having the Italian people in touch with their fatherland on both physical and spiritual levels permeated Fascist elementary curricula.[112] As the elementary textbook review committee wrote of *The Peasant's Book* (*Il libro del contadino*), a book for rural schools, it was chosen because it illustrated "a true *agrarian awareness* in the country," an essential element in the campaign to create New Italians.[113]

Because of the extreme importance of the ruralization campaign in Fascism's concept of the patria and the Italian race, the government mandated numerous resources directed toward the rural school population. It ordered the development of textbooks specifically for rural schools that placed a greater emphasis on the characteristics of each season; the Italian countryside and the important holidays; hygiene on the farm, including the dangers of dust and the importance of warm winter clothing; and important household chores that all peasant children needed to perform. Additionally, the National Association for the Interests of Southern Italy (ANIMI) required that every rural school provide a small plot of land on school grounds for a garden or animal husbandry, with which they could impart practical and up-to-date training to their students.[114] This organization also established its own rural elementary schools and held evening and weekend classes for older community members.

The ONB also played a critical role in the state's presence in rural Italy. Shortly after its inception, it began establishing experimental gardens and practical courses in agriculture; building youth centers and gyms; organizing vocational schools and evening classes; and erecting a Cinema del balilla in every municipality, where members could view films produced by the state film corporation, the LUCE Institute (Istituto L'unione cinematografica educativa).[115] These endeavors were deemed essential to the political development of rural areas where children and their parents were largely sheltered from the reach of the central government and, therefore, required more intensive instruction in the goals of the new Fascist nation for the Italian race.

Educating young Italians in both urban and rural schools about their agricultural roots illustrated the essential connection of mind and body in Fascist education. Intellectual development was, for Fascist educators, inextricably linked to physical, moral, and spiritual development: "It is evident that an education of the mind prepares one for that of the heart and character. Physical education is therefore the best means for intellectual education, which is, in its turn, preparation for moral education."[116] Educators and officials believed they could manipulate certain physical characteristics to create a stronger, more powerful, and more disciplined race. The physical education and ruralization movements were significant aspects of this bonifica umana and molding of italianità; equally important were the campaigns for popular hygiene and health.[117]

In elementary schools, and especially in rural schools, health education took precedence over most other subjects. One of the leaders of the rural education movement, Alessandro Marcucci, wrote that cleanliness demonstrated "the dignity of the life of the nation."[118] As with similar movements in other western European countries, basic lessons in washing one's hands and face and keeping one's space clean were common in the Italian elementary classroom, but the state also assigned a sanitary official or doctor to every public school in order to perform monthly health inspections of the buildings, students, and teachers.[119] Moreover, even before beginning daily prayers, teachers monitored the personal hygiene of their students as a critical component of the greater racial campaign. These efforts were meant not only to regulate the germs that were coming into the classroom but also to instill a sense of discipline and orderliness in the minds of the students. According to the materials for one convention on public health, "the word 'clean' must acquire the highest honor for the Italian child, not inferior to that of 'good,' 'diligent,' and similar words! 'Clean' is not actually a word that simply refers to a physical quality, because it indicates an exquisitely moral endowment: the sense of decorum and respect for oneself and others."[120] Outside the classroom, vacation-time textbooks had numerous tips for a healthy summer and therefore numerous warnings about activities that, in the opinion of the ministry, could make children sick and potentially kill them, such as standing in a cold breeze after exercising or drinking excessively cold liquids in the hot weather. Officials were convinced that diligence toward such considerations would raise the physical and moral health of the nation and, therefore, the race.

Clearly the concept of patria—and through it, italianità—could not be reduced to a series of physical, cultural, behavioral, or political characteristics. Educators and officials wished to impress on Italians the complexity and richness of their racial identity. The elementary curriculum of the 1920s reflected the efforts of educationalists and officials to adapt familiar resources and references from Liberal Italy to the new goals and methods of Fascism. The regime's struggle with its own identity could be heard in the variety of voices clamoring within the MPI and the state at large, the array of textbooks read and approved for publication, and the constant revisions of laws and organizations in these years. Nevertheless, there were essential lessons about the linguistic, historical, and cultural heritage of the Italian population that maintained curricular importance for all educational and political officials; italianità, while drawing much from the physical landscape of the kingdom, was not wedded to it. Creating a New Italian who was in touch with the characteristics that both unified the people of the peninsula and islands and made them superior to other peoples around the world was essential to preparing young Fascist students for the real work that lay ahead of them: to embody and perpetuate these ideals, leading the race and the nation to a new height of Italian glory at home and abroad. Fascists would not be satisfied that these lessons alone were enough to transform the population and the nation-state into its Fascist form, but they would remain cornerstones of the campaign throughout the *ventennio*—the twenty years of Fascist rule.

Two

"Fascistizing" the Nation and Race, 1929–34

From Instruction to Education

When visitors arrived at Rome's Exposition Center (Palazzo delle esposizioni) on October 28, 1932, for the opening of the Exhibition of the Fascist Revolution (MRF), they faced an overwhelming image of the regime's power. Four copper *fasci littori* rose twenty-five meters into the air, and three massive entryways beckoned them in to experience the height of Fascist cultural and political supremacy.[1] According to the Italian observer Ercole Di Marco, the building itself appeared to be "a monolithic block from which one idea springs: the ideal and authentic unity with which today the Italian people feel connected."[2] Marking both the tenth anniversary of the March on Rome— the *Decennale*—and the influence of the Fascist Revolution as a whole, the dramatic exhibit displayed the finest of Fascist propaganda. The government commissioned more than twenty artists and architects to fill twenty-three rooms with photomontages, sculptures, collages, sound clips, and quotes that surrounded visitors with visions of the Great War and achievements of the Fascist movement. As historian Marla Stone has explained, the displays "played out a cycle of crisis, redemption, and resolution" that embodied recent Italian history.[3] Fourteen rooms illustrated the state's imagining of the Italian success in World War I, the postwar crises that led to the rise of Fascism, and the Fascist Party's successful seizure of power. The remaining rooms depicted the historical, cultural, and political elements that united Italians and that, with Fascism at the helm, would lead the race to international glory.[4]

Mussolini deliberately opened the exhibition shortly after he inaugurated the nearby and newly created Via dell'Impero, or Imperial Road (now the Via dei fori imperiali), which had required the removal of forty thousand cubic meters of earth to reveal the surrounding layers of the city's rich history. This central example of Mussolini's plans for the reorganization of the Eternal City passed from the Coliseum, directly over and through the ancient Roman forums of Trajan, Augustus, and Nerva, and ended in the Piazza Venezia, home to both the Vittorio Emanuele II monument and the Duce's office.[5] Its construction and subsequent use as a primary route for party parades literally connected the remains of ancient Rome to the symbol of the Risorgimento and the heart of the Fascist state.[6] Together with the MRF, it established a foundational narrative of Fascism's power and illustrated the strength and unity of the Italian race.

It is not surprising why the MRF and its surrounding celebrations have been the subject of much scholarship since its 1932 opening; to Fascists, observers, and subsequent historians, the exhibit, as the famous Italian journalist and art critic Margherita Sarfatti argued, was not so much "an exhibition" as "a demonstration" of the Fascist Revolution.[7] It was also an interactive lesson in the ways Fascism was rejuvenating the grandeur of the Italian race. Di Marco explained in his article that Mussolini envisioned this showcase as "the most lively *school* of Fascism that would teach Italians, particularly the young generations—to whom we will have to entrust the light that was lit in October 1922—how much blood the success of our new life cost; that there is no victory without sacrifices; that, when necessary, one must willingly sacrifice one's life for an idea; and, finally, that the heroic spirit of our razza is as native to us as the sun is to our lands."[8] His portrayal of the exhibition as a school designed to expose all Italians to both the fundamentals of Fascist italianità and the more general lessons of the Fascist state is critical to the MRF's importance in the history of the ventennio. No longer were Italians simply to memorize facts and figures; no longer were they to learn solely within a classroom. The limited instruction of the elite within yesterday's school was transformed into the holistic education of the race through Giovanni Gentile's principles of organic and active learning.

The Duce made this vision most apparent with his measures to encourage as many people as possible, especially students, to visit the show. The government closed schools from October 24 to November 5 so that entire families could view the MRF in its opening days; and with subsidies from the Fascist Educational Association (Associazione fascista della scuola), it offered elementary schools numerous incentives to visit an "exhibition that gathers the documents and relics of a period of history so full of events that contribute to the glory of Italy" throughout its two years on display.[9] Additionally, train fare to the capital was reduced for everyone, and publicity abroad urged tourists to come see the restored birthplace of the Italian race and the successes of the revolution.[10] Over the course of its showing, almost 4 million people visited the Palazzo delle esposizioni and took in not only the magnificence of the gallery but also the grandeur of Fascist Rome.

Ultimately, then, the MRF embodied the political and cultural moment Italians found themselves in at the beginning of the 1930s; the party maneuverings of the 1920s had successfully transformed the Fascist movement into a one-party regime. In an address delivered to the overwhelmingly defunct Camera dei deputati on May 26, 1927, known as his Ascension Day speech, Mussolini simply put into words the reality that measures of his first seven years in power enabled: "Opposition is foolish—pointless in a totalitarian regime such as the Fascist regime."[11] Moreover, what separated Italian Fascism from a number of other popular movements in Europe at the time, according to Mussolini, was its refusal to become "complaisant" and its gradual but ever-increasing "radicalization" of policies and practices.[12] It was the development of the Fascist concept of totalitarianism that most profoundly defined the ambitions of the regime in the first half of the 1930s: by 1929 the government had banned all political parties other than the PNF; had drastically censored the press; had overseen the expansion of the economic and agricultural campaigns for autarky; and had established many of the state institutions aimed at merging the public and private spheres of Italian society.[13]

As part of this totalitarian transformation, Mussolini had even officially resolved the acrimonious relationship between state and church that lay in the bedrock of Italian unification. With the signing of the Lateran Accords in the summer of 1929 came the creation of the autonomous Vatican City and the establishment of Catholicism as the official state religion. In return, the Holy See formally recognized the sovereignty of the Italian nation.[14] In brief, Mussolini had successfully allied the state with the church for the first time since the kingdom's creation in 1861, giving the image of a unity of purpose and allowing the majority of Italians to feel they could legitimately engage in national politics while remaining faithful to the church.[15]

All these efforts to create a totalitarian state convinced a majority of Italians of Mussolini's authority—or at least of the impossibility of successful resistance to his regime—and led to perceived political calm in the early 1930s.[16] As one former Balilla member wrote in his memoir, "For children of my age in those years, to be Fascist was the natural state, like being Italian or having white skin."[17] Between 1929 and 1934, despite the arrival of increased fiscal limitations that resulted from the global depression, the state used its temporary but valuable hegemony, as well as its increasingly totalitarian policies, to focus its efforts on transforming the population into New Italians and preparing to conquer a new Roman Empire. In other words, it focused on Fascistizing the Italian nation. And the Exhibition of the Fascist Revolution illustrated the political culture and vision of italianità that was to infuse every aspect of life in a Fascist Italy.

One of the fundamental ways the state worked to Fascistize its campaign for bonifica umana was by creating a totalitarian racial education for the youngest members of Italian society. In essence, the efforts such a project entailed emphasized the message that Italian racial ideals were the same as Fascist ideals; to embody the ideal Fascist was to embody the ideal Italian. The state articulated its vision for a Fascistized society in this period through a series of reforms, most notably mandating national textbooks and transforming the Ministry of Public Instruction (MPI) into the Ministry of National Education (MEN). These changes, along with the continued expansion of state efforts to maintain a presence in all aspects of daily life, ensured that ever-growing numbers of Italian children had access to the lessons required to Fascistize the Italian race.

Defining a Fascist Society in the Early 1930s

What did it actually mean to "Fascistize" the Italian population during this period? In the same speech that Mussolini declared Fascism a totalitarian regime, the Duce expressed the primary targets of his Fascist Revolution as comprising three categories: first, improving the demographic situation in Italy, both in terms of enhancing the physical health and increasing the overall numbers of Italians; second, expanding the administrative infrastructure of the nation; and third, clarifying the political directives for the future of the state.

It is notable that the first of the Duce's concerns was the health of the race, both in terms of quality and quantity. In the most sweeping terms, Mussolini announced his intention to increase the Italian population from 40 to 60 million by midcentury.[18] He joined Italian demographers and politicians in voicing a growing concern about the decrease in the Italian birthrate and its impact on the nation's ability to fulfill its moral, cultural, and political obligations. By increasing population numbers, Fascists argued, the stronger race could direct the salvation of Italian and European civilization.[19]

In order to reach its desired population numbers, and with them biopower, Mussolini enacted a series of pronatalist incentives.[20] Already in January 1927 the regime announced a tax on all bachelors over the age of thirty-four. This tax was doubled the following year and increased by another 50 percent in 1934.[21] The revenue from these taxes, Mussolini declared, would be used to fund other pronatalist policies, such as reduced train fares for honeymooners.[22] Longer prison sentences were also established for any individuals performing or seeking abortions.[23] And though government debates over the regime's legal stance on homosexuality ended with the decision that it was outside the purview of secular law, historian Lorenzo Benadusi has clearly shown how surveillance and punishment of suspected "pederasts" increased in late 1920s and 1930s.[24] Additionally, Mussolini borrowed from Italy's Catholic tradition of Mothering Sundays to demarcate December 24 as the Day of Mother and Child (Giornata della madre e del fanciullo) beginning in 1933. Coinciding with the celebration of Christianity's most sacred mother and child, the Fascist holiday called for ceremonies to award demographic honors to the most prolific families in each province and region.[25] The voice of the ONMI, *Motherhood and Childhood (Maternità ed infanzia)*, explained that December 24 was a day marked for "the solemn spiritual exaltation of the supreme values of the stirpe."[26] More explicitly, another journalist wrote that it was a celebration of "the mother, the sublime creature and giver of life . . . the eternal smile of the earth, the joy of the family, and the unyielding hope of the nation."[27] That same year, the Fascist Union of Prolific Families established its official journal—*The Fascist*—a monthly periodical that was "to protect the fundamental virtues of the razza."[28] In short, the protection of mothers and children provided for the life, renewal, and future of the Italian race by preparing abundant, healthy, and vigorous generations of New Italians. As Emilio Alfieri wrote, "All that we do for the defense of motherhood and the protection of childhood ensures the life of the stirpe, and supports its development, strength, and splendor."[29]

Encouraging the birth of increasing numbers of healthy Fascist babies would not do the fatherland any good without the assurance of their survival through childhood, however.[30] Mussolini began his urgent call for Fascism to address the physical aspects of the race's health, exclaiming, "Someone long ago argued that the state should not worry about the physical health of the people. . . . This is a suicidal theory. It is clear that, in a well-ordered state, the care of the physical health of the people must be the first priority."[31] As one might expect, the ONMI played an important role in the reduction of child mortality rates. Billed as "the most powerful instrument of the ingenious demographic policies" of the regime,[32] the ONMI worked "to create a social and sanitary education among the masses that continually reinforces the structure of the razza materially and morally."[33] With the encouragement of the central government, the ONMI continued to expand its programs for public health and hygiene in the form of mobile health clinics, outdoor schools and camps, mothering courses, and nursery schools.[34]

Of course, the movement to support maternity and encourage higher birthrates had been an integral part of the Fascist project for bonifica umana since the Duce's rise to power and, moreover, was prevalent throughout western Europe and North America. However, rhetorical and "scientific" shifts took place among Fascist officials, pedagogues, and medical professionals during the 1930s that emphasized growing concern not just for the quantity of Italians produced but also for their "quality."[35] Mussolini believed that the racial situation was bleak, suggesting that social diseases—seemingly pervasive ailments, such as tuberculosis and alcoholism, that threatened the fabric of Italian society as a result of moral degeneracy and bureaucratic limitations—were on the rise. He called for the state "to look out for the destiny of the razza, ... to heal the razza, and to begin to do so from motherhood and infancy."[36] It was not surprising, Mussolini continued, that the rise of social diseases was accompanied by a rise in urbanization and industrialization. Urbanization sterilized the population, he cried. "I do not acknowledge any healthy industries in Italy; those industries that are healthy come from agricultural and maritime work."[37] Italians needed to embrace their roots and strengthen the race in part through the historically Italian occupation of agricultural labor.

Leading Fascists of the early 1930s who supported such arguments were particularly taken by the racial theories of Nicola Pende—public intellectual, national senator, endocrinologist, and, most recently, Italian guardian of the medical field of "constitutionalism." This rather short-lived pseudoscience held at its core the theory of orthogenesis—that is, the notion that one can influence the evolution of a species through the development of specific characteristics within individuals—and claimed to utilize the fields of anthropology, sociology, and pathology to understand and ideally fix abnormalities in human physical and psychic growth. One of the field's principal tenets was that environmental factors played a crucial role in the development of the human constitution.[38] For example, if children grew up in healthy, disciplined environments, they would grow up to enjoy discipline, work, and devotion.[39] This argument led to Pende's special interest in constitutionalism's potential success among the various "ethnic" populations of Italy to create a population that adhered to a more uniform identity.[40]

In support of Pende's theories, the regime maintained that the majority of Italian children had the potential to become ideal Fascists. More to the point, administrators still did not want to abandon those children who were institutionally termed "abnormal." In 1933 the ONMI's president Sileno Fabbri broke down the general concept of juvenile delinquency into four subcategories, each characterized by a different degree of "recoverability" (or compatibility with Fascism): psychologically abnormal children; morally and materially abandoned children; homeless children; and actively delinquent children (investigated, condemned, or liberated from prison). Fabbri believed that improving and controlling the environment in which children lived could curtail juvenile delinquency, particularly among those children categorized in his second and third groups. The projects and personnel of his organization, Fabbri maintained, addressed the needs of these delinquents—those who had the greatest potential for eventually contributing to the Fascist project.[41] By the mid-1930s, in fact, the leadership of the ONMI demanded greater care for these children because of their potential threat to society if the firm hand of the Fascist administration did not supervise them.[42] Those children who were considered "*uneducable* abnormals"— primarily classified in Fabbri's first and fourth categories—were largely confined to classes and activities designed particularly for their supposed needs. It is unclear, however, to what extent even these delinquents were selected because of legitimate developmental or intellectual disability or because they were the objects of social, physical, or psychological bias that had nothing to do with their intellectual or physical capabilities. One memoir written by a teacher of a third-grade class of such "exceptional" students indicates that perhaps only one of his thirty-one students was developmentally disabled; the others came from "unstable" families or lived on the streets, with little money and no enthusiasm for school.[43] Regardless, the education ministry and the ONMI were remarkably proud of the ostensible measures undertaken to leave no child behind, with the image of the Fascist state embracing and training all children of the fatherland to be active members of Italian society.

Fascistizing the Education System

The education system played a vital role in the campaign to form generations of Fascist Italians; it accordingly shared in both the shifts toward totalitarianism and the greater focus on the quality of Mussolini's children. The institutional and didactic changes that had taken place in the MPI and its auxiliary institutions during the 1920s saw their foundations in Gentile's idealism and Western pedagogical views at large. However, beginning in 1928 and 1929, fundamental changes in pedagogical language, methods, and goals separated the Italian system more significantly from Gentile's original project and broader Western trends. Legislation in 1928 proclaimed the educational system in charge of a "total" education of the Italian youth, emphasizing the importance of collaboration between schools and auxiliary organizations so that, together, they could ensure that Fascist principles reached children at all times.[44] Specifically, the reforms to establish nationalized elementary textbooks and to change the name of the Ministry of Public Instruction to the Ministry of National Education emphasized Mussolini's demands for greater control over the development of his children. Additionally, many of the organizations that had been established with discrete goals, such as the ONMI and the ONB, began to share more responsibilities, reflecting the idea that the spiritual, physical, and biological aspects of each Italian could not be divided but rather had to be approached holistically. Through these modifications, the government transitioned from instructing young Italians how to be successful, fit citizens to educating young Fascists to embody the ideals of italianità and fulfill the supposed destiny of the race and fatherland.

As always, at the head of this project was Benito Mussolini, whom the party depicted as the nation's father and teacher

who began "the true era of education in Italy, for the formation of the true Italian, capable of building the new life of the
nation."[45] In turn, the daily workings of the national education system required leadership that would unceasingly pursue
the Duce's aims. It turned out that this necessity resulted in a
fair amount of turnover throughout the ventennio, reflecting,
among other things, Fascism's continued struggles to define its
system of Fascistization. After Giovanni Gentile left the MPI in
the summer of 1924, Alessandro Casati, a staunch supporter of
Benedetto Croce's spiritual philosophy, headed the ministry
for six months. However, by January 1925, in the aftermath of
the Matteotti Crisis, Casati's allegiance to Crocean philosophy
and politics led him to resign and subsequently withdraw completely from politics. Much to Gentile's dismay, Pietro Fedele—a
trained historian and devoted Catholic who, according to Gentile, supported a much more dogmatic approach to education—
next headed the ministry. Discussing Fedele's appointment in
a letter to his friend and colleague Ernesto Codignola, Gentile exclaimed that it was clearly a betrayal of Mussolini's trust
in him and his more organic approach to education.[46] Despite
Fedele's regular clashes with Gentile over pedagogy, however,
his tenure from 1925 to 1928 did not signal the complete dismantling of the Gentile Reform. Still, it was clear that a vast
majority of Gentile's supporters had left the regime by the end
of the 1920s; a new line of academics who largely did not have
a background in education policy, but overwhelmingly supported the move toward a totalitarian system, came to the fore.

Giuseppe Belluzzo, the minister of public instruction from
the summer of 1928 to the fall of 1929, was the first appoin-
tee truly to indicate the regime's shift toward prioritizing Fascistization over Western pedagogical innovation. Unlike the
regime's first three education ministers, Belluzzo had absolutely
no background in pedagogy, or Crocean or Gentilian philosophy. Instead, Belluzzo came to the post in July 1928 as a former
Nationalist and an engineer who showed much greater interest in—and qualifications for—the expansion of Italy's economy than its education. He was an avowed "productionist" who
believed that Italy's industrial and agricultural growth would

only come with a concerted effort to develop new technologies. Appropriately, he played a significant role in Fascism's early efforts at autarky as the head of the Ministry of National Economy between 1925 and 1928. Then suddenly, and rather unexpectedly, he was tapped to head up the increased Fascistization efforts in the state education system.

In spite of his obvious lack of appropriate credentials, Belluzzo embraced the challenges of his new position; the minister soon approached Mussolini with a list of concerns about the Gentile Reform that he wanted to tackle to create a more Fascist system and more-Fascist children.[47] He focused these reforms primarily on areas that would most directly influence his own national priorities—in particular, the greater funding and oversight of trade schools in postelementary education—but he also championed the expansion of the rural and pre-elementary educational infrastructures and declared that the elementary experience needed "to educate children's spirits and conscience, to monitor their moral and physical development, and to form the future citizens of a fatherland that is strong and aware of its destiny."[48]

It was largely in the service of these goals that Belluzzo announced the first of the major institutional reforms heralding a new phase of totalitarian instruction at the elementary level: the development of state-mandated national textbooks. It was clear that the textbook selection committees of the 1920s had not solved the problem of standardizing the curriculum. In 1928 alone, there were 2,491 author submissions, and 338 were approved.[49] This obviously represented a much smaller number of acceptable textbooks than were available at the start of Mussolini's rule, but a truly Fascist education of the population required a single, national curriculum that unified the population and garnered support for the Fascist project.[50] Discussions about commissioning state textbooks, led by Minister Belluzzo, started in the fall of 1928.[51] The result of these deliberations was that textbooks for the transitional school year 1929–30 would need to conform to a strict set of written criteria that met the "historical, political, legal and economic demands clarified by October 28, 1922," and the first edition of comprehensive national textbooks would be ready for use the following year.[52] A subsequent article in the national newspaper *People of Italy* (*Popolo d'Italia*) reported the ministry's three goals for the commissioned textbooks as

a. To not keep children closed up in an artificial world without any relation to their lives, but instead to give them contact with reality . . .

b. To give children a sense of Fascism's magnificent renewal of italianità.

c. To form a Fascist education that isn't ephemeral or superficial, but that spontaneously springs from real life.[53]

According to one article reviewing this decision, the administration had "settled on regulations for the creation of state textbooks in order to give each elementary class the necessary instrument for the spiritual formation of the new Italian, eliminating the inconveniences that come with having to review and adopt textbooks."[54]

The law, formally signed on January 7, 1929, provided for a single textbook to be used in the first and second grades, while the third through fifth grades would each have a discrete text. Additionally, the ministry would appoint a triennial commission to review and update the texts as needed.[55] Nevertheless, many of the textbooks would already see a second edition in the 1931–32 academic year in an active attempt by the commission to comply more fully with national Fascistization efforts.[56] According to one journalist, "it was absolutely necessary to bring forth new books permeated by the spirit of the times and devoid of the old and outdated mentality."[57] Simultaneously, and a bit contradictorily, the ministry had also to keep in mind the textbooks of other "civilized" (Western) nations, continuing the Fascist tendency to compare Italy to, and theoretically triumph over, other Western powers, despite the ostensible desire to separate the Italian nation and race from all others.

The ministry first circulated the new, state-mandated textbooks in the 1930–31 academic year after a commission of eminent scholars and authors from various fields wrote and approved them.[58] One 1930 article in the state-run *Annals of Elementary Instruction* (*Annali dell'istruzione elementare*) explained that "this collection of state textbooks, we are confident, will work to secure valuable educational tools for our nation to help form the New Italian that the Regime and its Duce desire."[59] To such ends, the books contained a much more significant amount of original text than those of the 1920s. They still had some external passages—excerpts taken from famous authors, politicians, and other national heroes—but the great majority of the content was new, presumably to graft Italian ideals that had been emphasized in the 1920s onto an increasingly Fascist image of the Italian race and society. Consequently, Fascism was dramatically more visible in these books. Instead of the limited references to the revolution and the Duce of the previous decade, authors wrote and illustrated these new resources to instill a clear sense of both the nature and permanence of Fascism in their readers. In particular, the administration used the 1932 Decennale to highlight the accomplishments of the party and the state in school resources. Vignettes highlighted the most familiar Fascist policies and values; contained numerous references to the future of Italian civilization; and, most notably for this study, emphasized the superiority of the Italian race under Fascist leadership.

Belluzzo may have fronted the national textbook project, but he would not last long enough at the head of the ministry to see its launch in 1930. Despite his championship of Mussolini's Fascistization measures, his pedagogical conflicts with Gentile—who still worked as a close advisor to the Duce—and other educational idealists pushed him from the position in the fall of 1929.[60] In his stead came the medieval historian, affirmed Fascist, and Gentilian educationalist Balbino Giuliano. Even in this period of increased inflexibility, Giuliano's three-year tenure simultaneously proved Gentile's continued influence and the ever-present need for compromise in the Fascist regime.

Giuliano's inauguration as minister also accompanied the second major institutional reform of the late 1920s: changing the name of the Ministry of Public Instruction to the Ministry of National Education. This makeover indicated two important trends in Fascist education after the party's consolidation of power.[61] One trend was to focus on education as opposed to instruction. Instruction, as Mussolini explained in a 1936 text-book, "could be considered a private undertaking," one that focused on teaching simple material lessons in reading and writing and arithmetic. The new ministry title would instead, according to the same text, "reaffirm a principle in an explicit way: that the state does not simply have the right, but rather the obligation, to educate the people and not only to train the people."[62] Fascist education entailed developing the entire person and creating a New Italian in the image of the Fascist racial ideal. The regime therefore determined to incorporate and educate the physical, intellectual, and emotional characteristics of the Italian student in every aspect of daily life.[63]

Equally important to the change in ministry title was the insertion of the word *national*. This amendment highlighted the priority of unifying the system—throughout *all* the Italian regions—under one authority. More progress toward this goal was made at the start of 1934, when the ministry, under the leadership of the historian and lawyer Francesco Ercole since the summer of 1932, took administrative control of all elementary schools. This measure responded to what administrators deemed "a preeminent political necessity" and conformed to "the totalitarian and united concept of the Fascist regime."[64] No longer was the administration of elementary schools dispersed among state, state-associated, and private organizations. The Fascist regime controlled all laws and regulations regarding national elementary education. Such measures, the administration posited, could only improve the regime's efforts to create a New Italian and a New Italy in Mussolini's image.

In order to improve the quality of the Italian race, the regime needed to make sure that children were uniformly exposed to the most-effective lessons in the Fascist way of life; efforts to educate adults in the skills necessary to be successful parents— the center of any child's moral education—were proving inadequate in the eyes of the government. The private family sphere could not be trusted to effectively impart the characteristics of Fascism's New Italians. In the early 1930s, pedagogues published studies linking increased school attendance to a reduction in juvenile delinquency, and government-sponsored studies of the early 1930s found that a majority of the areas with high illiteracy rates also suffered from the nation's highest mortality rates due to pulmonary tuberculosis, malaria, and other diseases.[65]

Therefore, the national school system, the ONMI, and the ONB had the task of intervening and counteracting any real or potential threats to the Fascist lifestyle and the Italian race; they were essential to both decrease the nation's child mortality rates and provide healthy environments for the Italian youth in the absence of stable, or at least reliably Fascist, families. In response, the regime more rigorously enforced school attendance. And because public health officials maintained that juvenile delinquency was a predominantly urban problem, they urged the greater emphasis on the national ruralization and physical education movements.[66] However, state initiatives could not stop there. One pedagogue of the period wrote, "I would say that if the ONB wants to help reach its predetermined goal, which is to make the little citizen of today the New Italian of tomorrow, the ONB must begin to study the best way to physically improve the individual in order to physically improve the razza."[67] In order for children to be physically fit, they needed to be healthy; the ONMI and the ONB took particular interest in training teachers to educate children about hygiene and social and personal health, distributing medicines in rural schools, and organizing exhibitions and conferences on these topics. In other words, by 1934 the state school system, the ONB, and the ONMI were collectively seen as the primary social prophylaxis against juvenile delinquency through their development of the intellectual, moral, and physical strength of the Italian youth and, therefore, the future of the Italian race.

Having administrative control over the educational system was not enough, however; if the school system was to have such a great influence on the moral, spiritual, and physical formation of New Italians, then its teachers needed to be the purest examples of Fascist morality and the Italian race. It was imperative for Fascism's messengers to adhere to and exemplify the Fascist principles and behaviors they were to instill in their impressionable pupils. As in the mid-1920s, officials called for the greater involvement of men in the profession, particularly as some observers began to refer to educators as an army fighting for Italy's moral protection.[68] Furthermore, in 1928 the government dismissed significant numbers of teachers in Italy's border regions who supposedly did not adequately speak standard Italian.[69] Likewise, teacher transfer requests to those regions were denied if the administration believed the applicants were not Italian enough to be appropriate role models.[70] And by 1929 Mussolini required all teachers to swear an oath of loyalty to the regime.

In an aspiring totalitarian society, it was also not enough simply to embody the New Italians in the classroom: the MEN also began making demands on the private lives of its teachers. Both male and female teachers needed to lead "pure" lives, which necessitated either celibacy or marriage.[71] By 1933, Minister Ercole announced that during the school year teachers were to spend Sundays "as a brief truce from normal activities," but certainly not as a time for relaxation. Occupying one's time in that way, in the words of the official bulletin, implied "idleness and the wasting of energies."[72] Additionally, Ercole required teachers to divide their time equally over school vacations between their own families and the activities orchestrated by the ONB.

So all teachers had to personify the New Italian, but such a requirement entailed even more rigorous standards for Italy's female teachers. In a 1929 ministry circular, Belluzzo demanded that female teachers (and their female students) needed to "dress themselves with the moral seriousness and discipline that Fascism encourages in the life of the nation." In all respects, female teachers needed to be "an example and model of moral austerity, of feminine restraint, of the highest correctness, so that young girls can have faith in them and can see the high ideal of maternity" that was the ultimate aspiration of any Fascist woman.[73] As an even broader measure, in 1931 the state Press Office demanded that all newspapers eliminate female images that were "too thin" or "masculine"—characteristics of what popularly became known as the crisis-woman (donna-crisi). Such women, who invariably worked outside the home and engaged in other supposedly degenerate activities, became synonymous with sterility and were therefore the most perilous type of woman to the Italian race.[74] It bears mentioning that no such decree was made regarding the physical appearance of male teachers or students.

Physical education was an essential, but complex, component of the campaign to perpetuate a sturdy Italian race and therefore required especially strong leadership training.[75] On February 5, 1928, the MPI opened the first Fascist School for the Training of Physical Education Instructors (Scuola superiore fascista per la preparazione degli insegnanti di educazione fisica) at the Central Military Academy of Physical Education in Rome.[76] That same year, and not very far away, Mussolini helped place the cornerstone of the Mussolini Forum (Foro Mussolini, now the Foro Italico, though very little has changed) just north of the Vatican, where the Duce imagined a new "sports city" would illustrate the centrality of physical education in his New Italy. Officials declared it would be the "biggest experiment in state education that history records," and it was here in 1932 that party officials unveiled the new home of the male physical education training school as the Fascist Institute for Physical Education (Istituto superiore fascista di educazione fisica).[77] In this grand complex that not only sanctified physical activity but also identified Mussolini as the heir to ancient Rome's glory through its name and design, the school staged many of its classes in the Stadium of Marbles (Stadio dei marmi), where sixty marble statues of youthful athletes surrounded a track and, inside, a grand parade ground. This stadium became the focal point in a dramatic compound of athletic and party facilities at the Mussolini Forum that continued to grow until the Italian commitment to war in 1940. As a whole, the Mussolini Forum was designed to forge educators and political leaders united by an Italian—Fascist—sensibility about the past, present, and future of the race; as one ONB publication pronounced, "it is a monument that reconnects us to the imperial Roman tradition. It will also eternalize the new Fascist civilization for centuries."[78]

The year the Fascist Institute for Physical Education moved to the Mussolini Forum, the state also opened the Fascist Academy of Physical and Youth Education for Women in the Umbrian town of Orvieto.[79] Like its male-centric counterpart, this institution involved a two-year course to prepare its students to teach physical education to children in the public school system and the organizations of the ONB.[80]

Two details about the founding of these teaching academies particularly illustrate this period in the evolution of Fascist racism: first, it showed the increased weight placed on physical education and Fascist "teacher training" in the minds of Fascist officials; second, it further evinced more-rigid conceptions of gender roles in Fascist society.[81] In 1930 the Fascist Grand Council, in conjunction with the Italian National Olympic Committee (CONI), announced the duty of Fascist organizations to limit the involvement of women in sports. While exercise was important for girls to maintain their form, lessons were to encourage the "mothers of the razza" to fight against the physical corruption that could result from *too much* activity.[82] Such perversion was easily exemplified, once again, by the infamously scrawny crisis-woman. While the progression of this piece of Fascist doctrine was most likely a gradual one, the formal institutionalization of separate training programs for female and male teachers indicated an enhanced desire to regulate and control the physical development of Fascism's New Italians. No longer were male teachers appropriate to train girls, and of course female teachers were not suitable to instill the values of strength and aggression in boys.

The regime's heightened concern for the provision of adequate role models was especially focused on Italy's rural communities. Praise for rural life—evoking the idealized values of a "traditional" peasant lifestyle and encouraging pride in a "simpler" existence—continued to be one of the primary themes in the elementary curriculum of the early 1930s. At the same time, pedagogues and politicians began to voice greater unease about the cultural, moral, and intellectual ignorance of Italy's peasant population. Elementary education was declared the most valuable weapon to combat these fears. Specific versions of the state textbooks were published for rural schools; to address the specific needs of Fascistizing the rural population even further, the regime established the Rural Radio Corporation (ERR) under the auspices of the Ministry of Communication, with collaboration from the MEN and the Ministry of Agriculture and Forestry. Taking inspiration from the initial success of a variety of radio programming during the 1920s, the national radio association (EIAR) launched a series of experimental, educational children's broadcasts in the spring of 1933. According to the press, the response was extremely promising, with an estimated 1 million listeners from all over the peninsula.[83] The particular objective of the ERR, as the name suggests, was to help Fascist principles "penetrate and conquer the countryside" through radio programs, accompanied by teaching manuals designed for elementary classes.[84]

According to one report, the first program included a dramatic reading of Giuseppe Fanciulli's "The Duce among Children" ("Il Duce tra i bimbi"), which, as the title indicates, depicted an interaction between Mussolini and some of his beloved children. The show continued with segments on Italian history, the Fascist Revolution, and national heroes.[85] The press immediately reported the popularity of these programs among students. An article on this new project explained that teachers had to mediate the students' interaction with each program at two points, before and after listening to the production: "Beforehand, in order to clarify the program for the child, and after, to relive that same broadcast so that it becomes a driving force and not an abstract lesson; that is, so that it is not reduced to a break in the day, without utility and application in school."[86]

The regime considered the radio an especially promising tool for the Fascistization of Italians because it could spread a single national message on numerous regional stations without the inevitable variations that came from relying on thousands of individual messengers. Furthermore, this message was spread with a single national language, thereby promoting Italy's linguistic unification.[87] When the ERR school broadcasts began in earnest in 1934, they hit the airwaves three days a week for thirty to forty-five minutes. Of course, the challenge of this sort of project was that it required access to radios, electricity, and cooperative teachers. The ERR, therefore, was also responsible for distributing monthly bulletins advertising upcoming episodes and including supplementary materials, as well as radios, within many of the most rural communities in Italy.[88] These measures, the regime hoped, would ensure or at least facilitate rural Italy's exposure to Fascism and the Fascist racial campaign, both in and out of the classroom.[89]

Fascistizing Education outside the Classroom

Radio programming was certainly not limited to the classroom, and its expansion into numerous afternoon children's shows in the late 1920s and throughout the 1930s illustrated the regime's continued concern about its access to children outside the walls of elementary school. Likewise, the party initiated successive modifications to increase the influence of the ONB and the ONMI in children's lives. Of particular note was the 1928 outlawing of membership in any youth organization other than the ONB (though membership to the ONB was still technically voluntary). There was one significant exception to this otherwise prime example of totalitarian action, however: the church's youth groups of Catholic Action (Azione Cattolica) were allowed to remain in operation as long as they limited their activities to enhancing knowledge of and connections to Catholicism and the church.[90]

The following year, in October 1929, Piccole and Giovani Italiane were placed under control of the ONB. The fusion of the two branches—the boys' groups of the Balilla and Avanguardisti and the girls' groups of the Piccole and Giovani Italiane—under a single authority secured the ONB's role as the party's most valuable vehicle with which to instill a "virile awareness" in Italy's male youth and feminine virtues in its female youth. The regime gave the ONB the responsibility of establishing a presence in every part of the peninsula, on the islands, and in the colonies as a representation of Fascism's determination to rejuvenate the race. Invariably, these chapters included a Balilla Center (Casa del Balilla) that served as a youth community center and a model of Fascist culture. Decorated with traditional Italian arts, these buildings often included a gymnasium, library, and outdoor garden, all of which were to help inculcate essential characteristics and skills in Mussolini's children.[91] The ONB also demonstrated its primacy within Fascist youth education as it continued to construct a network of cinemas, libraries, and playgrounds for Italy's children and to sponsor numerous rural schools and summer camps. As an example, ONB-sponsored rural schools grew from 477 in 1929 to 690 in 1930.[92] The purpose of all these institutions was, as one journalist explained, "to represent a natural gathering place for all children where they strengthen healthy friendships, functionally and spiritually learn the rules that the Duce has indicated for the Italian people, and face their first hardships and physical challenges."[93] This expanded presence of the state and its continued emphasis on the collective over the individual theoretically allowed Fascism's racial ideas to be reinforced time and again in Italy's children.

ONB and ONMI camps could not accommodate all children during summer vacations, however, and the extended period of time away from the classroom especially threatened to loosen the grip of Fascist principles on the minds of the young generations. To help combat such perceived dangers—alongside special summertime ERR programs—the ONB published a new series of summer vacation textbooks in the early 1930s. As Renato Ricci, the head of the ONB—and now an undersecretary of state for physical education and youth—wrote in the introduction to one such book, "A book to read for vacation? Absolutely! Vacations for every good Balilla mean relaxation but not laziness. He needs to strengthen his body and mind in order to return to school healthier and more active."[94] These books, more uniform than those written in the 1920s, were dispersed to all students of ONB-run rural schools for free.[95]

Ricci's opening message to the 1930 annual report of ONB activities encouraged the regime's further reliance on the organization in all of these influential facets of youth education. He informed readers that the previous year had been "characterized by feverish and tenacious work and by the daily, noble sacrifice of the thousands and thousands of Fascist educators and organizers—both passive and active—as only those can be who are possessed by a great conviction: *the Roman and Musso-*

linian future of the stirpe."[96] He concluded his introduction with the decisive statement that, finally, Italians had discovered the true function of physical education, "no longer . . . the futile movement of arms and legs of dubious utility." Though children were urged still to enjoy physical activity, Ricci explained, it was important to understand that it also had "a particular influence in the spiritual formation of the youth," which was undoubtedly a critical component of Fascism's racial campaign.[97]

Carried by this apparent momentum, Ricci's organization established nineteen new Balilla Centers, ninety-nine gyms, and thirty-seven playgrounds in 1931, indicating the continued growth of the ONB's influence.[98] However, Ricci explained in his official summary of the year's work, "The rise in membership numbers . . . is more than the result of the work of expansion and propaganda; it is both the effect and the indicator of the increasing sympathy with which the Italian people regard the Opera Balilla."[99] He insisted in this report, as in others, that membership in the ONB's groups indicated complete loyalty to the Fascist Revolution and its ideals. While no one can deny the fault in this logic, it must be conceded that the ONB's infrastructural and educational presence, and prospective influence, broadened significantly in this period of Fascist totalitarianism. With this infrastructural expansion came the concomitant intensification of the Fascist racial project.

Utilizing a Fascist Society

Mussolini had largely consolidated his political power by the end of the 1920s and saw the next phase of the process of national conquest in strengthening what he believed was his regime's cultural and political hegemony and historical entitlement. He had convinced his enemies and followers alike that dissent was virtually impossible. It was time, then, for the regime not to remain complaisant but to persuade the Italian race that its characteristic italianità not only unified the nation but also marked its superiority over all others. Government projects such as the MRF and the creation of the Via dell'Impero indicated the overarching goal of educating the Italian population in these beliefs, encouraging bonifica umana in all aspects of public and private life. The transformation of the Ministry of Public Instruction from a state organ in charge of "training" to one responsible for "national education" was not simply nominal but rather further indicated this move to create a holistic and truly Fascist educational system. The elementary-education mission changed to create not only healthy and fit Italians but passionate and motivated Fascists who would support the more aggressive goals of the Fascist state. The function of Fascism was, as one pedagogue explained, to create an Italy "ready for all of the requirements and all of the conquests, and capable of recovering, from Rome, even against Paris and Moscow, its civilizing mission in the world."[100] Such an accomplishment would, in turn, reestablish the Italian race as the predominant global power.

From Fit to Fascist

One of the principal resources for the Fascist primary school student was the *quaderno,* or exercise copybook. Often sporting a cover illustrating an important moment in Italian history or Fascist policy or an idyllic scene from the national landscape, this slim notebook offered children, teachers, parents, and officials a formal collection of each student's lessons and work. The words and images recorded in the quaderno do not necessarily indicate the student's internalization of the book's content, but they do provide a glimpse into how teachers and their pupils used class time and were asked to conceive of their collective identity.

An entry from one such source—displayed as part of a 1929 Florentine exhibition on Fascist education—helped its readers form an image of the ideal Fascist elementary classroom. Its third-grade author, from nearby Pistoia, began her account with a brief overview of the school, which was beautiful and clean. Her classroom, too, was airy, newly painted, and even had three windows. It was also small, with the foremost of the thirty student desks practically touching the chalkboard. Still, she explained, the room contained many beautiful things. On the walls "there is Jesus, to whom we pray; there is the flag we salute when we sing; there is the King and the Duce. To them we also salute and say 'Eia! Eia! Alalà!'"[1]

The walls also bore a memorial to Italy's fallen soldiers, in front of which students regularly laid flowers; and their teacher frequently added other pictures to the collection to aid her lessons. In addition to these images, the classroom was equipped with a thermometer, compass, gramophone, and small library, all of which were essential tools of modern pedagogy. Students were required to keep this classroom and these supplies clean, sweeping the floor and washing the desks almost every day, and to make sure they themselves were clean according to current hygienic standards. Outside the windows, students could see the schoolyard and its adjoining fields where they played when weather permitted. Our author concluded her sketch by underlining her joy at coming to school because she was so eager to learn.[2]

This portrait of a Tuscan elementary classroom illustrated the model integration of Fascist imagery and racial standards within the daily activities of the Italian primary school at the end of the 1920s. The Duce's theories about the role of the state in regulating the health of the race were at the core of the Fascist experiment, and the classroom represented the most effective means with which to articulate and strengthen the ideal characteristics of the Italian race. A manual from 1930 informed teachers, "One does not encounter resistance in children. Curious about the world that surrounds them, desirous to know the life and actions of adults . . . with travel literature or history, with visits to monuments, with excursions, their love for the nation will grow until this instinctive sentiment is transformed into moral obligation."[3] Therefore, the author declared, "to develop feelings of nationalism must be the goal of a truly patriotic education." As such, "every activity works for the gradual acquisition of spiritual strengths and practical abilities, in the end combining to form capable, proud, and daring Italians."[4]

Reflecting the Fascist ambition to create a more totalitarian society of New Italians, the education ministry and its ancillary organizations officially maintained their support of the Gentilian principles of active and organic learning to promote lessons and activities that cultivated every aspect of the young Italians' minds and bodies; such lessons were to mold strong and faithful members of the race. In the preface to another 1930 teaching manual, Cornelio Di Marzio proclaimed that "with physical education one prepares a soldier for the city, the *urbe*; with cultural education, it prepares a citizen for the fatherland." More importantly, Di Marzio went on to explain that these two facets of education were intertwined and, together, created a "synthesis exalting faith in something that transcends all of us and forms the religion of our very lives."[5] The spiritual language of Di Marzio's text underscored not only the fundamental role of religion in Italian education and society but more generally the holistic approach to Fascist pedagogy and racism. In support of this position, the administration continued to encourage teachers, as well as the leaders of Balilla and Piccole Italiane, to incorporate outdoor activities, visits to monuments, and field trips to exhibitions and museums into their regular programs. Furthermore, pedagogues stressed the importance of group activities, such as singing, sports, and camp life, as essential to the "re-education of the razza" by creating the sense of collective belonging that was deemed fundamental to the formation of ideal Fascists.[6] These sentiments were essential components of the education of the disciplined soldiers and prolific mothers who would carry the race to its supposedly inevitable glory. In short, such an education would infuse children with the "virtues of the Latin razza"[7] that were "indispensable part[s] of the improvement of the stirpe."[8]

The totalitarian aims and institutional transformations of the Fascist state between 1929 and 1934 translated into curricular modifications for the racial education program. The state worked to Fascistize the concepts of nation, race, italianità, and physical health, particularly within the new state textbooks, by taking on references to Fascism's role in unifying the nation and the need for a revitalized Italian race to expand abroad. Additionally, the regime called for the Fascistization of children's bodies through the disciplined practice of good hygiene and physical fitness. With the successful implementation of such lessons, the regime believed, both the nation-state and race would be prepared to expand to fill their rightful place in the world.

Fascistizing the Language of Italianità

The introduction of the concept of totalitarianism to Fascist rule clearly influenced the model of Italian society and the infrastructure of Fascist education, but it also subtly transformed official language about the nation, the race, and italianità. The

1920s' ideas of nation, fatherland, and race were still widespread
in Fascist rhetoric, but they frequently became embedded in
the more administrative idea of the state. That is, at the heart
of the definition of the Fascist nation was the state—the formal
infrastructure of the Fascist government and its many agents.
As an example, the prominent Fascist educator Angelo Cammarosano laid out a definition of the state (*lo stato*) in a 1930
article that identified three chief components: people, territory,
and government. He first described the people within the state,
who were "a group or society of men." He continued to explain
that "when these men are of the same razza, language, and religion, and they share traditions, customs, and ideals, we call them
part of a 'nation,' and that is to say that the people were born of
the same stirpe."[9] Cammarosano did not elaborate on the basic
concepts of razza or stirpe here, but he did go on to explain
that the state's territory, where "said people" resided, could be
considered a patria—"the land of our fathers"—when the people had lived there for a long time. As in the 1920s, these ideas
of nation and race were interrelated and often interchangeable. Finally, he addressed the government of those people, to
which all were "subordinate, under penalty of coercion," and
which gave the state a structure that differentiated it from the
broader ideas of nation or fatherland.[10] This characterization
of the state, which relied on a group of people with shared
historical and cultural characteristics—a race—typified some
of the more general shifts in the Fascist definition of the Italian fatherland and italianità that took place in the early 1930s.

As the last chapter discussed, there was also a demonstra-
ble shift in Fascist language that indicated a growing concern
in the campaign for bonifica umana for the quality of the Italian race as much as its quantity. Sileno Fabbri, president of the
ONMI between 1934 and 1937, wrote in 1933, "When one speaks
of the defense of the razza, one does not mean, nor should one
mean, only physical defense; instead, one must aim for both
moral and intellectual defense; that alone will improve quality as
well as quantity."[11] Articles and speeches by other Fascist bureaucrats and leaders of the demographic campaign also frequently
emphasized the need to improve or defend the race. One pub-

lic health official explained, "The peoples who lead, while they increase in numbers, also refine those selective virtues that create legions out of their great numbers instead of flocks.... A razza that is increasingly strong in muscle, brain, and civic virtues: that is the ultimate goal of the demographic program."[12] What is striking about this quote, in addition to the idea that Italians needed to be aware of their racial makeup, is the official's distinction between the *flocks* of people that weaker nations produced and the *legions* of individuals raised in stronger nations. This emphasis meshed well with the pedagogical rhetoric of the period that distinguished between instruction and education; at least in theory, the regime did not want mindless followers but rather conscientious and disciplined Fascists. The creation of such a population would require strengthening only the most valuable characteristics of italianità.

Yet while there was no doubt among Italian scholars that human races existed, many of them in the early 1930s argued against the idea that the peninsula and islands contained a single race. Instead, many supported logic in line with what Arcangelo Ilvento presented in a 1932 article: "Every people is formed through the historical processes of invasions and wars and the biological processes of encounters between the invaders and the invaded, by an amalgam of various sub-races, fused in the crucible of the nation, so that one can speak more of a stirpe in an historical sense than of razza in a biological sense."[13] In particular, many Italian scholars argued that Italy's regions had historically been composed of several races; but as Giuseppe Steiner wrote in his 1931 book on the culture of Fascism, "the Roman empire slowly equalized and fused all of these various Italic groups into one people that shared many particular regional characteristics, customs, and habits, but were not different enough to break the unity of the nation. Instead, they served to make the civilization more complicated and varied."[14] The theory that the combination of different races produced a more dynamic population pervaded Italian racial theory in the late 1920s and early 1930s.[15] Mussolini claimed in his 1932 interviews with Emil Ludwig, "Of course there are no pure races left; not even the Jews have kept their blood unmingled.

Successful crossings have often promoted the energy and the beauty of a nation."[16] Despite the growing usage of the terms *razza* and *stirpe* at the beginning of the new decade, then, the ambiguity of their definitions allowed the state—and particularly the education system—to continue manipulating them in order to refine the contours of Italian racial identity.

The frequent praise for Italy's regional diversity may have been based on the belief that it actually united the nation, but educational policies and curricular choices of the period indicated mounting apprehension about the tenacity of Italy's regional differences.[17] Alongside the ministry's 1929 transformation into the MEN, it began to decrease its emphasis on region-specific education. Instead of using personal connections to local cultures as a way for students to relate to their national identity—as Gentile's theory of organic learning had originally proposed—the MEN encouraged educators to place more weight on identifying first with the unified nation and race and second with the region. Students were officially forbidden to speak anything but formal Italian in the classroom, and the introduction of comprehensive national textbooks the next year included a secondary series of regional textbooks that was to be integrated only into third-, fourth-, and fifth-grade curricula.[18] These books were meant to supplement lessons on national history, geography, and culture in the upper grades, only after students had a solid foundation in the characteristics of italianità. Furthermore, students were required to prove knowledge of the primary physical, cultural, and economic characteristics of every region in the elementary school exit exams.[19] In other words, familiarity with Italy's regions was to enrich and deepen students' understanding of the nation at large but not to overshadow it with an exaltation of local heritage. Provincialism was to be banished once and for all. This change in the treatment of regional associations plainly illustrated the continued difficulties in the project to unite the disparate regions of the Italian Kingdom into one nation. Moreover, it demonstrated the regime's intensified campaign to complete that project by molding the race according to a Fascist definition of italianità.

Fascistizing Italianità through the Textbooks

This stage in the evolution of the Fascist racial campaign was clearly visible in the elementary curriculum that the newly minted state textbooks presented. Textbooks continued to highlight religious parables, Italy's innate beauty, and stories about famous Italians. More evident, however, was an emphasis on the history and the goals of the Fascist state; *romanità* (Romanness), the modern nation, and the PNF all became integral to the campaign to create a popular mentality of superiority and entitlement that would, MEN officials hoped, push Mussolini's children to support the aims of the state.

At this point in the ventennio, the Fascists had been in power long enough that they could, and felt the need to, show the regime's accomplishments in the rejuvenation of the Italian nation and race—just as the MRF illustrated. The first edition of the third-grade textbook described the Fascist transformation into a New Italy particularly succinctly: "Few years have passed since the March on Rome, and already the face of our Italy has completely changed. There are no more strikes, riots, or lack of discipline; instead, there is order, respect for superiors, peace between workers and bosses."[20] As the regime's tenure lengthened, its challenge would be to strike the delicate balance of asserting what it claimed were immense strides taken to resurrect the historic greatness of the race while also insisting on the perpetual urgency of the revolution: "October 28, 1922 was the beginning of [Fascism's] great work of renewal, which is not yet done, but has already changed the face of Italy."[21] The regime felt comfortable claiming a certain amount of success in its campaign to form the New Italian, but unceasing curricular emphasis on a glorification of the culture, history, language, geography, morals, and spirit that held the Italian population together—their italianità—indicated that it emphatically did not believe the revolution was complete at its tenth anniversary.

More than anything else, textual emphasis on the parallel histories of ancient Rome and Fascism exemplified the escalating drive to Fascistize the Italian student body and italianità. One of the most prominent images in the new textbooks—

and everywhere in Fascist Italy—was the fascio littorio.[22] It was no coincidence that the Fascist Party appropriated such a prominent icon of ancient Rome, evoking both the history and power of the classical civilization; like Mussolini's excavation of Rome itself, the PNF and regime utilized the fascio littorio's historic significance as a representation of the state's power over life and death in order to merge the past with the present.[23] A second-grade textbook described the more popular identity of the symbol as "the will of all Italians, which remains united in order to be strong and invincible."[24] Many books also included an object lesson about the fascio littorio. One such story described a peasant whose many sons often fought with each other instead of working together. Then, one day, a wild animal attacked one son, and his brothers did not come to help. When the father learned of this incident, he gathered his children together and presented them with a bundle of sticks. He explained, "Take one twig and you can break it easily; take two and you can break them with little work; take three and you can break them with a certain amount of effort . . . take five, six, ten, however—no matter how hard you try—you will no longer be able to break them. . . . So it is with you; as long as you are united and support one another, no one will be able to do you harm, and you will win. If you are divided, however, anyone will be able to offend and ruin you."[25] The icon was more than a mere appropriation of an ancient emblem; it was a physical incarnation of Fascist morality. This particular allegory reinforced the regime's core values of patriarchy, strength in unity, obedience, and loyalty.

Texts further highlighted Fascism's inherent bonds with Roman history with celebrations of Mussolini's 1923 announcement that April 21 was officially to be the birthday of Rome and a national holiday.[26] Of course, there is little evidence of what day the city of Rome was actually settled, but choosing April 21 as the official anniversary of Rome's founding further marked the national resurrection of the ancient Roman past as a central, unifying theme in the campaign to strengthen the Italian race and legitimize the Fascist state. As one author concisely explained, "For us, Fascism is a return to romanità"—the essence of ancient Rome and the basis for italianità.[27] Moreover, the Fascist significance of April 21 stretched beyond a commemoration of Romulus and Remus; it was also the regime's chosen replacement date for the Socialist Labor Day of May 1.[28] An author of the second-grade text explained, "Rome is the capital of Italy and once was the capital of the world. Benito Mussolini, who wants to reestablish the greatness of Rome in the world, has decreed April 21 is a national holiday: it is the celebration of the birth of Rome and the celebration of work."[29] On this important date, the entire Italian race was to celebrate the historical and social roots of italianità. And as was mentioned in chapter 1, the regime added the party's "calling to the colors," or leva fascista, to the celebrations of April 21 in 1927.[30] This ritual was, as Mussolini exclaimed in anticipation of its second iteration, "a most important moment for the educational system and the totalitarian and integrated preparation of the Italian man that the Fascist Revolution considers ... the most fundamental obligation of the state."[31] With this rite of passage—on the anniversary of Rome's origin and during the celebration of Italy's laborers—the Duce promised Italians the perpetuation of Rome's legacy and the fruits of their labor.

These rituals followed Mussolini's vague but emotional call for Italians to return to their "Roman, Latin, Mediterranean style."[32] In his 1932 book on the fundamentals of Fascist culture, renowned children's author Giuseppe Fanelli began with a description of Mussolini's push for the advancement of the Latin stirpe and the immortality of the Italian spirit even before his creation of the Fascist squads.[33] In part as a result, Fanelli argued, the "eternal spirit of Rome" infused the very core of Fascism. He concluded that it was not enough simply to applaud the successes of the contemporary regime; it was essential also to consider the Roman traditions on which the triumphs of Fascism relied. Underscoring this association was the increasing focus within elementary education on the racial continuities between the ancient Roman people and the contemporary Fascist population embodied in the idea of the Italian stirpe. As another writer proclaimed, "The Italic stirpe has always cherished the original characteristics of its healthy and prolific razza, since the characteristics of the Italian family, particularly in the countryside which the Duce has often exalted, have always been these: profound religiosity, unquestioned morality, attachment of fathers to their homes, complete dedication of the woman to her children and home. And then: a sober life, frugal tastes, simple desires, and modest habits."[34]

Given the growing presence of the terms *stirpe* and *razza* in the elementary education of the early 1930s and their implicit links to ancient Rome, it should come as no surprise that history played an ever-more prominent component of the Fascist primary school curriculum. One Fascist orator and scholar, Carlo Delcroix, wrote to Fascist children, "History is the greatest teacher of a nation, and the most maternal voice for a people.... For you children it must have an even greater purpose, more maternal and more important: to educate and ignite love and pride in the fatherland and the sweetest feeling of being and being able to say that you are Italian."[35]

Though historical anecdotes flowed throughout all elementary textbooks, the academic subject of history was limited to grades 3 through 5.[36] Third-grade students were introduced to the subject with a focus on modern Italian history, beginning with the Risorgimento and then discussing Italian unification and the Great War. The most consistent approach to this era was briefly to mention the preceding period of foreign rule and then to applaud the Italian movements for independence and unification.[37] The presence of foreign rulers on the peninsula and islands was, interestingly, often characterized as punishment for supposed weaknesses of the Italian race: "After the unification of the Italian nation and the emergence from misery and servitude—with which Italians harshly atoned for the faults and errors committed in the centuries when they were divided and clashing—it was blessed forever."[38] Fascists regarded the years after unification, then, as a time in which Italians reclaimed the land and power that had historically belonged to them but had been taken from them as a result of their own failings. Consequently, the supporters of the Risorgimento, united Italy, and World War I had fought for the recuperation of the race's natural property and influence.

The Fascist treatment of Italy's modern era in the third grade ended with a portrayal of the Fascist Revolution as the final step in the total redemption of the nation and race: "Today Italy, which was divided and subservient one hundred years ago, is one of the greatest powers in the world and presents an awesome display of discipline, work, and faith. The heroes and martyrs of the Risorgimento, Great War, and Fascist Revolution made the fatherland free, united, prosperous, and strong."[39] Though each iteration of the textbook contained a somewhat unique collection of historic personalities, there were some characters besides Mussolini and King Vittorio Emanuele III who consistently appeared in these books. Great protagonists of the Risorgimento, such as Giuseppe Garibaldi and Giuseppe Mazzini, as well as the poet and nationalist Gabriele D'Annunzio, were most often eulogized; but folk heroes of the Great War, such as Cesare Battisti and Enrico Toti, were also highlighted in order to demonstrate the ability of every Italian to sacrifice himself or herself for the glory of the fatherland and race.[40]

History melded with civics lessons in the argument that Italy's long-standing efforts to redeem the race were finally bearing fruit; nevertheless, students needed to continue the struggle so that the labors of their forefathers would not be wasted. Italy, the third-grade text announced, "now waits for you to grow, healthy in mind and body, in order to continue this work, in a way in which Italy will again be a splendid beacon of civilization; ready, like our fathers and our ancestors, if the fatherland calls, to run to arms, and to fall willingly, if its salvation and grandeur demand the ultimate sacrifice of you."[41] Mussolini's children could not afford to slacken their vigilance; only with continued effort and sacrifice would a new, Fascist empire establish itself in the world.

Students moved from studying modern Italian history in third grade to receiving an extensive education in the history of ancient civilizations in fourth. Such a topical transition suggested a belief that if students had a solid understanding of their most recent past, they could more easily understand the connections between it and Italy's ancient predecessors. The first national fourth-grade textbook described several societies of the classical world, including Egypt, Assyria, Babylon, and Israel, as well as a number of cultures on the Italian peninsula. Its approach to ancient Jewish history is particularly noteworthy considering the regime's anti-Semitic measures in the coming years. The book relayed the story of Abraham and then explained how ancient Jews differed from their Egyptian counterparts: "One reason was religious because the Egyptians worshipped many gods and gave them strange human forms with animal heads. The Jews, unique among ancient peoples, believed in one omnipotent God that did not take a corporeal shape. And their faith was so strong that they felt horror and disgust toward the people who worshipped idols. When Egyptian oppression became worse, a great leader, Moses, gathered all the Jews and led them to the Promised Land, Palestine."[42]

There are a number of possible explanations for the relative sympathy with which this piece was written, the first of course being that ancient Jews were the forefathers of Christians. Second, the text compared Jews to a "barbarian" African population that worshipped multiple gods. Third, the Fascist regime held no formal stance for or against modern Jews at this point—though there were plenty of anti-Semites within the party—and the author of this vignette might well have been able to write the story in whatever way he wanted. The absence of a similar narrative about the Jewish population of ancient Rome is striking, however.

More valuable to the racial education of Mussolini's young New Italians was the fourth-grade text's description of the early Latin population: "One of the smallest and poorest peoples in ancient Italy was that of the Latins. . . . They had a few poor families of herders and farmers, but they had great values and moral qualities. They were hardworking, frugal, and strong willed, of simple and pure customs, honest, faithful to their word, devoted to their families, religious, dedicated to ideas of justice and integrity."[43] The authors then made apparent the presumed correlations between the ancient Latins and the population Mussolini rescued in 1922: "Appreciate these values, children; they are the values of the worthy and the brave, and history, this history that I am telling you, teaches you that with and for these values, the small and poor Latin people did not just become the greatest people of the world, but also gave the world the highest forms of civilization."[44]

The descendants of these modest Latins, of course, were the founders of ancient Rome, who, according to the textbook, conquered the ancient world and brought civilization to Europe and the Mediterranean. Roman rule, one author explained, meant

> to keep many different populations obedient to the same laws; to assure peace, tranquility, and prosperity in this part of the world; to build hundreds of streets; to cast bridges over rivers; to construct ports; to found cities where there were savages and deserts; and to bring order, work, science, and civil society where savage tribes carried out a miserable life fighting fiercely among themselves. This was the benefit that Rome brought to the world as no one else was ever able to do: a benefit that secures eternal glory for Rome and should earn her eternal gratitude, because the grandeur of Rome was not simply a fortune dropped in the laps of a lazy people, it was not the violence of the armed, but it was earned by an army of virtue, with strong family values, with knowledge of the laws given to the world, with constant work and spilled blood and the life given with great generosity to all the lands in all the seas.[45]

The impulse behind the glorification of ancient Rome's empire was not simply born of a Fascist call for greater national pride and unity. Inherent in these texts was Mussolini's resolve to claim Italians' inherited racial superiority over other races and nations. Quoted in a book for elementary students, the Duce stated, "We respect other peoples, but our Italy, Balilla, is the most beautiful, the most holy, the greatest! No one will ever be able to equal the power of Rome, the heroism of our martyrs, the courage of our small and proud infantry, the impulse and audacity of our Black Shirts, the strong will of our workers."[46] According to this quote, the roots of Italian superiority were found in the history and spirit of the people.

However, a few pages later in the same book, the author again cited Mussolini, this time exclaiming, "It is Fascism that formed the new Italian, the Italian who is proud to be Italian in comparison to all the other peoples, more or less civilized, of the world."[47] In this second declaration, the strength of the race was only realized through the work and sacrifices of the Fascist Revolution. The juxtaposition of these two quotes and their seemingly divergent interpretations of the source of Italian superiority illustrates the persistent difficulties the regime faced in attempting to prove both the inherent preeminence of the people and the essential role of Fascism in the formation of that position. Ultimately, the message Mussolini and the MEN wanted to convey to their young Fascist followers was best defined by its simplicity and was most explicitly stated in a 1933 manual for Balilla squad leaders: "Italy is a great country and the Duce wants our people to affirm its superiority over all others."[48]

The fifth-grade texts repeated much of the material reviewed in the previous two grades, though their authors did attempt to place Italy in a more global historical context, primarily focusing on the peninsula's importance to European history but also to the larger Mediterranean world. Broken into two general sections—the medieval and modern periods—the state textbook spent very little time on any history before the emergence of the Renaissance. While vignettes about early Italic kings and the Crusades earned the space of a few pages, much of the book's first part focused on the great accomplishments of the peninsula's fourteenth- and fifteenth-century city-states. As one piece explained, "at this time, even though it was darkened by continuous internal strife and wars against foreign tyrants, Italy knew it was lighting the fires of a new civilization in the presence of the world. The arts and letters were reawakened to a fresh life by brilliant powers that raised the name of our fatherland to its ancient grandeur."[49] One of the greatest products of this era of artistic, mercantile, and intellectual preeminence was of course the great Genoese merchant and explorer Christopher Columbus, who, inspired by the achievements of his homeland's Renaissance, ushered Italy and the rest of the world into the "Modern Era" with his "discovery" of the Americas.[50]

In the shadow of these triumphs appeared the unpleasantness of the peninsula's foreign occupations. Bright moments of heroic Italian nationalism were still found in this long and dark time, but the fifth-grade text quickly moved on from the early modern period to bask in the accomplishments of the Risorgimento and the Kingdom of Italy. And of course these steps toward the reclamation of Italians' inherent glory culminated in the kingdom's greatest victory: Mussolini's March on Rome.[51]

What stood out as new to the fifth-grade curriculum was its discussion of Italy's first efforts as an imperial power; early settlements in Eritrea, Somalia, and Libya, according to the text, helped Italy "open new commercial avenues," provide work for her children, and keep foreigners from completely taking over the African coast of the Mediterranean.[52] This narrative merged perfectly with the state's campaign to promote Fascist expansion abroad, and its echoes infiltrated all elementary textbooks. Lessons presented national expansion as a matter of historical and irredentist entitlement as well as autarkic necessity. The fourth-grade textbook explained to its readers, "Italy, because of its location, should be the natural ruler of the Mediterranean Sea, into which it stretches like a long pier; and which was dominated by the Roman Empire, and then by the merchants of Venice, Genoa, Florence, Pisa, Naples, Amalfi, and Palermo."[53] According to Fascist rhetoric, both historic precedent and geographic dominance necessitated the reconquest of "intrinsically" Italian lands. Giuseppe Fanciulli encapsulated this belief in his book *The Great Italian Navigators* when he wrote, "We Italians have two fatherlands: our beautiful land from the Alps to the islands and the changing, immense ocean."[54] Though these calls for irredentism, colonialism, and autarky were already visible in the educational language of the 1920s, the curriculum and general propaganda of the early 1930s showed an elevated earnestness to address these concerns.

One cause of these more urgent calls for expansion was Mussolini's escalating desire to harness the international influence of Italians working and living abroad, particularly in light of the expanding global economic crisis. In essence, these Italian émigrés still belonged to the nation and had only emigrated out of economic necessity; they were natural members of the Italian race. It was the state's responsibility, therefore, to make room for them once again by expanding Italy's territories to the extent of its historical and racial entitlement.

State textbooks explained that the first step to drawing Italy's dispersed population back to the fatherland had been to increase national agricultural and industrial production in the 1920s. The relative success of Mussolini's autarkic campaigns had somewhat insulated the kingdom from the aftershocks of the 1929 economic collapse—with which the rest of Europe and North America continued to struggle—and allowed more people to find work within Italy. Such economic growth offset the losses of population, labor, and resources to other nations: "The government wants to increase work in the fields and workshops of Italy, so that the growing population can find, as much as possible, work and bread in their fatherland. That is why the government pushes and helps farmers to improve the mode of production through the Battle for Wheat; with the reclamation projects it hopes to make arable the lands that have been abandoned because they are swampy and malarial."[55] The texts further argued for Italians to *return* to the fatherland because their immigration to territories ruled by other governments often led to their cultural abandonment of Italian identity. The nation needed to grow economically in order to bring its members home and strengthen the race as a whole.[56]

In the early 1930s the regime put together a permanent exhibition in Rome on Italians abroad to increase awareness of the potential political and economic strength these emigrants could bring to the fatherland and race at large. This exhibit aimed to show the historical impact of Italians outside their national borders and simultaneously to highlight the renewed destiny of Italy's race.[57] Even with all of Fascism's reclamation and autarkic measures, the contemporary boundaries of the Italian nation-state were too limited to support 40 million Italians—let alone the 60 million Mussolini demanded by midcentury—and therefore the regime needed to expand its territory, in both Europe and Africa. One observer of this exhibition explained its message particularly well: "The Italian razza will grow and prosper in the Mediterranean that was the theater of our history for millennia."[58]

To excite the imaginations of Mussolini's children even further, books highlighted the thrills promised to the race's adventurous explorers. In 1931 Giuseppe Fanelli published a book, *Love of Faraway Lands: Explorations, Adventures, and Discoveries by Italian Pioneers in Africa*, which, as the title suggests, shared with its young audience the stories of Italian adventurers and missionaries. The explicitly romanticized vision of travel in the wilds of Africa—certainly not original to Italian literature—hoped to encourage young Italians to visualize a Fascist imperial future.[59] Fanelli wrote in his introduction, "Italy, which has never been second to any nation in the history of human bravery, has a great heroic group of explorers—illustrious figures to whom young Italians should look as one of the most noble expressions of our stirpe."[60] This volume took the opportunity to sing the praises of Italian exploration and colonization from the Roman Empire to the Fascist era but also to show how inferior and uncultured the peoples of Africa had been and continued to be. Fanelli reported that the Mombuttani culture still revered cannibalism, which "the nobility practiced and was the pride of the razza." Many other communities continued to practice slavery, which was an institution "as old as the world"—even the Greeks and Romans had practiced it—but which had never been "so terrible or ferocious an example of oppression" as in the modern cases of African slavery.[61]

As perhaps the most articulate example of the many layers to Fascism's rationale for expansion in the early 1930s, the third-grade textbook explained, "In Africa, Asia, and the Americas, there are great expanses of land, rich in natural resources, but inhabited by indigenous populations that are still barbaric or savage and who do not know how to exploit them." The author then changed tactics, explaining the entitlement to European expansion in light of such supposed ignorance in striking terms of physical appearance: "The white peoples, however, thanks to their civilization, understand the value of those resources and use them to develop industries and commerce in their countries, with which they increase their prosperity and power. It is therefore natural that white peoples have occupied those lands, in order to get the resources that are so important for the well-being of their countries, and to show the indigenous peoples the light and the benefits of a superior civilization." The piece then continued, describing united Italy of the late nineteenth century: "Our Italy did not possess any colonies, even though it had already risen to a level of great power. Its population exceeded thirty million. Its industries and commerce, always expanding, needed greater and greater quantities of those natural resources, of which, unfortunately, its own soil is poor. It was therefore of vital necessity for Italy to acquire colonial possessions."[62] Of course, such logic determined that the further population growth of the Fascist period would necessitate another expansion of Italian holdings.[63] In short, cultural, historical, economic, and racial imperatives came together to motivate the race in support of a campaign for Italian national expansion.

Fascistizing Italianità through Students' Bodies

As the 1929 transformation of the education ministry's title indicated, it would not be enough for Fascist educators simply to *instruct* their pupils about their inherited entitlement to global dominance; these children needed to be *educated* to embody the racial characteristics necessary to follow through on the mission of Fascism's New Italy. These future leaders needed to prove the race's birthright through the successful development of Fascism's physical, moral, and intellectual ideals. And by the early 1930s, Fascist administrators began to see positive changes in the health and strength of the young Italian population: "For some years now we have observed a considerable improvement in the razza: children that are growing like palm trees; sturdy, muscular adolescents, healthy in body, and for that reason, also in spirit, ready, willing, strong."[64]

The MEN continued to view physical education and public health campaigns as fundamental to these advancements in the Italian race, and lessons and training in such fields increasingly permeated the school day and extracurricular activities.[65] The regime urged every school to have playing fields so that all children could get out of their classrooms and into the sun. Games, seen as an important part of physical education, were also rigorously overseen by the regime; they were thought to prevent, or at least limit, physical defects that could be the result of limited physical activity.[66] The true benefit of physical education in elementary school, however, was, in the eyes of its proponents, simply to encourage the natural growth of the child. This attitude in and of itself did not differ from that of the 1920s in Italy or other western European countries; however, in the early 1930s, officials began inserting overt symbols of the regime's influence on Italian life into the lessons. Visibly distinguishing the Fascist system from broader Western trends, all physical education classes and competitions—for both boys and girls—began and ended with the Roman salute, and exercises included marching and commanding.[67] Such changes helped to insinuate Fascist culture further into the established field of physical education and the everyday activities of elementary school students.

Extracurricular outings, exercises, and lessons undertaken by the Balilla and Piccole Italiane were deemed necessary supplements to the elementary school experience.[68] As with all aspects of an Italian child's life, the activities undertaken by the ONB were to contribute to the formation of purely and completely Fascist members of the race who would ultimately become the leaders of the Fascist nation and empire: "Physical and youth education, in the Fascist state, is inspired by healthy educational standards, by discipline, by order, and by conscious bravery, in addition to the physical improvement of the stirpe."[69] Of particular note in this project was the increasingly significant role of military culture in physical education and specifically in the sections of Balilla and Avanguardisti. As the prominent textbook author Oronzina Quercia Tanzarella described, their members constituted "a true army of children that marches toward the conquest of the future."[70] The focus on military culture manifested itself in explicit ways—such as the groups' organization into Roman squads and phalanxes—and, more importantly, in the values encouraged among its recruits. Quercia Tanzarella continued to explain that the ONB was "an organized army with discipline and almost with military consciousness, with rigorous divisions and subdivisions, with its own regulations, and with precise hierarchies."[71]

These characteristics that the ONB promoted were not limited to its male divisions. Girls, too, were encouraged to develop standards of order, discipline, and loyalty; and a military vocabulary and order worked well to inculcate these key sentiments in all Fascist children. The gender differentiation more obviously took shape in the activities and imagery used to frame the activities of the Balilla and Piccole Italiane. While boys were ever more exposed to camping, hunting, fishing, and other pursuits to make them more proficient outside the home and within the culture of the military, girls were exposed to "rhythmic" exercises and courses in first aid and child care to prepare them for the rigors of marriage and motherhood. Girls, in short, were trained to defend the home front and support the boys in what was increasingly becoming clear would be their military future.

Additionally, concerns for a child's physical environment increasingly played a role in the prospective strengths or weaknesses of the Italian youth: "Various conditions and habits of life, environmental conditions, states of mind, etc. can profoundly change the individual physical-psychic makeup"; and the MEN and the ONB needed to manage such factors as much as possible.[72] Textbooks were filled with recommendations (and admonitions) that would lead students to embrace healthy lifestyles:

> To grow up healthy:
>   Wash early and breathe in the pure air of the morning.
>   Wash well and often during the day and do not ever forget to wash your hands before eating.
>   Do not drink cold water and do not stand in the wind when you are sweating.[73]

Beyond simple instruction, however, teachers started promoting competitions to raise awareness about personal hygiene and health. Many schools implemented additional policies to encourage personal hygiene, such as providing students with uniforms and personal toiletry kits (which included a washcloth, soap, a comb, a toothbrush, and a nailbrush), and classrooms with informative posters and first aid kits.[74]

Clearly, the importance of maintaining a healthy physical environment extended to the student's personal display of discipline, strength, and hygiene. Members of the Balilla organizations had always worn uniforms, but the 1928 ban of all other youth groups (except those associated with Catholic Action) forced the significant expansion of its membership and of the visibility of its uniforms. The fact that these uniforms reflected one's age and gender, as well as the season and occasion, meant they mirrored Italy's professional military uniforms.[75] Indeed, organization leaders and textbooks encouraged students to view their uniforms as illustrative of their role as servants to the fatherland and race. Boys were given to believe that they were playing their part—even at a young age—to protect the nation and should be willing to do so with arms, if necessary. As a character in the ONB textbook written for first graders on vacation exclaimed:

> How wonderful my Balilla uniform is: a black shirt, blue tie, and a fez with a golden eagle.
>
> When I wear my handsome uniform I feel my heart beat faster because of the joy of already being a little soldier.
>
> I raise my arm and promise to give honor to the "holy Black Shirt."[76]

Likewise, Piccole Italiane, dressed in their black skirts, white blouses, and black berets, were encouraged to think of themselves as essential members of this military, dedicated to the health and safety of their families and their fatherland. All together, these children were the sturdy New Italians who would be the envy of the world.

The gendered distinction in physical education and among ONB uniforms supported the gendered duties boys and girls were expected to observe. Though all children were expected to be obedient and devoted Fascists, by the early 1930s, their separate social and political obligations were delineated in the first years of public education. The report cards for the young Franca Rizzi of Foggia outline the variety of courses required of her in elementary school. In addition to the primary academic subjects of religion, reading and writing, math, Fascist culture, and hygiene, Rizzi was obligated to take part in regular lessons in home economics and manual labor each year.[77] Even more important to the successful future of Italy's young girls was adherence to the catechism of the Piccole Italiane.

The Piccola Italiana must prepare herself to be the Fascist woman of tomorrow: this is the discipline she must follow.

I. To fulfill her duty as daughter, sister, student, and friend with joy and happiness, even if that duty is sometimes difficult.

II. To serve her fatherland as if she were the greatest mother, the mother of all good Italians.

III. To love the Duce, who has made the fatherland stronger and greater.

IV. To obey her elders happily.

V. To have the courage to oppose those who suggest bad things and mock honesty.

VI. To educate her body to compete successfully and her soul not to fear pain.

VII. To flee stupid vanity, but to love beautiful things.

VIII. To love work, which is life and harmony.[78]

Italian girls had the challenging task of being both attractive and solicitous members of society while also, as point 7 of the catechism stated, avoiding any behavior that might be interpreted as vain. Educators and officials began more vociferously to criticize what they believed was the excessive vanity of society and the ways in which such values hampered the abilities of Fascist women—and therefore men—to perform their national duties.[79] Piccole Italiane, in essence, were meant to serve their race, nation, and family—in that order—every moment of their lives. They were to submit their body and spirit to the values and will of the Fascist state so that they, in turn, would become model mothers.[80]

The regime dictated that the three rules of conduct for a Piccola Italiana were propriety, discipline, and generosity: "These qualities are necessary for anyone who wants to become the perfect Fascist woman, who is a strong [*militante*] force in the regime, the custodian of the traditions of the stirpe and of the Fascist ideas about governing the home, raising and educating children, and assisting family and neighbors."[81] Noteworthy is the author's use of the word *militante* to denote "strong" or "forceful," even in the context of feminine ideals; Fascist girls and women, too, were seen as a united force, devoted to the support of the masculine army that was to carry out the will of the fatherland and race.

The multifaceted approach to the racial education of Mussolini's children reflected the totalitarian efforts of the regime at large. The Ministry of National Education created a unified elementary curriculum in its new state textbooks that continued to underscore the common characteristics of italianità but increasingly highlighted the factors that made the *Fascist*—not just the Italian—race historically, spiritually, and politically superior to all others. The ONB and ONMI, too, urged parents and their children to shed the unhealthy habits of the past and embrace the discipline, strength, and pride that came from a truly Fascist lifestyle. By combining an education in Italians' illustrious imperial past with its present demographic, economic, and moral needs—as well as the cultural and moral inferiority of other peoples—the regime further delimited its requirements of the New Italy and laid the essential groundwork for the conquest of its imperial future.

Three

Resurrecting the Roman Empire, 1934–38

5

Libro e moschetto, fascista perfetto, 1934–36

Shortly after replacing Francesco Ercole as the minister of national education in January 1935, Cesare Maria De Vecchi di Val Cismon addressed the regime's finance committee about his ministry's budget. Of utmost importance to De Vecchi in this presentation was to remind his fellow Fascists of the education system's extraordinary significance in the greater Fascist project. What was this project in the thirteenth year of Mussolini's revolution? As the minister declared, it was, and always would be, imperial. Of course, this in and of itself was "not a new or revolutionary affirmation, nor [was] it merely a rhetorical and sterile exaltation of racial pride." It was a return to the essence of the Italian civilization, which was why "all of our spiritual strength revolves around the unfaltering cornerstone of romanità, a cornerstone that is unfailingly imperial."[1] The MEN found itself at the center of this mission, he continued, as "school is the meat of the meat and the blood of the blood of the state. It is the state itself."[2] It had the essential task of preparing Benito Mussolini's children to seize their imperial destiny. Given the immense value of this undertaking, it was imperative that the regime extended its funding of the ministry and all of its auxiliary organizations, as a "warrior's education cannot actually begin simply with one particular discipline. . . . The duty and honor of the school is the complete formation of new Italians, making the Italian, the son of Rome, spring from its civil, political, and military education."[3]

De Vecchi's appointment to the MEN and his perspective on the role of the education system in Fascism's undertaking illu-

minate much about the political and pedagogical moment of
1935: Italy's renewal of the Roman Empire was at hand. Like
many of Mussolini's later education ministers, De Vecchi had
no background in pedagogy or education policy. However, he
did have credentials that were much more valued at this point:
he was a Fascist of the first hour and an experienced colonial
bureaucrat.[4] A veteran of the Great War, the lawyer from Piedmont had joined the Fascist squads during the earliest days of
the movement, and in 1922 he marched into Rome alongside
Mussolini as one of his quadrumvirate. The four men honored
with such membership—De Vecchi, along with Michele Bian-
chi, Emilio De Bono, and Italo Balbo—were considered Mussolini's four most trusted colleagues, and each subsequently
became a foundational member of the regime. For his part,
De Vecchi spent much of the 1920s as the governor of Italian
Somaliland; after the historic signing of the Lateran Pacts in
1929, he became Italy's first official ambassador to the Holy
See.[5] He would serve as the minister of national education for
less than two years (1935–36), but the placement of one of the
Duce's most trusted generals and colonial officials as the nation's
chief pedagogue reflected the regime's demand for an educational system that could mold and mobilize a race of imperial
soldiers. In the words of one historian, he was considered to
have the military style inherent in true Fascism.[6]

Since the Fascists' rise to power in 1922, international relations
had played an important role in the regime's development; but
as some historians have argued, the state focused much more of
its attention during the 1920s and early 1930s on domestic and
colonial affairs. The regime's confrontation with Adolf Hitler's
speedy rise to power in 1933 and his rapid implementation of
an aggressive racial campaign, however, could only have demonstrated to Mussolini the continuing need to impress Italy's inherent grandeur on the world.[7] From the Italian perspective, many
of the comments Mussolini and the PNF made about race and
the racial makeup of the Italian nation in the 1930s could be
read in conversation with their German counterparts.[8]

What most obviously differentiated Nazi racism from Fascist racism in the mid-1930s was its racial categorization of

Germans as Aryans, Nordics, and, well, Germans. More significantly, however, Nazi racists placed priority on the argument that somatic characteristics were the manifestation of mental and moral characteristics; they believed one could identify the nature of an individual—or an entire group—with a glance. Such connections between physical and moral or intellectual attributes allowed Nazis to develop a much more superficial racial campaign. That is, external traits—as opposed to Fascism's more nebulous spiritual traits—supposedly became the chief measure of German racial fitness. Of course, the fact that many of these physical characteristics—most notably of Jews—were invented meant that the Nazi regime had many of the same difficulties distinguishing Germans from non-Germans that the Fascist regime did within Italy. Finally, Nazi racism diverged dramatically from its Fascist counterpart with its determination to purge German racial weaknesses through negative eugenic policies, such as sterilization and euthanasia, and not simply through positive, pronatalist initiatives.[9]

Nevertheless, one must not place too much responsibility for Mussolini's decisions in the hands of Hitler—or global politics and personalities more generally—as it risks eclipsing the role of Fascism's long-standing racial and imperial objectives and the evolution of the regime's efforts to realize them. The expansion of the Italian nation-state and the creation of a second Roman Empire were critical components of the regime's racial project as clear evidence of Italians' military, political, and racial strength. More to the point, a well-developed belief in racism and its corollary of a racial hierarchy was an essential prerequisite of the Fascist, or indeed any, modern imperial mission. An active imperialist campaign only served to reinforce those beliefs. Thus, a successful colonial undertaking in the Kingdom of Ethiopia, ruled since 1930 by Haile Selassie I, presented the ideal next step in the state's resolution to intensify the Fascist racial campaign.

Fascists had worked to establish a martial and imperial ethos within Italians from Mussolini's initial ascension to power. Still, the period between 1934 and 1936 witnessed a surge in efforts to shape a disciplined race that could accomplish two interrelated goals at the heart of the Fascist undertaking: the expansion of the kingdom's borders and the reestablishment of Italy as one of the world's greatest powers. The accomplishment of the first goal was necessary in order to achieve the second; but in order to achieve either of them, the Italian race as a whole needed to embody the greatest strengths of italianità. Ferdinando Loffredo, a rising star in Fascist eugenics, defined Fascism as "a revolution that is creating, and wants firmly to impose on the world, a new civilization. It is a revolution that works in a country for which the people constitutes the greatest wealth."[10] Shaping the population—its "greatest wealth"—to personify the ideals of that new civilization was the most essential step toward expanding the race and Fascism beyond the confines of the Italian nation-state. And as Mussolini saw the opportunity to establish a second Roman Empire loom before him in the mid-1930s, completing the prerequisite of creating an orderly, united, and powerful race of New Italians became increasingly urgent.

The educational efforts of Fascism's first twelve years had established the infrastructural and ideological framework to cultivate Italian children aware of and actively embodying the cultural, spiritual, and physical attributes of their race. They had concentrated on developing this sense of racial unity and superiority among those individuals who were positively designated as Italians. In other words, the regime had been more concerned with clarifying who *was* Italian than who was *not* Italian. As part of this goal, it had been the obligation of the education system to help young Italians define and embrace their racial entitlement to empire. However, the Duce's mounting impatience for greater international prominence required an intensified effort in this campaign to strengthen the Italian race. Such escalation demanded the continued promotion of the increase and improvement of Italians but also a critical demonstration of their dominance over enemies and inferior societies.[11]

Of course, the Fascist Revolution always had enemies. In the early years of Fascism, its prime targets were political anti-Fascists—above all Socialists and Communists but also Liberals and Masons. And while those enemies were targeted throughout the Fascist era—as well as a growing list of others, such as homosexuals, Slavs, alcoholics, religious minorities, and other enemies of Fascistization—by the mid-1930s the regime also increasingly turned its attention to the identification of individuals and groups it designated as "foreign," "bourgeois," and marshaled against Italy's rise to political, economic, cultural, and racial primacy.[12] By this point, foreignness applied to homosexuals, Roma, Slavs, unmarried adults, and immigrants within Italy's boundaries that affected the quality of the population just as much as to individuals and groups living outside the nation. Nonetheless, increasing an Italian colonial presence outside the peninsula would further help delineate the characteristics that unified Italians and demonstrate their superiority over others.

Unquestionably, the pedagogical decisions of the second half of the 1930s built on those of the 1920s and early 1930s. Still, the policies and rhetoric of the period between 1934 and 1936 experienced significant radicalization amid the heightening sense of urgency to answer supposed domestic needs and foreign threats, especially in light of the global economic depression that had shocked much of Europe in the years since late 1929. In particular, the educational initiatives that Ministers Ercole and De Vecchi established between 1934 and 1936 aimed to expand the regime's totalitarian project even further and to train Mussolini's children to take part in the nation's impending seizure and subsequent protection of the second Roman Empire.

The institutional and pedagogical modifications of this period by and large reflected the slogan *Libro e moschetto, fascista perfetto*, which was increasingly central to youth education in these years. Awkwardly translated as "a book and a rifle make a perfect Fascist," the phrase succinctly conveyed the two broad categories of education Mussolini's children were meant to receive in preparation for their roles as the leaders, providers, protectors, and mothers of a second, Fascist, Roman Empire: intellectual understanding and physical preparedness. As one writer explained in a 1936 article, students were meant to develop a "sense of national pride and, above all, love of Fatherland that would make one willing to sacrifice and dedicate oneself completely to the security, strength, and power of the Motherland

[*Madre-Patria*] according to the increasingly realistic concept that the nation was an impending force of expansion in the world."[13] The educational policies of these years continued to increase state control over the development of young Italians, especially with the growth of the ERR and the 1935 institution of the Fascist Saturday. Additionally, the elementary curriculum further increased its emphasis on expanding the Italian race and Fascism abroad, primarily in the form of imperialism; and the ONB expanded its efforts to prepare young Italians militarily for their inevitable conquest and control of a second Roman Empire. All of these adjustments to the elementary education of Mussolini's children conformed to a more definitive and aggressive set of racial characteristics. Still, these maneuvers in no way represented changes of direction in the Fascist mission. On the contrary, this period of increased militarization and aggression represented an intensification of Fascist campaigns that educational policies and texts had framed since 1922.

Supplying the Books and Rifles

The author of a 1936 curricular guide for rural schools introduced his material to readers by reminding them that Mussolini taught Italians about "the experience of the civilizing mission" and the purpose of "a new Italy, a greater Italy" by way of the classroom.[14] While the efforts to instill a "colonial mentality" in Italian students had punctuated Fascist education for the entirety of Mussolini's rule, by 1934 they had visibly appropriated a front seat in Mussolini's national and racial projects. If he was to conquer a second Roman Empire, the Duce needed to ensure a popular acceptance of the race's imperial imperative; as such, he intended for his young students to absorb their lessons and then share them with family and community members. The regime believed that students, more than anyone else, could influence the spirits of their elders with their admirable examples, especially within the nation's more inaccessible peasant populations.[15] Thus, developing acceptance of the Fascist imperial program among elementary students was an essential step in creating an imperialist Italian nation-state and race. Consequently, Ercole and De Vecchi's reform efforts focused on increasing access to the state's imperial messages.

Of utmost importance in this mission, therefore, was the continued expansion of educational resources in rural Italy. To that end, in 1935 the ONB announced its determination to ensure the availability of fourth-grade classes in all rural schools under its jurisdiction.[16] In theory, the MEN—and the MPI before it—had long required rural schools to have all *five* elementary grades available to its students. Until 1935, however, the obligation largely remained limited to paper. One contributor to the *Annals of Elementary Instruction*, Renato Marzolo, emphasized the practical advantages of expanded schools, writing, "Families now have the option to leave their young children in school and entrust them to older students for a longer period of time," allowing parents more time to work for the good of the nation, free of child-rearing obligations. More important to the Fascist project of developing New Italians, Marzolo explained that the "institution of the fourth grade has also shown itself to be very useful for reinforcing the lessons taught in the lower grades and entrenching in students the habit of reading books and newspapers, even without the guidance of their teacher."[17] Once again, the longer the state could maintain regulated influence over its student population, the greater the likelihood that Fascist lessons were learned and Fascist habits were established.

With like purpose, the educational programming of the ERR began in earnest in 1935.[18] Another article in the *Annals of Elementary Instruction* announced that the ERR had already distributed 4,563 radios across the nation as of February 1935, which, according to the author's mathematics, made its programs available to an impressive 1,069,351 students. While the accuracy of those numbers is questionable—they suggest that each radio was accessible to an average of 234 students—state statistics collected in 1976 claim the state budget for radio programming in Italy almost doubled between 1936 and 1940, from 697,062 to 1,329,723 lire.[19] Such an increase in spending clearly indicates the rising importance and use of radio broadcasting in the ever-expanding Fascist propaganda machine during the second half of the 1930s.[20] The ambition of the ERR, the author of the *Annals of Elementary Instruction* article reminded his readers, was to help the rural masses realize they were "the beating heart of the Fatherland." Once the state had rid the peasant population of any "feeling of isolation" or inferiority in relation to the nation's urban populations, he explained, it would comprehend its immense value to Italy and Fascism's project to create a second Roman Empire.[21]

The state's attention to the spread of a technological and bureaucratic infrastructure throughout the nation did not exclude a continued reverence for agricultural life. Much like officials in other parts of Europe, such as Germany, France, and many of the new nation-states in southeastern Europe, Fascist educators and politicians persisted in encouraging Italians to move back to the countryside and embrace the agricultural heritage of the fatherland and therefore some of the deepest roots of italianità.[22] And as elementary school acted as a crucible in which the raw and precious inheritance of the Italian youth became refined and strengthened, one pedagogical article reminded its readers, "Where a rural school emerges, clean, spacious, cheerful . . . it raises a beacon of civilization; it firmly plants a sentinel of the New Italy."[23] The real concern for the rural population, therefore, stemmed from the regime's increasing desire to have all Italians receive the same information—that is, to control, more and more, the substance of each and every child's education. While the administration had to rely on teachers and their individual personalities for a great majority of lessons, it fought to make the input—and then the output—of the schools as uniform as possible. The expansion of educational radio programming was a logical result of this impulse.[24]

Further supporting these totalitarian aims, state textbooks continued to pull away from regionally specific lessons and aimed to present a single national curriculum. Occasional lessons in local dialect, tradition, or history still emerged from regional versions of the texts, but overall the material focused far more on nationally unifying factors. In particular, the campaign to make the national language predominant among Italians persisted; as Carmela Toscano succinctly explained to her

Balilla and Piccole Italiane readers, a shared language "tight-
ens the bonds of solidarity and makes one more strongly feel
love for the country."[25] Of course, language was only one manifestation of the Italian racial character, and similar efforts in
the fields of history and culture were likewise directed toward
Italians' unifying racial features.

To the occasional complaint that a national textbook was not
useful in a country with such dramatic regional diversity, the Fascist pedagogue and head elementary school inspector for the
MEN Piero Bargellini declared, "Every man has a core of humanity that does not change with variations in countryside; he has
a core that does not alter even with the changing of historical
events; he has a spiritual foundation that he never loses."[26] Bargellini continued, evoking the dangers of liberal Europe and Com-
munist Russia, "Every initiative that comes from Rome must
have a universal character. Without this character, the Roman
initiatives and missions do not mean anything more than those
from Paris or Russia." With its national uniformity, the state
textbook "overcomes all of the complaisance of folklore, all of
its psychological preciousness, all of its descriptive laziness and
environmental particularities."[27] Again, if the Duce was to create a second Roman Empire, he needed to create a united home
front, spiritually as well as politically. Only then could Italians
truly prove their racial supremacy over all other peoples.

In addition to the state textbooks and radio transmissions, the
regime encouraged the publication of multiple new national
youth-oriented periodicals to inform student populations
of events and issues of national concern. While *Fascist Youth*
(*Gioventù fascista*), a bimonthly magazine of the PNF, had been
published since 1930, it was geared toward an older student readership. The weekly magazine *Il Balilla*, founded early in 1934,
became a much more important and prominent publication
for the younger, primary school–aged readership. According to
reports in the official bulletin from the MEN, each issue contained illustrations, photos, and descriptions of recent Fascist
achievements, current events, historical vignettes, and national
hagiography. The publication was, Minister Ercole explained,
crafted with "a pure spirit of italianità" and would therefore be

an essential resource for elementary educators taking on the "lofty mission of the spiritual formation of the Fascist youth."[28] The ministry, on behalf of the regime, highly desired its wide distribution, and multiple announcements in MEN bulletins expressed the strong suggestion for elementary schools to subscribe.[29] In theory, such resources would inform students about their nation-state and race, as well as the world around them, making them aware, in the words of historian Benedict Anderson, "of the hundreds of thousands, even millions, of people in their particular language-field," strengthening the entity of "the nationally imagined community."[30] In turn, these readers would feel more personally connected to the goals and demands of the Fascist state and, of particular concern to this chapter, the conquest and protection of a second Roman Empire.

A much more sweeping and far-reaching initiative with similar intent was the mid-1935 creation of the Fascist Saturday (*sabato fascista*). With this reform, the national workweek officially ended at lunchtime on Saturday. Thereafter, all Italians were to partake in one of the multitude of Fascist extracurricular organizations that most commonly put them in contact with the rifles that were becoming a growing presence in daily life. In terms of Fascist elementary students, they were to report to their section of Balilla or Piccole Italiane for various "instructional activities," principally military education.[31] Because membership in the ONB organizations was still officially voluntary, the regime placed growing pressure on teachers to enlist students in their ranks.[32] Of course, obtaining student subscriptions was also purely "voluntary," but a teacher's ability to increase the numbers of ONB members among his or her students was prominently mentioned in annual reviews.[33]

During these Saturday afternoon meetings, children took part in athletic competitions and local parades, visited local exhibitions, participated in community service and commemorations, and departed for camping trips and other outings. As one fourth grader, Antonio, wrote in his school diary in April 1939, the Fascist Saturdays were when "we learn to be real Italian Fascists and to follow the orders of the Duce, above all by studying and being proud in the face of those who threaten our dear and beautiful Fatherland."[34] Italians were to be Fascist at all times, and the Fascist Saturday ensured that the regime could monitor even more of the time spent outside of school.

With these changes to the ever-expanding educational infrastructure of Fascist Italy, the regime increasingly ensured the distribution of those books and rifles that were so necessary to the development of Mussolini's New Italians. Of course, supplying all Italian children with the basic materials for their Fascist transformation was only the first step; the messages and training that went along with those resources would determine the quality of their racial rejuvenation.

Arming Italians with Ideas

Embracing the idea that Fascists needed to be educated both mentally and physically to meet the global demands of a superior Italian race, educators first needed to inculcate faith in the need for a second Roman Empire. As De Vecchi proclaimed to Italian children at the end of the 1934–35 school year, they needed to work "Romanly" (*romamente*) for the nation and race: "As you already know, [to work] Romanly means [to work] like those who desire to work, who know what they want for themselves and for Italy, and who do not fear fighting one or all in order to conquer their destiny."[35] The general themes of elementary textbooks geared toward developing New Italians who would work Romanly did not much change in the mid-1930s. They continued to underscore connections between ancient Rome and modern Italy, the religious and secular heroes of Italian history, the great and small achievements of the Fascist regime, the physical characteristics of the nation-state, and the equation of the New Italian with the faithful Fascist.[36] Additionally, however, texts demonstrated the increased attention and significance placed on teaching students about Fascist aims outside the borders of the Italian peninsula and islands, as well as the heightened emphasis on the persecution Italy had suffered and continued to suffer at the hands of foreign powers.

Reflecting this sharpened focus on the extramural ambitions of the regime, textbooks expanded the number of lessons and vignettes on Fascist goals for national autarky, irredentism, and colonialism. The first order of business was to stress the continuity of Mussolini's goals for the Italian race and nation-state—that is, to show that the present aims of the regime had always been considerations of the Duce. In 1935 the author Giuglielmo Strata explained to young members of the ONB that national expansion had been one of Mussolini's lifelong goals. According to Strata, Mussolini had traveled and worked abroad as a young adult in order to learn about different peoples and cultures but was ultimately expelled because of his strong irredentist views.[37] Regardless of the inaccuracy of such a narrative, its critical message lay in its emphasis on the Duce's selfless efforts for national redemption, even at a young age. More generally, Strata's anecdote asserted that the increased Fascist stress on the expansion of Italy's borders echoed the regime's long-term ambitions.

As part of this larger campaign, educators were also tasked with demonstrating Italy's entitlement to the irredentist regions of Trentino-Alto Adige and Venezia Giulia, as well as Dalmatia, after the Great War. Again according to Strata, until their "return" to the fatherland, the spiritually—racially—Italian residents of those regions had suffered under foreign oppression.[38] The power of this rhetoric was twofold. First, it presented postwar irredentism as a continuation of the Risorgimento and its mission to unify the disparate regions of the nation.[39] Second, it clearly identified Italians as needing to protect themselves against aggressive, foreign enemies. Nationalist and irredentist content had been present in educational texts prior to and throughout the Fascist era, but the new thrust of these pieces lay in the predominantly negative portrayal of other European powers in contrast to the benevolent—even altruistic—aspirations of the Fascist regime.

Beyond educating Italian children of the need to reclaim "Italian" lands from foreign occupiers, elementary education of the mid-1930s had the goal of clarifying the state's mission to reappropriate a more significant imperial—and not just national—presence in the Western world as part of the Italian race's birthright. Italy had maintained African colonies in East Africa since the 1880s and further established its authority in Africa after the 1912 takeover of Libya from the Ottoman Empire. However, these three colonies combined were apparently not noteworthy enough to allow Mussolini's claim of commanding an Italian empire. To achieve such an appellation, Italians needed to show clear dominance over the last remaining autonomous kingdom on the continent of Africa: Ethiopia. Italy's elementary textbooks, pedagogical journals, and student assignments argued that such a conquest would prove to the world the Fascist nation-state's military, political, and racial preeminence.[40]

Especially important to a regime preoccupied with its place in history, such an enterprise would lead to national and racial vindication for the historic embarrassment incurred at Adwa in 1896. This battle, which cost the Italian military and state much more in pride than financial and personal losses could indicate, was the only successful attempt in modern history of an African power to keep European forces from occupying its land.[41] A Fascist victory over the same kingdom thus had the potential to confirm Italians' military and racial prowess. The cover of one student copybook drove home this imperative with the illustration of a Fascist soldier picking up a rifle from the skeleton of a countryman collapsed next to a tombstone inscribed "Adwa, March 1, 1896." Above, a quote from Mussolini declared, "We have old and new debts to settle: we will settle them."[42] Just as important, an Italian rout of Ethiopia's forces in the 1930s would definitively prove Fascism's might in an area where Italy's former Liberal state had clearly and utterly failed, further proving Mussolini's overwhelming value to the Italian nation and race.

A military campaign against the Kingdom of Ethiopia would also nourish the long-standing Fascist principle that struggle actively unified the Italian race; a collective battle against an other provided a perfect opportunity for the race to further define italianità.[43] Educational texts increasingly distinguished Italy from other nations and races through terms of inferiority and superiority; one text reminded members of the ONB of the much-revered nineteenth-century nationalist Alfredo Oriani, who declared, "The superiority of our razza awards Mediterranean Italy . . . a predominance over those of France and Spain."[44] A published letter from an elementary school student to Rodolfo Graziani—the general in charge of the southern campaign in the 1935–36 Italo-Ethiopian War—reflected the value of such sentiments in a war for an Italian empire. In an effort to motivate Graziani to continue his work, young Filomena Boffoli explained:

> The foreigners who are jealous of us try in vain to starve us with their sanctions, but they don't know that they cannot subdue a brave people, a great people, without great difficulty. No one can conquer us because the Italian army is united, ready at a nod from the Duce. The sanctionist nations say that they are civilized, but if they truly were, they would not have applied sanctions to a people that marches to Ethiopia, a barbaric and primitive land, to liberate the poor slaves from the yoke of their leaders. But as long as we have intrepid generals like you, for whom nothing is impossible, we will not fear the sanctionists or the barbaric Abyssinians.[45]

The sense of pride, outrage, and entitlement in this short letter reflected perfectly the emotions that the Fascist government desired of its people—toward Ethiopians and anyone else who stood in Italy's way.

The successful conquest of Ethiopia would officially allow Mussolini to initiate the era of a second Roman Empire and expand Italian influence abroad; a resurrection of the great Roman Empire would plainly illustrate the racial, economic, and political strength of Fascist Italy to all.[46] In addition to proving and enhancing Italian racial superiority domestically, Fascism's imperial project had the critical aim of demonstrating Italian supremacy abroad. At the very roots of the Fascist Revolution was a search for national respect—and fear—from the international community; in light of this objective, the aim of the mid-1930s was to give the world concrete examples of Italian strength. Giovanni Gregorio, writing in *Fascist Youth* early in 1935, explained that imperialism was the most powerful expression of an expanding state and that "all strong peoples have wanted and created empires." In short, the Fascist state was obliged to create an empire. He continued, "The strength of its ideas; the intelligence of its leaders; the needs of the nation;

the traditions and geographic position of Rome; the discipline and military power of the young generations; the genius of the Duce—these are the ... reasons for believing in this superior civilization."[47] Of course, it could only be a superior nation, led by a superior race, that would be able to successfully revitalize an empire that was the touchstone of civilization for all Western powers.

All these ambitions were overlaid with the sense of racial obligation discussed earlier in this chapter; as another article in *Fascist Youth* most clearly expressed, "Forty years ago, reckless officials and unlucky military heroism forced Italy to experience the first Adwa. Afterward, a chorus of voices was heard in Europe lamenting the repercussions that European prestige—that is, the prestige of the white race, the expression of civilization—had suffered following the Ethiopian victory. For all of this, Italy carried the responsibility of not knowing how to erect a bulwark for the untouchable white superiority."[48]

It was imperative for Italians to redeem themselves and demonstrate their innate superiority—under Fascist leadership—over the last remaining independent African kingdom. Despite the fact that imperialism carried great responsibilities and occasional challenges, another author noted, "these difficulties will always be overcome by the New Italian; it is also true that the colonies form our will, expand our horizons, and provide new inspiration for hard work."[49] The strength and superiority of the Italian race would grow with its colonial holdings; any and all difficulties were simply additional opportunities to prove the worth of the New Italians.

An even more obvious rhetorical example of Fascist instruction in the superiority of the white Italian race and its clear entitlement to imperial rule was the opening story in Giuseppe Fanelli's 1935 textbook for fifth graders, *The Most Beautiful Flowers*:

> Almighty God created white men and black men. He gave them two precious gifts and said, "Here is gold, and here is writing—choose which one you want!"
>
> The Blacks, greedy and not very insightful, yelled immediately like noisy children, "We want the gold! We want the gold!"

"Take the gold," Almighty God said; and the Blacks had the gold. Writing remained for the Whites.

Each group used its gift as best it knew how. The Blacks, occupied with mines, extracted gold; the Whites, occupied with books, gave themselves to studying the sciences.

What happened after a century? The Whites invented machines, built boats, learned the art of war, and traveled. The Blacks continued to dig up gold, but they did so for the Whites.[50]

This story—which clearly delineated the existence of a racial hierarchy based on physical characteristics, supplemented, of course, by spiritual distinctiveness—had appeared in earlier textbooks. Its position as the introductory text of this schoolbook, however, illustrated the greater importance of its message to the goals of the Fascist state and primary school curriculum.

A decisive military defeat of the Ethiopian forces would be essential to Mussolini's objective to prove Fascist and Italian might, but so would a strong and moral approach to subsequent Fascist rule. While Mussolini wanted to be feared militarily, he also wanted to demonstrate that Italians were wiser colonial rulers than the great powers of France and Great Britain.[51] Blending concepts of racial superiority with the Catholic notion of redemption, Italian imperialists argued that they would not simply exploit Ethiopia for economic resources or use the military occupation for strategic purposes. Italian colonists would truly benefit East Africa through widespread economic, political, and moral improvement.

The fact that some Ethiopians still practiced slavery became an invaluable asset to Fascist claims for colonization: the Fascists would free Ethiopians from bondage.[52] Though the League of Nations had accepted Ethiopia's membership in 1923—thereby formally recognizing its political sovereignty—the kingdom's continued reliance on the institution of slavery meant that its admission remained provisional; this tenuous relationship between Ethiopia and the international West left room for the Italian popular press to declare Ethiopia unworthy of political autonomy and to justify a military takeover by a morally superior nation and race.[53] The cover of another school copybook illustrated this mindset with a vivid image of Italian soldiers overseeing Ethiopian allies breaking the bonds of grateful slaves under the simple yet powerful title "Civilization."[54] Hypocritically, though unsurprisingly, the Fascist regime declared all Ethiopian slaves free shortly after their initial invasion and then immediately ordered Italian troops to force many of them into the service of the Italian military.[55]

The continued refusal of the League of Nations to support an Italian invasion of the East African kingdom did nothing to hinder Fascist determination and in fact served to heighten popular support for Mussolini's crusade for imperial glory, perhaps indicating at least partial success for the regime's education campaign.[56] Indeed, the league's announcement of sanctions against Italy after the October 3, 1935, invasion of Ethiopia (which did not include the one thing that had the potential to prevent a military engagement, oil) significantly enhanced support from devoted Fascists—as Filomena's letter to General Graziani demonstrated—as well as from previously self-identified anti-Fascists.[57] Renzo De Felice argued that the Italo-Ethiopian War between October 1935 and May 1936 marked the high point in popular support for Italian Fascism, and Victoria De Grazia has subsequently added that the lead-up to and duration of the war provided the best example of Fascist mass organization at work.[58] The regime built an expansive media campaign that asserted the nation's ability to overcome the so-called barbarity of the league and its supporters. To accentuate the effects of the sanctions—or, in Fascist terms, the stoicism of the Italian nation in the face of those economic sanctions—some periodicals actually recorded dates in terms of how long Italy had been sanctioned. For example, alongside January 6, 1936, editors parenthetically noted "Fiftieth day of the economic siege."[59] Such additions to daily life encouraged a collective sense of attack and defiance, uniting Italians and promoting support for the regime that would protect Italian national interests against their enemies.

Capitalizing on this rising sense of national and racial unity, Mussolini followed his initial invasion of Ethiopia with a series of Days of Faith (*Giorni della fede*) to emphasize the value of every Italian in the successful execution of the East African cam-

paign. First held on December 18, 1935, and followed by numerous others, the Day of Faith called on Italians to donate any
and all gold objects to the state to help fund the troops in East
Africa. The name given to this day of "voluntary war contributions" was clever, as *fede* referred both to the faith participants
displayed in the Fascist project and to the wedding rings that
were a primary donation to the cause. In place of their symbols
of marital commitment, Italians received steel rings engraved
with the words "For the Fatherland," formalizing what had been
a major goal of the totalitarian regime: training the populace
to prioritize the fatherland over the family.[60]

The success of such events hinged on popular outrage over
the international community's denial of Italy's right to colonial expansion.[61] Mass publications further stoked the fires of
popular backing by issuing lists and photographs of the individuals and families who had given their savings to the national
cause. Children's magazines were especially adept at highlighting the youth contributions to such programs.[62] One student
wrote to Renato Ricci in an album her class put together for
the head of the ONB that she was delighted Italy was not suffering from the sanctions imposed by England and its "bad"
friends because of the contributions she and her classmates
had made.[63] Periodicals also ran articles about the donations
and support from Italians abroad—especially children—whose
offerings "were the purest testimony of the spiritual force of
the Fascist Fatherland and of the renewed conscience of its
children."[64] As De Vecchi's address to the finance committee
had affirmed in the early days of 1935, the education system—
and Italy's youth—was at the heart of Fascism's imperial project. These propaganda measures and other initiatives within
the education system were used to combat what one author in
Motherhood and Childhood termed "egotistical individualism."
The journalist further explained, "The individual, the building
block of the state, must work toward moral and physical perfection in relation to his functions within the state" in order
for each person to participate in building "the glorious future
of the nation."[65] National, and racial, unity was essential to Fascist success both at home and abroad. Therefore, the perceived

success of state actions such as the Days of Faith both echoed Fascism's pedagogy for the previous thirteen years and, as the Duce would claim, allowed Fascism to achieve a "totalitarian victory" in Ethiopia.[66] He would officially declare the creation of the Italian Empire on May 9, 1936.

Arming Italians with Rifles

Concurrent with the need to bolster a popular sense of imperial entitlement in the lead-up to the Italo-Ethiopian War was the necessity of educating students in the physical demands of a Fascist empire. And while the regime nominally paid lip service to Gentile's original principles of organic and active learning in these years, the pragmatic concerns of the state to develop successful soldiers, leaders, and mothers clearly outweighed its desire to adhere to the philosopher's pedagogical ideals. Stated simply, the official stance of the MEN and its auxiliary institutions was that the overarching purpose of educating the Italian youth was to serve the state and, through it, the race.[67] As one 1934 ONB publication reminded its young readers, "the order, discipline, and silent work that are at the foundation of the Fascist state will find in you a faithful follower even at gatherings, in the field, and at the gym."[68] And at least in some classrooms, such a lesson was driven home; one unnamed student wrote in his notebook, "To reach the goal, there is only one job: to work; and there is only one obligation: to obey. To work and to obey is required of all Italians big and small, who know their role in the world."[69] The concept introduced in 1934 that there was no distinction between a Fascist citizen and a Fascist soldier—Italians were, in fact, citizen-soldiers—defined the contours of the youth's obligations most obviously.[70] Strata declared in his 1935 book, *The Fascist Fatherland*, "Fascism arose with the precise goal of reevaluating war and victory, of reinvigorating a love for the Fatherland in its citizens, of making the Fatherland strong, respected, and feared, and of increasing its prestige abroad. In order to reach all of these noble goals, Fascism gave the nation the soul of a warrior."[71] Consequently, one of the most striking steps in the evolution of Fascist education during the mid-1930s was a significant increase in the militarization of youth culture in daily life, and particularly on Fascist Saturdays.

At the end of 1934 the regime passed a law necessitating the inclusion of courses on military culture in all Italian schools.[72] In response, one journalist wrote to his young Fascist readers, "Now military culture enters the schools, and not through the window or the back door, but with full honors. It comes to take the place it is due—and should have had for a long time now—next to the old and venerable doctrines that we hope will not turn up their noses at the newcomer, who is young, lively, and brilliant."[73] With such martial qualities, Fascist Italy and the Italian race would be able to maintain and expand its prestige throughout the world.[74]

In accordance with this new law, all elementary students received a premilitary education with literature and activities designed to excite students about the armed forces and encourage them to enjoy competition. This education in military culture was to give the youth a "heroic spirit" and pride in their race, as well as to prepare them for battles in defense of Italy's presumed destiny.[75] Again, the justification for such preparation was not merely hypothetical; Fascist texts and pedagogues raised the specter of the past to make clear the obligations of the future. Carmela Toscano simply stated, "The course of history has always shown us that strength was the principal element of conflict and victory."[76] Another article, directed more clearly to the conscience of its student readers, asserted that the youth "must fight to continue the work of innumerable generations of Italians who, in every era, fighting with spirit and with muscle, suffering, sacrificing themselves, have kept the Fatherland alive and made it the source and center of world civilization."[77] The Italian inheritance would impel young Italians to protect and perpetuate the accomplishments of their forefathers.

In order to be a good Italian, therefore, one had also to be a good soldier, and this applied in very serious ways both to boys and girls. The regime needed Mussolini's children to learn to read and write and understand the fundamental nature of the race and nation-state, but it also required them to know how to protect that race and nation-state against any and all

enemies. Sport was no longer an end unto itself but was critical to the military preparation of the race.[78] More directly, the
oath that was compulsory for all members of the ONB stated,
"In the name of God and Italy, I swear to follow the orders of
the Duce and to serve the cause of the Fascist Revolution with
all my strength and, if necessary, with my blood."[79] If students
internalized the demand that the needs of the collective—both
the nation-state and the race—must transcend the needs of the
individual, Italians would be able to claim their intrinsic primacy in the world.

As its oath indicates, the ONB was vital to the military education of Italy's youth. In De Vecchi's 1935 address to the regime's
budgetary committee—parts of which opened this chapter—
the minister extolled the accomplishments of the ONB alongside those of the MEN. He explained that ONB programs led to
the "military and civic education of the entire Italian youth"
and clarified that this "Roman" "character is the austere and
necessary foundation for the life of a people that wants to conquer its future, the character which is indispensable to Italians
who ... are recovering a spiritual unity in a hardworking way
of life that is an example to the world."[80] The military education
the ONB imparted was primarily "a discipline of the spirit" that
underscored the superior might of the Italian race.[81]

In order to appreciate the international implications of the
Italian race's martial superiority, a necessary component of
effective youth education was the elementary understanding
of social Darwinism. In that regard, one teacher articulated
that "history is a selective process and only those who retain
the masculine character of their spiritual form survive."[82] It was
this idea of the "masculine character" of cultural survivors that
most prominently directed the lessons in military education
for boys during this period. Between 1934 and 1936, gender
designations, like racial distinctions, became even more pronounced. Articles tended to combine discussions about the need
for military education with the familiar description of physical education as an "education in manliness." Accordingly, the
purpose of the ONB was to "increase the virility and morality
of the razza."[83] Manliness was synonymous with strength and

power, the characteristics with which Fascists most wanted to imbue the Italian people.

Developing the masculinity of the Fascist race was contingent upon also strengthening Italian femininity—that is, the regimentation of women's roles as homemakers and caretakers. The textbook for young girls training to be squad leaders in the Piccole Italiane explained that the "Fascist pledge obliges the Piccola Italiana to serve her fatherland in every moment of her life, growing healthy in body and in spirit in order to become a *Fascist woman*: a wise governess of her house and a teacher of civic virtues to her children."[84] More specifically, it addressed the need for Italian girls to be prepared for war: "Wars are inevitable in the history of peoples, and she needs to have a heart prepared for the most painful sacrifices for the honor and salvation of the fatherland." Again referring to the heroism of ancient Rome, the book continued to explain that "like the Roman woman, the Italian woman prepares herself for war by fortifying her soul with the memory of the glories of her fathers."[85]

In terms of physical education, these goals for Italy's young girls meant that, as one pamphlet for the English-speaking world explained, "physical training is organised chiefly for aesthetic purposes, intended to make the bodies of the growing women slim, graceful and generally strong. Exercises which are likely to cause physical strain have been banned, games and sports being taught and competitions arranged with a view to safeguarding the physical and moral health of the members."[86] Just as texts in the early 1930s explained, those of the mid-1930s argued that appropriate exercises—such as rhythmic dance and tennis—would create healthy and strong mothers. Unlike Nazi Germany, where women were encouraged to be athletic and muscular, Fascists believed that an "overemphasis" on athleticism could lead to the immoral "masculinization" of women, as it had in many other countries, such as the United States and Great Britain.[87] According to one article, such a process affected a woman's sentiments and consciousness of "her fundamental mission": motherhood.[88] Therefore, it was essential to find the right balance of femininity and physical health, because, as the author continued, "the habits of the sportsman are never accompanied by the tendency to grumble, be superficial, or become embittered—defects that, as is noted, determine ninety percent of marital unhappiness." Furthermore, "physical health gives the optimism, courage in adversity, serenity, and capacity to understand an exhausted man and to work with him."[89] Too much aggression, independence, and strength, however, and the institution of motherhood—the very bedrock of the race's future—would be in peril.

The Perfect Fascist

Still in the middle of the 1930s, the Fascist regime and its collaborating racial scientists struggled to find a theory of race that adequately addressed the diversity of the Italian nation-state and the goals of the Fascist Revolution. Most frequently, authors talked about a more generic "white" Italian race, the importance of Italian racial hybridity, or the popular concepts of a unique Latin or Mediterranean race that emphasized spiritual and historical commonalities.[90] While Italians could not ignore the confidence of racial propaganda coming from the new German regime, most state-sponsored "scholars" refused to engage seriously with the more strictly "scientific" theories of race, Aryanism, and the negative eugenics the Nazis employed.[91] Instead, much like their French contemporaries, Fascists upheld the official position that the entire spiritually connected Italian race could, as a whole, be improved through pronatalist policies and, more generally, a campaign of bonifica umana.[92] State-sponsored racial scientists and eugenicists did not claim that italianità was not facing challenges, but they did maintain that those threats largely remained outside the Italian race. They believed there were few contaminants within the race that needed to be expunged, as Nazi eugenicists frequently argued regarding the German race. In fact, juvenile delinquents and criminals were most frequently characterized as being either foreign to the Italian race or victims of poor parenting.[93]

Nevertheless, the regime needed to remain vigilant; a 1935 text commemorating the tenth anniversary of the founding of the ONMI characterized one of the most important missions of the organization as unifying Italians under a single set of goals to improve the race. The memorial book portrayed the ONMI's ongoing efforts to protect mothers and children in terms of safeguarding the racial interests of the state: "ONMI is an organization for the physical, psychic, and moral protection of mothers and children, placed within *preventive medicine* and directed toward the important goals of the *demographic policies* of the Fascist regime."[94] In addition, the text explained that the biopolitical concerns surrounding the health of mothers and children could not be simplified: "The projects that the Regime has assigned ONMI ... can attest to the vast and multifaceted range of the organization's activities ... for the reinforcement of the stirpe, projected through the centuries and which is understood as a substantial and fundamental element of a never-ending conquest of spiritual, political, and social virtues."[95]

Mussolini and his state continued to navigate the delicate balance between proving the great successes of the revolution and reminding the population of the work that lay ahead. The age of the second Roman Empire was at hand, as was definitive proof of Italy's racial, political, and military superiority in the world. Therefore, alongside the commemoration of ten years of work, the ONMI strongly urged its followers that a decade was not much time and that Italians had still much to do. The success of Fascism's next stage depended on racial strength both through quantity and quality. Numbers were critical to the strength of the military, the empire, and the legacy of Fascism, but only insofar as those Italians adhered to the purest qualities of italianità. Still, the complex set of demographic measures this project of bonifica umana entailed were not set in stone even fourteen years after Mussolini's March on Rome; the revolution would continue to require renegotiation to ensure the best path toward a powerful second Roman Empire.

La Patria non è una illusione,
la Patria è la più grande, la più
umana, la più pura delle realtà.
MUSSOLINI

Quaderno

1. The cover of a copybook depicting Benito Mussolini bending over a group of children. In the lower-left corner, Mussolini is quoted as saying, "The fatherland is not an illusion, the fatherland is the greatest, most humane, and purest of realities."

SOURCE: Notebook, *Quaderno*... (Florence: S. I. Castello S. A., c. 1938). 8¼ x 5⅞ inches (21 x 15 centimeters). Wolfsonian–Florida International University, Miami Beach, Florida, Mitchell Wolfson Jr. Collection. XX1990.1948.18. PHOTO: Lynton Gardiner. Published with the permission of the Wolfsonian–Florida International University (Miami, Florida).

2. The cover of a copybook with an illustration of Piccole Italiane, the youth group for girls between the ages eight and eleven. In the background, a drawing shows members of the ONB entering the Mussolini Forum in Rome. The text in the upper-right corner reads, "The hopes of Italy: Piccole Italiane."

SOURCE: *Quaderno di… Speranze d'Italia Piccole Italiane* [Notebook of… Hopes of Italy Piccole Italiane] (Italy: CIPS, c. 1938). 8¼ x 5⅞ inches (21 x 15 centimeters). Wolfsonian–Florida International University, Miami Beach, Florida, Mitchell Wolfson Jr. Collection. XX1990.1948.12. PHOTO: Lynton Gardiner. Published with the permission of the Wolfsonian–Florida International University (Miami, Florida).

3. A poster advertising ONMI's 1936 celebration of the Day of Mother and Child on December 24, year XV. A mother and father hold their child between them, looking toward a new dawn.

SOURCE: Marcello Dudovich (Italian, 1878–1962), designer, *Giornata della Madre e del Fanciullo. Anno XV* [Day of the Mother and Child. Year XV] (Rome: Opera nazionale per la protezione della maternità e dell'infanzia, 1936). Printed by Grafiche IGAP (Impressa Generale Affissione Pubblicità), Milan and Rome. Offset color lithograph. 54 x 38¼ inches (137.2 x 97.2 centimeters). Wolfsonian-Florida International University, Miami Beach, Florida, Mitchell Wolfson Jr. Collection. 84.4.11. PHOTO: Bruce White. Published with the permission of the Wolfsonian-Florida International University (Miami, Florida).

4. The cover of a copybook with the title "Civilization," depicting an Italian soldier overseeing Ethiopian military allies breaking the bonds of slaves after the Italian victory in 1936.

SOURCE: *Quarderno di... Civiltà* [Notebook of... Civilization] (Milan: Pizzi e Pizio, c. 1938). 8¼ x 5⅞ inches (21 x 15 centimeters). Wolfsonian–Florida International University, Miami Beach, Florida, Mitchell Wolfson Jr. Collection. XB1992.2231. PHOTO: Lynton Gardiner. Published with the permission of the Wolfsonian–Florida International University (Miami, Florida).

5. One of Aurelio Bertiglia's postcards using juvenile caricatures to depict an idealized course of the Italo-Ethiopian War. Here Ethiopian civilians raise their hands in Fascist salute to Italian soldiers.

SOURCE: Aurelio Bertiglia (Italian, 1891–1973), illustrator, [Ethiopian children saluting and surrendering to Italian children in colonial military uniform]. 3½ x 5½ inches (9 x 14 centimeters). Wolfsonian-Florida International University, Miami Beach, Florida, gift of Steven Heller. XC2008.07.17.206.5. PHOTO: David Almeida. Published with the permission of the Wolfsonian-Florida International University (Miami, Florida).

6. A poster meant to accompany an ERR episode of the educational program titled "How to Become Physical Education Instructors." It originally aired on March 9, 1938. The poster intersperses images of students performing various exercises with those of the Mussolini Forum in Rome.

SOURCE: Oreste Gasperini (Italian), designer, *Come si diventa insegnanti di educazione fisica. Ente radio rurale. Radioprogramma scolastico N. 60* [How One Becomes a Teacher of Physical Education. Scholastic Radio Program N. 60] (Rome: Ente Radio Rurale, 1938). Printed by Tumminelli, in Rome. Offset photolithograph. 27⅝ x 39½ inches (70.2 x 100.3 centimeters). Wolfsonian–Florida International University, Miami Beach, Florida, Mitchell Wolfson Jr. Collection. XX1990.2989. PHOTO: Silvia Ros. Published with the permission of the Wolfsonian–Florida International University (Miami, Florida).

6

Educating Rulers for the
Second Roman Empire, 1936–38

In the aftermath of the Italo-Ethiopian War, the internationally known illustrator and graphic designer Aurelio Bertiglia
produced a series of postcards depicting scenes from the recent
Italian conquest. As a set, the five cataloged in the archive of
the Wolfsonian library in Miami Beach, Florida, present a particularly revealing interpretation of Italy's occupation of the
kingdom; they portray the Italian presence in Ethiopia as one
characterized by strength, charity, and popularity, just as the
regime had so anticipated on the eve of its invasion.[1]

Each frame illustrates Italian soldiers interacting with a variety of Ethiopians, both soldiers and civilians. Of special note is
that all of Bertiglia's subjects are children. Every one of them
exhibits the juvenile features of outsized heads and eyes, small
noses, rounded cheeks, and shortened bodies. Indeed, the Italian
soldiers even wear a mixture of official military attire and ONB
uniforms. In the first postcard, three Italian soldiers kick baby-
faced caricatures of Emperor Haile Selassie and his entourage
down a hill. The Italians sport relaxed smiles as they perform
their duty, in stark contrast to the terror inscribed in the eyes
of their victims. In this illustration, as well as the others, almost
all the Ethiopians wear traditional dress—including *shamma*
(cotton cloaks), robes, and headdresses—and carry spears and
shields. Meanwhile, the second postcard depicts a single Italian child soldier holding an Italian flag, while a combination
of four young Ethiopian royals and commoners supplicate the
new authority on their knees, some with looks of resignation,
others with looks of admiration. The third drawing portrays

three Italian soldiers breaking the iron chains of a slave as an
Ethiopian woman looks on in amazement. The fourth furthers
this notion of Italian altruism with the image of two young
Italian soldiers distributing food among their new Ethiopian
subjects. Italian flags fly from the mud-and-straw huts in the
background, just as they do in the previous picture. The final
postcard in this series captures a scene in which two Italian soldiers walk away with their national flag. In the background, a
young Ethiopian holds aloft a white flag of surrender. He and
three others in the foreground face the Italians and raise their
right arms in Fascist salute. This image appears to complete the
set of five by wordlessly conveying to its viewers not only that
Italians had successfully conquered Ethiopia but also that the
local population was grateful for the foreign presence. Mussolini's empire was born.

Growing up in the northwestern Italian city of Turin in the
1890s and early 1900s and largely teaching himself the artistic
skills that would form the backbone of his livelihood, Aurelio Bertiglia began designing postcards (along with musical
scores, fashion, and commercial graphics) in the early twentieth century. Throughout his prolific career, he was notable
for his frequent use of children as subjects. Editors and politicians began to notice his work during the Great War, when he
made a significant number of anti-German and anti-Austrian
postcards.[2] Being politically savvy, Bertiglia quickly designed
Fascist uniforms for his subjects after Mussolini and his Fascist
Party came to power in 1922.

Though Bertiglia used young children in a vast array of subject matters, they particularly add important layers of meaning
to the series of tableaus discussed here. Western art and propaganda had long depicted colonial subjects as children in order
to convey their assumed racial immaturity and the necessity
for foreign oversight.[3] Such a message seems inherent in the
simultaneous displays of ignorance and helplessness among the
Ethiopians Bertiglia drew. At the same time, the artist's use of
children to represent Italian soldiers helps underscore the significance of youth to the Fascist colonial mission. As school
textbooks had expressed to their readers for over a decade, it

would be Italy's children who would reconquer the world and establish the New Roman Empire. Mussolini had informed students in the 1920s, "You are the dawn of life; you are the new promise of the Fatherland. You, o children, must be the faithful custodians of the heroic civilization that Italy is creating with work, discipline, and harmony."[4] In short, these five postcards visualized the central role of Mussolini's children in the successful conquest and protection of a second Roman Empire.

Bertiglia's images actually illustrate several critical themes of this latest phase in the Fascist racial campaign in a casual and, theoretically, an ephemeral format; used to relay brief messages, these postcards were simply part of the everyday experience of Fascism. As commercial products, they needed to appeal to a wide-ranging audience of consumers. Thus, one can assume their messages were at least not particularly controversial and at most broadly supported. In addition to emphasizing the continued importance of the Italian youth to the national and racial projects, Bertiglia's five postcards highlight the fundamental Fascist arguments for the value of an increasingly militarized Italian population; the need for an empire to realize Italy's true potential; and the role of that empire in the development of more-exclusionary concepts of Italian racial identity.

While the period 1934 to 1936 had worked to strengthen the regime's totalitarian control over the development of an imperial ethos in preparation for the Italian conquest of Ethiopia, the years 1936 to 1938 were largely spent defining what it meant to be a Fascist imperial power for the Italian race, its subject populations, and the wider international community in the aftermath of Ethiopia's conquest. The Italo-Ethiopian War had significant legal and social consequences in the realm of imperial racial policy, which found echoes in the regime's latest modifications to domestic elementary education. These changes, enacted under the ministerial leadership of Giuseppe Bottai, reflected the development of lessons about the rights and responsibilities associated with ruling the New Italian Empire as well as subtle shifts in domestic racial theory and goals for physical education. Ultimately, Bertiglia's themes and the new imperial undertaking not only defined the contours of the Fascist racial project between 1936 and 1938 but also reinforced the state endeavors toward bonifica umana that had been developing for the previous fourteen years.

Defining the New Empire in the Horn of Africa

The military campaign that pitted Italy's troops against those from the Kingdom of Ethiopia for seven months between October 3, 1935, and May 9, 1936, was relatively short but extraordinarily brutal.[5] Taking advantage of a minor border skirmish at WelWel (the town was actually about 150 miles from the Ethiopian border with Italian Somaliland) that took place ten months earlier, Mussolini had directed his generals to invade Ethiopia and initiate an imperial project that he had been developing at least since 1925.[6] Many of the Italian soldiers who marched on Adwa and into Addis Ababa had come to maturity under the watchful eye, forceful words, and coordinated exercises of Fascism's integrated educational system.

Indicating the immense political importance of the campaign—even at the expense of its tactical efficiency—Mussolini had appointed the militarily inexperienced and timid sixty-nine-year-old quadrumvir Emilio De Bono to be commander in chief of the Italian armed forces in Africa and the Ethiopian campaign. (It is significant, however, that Mussolini quickly recognized his poor choice of commander and in December replaced De Bono with the much more skillful and brutal, but no less politically valuable, governor of Libya, General Pietro Badoglio.)[7] Meanwhile, General Rodolfo Graziani led the troops from Italian Somaliland into the fray from the south and east. Graziani, unlike De Bono, had amassed significant experience in colonial warfare and administration as the commander of Italy's "pacification" efforts in Libya during the 1920s and early 1930s. Since 1934 he had served as the governor of Italian Somaliland.[8] This combination of politically appointed and morally bankrupt leadership of the Italo-Ethiopian War would presage much of the Fascist administration in East Africa.

Furthermore, the Duce had long been aware that Italy's military and economy were in no shape to carry through a lengthy engagement in Ethiopia and planned accordingly. In his foreword to Badoglio's 1937 account of the war as it was presented to the English-speaking world, Mussolini explained that "the categorical imperative of the African war, as of all wars, was this: the war must be won; but, in the Ethiopian war, to this imperative circumstances added another, no less categorical imperative: the war must be won, *and quickly*."[9] More directly—at least according to General De Bono's official account in his 1938 memoir *Anno XIII*—Mussolini impressed on his first commander that "I am willing to commit a sin of excess, but never a sin of deficiency."[10] Consequently, by the end of October 1935, Mussolini had committed twenty-five divisions of the Italian and Fascist militaries (as opposed to the three De Bono had originally requested), tens of thousands of civilian laborers, and 2 million tons of matériel so that there could be no question of the war's outcome.[11] Italy's some 500,000 soldiers would ultimately clash with Ethiopia's estimated 350,000 troops.[12] And yet Mussolini went even further, ordering Badoglio to use any means necessary to secure an Italian victory, including the use of poison gas, civilian bombing, and biological warfare.[13] Emperor Haile Selassie made numerous visits to the Geneva headquarters of the League of Nations throughout 1935 and 1936 to inform the international organization, and the world, of the Italian war crimes against his kingdom.[14] Among the offenses Selassie enumerated—and scholars have subsequently confirmed—were the widespread use of poison gas, the aerial bombing of Red Cross hospitals, the murder of religious leaders, and the imprisonment of hundreds of other spiritual and political representatives.[15] Such tactics did not end with Mussolini's May 9, 1936, declaration of Ethiopia's membership in the Italian Empire. Shortly thereafter Mussolini named General Graziani as viceroy of Italian East Africa (Ethiopia, Somalia, and Eritrea), where he would earn a local reputation for being indiscriminately brutal toward Italy's colonial subjects, particularly after the 1937 failed attempt on his life.[16]

Without delving too deeply into the details of Italy's flimsy facade of civilized rule in Africa, it is evident that both the objectives and reality of Italy's occupation of Ethiopia generated increasingly exclusionary concepts of italianità. Of course, enforcing a racial hierarchy within Italy's colonies had been a political objective since the Liberal era.[17] Nevertheless, the language regarding and treatment of "non-Italians" after 1936 were uncompromising in their hierarchical, discriminatory, and aggressive nature—in Africa and also at home. In addition to the violent ordering of the newly conquered Ethiopia, the Fascist administration worked quickly to establish a more expansive and rigid colonial legal system throughout Italian East Africa. Italy's management of the region had always depended on the maintenance of social categories overwhelmingly defined by family lineage and physical characteristics; however, in 1937 and 1938 these racial classifications helped define an exhaustive codex of segregationist policies.[18] The result of this legislation was, according to historian Giulia Berrera, one of the most comprehensive racial programs in any colony within Africa.[19] As in many other parts of colonial Africa—and parts of the United States—at the time, the state enforced racial zoning and anti-miscegenation laws, but it did so with extremely detailed laws and decrees, legally regulating almost every interracial interaction in Italian East Africa, much like the apartheid policies of South Africa in the second half of the twentieth century.[20] For example, Ethiopians were to salute all Italians upon threat of physical violence; restaurants and other establishments serving Italians were not allowed to hire Ethiopians; theaters were strictly segregated; and Ethiopians could never hire an Italian.[21] Finally, education was largely withheld from the African-born populations of Italian East Africa.[22]

Despite contemporary and subsequent justifications, this legal system was the result, Barrera argues, not of local experience and settler demands but rather of governmental decree from Rome.[23] Italian colonists, too, faced significant—primarily monetary—penalties if officials ever caught them damaging the integrity of the race; they were not allowed to work for or live with Ethiopians. At the same time, any Italian publicly caught committing a crime could not be punished, as that would undercut the superiority of the race. Historian Alberto Sbacchi has explained that "Italian emigrants to Ethiopia were to be educated to think of themselves as superior to, but not dominant over Ethiopian subjects. Ethiopians were not to be held in contempt, but there was to be a clear differentiation and separation between 'whites' and 'blacks.'"[24] Thus, the regime also launched a widespread campaign to educate colonists about the serious danger that interracial relations, and the children that resulted, presented to the health of the Italian race and the strength of the Fascist state. The famous contemporary anthropologist and explorer Lidio Cipriani confidently proclaimed that Africans were obviously not as developed as whites and that to treat them as equals was to run a grave risk for Europeans. And since women were the most important "depositories" of heredity in every culture, "under absolutely no circumstances should white women destroy the treasury of possibilities latent in her by favoring men of color."[25]

The central political and cultural position the Catholic Church held in Fascist Italy certainly meant that its doctrine worked its way into the rhetoric of Italian imperialism. As evidenced in Bertiglia's five postcards, the juxtaposing concepts of conquest and salvation both found voice in Fascist discussions of imperial war and colonization, underlining the regime's equally strong desires to be perceived as a powerful military state and as a superior racial and imperial power. Just as Fascist mouthpieces proclaimed the efforts toward a domestic Italian bonifica umana, such language was employed to suggest the potential for the redemption of Italy's colonial peoples and their underutilized lands. In fact, some educational texts described the takeover of Ethiopia as commensurate with the Fascist reclamation projects in southern Italy: "The Duce had ordered the army and the Black Shirts to carry the Tricolor into Abyssinia, where he wanted to colonize those abandoned lands as he had done with the uncultivated regions of Italy."[26] Such articles mirrored the language of *bonifica umana* and *bonifica integrale* (comprehensive [land] reclamation) that the regime used to characterize many of its domestic projects.[27] The belief in the improvement of Ethiopia and Ethiopians obviously did not preclude the existence of racism. Rather, it was predicated on the basic concept of a hierarchy among peoples that was first and foremost inherited—Ethiopia's autonomous political, religious, and economic practices were obviously viewed as inferior to those that Italians could impose. Therefore, regardless of any abstract idea that Italians could "improve" or "save" their colonial subjects, the primary concerns ultimately remained to destroy indigenous Ethiopian autonomy; to create a feudal relationship of racial domination; and, thereby, to teach Italians and Africans to respect the superiority of italianità over any other racial category.[28]

The fact that politics in Rome highly influenced the development of colonial policy is not meant to imply the lack racism between Italian settlers and the indigenous populations of their African colonies; nevertheless, such a complex social and cultural situation raises serious questions about the role supposedly local, practical considerations played in the decision to develop this comprehensive series of race laws.[29] That is, it appears unlikely that such laws were direct responses to popular demand. More to the point, it draws attention back to the function of domestic Italian policy and racial rhetoric in the Fascist imperial projects and bolsters the contention of this book that racism is a prerequisite of colonial imperialism. Accordingly, understanding concepts of race and racism at home is necessary to develop a full understanding of the intentions and consequences of such ideas abroad. Of course, intent is not synonymous with result, but Fascist ideology does elucidate much about the regime's aims and methods to achieve results. And the principles and lessons conveyed to the Italian population through elementary education delimited much of the ideological approach to reach Mussolini's goal of Italian national and racial supremacy within and outside his new empire.

Defining the Fascist Empire for Italy's Children

Since 1922 the state had made it clear that Fascist successes were impossible without the appropriate education and support of Italy's children; it, therefore, had been and would continue to be imperative for the education system to instill a deep sense of faith and obedience among its students: faith in the power of Fascism, faith in the unity of the fatherland, faith in the supremacy of the race. The multitude of educational initiatives and lessons employed between 1936 and 1938 played a critical role in developing the regime's vision of Italian identity as an imperial force.[30] In particular, the work of Giuseppe Bottai (1895–1959), who took over the position of minister of education from Cesare Maria De Vecchi di Val Cismon in November 1936, heralded this new, even more uncompromising and political period in Fascist education.

Like his ministerial predecessor, Giuseppe Bottai was a World War I veteran (indeed, an officer in the famed Arditi), a trained lawyer, and a central figure in the 1922 Fascist March on Rome. After Mussolini's rise to power, he became one of the Duce's most respected colleagues, and the trajectory of his career reflected this status. In 1923 he founded the periodical *Fascist Critique (Critica fascista)*, which remained an important party publication until 1943. He also held numerous government positions, including deputy secretary and then minister of corporations between 1926 and 1929. During this tenure within the Ministry of Corporations, he authored the foundational document of Fascist corporatism, the Labor Charter (Carta del lavoro). After Mussolini's declaration of the Italian Empire, Bottai also briefly served as the first governor of Ethiopia before he was recalled to the peninsula to serve as minister of education.[31] Bottai's Fascist career demonstrates not only his thorough involvement with the regime but also the ways in which Mussolini used a small number of trusted collaborators interchangeably within his state bureaucracy. Somewhat in contrast to his German counterpart, Mussolini often acted less concerned with his appointees' specific expertise than he was with their loyalty to him and the Fascist project.[32]

Bottai was the longest-serving head of the MEN, and his view of education and its importance to Fascism's mission paralleled the increasingly radicalized theories of Mussolini's administration. Bottai wanted "a political school, aware of its relationship to the state, which requests that school initiate children into politics" since, in Fascist Italy, "there cannot be anything but the politics of the empire."[33] In fact, the reality and obligations of the new empire were to imbue every aspect of the Italian's life, and he tasked schoolteachers with satisfying this directive.[34] This express call for the greater politicization of the school system built on basic principles of the larger and longer-term Fascist project; at the same time, the militarization, centralization, and racial aggression that marked youth education under Bottai's tenure were unprecedented. According to one 1936 article in the *Annals of Elementary Instruction* titled "The Mission of the Schoolteacher," teachers of elementary schools had to be trained to instill three essential aspects of Fascist life in their pupils: military preparedness, religious faith, and productivity on behalf of the nation.[35] As one might imagine, the sense of urgency to impart more specific lessons geared toward these priorities sidelined Gentile's pedagogical ideals of active and organic learning.[36]

Most of Bottai's radical changes to the Fascist school system would not occur until his 1939 rollout of the School Charter (Carta della scuola), but the new minister did much during his first two and a half years in the ministry to further Fascism's national and racial projects. As part of the unceasing educational campaign to make students believe in the Fascist mission, educators were required to emphasize the racial imperative of Fascist imperialism for the economic, political, and spiritual success of Fascism and the nation. The need for an "imperial sensibility" within Italy's student population (and, consequently, its adult connections) had the dual function of teaching children to believe in their racial superiority and to strengthen and spread Italian and Fascist influence abroad.

Reflecting the superficiality of the Fascist desire to "redeem" colonial populations, domestic educational texts highlighted the familiar political and economic demands for the expanded Italian Empire. Giugliemo Strata claimed in his 1935 textbook—*The Fascist Fatherland*, published before Fascist victory had even been declared—that the takeover of Ethiopia would be "nothing but a territorial reconquest: constant and effective action regained these [lands] for the fatherland and has increased our farmland to absorb our emigrants (at least in part), tying them to us as if the lands were genuine provinces of Italy."[37] Vincenzo Meletti echoed these arguments and urged his young readers to take their part in these critical projects when he wrote, "Children have the duty not only to visit the colonies, but to go there to live in order to set up industrial and agricultural enterprises that are not possible in the Fatherland and which can create riches for the courageous and daring."[38] Colonies presented the opportunity to increase Italy's economic resources and absorb the Italian population that had, until recently, frequently migrated to Europe, Australia, and the Americas to find jobs and land.[39] In this way, Italy's "greatest strength"— its biopower—would not disperse to other, rival countries but instead would enhance Italy's strength at home and overseas through contributions to the greater Italian Empire. This motivation had been a focal point in Italian colonial theory and policy since the late nineteenth century, and Mussolini argued that the supposedly fertile land procured through the Italo-Ethiopian War would offer the best opportunity yet extended to a race desperate for land and work.[40] It would also help spread Fascism abroad, bringing Mussolini's goal to develop a new world civilization closer than ever before.

Practical considerations played their role in the development of an "imperial consciousness" among Italy's students, but they certainly did not eclipse the spiritual (racial) value an expanded empire had for Mussolini's children. In an article for *Fascist Youth* (*Gioventù fascista*), Umberto Nani exclaimed, "Yes, the empire does have its material benefits, but above all else it has spiritual benefits; it is not just the integration of new territories; it is not simply a solution to our material, economic, concerns, but more importantly it is the solution to our spiritual problem. It is an affirmation of civilization; of the obligation of a greater opinion of life; of an expansion of our spiritual influence in the world."[41] Because of its importance to Fascism's racial campaign, references to the Italian Empire permeated all aspects of Italian life, including children's pastimes, such as comics and games.[42] One pedagogue explained, "A people that has faith in itself, its great tradition, and its history, a people that knows how to reorganize itself on the remains of a three-thousand-year-old civilization in the midst of formidable difficulties and immense sacrifices . . . a people like ours that has the precise feeling of obligation to fulfill a missionary role in the world, must create its own imperial pedagogy and, through military education, make our power and expansion more secure."[43] Regardless of whether or not Italians would redeem their African subjects, the priority was to ensure the Italian Empire's primacy in the world, first through obtaining the unwavering support of its population and then by using that support to confirm its great racial strength.

The rights and responsibilities of Italy's "civilizing mission," too, had to be taught to Italians as early as possible, so that the present glory could be perpetuated and expanded for and in future generations.[44] Students needed to have a *permanent* imperial consciousness, which revolved first and foremost around a clear understanding of the superiority of italianità. The newly established empire constituted the focus of Giuseppe Fanelli's 1937 exercise book, *Balilla: To the Sun!*, designed for children on summer vacation. A number of its stories discussed the power of Italians and the incompetence or ignorance of Ethiopians.[45] Indeed, Fanelli reminded his readers that it "only took Italy seven months to conquer its empire," fighting against superstitious Abyssinians who ate raw (often spoiled) meat like beasts; hence, after their grand success, the Italian troops proceeded to share their knowledge with their conquered subjects by building hospitals, schools, and roads: "We want to bring civilization and well-being to those peoples made miserable by misfortune, ignorance, and the evil government of the Negus [Haile Selassie]."[46] Another prominent Fascist pedagogue, Nazareno Padellaro, explained that "to know how to instill in children the fair valuation of other peoples means giving them the healthy pride in being a part of a favored razza. This God-given privilege does not need to be verbalized, since it must constitute the atmosphere in which the mind of the child exists. Before admiring others, we must teach students to admire ourselves in our strengths and in the value of our mission."[47] According to the regime, while the lessons in racial superiority of the 1920s had developed a solid foundation of Italian strength, only an empire that utilized a clear racial hierarchy would establish the racial unity that would prove Italy's dominance in the world.

The preparation for, execution of, and results from the Italo-Ethiopian War thus had a very real impact on aspects of the

domestic educational system and curriculum, which continued to hold a key position in the campaign to define italianità and its racial power. In the fall of 1935 and certainly by the
time of the declaration of the empire, the regime promoted
much more exclusive definitions of Italian identity; they became
conceptualized ever more concretely as categories of "Italians"
and "non-Italians" with new, tangible examples of an other, a
process that Edward Said famously explored in his ground-
breaking work *Orientalism*.[48] In one of Mussolini's many victory speeches in May 1936, the Duce declared that Ethiopia "is
Italian by fact, because our victorious army occupies it. It is
Italian by right, because with the sword of Rome it is civilization that triumphs over barbarians, justice that triumphs over
cruelty, the release from miseries that triumphs over millena-
rian slavery."[49] The speech continued, declaring that the "Italian Empire was founded by men who, in form and character,
are truly Roman. And behind these men march proud Italian
and colored legions, perfectly lined up, profoundly faithful,
prepared to follow all of Rome's commands."[50] Once again,
this language suggested a resurrection of the classical Roman
army, employing a multitude of faithful citizens and colonial
troops, working for the re-Romanization of the world; on the
other side of the battlefield were hordes of barbarians, unworthy of the valuable resources they possessed. A "Roman" victory
over such opponents constituted the greatest image of Italian
supremacy in Fascist eyes.

At the same time, the language of Fascist educational texts
before and during this period—and even in the speech quoted
above—attests that the substance of the Fascist vision of italianità had not altered dramatically. The move from defining
Italian identity to include its population's many variations to
outlining the contours of italianità by excluding unwelcome
intruders maintained the ultimate goal of forming a sense of
national community and racial cohesion. There still remained
an emphasis on the need for each individual Italian to undergo
a "spiritual evolution"; every Italian needed to develop his or
her own internal discipline in order to fully personify italianità and best serve the nation and race.[51] School and govern-

mental administrators still stressed the now long-held belief in the historical and spiritual inheritance of italianità, which could best be illustrated by studying the national past. As evidence of the need for a broad understanding of this shared heritage—and particularly its rich imperial past—the regime organized an exhibition on romanità in 1938 for school children and adults alike on the occasion of the two thousandth anniversary of Emperor Augustus's birth. The retrospective focused on ancient Roman society, highlighting the cultural, martial, political—even totalitarian, according to historian Joshua Arthurs—accomplishments of the imperial power.[52] Such an educational showcase, like the 1932 Exhibition of the Fascist Revolution, acted as a public classroom, identifying some of the most valued bonds among Fascists.[53]

Of particular interest here was the substantial attention the exhibit gave to the legacy of ancient Roman education, youth organizations, and family values. More specifically, it emphasized the role of the family in the education of Roman children. Before the institution of formal schools, one reporter explained, "fathers taught their sons to have absolute respect for laws, the gods, honesty, temperance, humanity toward the conquered, and strength in the face of dangers and bad influences more through example than through words," just as Mussolini was doing with the children of Italy.[54] Organizers presented a similar narrative about the education young Roman girls received from their mothers in the critical "spirit of maternal dedication," which was certainly no less important than the education boys received.[55]

Additional displays described Roman youth organizations and compared them explicitly to those established under Mussolini. These groups were designed "to impart lessons in physical and moral education to their members in such a way as to prepare them for the military. It is this type of organization that the Regime has resumed with such vigor and success."[56] Ultimately, the reporter for the *Annals of Elementary Instruction* reminded his readers, "these were the principles that formed the glory and grandeur of the stirpe and, thanks to God, enliven the ranks of our young men in arms today."[57] Visitors were unmistakably meant to find comfort in the supposedly apparent connections and similarities between ancient Roman and contemporary Fascist societies.

The achievements of ancient Rome obviously remained a critical focus of elementary and popular history lessons, but Italy's modern history also continued to play a significant role in illustrating the characteristics of italianità.[58] In addition to relaying events of the Risorgimento, large segments of the textbooks were devoted to biographical anecdotes about the peninsula's most famous personalities, to "nourish in children the all-consuming nostalgia of greatness, the longing for virtue, and the appetite for glory" that would inspire students to make their own contributions to Italy's grandeur.[59] For the most part, these biographies did not deviate from those that had been honored in earlier texts; however, after the Italo-Ethiopian War, other important historical figures and Fascist players made their appearance, such as Italo Balbo and the sons of Mussolini (Vittorio and Bruno) who were decorated pilots for the Italian Air Force during the 1935–36 campaign. At the same time, few references were ever made to specific female role models, with the exception of occasional anecdotes about Queen Elena. Again, these short histories were to give students models to emulate as they were asked to protect and represent the empire in the years ahead.[60] The complete lack of female role models indicates the true focus of these lessons.

Ultimately, then, the regime's unceasing efforts to centralize and politicize its educational system worked in tandem with the campaign to ensure a widespread "imperial consciousness" among Italy's children. The primary message such a collaborative project expressed was that the expanded Italian Empire proved the exceptionality of the Italian race. Those who belonged to the Italian race were members of a privileged collective. They were also members of an *exclusive* collective—not everyone shared the characteristics necessary to fulfill the obligations of the Italian mission. And it was critical that the members of such an honored race maintain its strength through the exclusion of any potential weaknesses or threats. In other words, educational materials from this period embraced more-explicit lessons in the glory of the Italian race and the great value of one's *inclusion* in the collective. This shared privilege was presented in clear comparison to and as a result of the exclusion of Italy's internal and external enemies.

Defining the Future of the Fascist Empire

Concurrent with the growing trend of defining Italians by excluding an increasing number of non-Italians, the Fascist regime spent more resources strengthening the health of imperial Italy's future leaders during this period. Certainly the themes that had saturated the demographic campaign throughout the Fascist era remained intact—the power of numbers and the expansion of public health resources continued to drive the initiatives of the ONMI and Fascist youth organizations.[61] At the same time, an intensified effort to refine the concepts of racial health and italianità was based more heavily on supposedly objective and scientific standards.

Many long-time Fascist collaborators continued to use vague terminology to define the race, as educationalist Alessandro Marcucci did when he explained that it was the beauty of "the great Latin blood" that characterized the Italian stirpe; at the same time, new state-sponsored scholars began to raise their voices, calling for more "scientific" and "quantitative" approaches to the state's racial campaign.[62] This was the beginning of Lidio Cipriani's ascent into the regime's circle of most trusted racial scientists. In response to his proposal to conduct a national census of people of "color" living within Italian borders, the director of Fascism's Central Office for Demographics admitted that "the motivation for such a proposal is to fix the mixing of different races, which anthropologists have shown indicates a decline of the stirpe, as it has been observed in other nations that have elevated people of color to the same social level as whites."[63] Such commentary indicated a growing attention toward more-rigid concepts of Italian and non-Italian groups within the national borders. Moreover, it revealed that "anthropological," or physical, characteristics—supposed indicators of moral and intellectual capabilities—were of primary importance to these narrower definitions. Certainly Nicola Pende had long been calling for increased emphasis on the physical construct of the Italian race, but King Vittorio Emanuele III's May 1938 order for the construction of an "Institute for the Bonifica Umana and Orthogenesis of the Race" further indicated the official embrace of more-biological definitions of italianità.[64] Nevertheless, unlike its German neighbor, the Italian regime still did not consider employing negative eugenics (abortion, forced sterilization, or euthanasia) on undesirable members of the Italian race.[65] Furthermore, little, if any, of this conversation was evident in the lessons of Italy's elementary education.

The pronatalist movement remained an essential component of the regime's campaign for bonifica umana—despite and because of its contracting definition of italianità.[66] After 1937, marriage and children were made a requirement of anyone applying for a government position.[67] Auxiliary organizations continued to focus their attention on the Fascist education of mothers and their children, but they also developed more rigorous programs to help train and care for them on a much more pragmatic level. They expanded the numbers of traveling and rural clinics, lactation stations, summer camps, climate colonies, and nursery schools and also increased the distribution of medications and availability of exhibitions on preventive health measures. The most significant example of this latter initiative was the 1937 National Exhibition on Summer Colonies and Child Health launched in Rome's Circus Maximus, part of which was to remain a permanent fixture for children and health clinics during the summers.[68]

Likewise, the regime continued to place great importance on the Day of Mother and Child. Journals and pamphlets honoring the day continued to use the influence of historical examples to prove the critical importance of the family and familial inheritance in the larger biopolitical and spiritual goals of the state. The author of a booklet in honor of the occasion, titled *On the Threshold of Life*, explained, "Napoleon Bonaparte said the education of a child begins one hundred years before his birth. . . . To leave one's children an inheritance of health, sobriety, simplicity, healthy and pure habits, as well as love for the ideal saints of religion, family, country, and work; to succeed in instilling in the soul of one's descendants an instinctive disgust and an invincible antipathy for all that is depraved, sought after, refined, affected in the habits of body and spirit; this is what parents should intend to see not only in their children, but also in their grandchildren and great-grandchildren."[69]

Keeping such obligations in mind, the Day of the Mother and Child gave Mussolini and his regime the opportunity, as another author explained, to celebrate "bountiful motherhood, integrated [state] assistance, and the triumph of the razza's potential, a drive which required the efforts of the entire nation to increase its numbers." In this particular article, the author emphasized the fact that Mussolini had done much to save the "white" race: "The scrutiny the Duce directed toward the world was something engraved with harsh lucidity in the souls of all those who are aware of belonging to a white 'razza' as much as a white 'civilization.'"[70] Coming on the heels of Mussolini's victory in Ethiopia, this article bolsters the argument that more supporters of the regime had begun infusing their concepts of italianità with the simplistic language of physical difference; that is, they relied more on a duality of difference: black and white, Italian and non-Italian, us and them. Just as notable, however, was the argument that the new Roman Empire would only be successful if the Italian race could fulfill the responsibilities such an undertaking required, and healthy Fascist families were the building blocks of this mission.

To defend the family, therefore, was to defend the development of the race and guarantee the future of the Italian Empire; as a result, texts geared toward schoolchildren were intent on expressing the importance of the family and eventually creating their own.[71] Vincenzo Meletti explained to his readers, "You have heard many times, Balilla, that Fascism favors the formation of new families in all ways; it prefers and awards the most numerous, advises men to wed, makes those who do not wed pay taxes, gives marriage and birth awards and transportation discounts for newlyweds who go to Rome on their honeymoon—even those coming from abroad. This way our population has been able constantly to increase in number."[72] The family was responsible for the initial education of the spirit and the development of a sense of responsibility to the state. It was also the first line of defense against poor habits and anti-Fascist beliefs.

Still, the regime was looking for more-quantitative methods with which it could look after the racial health of the population in a more centralized capacity, and in the mid-1930s some Fascist administrators proposed the creation of a biotypological dossier (*cartella biotipologica*). According to one account, this document would consist of a card color-coded to identify the specific Fascist Party organization to which the cardholder belonged. More interesting to the evolution of Fascist eugenics was the fact that each of the four sides of the card would contain a piece of medical, physical, or intellectual information about the cardholder. Two sides of the card would show the family situation of the student and his or her health history, as well as ethnographic details, such as the color of skin, eyes, and hair and the form of the nose, eyes, and hair. The third side would share the student's level of physical development with any teacher or doctor who requested to see the document. The card would reserve the last side for the results of an anthropometric exam that was to be updated every semester between the ages of six and thirteen. In essence, this exam simply measured the height, weight, and body mass index of the student.[73] To Fascist officials, however, its results, and the card in general, would represent "a precious and brave contribution to social medicine, that is the branch of medicine that studies the individual as a building block of society; it carries a very important contribution to preventive medicine and represents a precious field for the sociologist, the educator, and the legislator, whose efforts must converge in one goal, that is the reclamation of the razza."[74] Thus, the physical and mental characteristics of the race would, for the first time, be simplified to fit on four sides of an identification card.

There is no evidence that this proposal was ever acted on, but in 1936 the administration did create "the personal booklet of the citizen-soldier" (*libretto personale del cittadino-soldato*) that every Italian male over the age of eleven was to carry for the entirety of his military career. Like the biotypological dossier, the personal booklet included all essential information about the individual's party associations, physical and mental health, and general activities, to be available upon anyone's request. To lose the booklet was punishable by fine and possible censure.[75] With this booklet, the regime merged its long-standing concerns for the physical and mental health of the race with an increasing emphasis on quantifying the qualities that made each individual racially fit.

Obviously, then, the physical health that consistent exercise, discipline, and hygiene could bring was essential to the health of Italy's future leaders. In 1936 the PNF published *The Citizen-Soldier*, a book that emphasized the importance of physical and moral preparation of the youth that the term *citizen-soldier* encapsulated.[76] This manual reminded its readers of their twin obligations as Fascist citizens and soldiers that had first been explicitly declared in 1934. It also verbalized the parallel purpose of the youth organizations as an essential component of the campaign to protect the stirpe in "its survival, essence, and health." More generally, the guide's author continued, the "demographic campaign is at the forefront of this project, it is the first priority of this movement."[77]

According to the regime, the effective implementation of physical and military education in the 1920s and 1930s had been crucial to the successful resurrection of the Roman Empire. A month before the declaration of the Italian Empire, in April 1936 the regime celebrated the tenth anniversary of the founding of the ONB. In a speech made from his balcony at the Palazzo Venezia to hundreds of ONB members below, the Duce cried, "All Italians participate in your joy and celebration, while the world admires you because it sees an expression of the perennial youth of Rome in your discipline, tenacity, and courage."[78] The African campaigns had served to prove the efficacy of the programs, encouraging an intensification of their efforts, preparing for the continued successes of the race. In celebration of this anniversary and the success in Ethiopia, one article stated, "There is another conquest, which is more beautiful, more important: the new face of the Italian youth, proud and brave, strong in body and in soul, already tested in the heroic climate of the African undertaking . . . who learned in the ranks of the Opera Balilla to sleep in a tent and to use a rifle."[79] In short, as another author wrote succinctly, "it is from [the children's] hands that must come the new history of Italy."[80] The older generations were not creative enough; the young generations had the passion and spiritual richness that were required of the revolution. Still, the regime needed to make sure all these attributes were appropriately directed. As another guide to young Fascists instructed, "Wear the Black Shirt that the Duce gave you with joy and dignity: it reminds you of the bloody torment of expectation, the tremendous endeavors of the present, and the greatness of the future."[81] With such a mindset, Mussolini's children could claim the future as their own.

Physical and political education for both boys and girls lay at the center of the Fascist youth organizations.[82] The administrators regarded physical education "as a higher priority . . . not just as mechanical exercise for its own sake, but as a joyful and free strengthening of individual energies to serve the collective national discipline"; and they clarified, as was most important to the government at this point, "through physical exercises one forms a Fascist character, and gymnastics is naturally a part of military preparation."[83] The purpose of these organizations was increasingly pragmatic, training their members to face with dignity and honor the challenges of belonging to an imperial power.[84] Carmela Toscano explained, "The man who is not used to overcoming difficulties would quickly flee when perhaps real danger decides the destiny of the fatherland."[85] Such behavior was not acceptable for the race of citizen-soldiers Mussolini so depended on to uphold the glory of the Italian Empire and race.

While girls would not be directly exposed to the military education that was required of Italy's boys, Meletti emphasized the physical duties required of Italy's young girls in his text *The Fascist Book for the Piccola Italiana*. The primary argument of the book was that Italy needed young women—the mothers of tomorrow—if it were to prove its greatness to the world; they were needed to care for the nation's present soldiers and pass on the great Italian civilization to the soldiers of the future.[86] Since Fascism's earliest years, the guiding purpose of girls' education was to prepare them to be perfect wives and mothers; at this stage in the ventennio, this aim was even more directed. As a telling sign, at the beginning of the 1937–38 school year, one of the primary educational journals in Fascist Italy, *The Rights of the School*, established a special section each week titled "Women's Pages," which included articles on women's fashion, obligations, and moral ideals, highlighting the model characteristics of the New Italian woman. The successful development of Fascist wives and mothers was just as important as the successful training of an Italian army.

As even further evidence of the extreme importance the regime placed on the physical health of Italy's youth—both boys and girls—the first of the more significant changes that Minister Bottai enacted in the early years of his tenure was the reorganization of the Fascist youth associations. The first day of year XVI of the Fascist Era (October 29, 1937) marked the birth of the regime's newest organization, the Fascist Italian Youth (Gioventù italiana del littorio, or GIL), with which all the youth divisions were placed under the direct control of the PNF, instead of having the youngest sections under the direction of the semiautonomous ONB and the older groups under the leadership of the Fascist Party.[87] Such a move was plainly meant to further centralize and standardize the Fascist youth movement. An article in the illustrated monthly magazine for Mussolini's newspaper, *The People of Italy*, explained that the new organization meant that "the children of every age now form a homogenous union of powerful forces and of command, and will be more greatly fueled by the living spirit of the Revolution."[88] Furthermore, the GIL, under the guidance of the former party secretary Achille Starace (and for the first time in more than ten years, not Renato Ricci), called for the mandatory membership of all Italian children between the ages of six and twenty-one.[89] These more demanding membership regulations required the creation of another youth division for six- to eight-year-olds called the Children of the She-Wolf (Figli della lupa), a name that once again evoked the Rome of its mythical founders Romulus and Remus. With the motto of the new

overarching institution—Believe, Obey, Fight—the principles
of the more centralized Fascist youth movement were solidified
and expanded to include a greater portion of the population
while simultaneously excluding those who were definitively
marked as non-Italians.

The 1937 transfer of the administration of all youth organizations to the PNF did not indicate a change in the groups'
goals, however; the GIL served the same purposes as the ONB
and maintained the names of its preexisting divisions. One pedagogue explained the centrality of the GIL to the Fascist project
when he wrote, "Alongside the school, which has been completely renewed in method, aim, and structure, the great organization of the National Fascist Party is the Gioventù italiana
del littorio, which in all its various sectors is not just a gymnasium for physical education, but above all is an arena for the
moral preparation of children; the beginning, in a civil and
human sense, of a full life for the new generations, of a life of
work for their families and their fatherland."[90]

At the same time, texts highlighted the heightened regimentation of the GIL and its contribution to strengthening the
Italian race as it was conceived of in more exclusive terms. Of
increasing importance to the Fascist characterization of the Italian was the perception of uniformity among all Italians. After
years of encouraging pride in the great variety of regional and
individual differences in the population, books and illustrations now increasingly emphasized the great homogenizing
effect of a uniform. In Gherardo Ugolini's 1936 story, *I am a
Balilla!*, written to inspire Italian children abroad to join Fascist youth organizations in their adopted countries, the hero
of the book dons the uniform of the ONB. An Italian living in
Argentina, the child expresses his great amazement at the lev-
eling effects of the Balilla uniform, claiming that all the members "seemed equal." More specifically, "when they have other
clothes, the students seem to be from all different backgrounds,
as if they are not all from the same razza and their diverse conditions made them strangers to one another." The uniform, on
the other hand, had the result of displaying the unifying features of what might otherwise be considered unique individ-

uals: "Once in their divisions, it could no longer be said that the pupils were grouped into those who were poor and those who were rich. They were Balilla, they were all equal; to see them, to me they seemed even better than before."[91] Such was the ideal sentiment from belonging to the standardized ranks of the Fascist youth movement: Italians shared a single identity, a unified purpose, a superior strength. Such characteristics were to demonstrate clearly Italy's position as one of the great nations and races of the world.

Such a vision of the ranks of Fascism's future leaders communicated the perceived success of the intense period of Fascistization in the early 1930s and the apparent triumph of the education system's efforts to instill a Fascist, imperial consciousness in the minds of its wards. The four years between 1934 and 1938 initiated the much more public pursuit of Mussolini's international goals for his race of New Italians, and the period's latter half clearly focused on defining the imperial future of the Fascist nation and Italian race. The rhetoric and mindset that took the Fascist military into Ethiopia and prepared the population for the responsibilities such a privilege entailed mirrored the pedagogical policies and institutions that had educated the nation for at least the previous twelve years. They also created the foundation on which Mussolini and his hired scientists could construct the most exclusive definition of Italian national and racial identity and the most aggressive phase of Fascist racism in the coming months.

Four

Ensuring the Empire's Immortality, 1938–40

Enforcing the Racial Ideal

Benito Mussolini's 1936 declaration of a new Italian Empire marked the achievement of a significant long-term goal for the regime, but the Duce certainly did not see it as the endgame for Fascist Italy. Rather, it signaled the beginning of a new era in Italian history.[1] The successful conquest of Haile Selassie's Ethiopia supposedly verified the rejuvenation of the Italian race Mussolini and his regime had worked to inspire for the previous fourteen years; it solidified the return of Roman dominance that had once defined the Western world. The project then became—in the years between when Vittorio Emanuele III received his new title as emperor and Italy entered World War II—to develop a race of New Italians who identified as entitled imperialists just as much as conscientious nationalists.[2]

As the preceding chapters have shown, the regime steadily developed increasingly totalitarian policies and restrictive racial rhetoric in order to further delineate the contours of a healthy Italian race. The period from 1938 to 1940 was no different in this regard; indeed, it faced some of the most dramatic legal and bureaucratic shifts in the Fascist racial campaign to identify and improve the race in the swiftest and most effective ways possible. Italy's imperial campaign in Ethiopia had come out of a longer and more ambitious racial project, but it also triggered an acceleration of the state's exclusionary dictates for the Italian race. The codification of racial segregation in Italian East Africa (AOI) shortly after Mussolini's May 1936 victory speech had largely resulted from preexisting understandings of race and colonial rule and especially from the perceived inability of Italians to honor their racial superiority outside the peninsula. Similar frustrations with the lack of sufficient progress in Italians' racial strength and awareness—despite the proclaimed successes in Ethiopia—were likewise articulated in the most radical and restrictive racial policies yet seen within the borders of Italy.[3]

Of perhaps greatest significance in this latest stage of the Fascist racial campaign was the July 14, 1938, article in the *Giornale d'Italia* titled "Italian Fascism and the Problems of the Razza," which announced, "Human razze exist." Allegedly written by a group of racial scientists and laying to rest a long-standing debate among Italian politicians and academics, the article explained, "The existence of human razze is not an abstraction of our spirit, but rather it corresponds to a reality that is unique, material, and perceptible with our senses."[4] This was the first of ten points enumerated in the document, later dubbed the Manifesto of Race, that many, perhaps even most, scholars and observers have declared the cornerstone of Fascism's official domestic racial policies.[5] Of course, the document's insistence on prejudice against so-called inferior races within Italian borders was not especially novel in pragmatic terms, since the regime had consciously discriminated against Slavic and German speakers, as well as other "non-Italians" since the 1920s. Instead, the component that appeared to be the most dramatic theoretical departure from previous Fascist doctrine was its identification of physical biology as the most important factor in the Fascist definition of race, thereby providing a "scientific" justification for future racial laws. Further, what writers have widely cited as the most jarring aspect of the manifesto was its clear articulation that Italians belonged to the Aryan race and that any Jews who lived in the empire were not members of that race.

Combined, these decrees and the ensuing racial regulations legally transformed the experience of Italian Fascism throughout Italy and its colonies; despite the new "scientific" thrust of the language, however, its theoretical substance ultimately did not prove to be a remarkable departure from the foundational concepts of race—and particularly the Italian race—that Fascist officials had articulated for at least the previous sixteen years and that would remain intact for the remainder of Mussolini's time in power. Certainly, a new and significant wave of discrimination, violence, and suffering throughout the empire resulted from the racial policies of the late 1930s. The supposedly scientific underpinning of this latest stage in Fascist racism affected the lives of millions of non-Italians and Italians through new economic and political restrictions and more aggressive eugenic measures. At the same time, the Fascist education system—and many of the state's other institutions—had worked from the earliest days of Mussolini's rule to instill concrete conceptions of Italian racial identity and to form New Italians who could assert Italy's racial prowess in perpetuity. The successful integration of this latest and most aggressive layer of criteria into Italian identity directly depended on popular familiarity with Fascism's racial principles as educators had, in theory, explained to young Italians throughout the ventennio. And while the school system, too, underwent noteworthy bureaucratic changes in this period—particularly in response to Giuseppe Bottai's 1939 School Charter—the regime still promoted the central role of the inherited Italian spirit as the core of the Italian race.[6]

Mirroring this steady accretion of racial theory and legal discrimination, Fascist officials found themselves simultaneously arguing for the consistency of Fascist racial doctrine and the novelty of the 1938 and 1939 racial policies. Writers insisted that the "Fascist demographic policy, in reality, though not separate from its secular roots in the Roman and Italian tradition, is nevertheless something completely new, original, revolutionary."[7] In short, rather than completely transforming the substance of Fascist racism, the ideas of the Manifesto of Race and their legal consequences pronounced the latest layer of specificity within a body of principles that had been in constant evolution since the establishment of the Fascist state in 1922.

Expanding on the Manifesto of Race

Without a doubt, the official declaration that race was a biological category and that Italians belonged to the Aryan race was a substantial departure from previous Fascist rhetoric and established the foundation for a new direction in Fascist racial law.[8] Of course, modern theories of race had depended on some conception of biological inheritance at least since the Enlightenment. For the first time under Fascist rule, however, the Manifesto of Race formally declared physical characteristics as the *most* important component that composed the category of race.[9] Even in light of the obvious intensification of Fascist racial policies in the decade leading up to the publication of the manifesto, the social, economic, and political consequences of this new language were striking. In October 1938 Mussolini and the Fascist Grand Council released its own Statement on Race, which officially declared "the urgent reality of the racial problems and the necessity of a racial conscience following the conquest of the empire." For sixteen years, the document reminded readers, the state had pursued the quantitative and qualitative improvement of the Italian race, and all that work had the potential to be compromised if the regime did not address the threats of miscegenation and other "debasements" currently present in the empire.[10]

Consequently, the regime established new legal codes in August, September, and October 1938; Italians were no longer allowed to marry anyone from the Hamitic, Semitic, or other non-Aryan races. Furthermore, marriages between Italians, as well as between Italians and foreign Aryans, could be prohibited at the behest of the Ministry of the Interior if they were deemed detrimental to the health of the race.[11] Prior to a civil marriage, all men and women needed to prove their "racial purity"; in this way, the racial scientist Guido Landra believed, "the race is radically defended from all causes of biological, political, and spiritual degeneration that results from miscegenation."[12] The celebrated Fascist educator Paolo Orano further explained that the Fascist state had always "been in the vanguard of nations in the decisive will to redeem the race and rid it of degenerative habits and pernicious doctrines."[13] Not just anyone could marry—only those Italians who could protect and strengthen the race as a whole could gain that right. In their broadest sense, these were racial laws that, like Fascism's previous racial policies, pitted Italians against so-called non-Italians.[14]

As part of this more expansive project to ensure the full Fascistization of the Italian race, the state also passed a number of cultural laws in 1938 and 1939 that further prescribed the behavior and appearance of the New Italian. Primary among these new laws was the announcement that all Italian troops and youth organizations were required to march using the *passo romano*. According to Mussolini, this "Roman" version of the goose step had the dual purpose of creating an even greater, more uniform national military culture while also recalling, once again, the proud history of ancient Rome.[15] Additionally, Mussolini announced the replacement of the pronoun *voi* for the formal mode of address *Lei* in referring to the second person singular. While a seemingly subtle change, the attempt to reformulate the basic terms with which Italians communicated—creating a classless style of speech—connoted yet another way in which the Duce hoped to create the New Italian and the new Italian Empire.[16] It was clear that even after sixteen years in power, the Fascist regime still had grave concerns about the success of its campaign for bonifica umana; combined with the new marriage laws, these practices were meant to accelerate the process.[17]

In spite of these more universal racial policies, many contemporaries and subsequent scholars have identified the racial legislation of this period as first and foremost anti-Semitic, largely in response to the numerous measures that specifically affected Italy's domestic and foreign Jewish populations. The Grand Council's Statement on Race argued that the immigration of foreign (Jewish) elements, particularly since 1933, had impaired the Italian Jewish opinion of and relationship with the regime; and because state policies needed to reflect the urgent necessity for national unity, any Jewish influence on the Italian race needed to be neutralized.[18] Thus, all foreign Jews who had settled in Italy after 1922 were obligated to leave or transfer to one of a number of internment camps, many of which were already well established.[19] Jewish nationals were no longer allowed membership in the PNF, entry into the military, responsibility in any munitions industries, or management of Aryan domestics.[20] There were certain exceptions to these requirements, particularly for Italian Jews (and their families) who had participated in the Fascist Revolution or any national war or who had joined the PNF before the March on Rome,

but the regime would withdraw these exemptions by the time
Italy entered the war in June 1940.[21]

Many scholars have contended that the Manifesto of Race
signaled the beginning of the domestic Fascist racial campaign
because of these substantial legal developments. And yet this
book has shown that racism was a crucial component of Fascist
ideology at least since 1922. Therefore, perhaps what is most useful to understanding the role these latest developments played
in Fascist doctrine is a look at the logic exposed in the Fascist
Grand Council's own Statement on Race. In this document, a
one-sentence paragraph stated, "The Jewish problem is nothing but a metropolitan aspect of a problem of a more general
character."[22] In other words, the anti-Semitic portions of these
new racial laws merely represented another facet of the regime's
larger and longer-term goal to refine and strengthen the Italian race. In fact, even as the first anniversary of the Manifesto
of Race passed in the summer of 1939, officials and the press
continued to emphasize the ultimate goal of the new racial
policies as primarily "to elevate our prestige as Aryans and as
Romans," not, it would seem, as anti-Semites.[23] Such rationale
is supported both by evidence from the previous sixteen years
of Fascist rule and the elaboration of racial policies and education over the following two.

Racial Theory in Response to the Manifesto of Race

In writing about the Manifesto of Race, the sitting secretary of
the PNF in 1938, Achille Starace, stated, "Even in this field, the
regime has followed its fundamental course: first action and
then doctrinal formulation, which should never be considered academic—that is, an end in and of itself—but as a decisive action as part of a greater political clarification."[24] Even
at this late date in the regime, the Fascist principle of "action
over words" remained in practice and quite useful to a state
that continued to feel its way through the creation of its ideal
Italy and Italian race. Certainly, the newest racial legislation
changed the political and economic lives of Italians and non-
Italians throughout the peninsula, islands, and colonies. Nevertheless, a closer look at how scholars and officials worked to

define the category of race in the years 1938 to 1940 indicates a much more semantic shift in, rather than significant theoretical reevaluation of, Fascist racism.

Despite the supposedly clear-cut definitions articulated in the manifesto, other scholarly articles and official documents of the period suggest there was still quite a bit of racial theory for Fascist scholars and officials to debate. Mussolini and representatives of his state had used the term *razza* throughout the Fascist period—and indeed some linguists even argued for the Italian roots of the very concept—but the new scientific thrust of the word appeared to require a more in-depth look at its meaning and the role it played in Fascist doctrine.[25] Giacomo Acerbo—the prominent Fascist economist, party official, and author of the 1923 law establishing the legal framework for the Fascist takeover of the Italian parliament—explored these questions in his 1940 treatise on the fundamentals of Fascist racism. In this ninety-five-page essay, Acerbo explained that there were actually four generic classifications of racial theory: popular (or pseudoscientific), historical, naturalistic, and spiritual. Still, he claimed, there was a common starting point for all these interpretations: all of them "assign somatic, linguistic, and cultural properties as characteristics of a particular group."[26] As a whole, then, Acerbo effectively echoed long-standing Fascist views of race by explaining that the components of a race were physical, historical, cultural, and spiritual all at once. Additionally, he argued, the Fascist application of all four classifications had the fundamental aim "to preserve the ideal and spiritual substance of our stirpe."[27] In essence, the particulars of the definition of race did not matter nearly as much as the intent behind its use.

Supporting this definition that argued for the equal importance of a race's physical, spiritual, cultural, and historical attributes, an article in *The Rights of the School* proclaimed, "Anthropologists agree with the designation of the term *razza* as a human group that has the same anatomical and physiological characteristics. . . . But anthropologists also agree that every razza has its own predetermined psychological and linguistic characteristics that, combined with the physical characteristics, distinguish human categories with greater precision."[28] Physical traits were the most obvious racial designators, but they were certainly not the only ones.

Nicola Pende, founder of the eugenic pseudoscience of constitutionalism and a prominent supporter of Nazi racism, also agreed with this analysis of race and, in the remarkably turgid prose of one 1938 article, used it to discuss the specific example of Fascist policy. According to Pende, the Fascist state had always allowed for many ethnicities (racial subdivisions) within the Italian nation, but it wanted to impose on its people an understanding of the "Italic" race as a *spiritual type with a biological foundation.* Explaining this need further, Pende echoed long-familiar racial rhetoric: "The biological Italic type, which has many original racial elements, in the course of its history, is physically and psychologically nothing less than the *progeny of Rome*, because it is mother Rome that for millennia knew how to assimilate and amalgamate peoples of European races that were morphologically and psychologically different, in order to form a *romano-italico type*, that persists from the time of Roman Italy, and that has an ethnic profile in a biological sense, which cannot be confused with other national types, even in the great sphere of Latin families."[29]

Despite the new veneer of biological determinism on the Fascist definition of race and the new classification of the Italian race as Aryan, the familiar language of Italy's historic and spiritual inherence maintained its presence in much of the Fascist racial literature.[30] Fundamental to all these definitions was the clear goal of distinguishing one racial category from others. Carlo Pino, in his January 1939 article in the party journal *Hierarchy* (*Gerarchia*), explained that the regime's racial policies were "inspired by discrimination, which is a derivative of racial pride; however, this pride can only draw power from the objective appraisal of other races."[31]

Proponents of the Fascist demographic and pronatalist campaigns continued to write most emphatically about the less visible—spiritual, historical, and moral—constituents of razza. One author for the onmi periodical *Motherhood and Childhood* asserted, "I have said that civilization and history have made the idea of razza possible. Let me explain: razza is a reflection of a specific people ... in order to recover its ideal unity, it does not matter whether it is based upon blood or spirit."[32] Another author explained that, in Fascist doctrine, race "is not a simple anthropological or biological concept, but it is all of our humanity, material and spirit, that is realized in the family." To expand on this idea, he continued to explain that the "racial and demographic policies in Italy are two aspects, or perhaps the same aspect, of one reality, since all of the adopted measures for an increase in population were accompanied by measures for the defense of the razza."[33] Ultimately, then, these spokesmen for the regime's demographic campaign reasserted the essential collaboration of spiritual and physical strength in the rejuvenation of the Italian race.

As part of this larger discussion of the definition of razza, writers in the last years of the 1930s frequently made a clear distinction between the concepts of race and nation, despite their close connections; moreover, they overwhelmingly emphasized the priority of protecting the race over the nation. As one party article explained, "A people is not truly a people if it does not have a sense of nation. At the same time, a nation cannot emerge in the world if it does not have a sense of razza." The article clarified further, "The most basic nationalism exists in a pride for one's blood."[34] More to the point, the editor of *In Defense of the Race* (*La difesa della razza*) and one of the most vocal racists of this period, Telesio Interlandi, simply declared, "The concept of razza supersedes that of nation."[35] These declarations of the explicit and unquestionable supremacy of race over nation were new to Fascist rhetoric, though, by and large, the individual meanings of the terms still appeared to overlap substantially.

The theories and definitions of individual officials and scientists give us a sense of the intellectual debate surrounding this newest phase of Fascist racism, but they ultimately remain only pieces in the larger picture of Fascist rhetoric and policy.[36] Educational texts of the period 1938 to 1940, on the other hand, provide important, and in many ways more accurate, insight into the fundamental messages the government wanted the population to absorb about race and nation. These textbooks, teaching manuals, and pedagogical journals further highlight the gulf between the legal ramifications of the manifesto and the relatively consistent elementary education in the principles of Fascist racial doctrine.

Still in 1940, when the PNF published the second and final volume of its guide to political education for students in elementary school and middle school, which was aptly named *The Fascist's Second Book* (*Il secondo libro del Fascista*), the matter of finite racial categories was still not settled. While the first volume of this Fascist catechism, published in 1937, had focused its lessons primarily on the Fascist Revolution, Party, and state, the second volume laid additional emphasis on educating its audience about the specifics of contemporary Fascist racial theory and policy. The author explained, "The existing physical and spiritual differences between the principal razze, the secondary razze, and the various stirpi of a single razza are dependent upon a considerable number of factors, not all of which have yet been identified."[37] Of course, the admitted complexity of the subject in no way negated or even lessened the importance of the "evident inferiority of certain races" and the need to protect the Italian race from such contaminants.[38] This lesson, printed in a book meant to convey the official party creed, well illustrates the fact that the question of terminology, particularly the definition razza, continued to occupy the time and energy of numerous officials and educators.

The author of *The Fascist's Second Book* later outlined the nature of Italy's racial constitution to the nation's youth using a familiar story: "In the expansion of the Roman Empire, and after its collapse, other peoples still belonging to the white razza and predominantly of Nordic origin came to Italy, entering the orbit of Roman civilization and the racial unity of the nation."[39] The text then injected this long-established historical narrative with the new equation of Italians with Aryans when it explained that the "Mediterranean basin was and still is the sphere of the greatest splendors of this continuity of the Aryan primacy, with Greece, Rome, the Renaissance, and Fascism."[40] Notwithstanding this new racial classification, the account maintained the familiar argument that select (ancient) foreign races did not contaminate italianità but rather were absorbed into its essence, enriching and strengthening it. Just as striking was the suggestion of similarity between the legacies—historical, cultural, and racial—of ancient Greece, ancient Rome, and Fascism. The strength of Fascism and its New Italians was not confined to the borders of the Italian Kingdom or the current reign of the regime. It was an identity that was far more expansive in its presence and power.

Another text geared toward illuminating the fundamentals of Fascism to the party's youngest members added to this discussion by actually merging the concepts of razza and nation. This 1939 booklet created for the Turin section of the GIL posed the question, "What is the Italian nation?" In response, the text explained, "It is the entirety of all Italians who, belonging to the same razza, recognize themselves as united by the same traditions and aspirations; that they worship God in the same language, that they want to obey the same state authority."[41] While this abbreviated definition of the Italian nation did not explain the term *razza*, it very clearly relied on the principle that a nation's population was defined by inherited characteristics—an idea that did not differ dramatically from lessons earlier in the 1930s.

Finally, in his 1940 book *La scuola del Balilla*, Giuseppe Giovanazzi argued for the great importance of prioritizing the Italian race—and nation—over Italy's many component regions once and for all. He remarked that while children were children everywhere, in Italy they also had to become Italian. Such an Italian child could be described as "he who plays and enjoys himself, sings and draws, recites and dances, reads and writes and counts; but always, whether he marches in line through the streets of the fatherland or works in the serenity of the classroom, he feels and thinks, and gradually he strengthens in his feelings and thoughts the idea of being Italian, a conscious part and participant of a great community, whose glorious history confirms the faith and guarantees the right to a greater future." Giovanazzi concluded, "Why should a regional spirit be emphasized in the child when it clearly has forfeited its place to the national spirit?"[42] In fact, the reasons for eliminating region-specific lessons in elementary textbooks were so obvious to the author that it was *"unnecessary to speak of them."*[43] Italian collective identity now more than ever needed to focus on racial and national characteristics; and in the words of Giovanazzi, "Italy, for our child, means Fascism: that which Fascism has made and continues to make valuable; that which it makes and prepares, in our souls as much as our labors, in order continually to render the future Italy more glorious."[44] This rationale for a more focused model of italianità reflected the theory of this latest phase of Fascist racism, but it also appeared to sound the death knell for Gentile's principle of organic learning, which had been increasingly under attack over the course of the 1930s. Mussolini's sustained anxiety about the lack of unity within the Italian race, while not upsetting the bedrock of Fascist racial pedagogy, would urge the reevaluation of the state's elementary education system just as it would the nation's racial legislation.

Bottai's School Charter: Reorganizing the Educational System

The elementary school system was consistently a vital instrument of the Fascist racial campaign; in these last two years before Italy's entanglement with the Second World War, its mission appeared to take on increasing urgency. The regime viewed the earliest stages of one's education as the time when, as the children's author Nazareno Padellaro wrote, students recognized their responsibilities to the state and the "ideal of collaboration for the grandeur of the fatherland." The students were "rigorously pure" in a racial sense, as they generally had not yet encountered the corrupting forces of foreign races, political enemies, or vices. Therefore, they could and needed to learn about their place in building up the power of the nation. Padellaro persisted, "Oriented toward this principle, the Italian school does not ask much more of the students than to prepare themselves and learn, except to live the life of the fatherland in every gesture, in every emotion."[45] In particular, many pedagogues viewed a child's earliest years in school as the most important for his or her education, as they constructed the cultural and social framework for the future citizens of Italy. More to the point, Minister of Education Giuseppe Bottai explained in a memo to school officials, "In the earliest stages of school, with the means to form the minds of children, one will be able to create an appropriate climate in which to form an early, embryonic racial consciousness, while in middle school the more elevated mental development of the adolescents—already in contact with the humanistic tradition regarding the study of classical languages, history, and literature—will allow for the fundamentals of racial doctrine to establish their hold."[46] The enduring goal of creating generations trained to think in terms of Fascist racial ideals—physical and moral strength, obedience, courage, virility, and discipline—had acquired a renewed sense of importance in elementary education.

In the years 1938 to 1940, Bottai and the MEN contributed to the regime's racial campaign with two related projects that reevaluated the education system's own policies and infrastructure. First came new rules in 1938 to discriminate more aggressively against so-called non-Italians, and second was Bottai's second major piece of Fascist legislation, the School Charter (Carta della scuola), which adjusted the educational demands on Italians to develop more successfully into faithful and productive New Italians.

In some ways, the simpler task in front of Bottai was establishing education policies in line with the new racial, and especially the new anti-Semitic, legislation. Mere weeks after the publication of the Manifesto of Race, Bottai wrote a memo refusing all future requests for travel abroad to individuals who wanted to represent the nation in any way—such as attending a conference or program of study—and who did not belong to the most updated definition of the Italian race.[47] Then, in early September, he signed off on a number of decrees regarding the "defense of the race" in the public schools. Jews were no longer allowed to attend public or semipublic schools, and the government ordered the establishment of separate, exclusively Jewish elementary schools.[48] Textbooks authored by non-Italians were no longer allowed in circulation within Italian schools.[49] Jewish teachers, too, were required to relinquish their positions immediately, as were Jewish academics, though at this point Jewish university students were allowed to continue their studies if they were already registered in a program.[50] Such policies were, in theory, to rid the school system of the most obvious examples of non-Italians.

The second piece of this two-pronged educational attack on the remaining weaknesses within the Italian race was a bit more complicated, and Bottai would not publicize his comprehensive approach to the problem—his School Charter—until 1939. However, the underlying aim of this more encompassing project—and of the Fascist racial campaign more generally—was no surprise: to instill in all Fascist students the ideals of the New Italian and the demands of the New Italy. In a circular written for educators and school officials at the end of 1938, Bottai reminded his personnel, "The Fascist school is the place in which the youth of the new spirit of the peninsula is born and called to unite . . . in order ever more profoundly to understand the reasons for living as men and citizens." Therefore, he continued, it was the obligation of all who supported the school system to teach their wards the "Fascist style"—that is, manliness (without apparent regard for femininity), severity, strength, and dignity—so that these young Italians could prepare to lead the Italy of tomorrow.[51]

When Bottai did unveil his charter—what would be the most significant overhaul of the Fascist education system since the 1923 Gentile Reform and of which he was quite proud—the legislation intensified the MEN's Fascistization efforts in two ways: first, by further centralizing school administration and, second, by further politicizing the lessons to which students were exposed at school.[52] As Bottai wrote to Mussolini on February 4, 1939, "For a reform *in* the system, of this or that gadget, a law can suffice; for a reform *of* the system, one needs a clarification of principles, each one of which is an introduction to an array of laws."[53] The legislation aimed to ensure a totalitarian educational system, bureaucratically as well as pedagogically; the MEN required the schools, GIL, and community at large to work together to mold the New Italians, who would one day lead the nation and race. The MEN billed the School Charter as a complete redesign of the education system, creating a structure of public institutions that would more effectively train New Italians of the New Italy.

Conceptually, the charter paralleled the organization of Bottai's 1927 Labor Charter (Carta del lavoro) in its twenty-nine chapters that reorganized the Fascist school system, and the majority of the charter addressed infrastructural modifications to the education system.[54] In many ways, this document merely codified changes to the educational infrastructure that had been taking place over the previous decade against great protest from educational idealists such as Gentile. Nevertheless, taken as a whole, the changes that the charter demanded were significant enough to warrant their implementation over two years. The regime would devote the first year to renovating completely the nation's nursery, elementary, vocational, and artisan schools.

For the first time, preschool was required for all children between the ages of four and six, and the new elementary school curriculum consisted of only three grades, generally for students between the ages of six and nine. The spiritual education, on which Gentile had focused so intently in the 1920s, still played a critical role in the elementary phase of an Italian's education, but the reforms Bottai and his charter laid out very much responded to the increased sense that most Italians' obligations to the state required them primarily to develop practical skills in order to make tangible contributions to the empire. Therefore, after the third grade, students were expected to attend a vocational school (*scuola del lavoro*) for two years—where they received early training in the professions they were encouraged to pursue—in addition to continuing their studies in core academic subjects. After this program, students who passed placement exams could continue on to classical middle schools.

Those students who did not plan to go on to a classical middle school were to train at a craft school (*scuola artigiana*) instead of the more basic vocational school, and it was the aim of the MEN that a much larger proportion of Italian students take this path to be truly productive members of the empire. One observer of these changes remarked that elementary education "prepares to discharge its responsibility as a totalitarian school, drawing upon its energies in the indestructible desire to bring the entire Italian population to a level of civil maturity that corresponds to the projects it carries out today and, even more importantly, tomorrow."[55] At these craft schools, students would learn the essential skills needed to join the nation's workforce, usually as factory workers, farmers, or day laborers, as soon as they met their educational requirements.[56] According to Bottai's published diary, when he and Mussolini discussed the charter, Mussolini commented, "If I understand this correctly, and I believe I do, you want even little gentlemen to learn how to get their hands dirty. I like it!"[57] This rhetoric diverged from the organic education that Gentile prescribed for elementary education in the early 1920s, but it continued an objective of the 1923 Gentile Reform for the upper schools to professionalize the youth at an earlier age, reducing the number of students in higher education and expanding the national workforce more quickly.

The School Charter also devoted a section to the subject of girls' education, both despite and in response to the emphasis on "manliness" in Fascist education. It plainly stated that "the social goal and mission of the woman, distinct in Fascist life," required separate institutions.[58] The pedagogue Antonino Pagliaro helped articulate this position when he explained that the role of Fascist education for girls needed to reflect women's position in Fascist society at large and to reject "the absurd presupposition of equality with that of the man." Above all, Pagliaro summed up, the charter's prescriptions for gendered education honored the position that the woman was the guardian of the "spiritual assets" essential to the continuity and strength of the Italian race.[59] Just as interesting, the charter explained that the three-year educational program designed specifically to prepare girls for their role as homemakers and teachers (if they were to enter a profession) began only after the completion of elementary and vocational school. Whether because of racial or practical considerations, Fascist educators continued to believe in the value of young Italian girls learning basic academic subjects, a fact that is often, and understandably, overlooked in light of Fascism's overwhelmingly misogynistic outlook.

While the charter addressed the issue of gendered education, it perhaps surprisingly avoided the subject of rural education, even though educational texts and mass propaganda continued to encourage a national ruralization movement. At least part of this omission must be attributed to the fact that this important aspect of national education received separate orders for reorganization in late 1938. On October 14, 1938, the government passed legislation further delineating the goals of the rural school system and signaling the state's relentless desire for more control over the rural population. As the MEN report explained, "Rural schools must serve the rural population, and this is a conquest that imposes specific organizational forms and programmatic differences from the general school system. This is not to say that the rural population is inferior to other citizens. It does, however, comprise a category of workers that has a right to a school of its own, with an academic system appropriate for its professional goals."[60] Subsequently, the government announced that each rural school was to have no fewer than twenty and no more than 250 students at a given time, limiting the teacher-student ratio and expanding the rural school system. In turn, the MEN established 169 rural directorates, each one overseeing forty-five to fifty schools.[61] Furthermore, at the end of the 1938–39 school year, Minister Bottai informed all rural teachers that a series of courses on Fascist culture would be instituted especially for their edification and, through them, the edification of their students.[62]

Such modifications to its structure continued to centralize and politicize the education system for a portion of the population that had always been less accessible to the regime and its demands. Fascism, one journalist wrote, "as the restorer of the strength and dignity of the nation, as the undaunted glorifier of the bright sources of the grandeur of the stirpe," had focused great attention on the land and "the robust farmers, who are the fertile custodians of the purity of the razza."[63] According to the Fascist state, the rural population remained the greatest carrier of italianità; and while the authenticity of its italianità needed to be protected, it also needed to be molded enough to embody all Fascist ideals. This demand necessitated an educational infrastructure only possible with the products of modernization. One author clarified the resolution of this conflict as resting in the moral education of the people: "It is not enough simply to live on the land, as a peasant, to retain unaltered characteristics of the razza.... Whoever renounces the city ... must be supported by that moral well-being that can only give a true sympathy, not occasional, not partisan, not academic, but constant, sincere, and productive, as part of the people who live in contact with the most evolved form of life."[64] It was not enough to live in the countryside, the regime contended; the rural population needed to be trained in the morals that would enable them to absorb and appreciate the benefits of their rural life.

Finally—though also not specifically mentioned in the legislation of Bottai's School Charter—the nation's summer and climate colonies continued to play an essential auxiliary role in the school system and the national public health campaign. Now almost entirely under the auspices of the GIL, these camps had expanded considerably since they were first established; one journalist reported that in 1938 their numbers had risen to five thousand, servicing approximately eight hundred thousand children in that year alone. And there were more plans to expand, particularly into the new colonial territories of East Africa and Albania.[65] As always, these camps were meant to expose children—and especially urban children—to the health benefits of the outdoors but also to reinforce the lessons of the classroom in discipline, hygiene, history, and pride that had "such great effect on the spiritual formation of their campers."[66]

All these bureaucratic changes—or expansions—to the education system were meant to service the second, larger goal of the School Charter and, as the previous chapter illustrated, Bottai's mission as minister of national education: to politicize the education system as part of Mussolini's totalitarian project for the Italian race. While such an objective had been discussed since the rise of the regime, the charter made it official that education was no longer a process individuals undertook; students had to embrace it as a small piece of the Fascist collective.[67] The pedagogue Giovanni Giovanazzi argued that the old school system had lacked passion; in response, the charter inspired "the moral, political, and economic unity of the nation" through state education.[68] As such, the charter's first proclamation stated, "In the moral, political, and economic unity of the Italian nation ... the school—the first foundation of solidarity among all social forces . . .—forms the human and political awareness of the new generations." Such a directive, the statement reminded its readers, was inspired by "the eternal virtues of the Italian razza and its civilization."[69]

The charter's second section followed this affirmation of the school system's national significance with the introduction of what it determined was the regime's new notion of "scholastic obligation." Meeting one's academic commitments had become just as important as fulfilling one's military service—in fact, honoring the first would be excellent preparation for the second. Moreover, the larger purpose of such a scholastic obligation, according to Bottai, was to have each student "integrate and follow his education on a political and an athletic-military plane."[70] The school system and the GIL, in the words of the charter, "formed a united instrument of education."[71] Bottai and the MEN viewed these combined efforts as central to "the formation of the political and military man of Fascism."[72] This partnership was much more obvious after the 1937 decree mandating that all children belong to a Fascist youth organization. Physical education was labeled a critical element of the academic schedule and was given parity with all other subjects.[73] Giovanazzi further explained that, jointly, schools and the GIL responded to all the needs of the young spirit: "passion, aspirations for improvement, love of risk, need for personal initiative, courage in voluntary discipline, the body always dominated by the spirit . . . religious and Fascist faith, concrete sense of humanity."[74] These were the characteristics that were to be emphasized in the future leaders of the Fascist empire.

Beyond these two expansive state organizations, the School Charter also emphasized that the effective education of Italy's youth depended on the participation of each student's family and the community at large. The seventh chapter of the new legislation pointedly reminded Italians of the essential role the Italian family played in educating and strengthening the nation and race. It bears noting that such stress on the importance of the family inadvertently brought attention to Fascist fears about its relative lack of control over this realm of the young Italian's life.[75] This was not a new concept in Fascist political and educational philosophy, either in theory or in practice. Still, the reiteration of the state's expectation that all social institutions, including the family, were responsible for furthering Fascist educational goals confirmed the totalitarian aim of the Fascist state at large.

In part as a response to such continued concerns regarding the extent of state control over private life, the ERR continued to be influential in both the centralization and politicization projects of this latest phase of Fascist racism. Its mission was to ensure a broad reception of key political and cultural propaganda and to bypass the subjective filters of individual families and teachers. What is perhaps most interesting about the scholastic broadcasts during this period is that the Commission for Elementary School Radio Programs decided not to "dedicate any individual program to racial propaganda." The official statement, printed in the introduction to the radio transcripts for the 1938–39 academic year, did, however, encourage teachers to "draw conclusions from the programs that praise our heroes and the activities of the regime, in order to heighten the students' pride in their race that is the foundation of our great future."[76]

In addition to the weekly programs of the ERR, the state's umbrella broadcast corporation, the Italian Organization for Radio Programming (EIAR), also produced a number of radio programs for Italian children that addressed both their mental and physical education.[77] Officials from the EIAR wrote in their annual report for 1938–39 (year XVII of the regime) that "the advantages of these radio programs are evident and undeniable in terms of national education, mass unification, and disciplined uniformity in political and social life."[78] To educate Italy's children in such a manner, radio stations began each day with stretching exercises at 7:45. At lunchtime they summarized the news, and at 4:40 p.m. they broadcast a show known as *Comrades of the Balilla and Piccole Italiane*. The contents of this latter show varied each day, but all episodes were to have the listeners' "intellectual and cultural life as motivation." The secondary, though no less important, role of the program was to "practically establish relationships, contacts, and exchanges between children of various provinces and regions, contributing to that reciprocal awareness from which friendship is born."[79] In addition to programming for classrooms of all ages, GIL outings, and parents, the ERR and EIAR also teamed up to develop special transmissions to and from the various summer and climate colonies throughout the peninsula and islands to remind everyone of their great importance in the Fascist racial project.[80] Hence, though the regime did not harness the educational power of radio technology until the 1930s, it worked diligently in those years to make up for lost time.[81] The expansion of national radio broadcasts—and the radios that aired them—coincided very purposefully with the attempts to reduce attention to Italian regionalism and, more generally, with the Fascist necessity of reaching and influencing as many Italians as possible.

Thus, 1938 and 1939 witnessed a sizeable number of legal and institutional transformations within the Fascist state to adhere to more-restrictive ideations of the Italian race and racial fitness that followed the publication of the Manifesto of Race. Yet a closer look at the discussions surrounding the evolving definitions of race in this period shows little substantive change in Italian racial theory. Even Giuseppe Bottai's 1939 School Charter, which represented the latest call for a totalitarian and politicized education system that trained students to embody ideal New Italians and to exclude designated non-Italians, while making a number of infrastructural changes, largely reflected pedagogical reforms that had been in development throughout the 1930s. The modified and expanded education system demanded the active participation of a variety of bureaucratic tools; pedagogical methods; and politically trained personnel within the MEN, its auxiliary institutions, and families throughout the empire. It also called for a revitalized curriculum to enforce the legal and theoretical principles enumerated in the Manifesto of Race and subsequent racial legislation. The curriculum that resulted in the 1938–39 and 1939–40 academic years, however, was composed of lessons remarkably similar to those developed well before the infamous July 14 publication.

8

Enduring Principles of Italian Racial Identity

Antonio began his fourth-grade journal with an account of his first day of school on October 17, 1938. The young student from the small village of Soleto, just fifteen miles outside of Lecce in Apulia, first described the school administration's inaugural address, at which "all the Balilla and Piccole Italiane were gathered in the building and Miss D'Astore gave a speech about 'race and autarky.'" Miss D'Astore began with a reminder that it was very important for all students to "contribute to the battle for autarky" by collecting and donating unneeded objects, from which the nation's workers could make many important materials. She explained, "currently in Italy many people are studying how to produce the materials that we used to import from abroad. We must learn to make them ourselves, so that we do not need anyone." Miss D'Astore then moved on to discuss the nation's "racial problem," first by reminding her audience of all the wonderful heroes the Italian race had produced, such as Guglielmo Marconi, Francesco D'Assisi, Gabriele D'Annunzio, and Christopher Columbus. She followed this list with the pronouncement that "we must begin already as children to make ourselves worthy of our race, distinguishing ourselves through our conduct, hard work, and education." After this short homily, Antonio wrote, all the children applauded, moved to the church to "receive benediction from the Holy Spirit," placed a wreath on the local memorial to fallen soldiers, and finally cried out, "To us!," before retiring to their respective classrooms.[1]

This short account of a small town's celebrations for the coming school year depicts a fair amount about the regime's educational and political interests in this late prewar period. Most plainly, according to Antonio's description, there was a continued sense of urgency to prove Italy's power, manifested in both economic self-sufficiency and racial strength. The vigilant participation of children and their families at school and at home was paramount to the success of each project. As it had been for the entirety of the Fascist regime, the primary thrust of the elementary curriculum was to articulate and implement the Fascist ideation of the New Italian: a faithful, healthy, strong, humble, hardworking individual who lived not for his own benefit, but for the glory of the Italian nation and race. It bears noting, however, that Antonio did not report any mention of a "Jewish problem" or other racial threat in Miss D'Astore's initial commentary on race. What appeared to be a more important part of the teacher's opening message were the calls for collective proactivity and the ceremonial undertakings after her speech; the integration of Catholic faith, public remembrance, and collective celebration were deemed essential parts of the effective development of New Italians.

The lessons articulated in the elementary school textbooks between 1938 and 1940 overwhelmingly supported these essential themes of the Fascist educational mission, even in the great shadow of the Manifesto of Race. In spite of multiple publications and many minor edits throughout the decade, the fundamental lessons of the 1931–32 textbooks remained. The historian Mario Isnenghi has argued that by 1938 the Ministry of National Education decided many of the original lessons from the early 1930s had been well implanted in the minds of students, and the establishment of the racial laws and the School Charter urged the release of a "second generation" of Fascist state elementary textbooks.[2] Certainly Bottai's legislation reaffirmed the state's role in overseeing the production of all elementary schoolbooks, particularly in light of the increased demands on the school system. All textbooks had to be purged of Jewish authorship, and texts needed to assert the benefits of racial discrimination.[3] Even in light of Insenghi's argument and some textual changes, however, almost all the themes in the texts of this second generation remained consistent with those of the first. Ultimately, elementary lessons between 1938 and 1940 echoed language and imagery from throughout the 1920s and 1930s; the concepts of discipline, physical and spiritual health, and national consciousness that had consistently been components of the Fascist campaign for bonifica umana were now quite familiar to students and teachers alike. Nevertheless, observers can still see the influence of the Manifesto of Race in the calls for heightened vigilance among Mussolini's children to strengthen their bodies and minds and defend against growing numbers of enemies.

The Historical Primacy of the Italian Race

History continued to play a central role in the elementary school curriculum, especially the focus on the historical brilliance of the race, the successes of the regime, the civilizing mission of Italians, and the overarching racial unity of the nation. When texts approached world history, they did so in terms of its racial makeup and especially the impact Italy—principally ancient Rome—had on the various races of the world. An increase in this type of material is where we see the greatest influence of the new racial legislation on elementary lessons. The regime considered it imperative that texts and teachers imparted the history of the major world races and especially of the so-called Aryan and Italic peoples, from whom modern Italians descended. Once these broad histories were understood, teachers could then discuss how inferior races, especially the Jewish race, had "infiltrated" and mixed with all other civilized peoples.[4] The creation of the new empire, too, increased Italy's contact with other races, and texts needed to explain how Italy had consequently developed policies to defend the integrity and purity of its stirpe from dangerous racial contaminations and "fragmentations" as well as from the supposedly well-known anti-Fascism of the Jews.[5]

Despite the presence of this more critical content, the bottom line of most world history lessons remained, in the words of Nazareno Padellaro, "as long as Rome lives, the world will live." This aphorism, he claimed, came from a time when "hordes of barbarians were sowing ruin and death" throughout the known world. Those, and any other, barbarians would always be vanquished as long as they kept "forgetting that Rome is sacred and invincible." When it mattered, Rome and its descendants would rise to the top. Padellaro ended the selection by reminding his students, "Why do we not celebrate the births of other cities, even larger and more populous cities? Because other cities are born and then die. Rome will always be reborn, just like the sun."[6] In short, even the lessons of these second-generation textbooks confronted the matters of race much in the same way those from the previous generation had. One student expressed her own internalization of such a lesson when she wrote in her school journal that she was proud to be a Piccola Italiana because she had pride in her nation, which had "already been glorious in Roman times and now wants to become the dominator of the world again."[7]

The second-generation textbook furthered this discussion of Italian racial superiority through the manufacture of a closely related lesson regarding what the regime characterized as the historical (and present) evils of foreign powers and the strength that united Italians against them. One ERR program featured a radio play about a small town outside Milan in the thirteenth century that had to fight against foreign occupiers. In a secret meeting to discuss the town's resistance, a representative from Milan appealed to the crowd, "Brothers! . . . Emperor Barbarossa now considers Italy his own; and only a devastating illness among his soldiers has held him back from besieging and destroying Rome! Every city that has had the courage to oppose him has been besieged, burned, and destroyed. . . . The cities that Barbarossa has not destroyed, he has stripped of every freedom and every valuable, while the soldiers mistreat the people." The barbarous acts of the Holy Roman Empire's forces had wreaked havoc in the peninsula, which, according to this piece, was a united entity in the minds of Italians, even at this early date. In response to his call, the townspeople cried, "Enough! Out with the foreigner!" The representative answered their zeal with the warning that "if the emperor still finds our cities divided and at war among themselves, he will win them easily." He continued, "If, instead, we all unite against him, we can fight him and drive him over the Alps for once and for all!"[8] The transparent message of Italy's strength in unity was a powerful one for its listeners, chiefly because of its stress on students' obligation to consider the collective over the individual. At the same time, the story also highlighted the dangers of foreign elements on the peninsula—in this case, interestingly enough, the Germanic Holy Roman Empire—and around the globe. For much of the 1930s, elementary education had expanded its emphasis on Italy's role in the world. The mounting tensions within Europe in the second half of the 1930s increased the regime's interest in educating the public about the threats foreigners—even supposed allies—presented.[9] Subsequently, the continued presence of such threats served to justify a variety of Fascist projects—such as the increasingly aggressive racial campaign—and their goals to protect Italy's national and racial communities.

Often the stories of individual heroes were used to further the concept that Italians, as individuals working on behalf of the race, needed to protect the nation against outside threats. Biographies of the royal family and popular Fascist leaders were most prominent in this respect. The story of Balilla, too, continued to occupy a central role in the Fascist narrative—the 1939 edition of the third-grade textbook even began the school year with a version of this foundational myth.[10] It was in their capacity as the protectors of the fatherland—most explicitly as soldiers—that these personalities were highlighted, offering role models for the future heroes of Italy. One pedagogical article reminded its readers, "The celebration of heroes should never contain a sense of satisfaction or sufficiency. It must nurture in children the inspirational nostalgia for grandeur."[11] As a clear illustration of this aim, the "Decalogue for the Militant Fascist"—somewhat of an abridged version of the Fascist catechism, printed in the front of one GIL manual—ordered its young readers always to remember those Italians who had died for the revolution and empire; all Italians needed always to be willing to sacrifice their own lives for the protection and glory of the nation and race.[12]

Perhaps unsurprisingly, then, the pedagogical importance of modern Italian history and the nation's longtime quest to unify all Italian territories was perhaps greater than ever before in this two-year period. Such lessons reminded students that Italy's recent history was the catalyst for the Fascist rebirth of the nation and race. Therefore, stories about the First World War were quite visible in these textbooks. They once again emphasized the honor of Italy's soldiers, but now they also highlighted the betrayal Italy had suffered at the hands of its one-time allies. One narrative of the Great War and its aftermath, entitled "The Enthusiasm of a New Life," related that "after three and a half years of sacrifices, Italy had triumphed. Trentino and Trieste were freed. Other very Italian lands had hoped to reconnect themselves to the fatherland. But how! At the moment of peace, the nations that had fought at our side, against the same enemies, gave themselves the lion's share of the territories." The piece further explained that it was only the Duce who was able to claim the territories that were rightfully Italian. Only he "knew how to instill in our people his energy, his desire to work for the grandeur of the fatherland."[13] Whereas lessons at the beginning of Mussolini's reign focused exclusively on the heroism of Italy's military—when the experience of World War I was so fresh—now texts could explore some of the deeply felt losses of the war; Mussolini would right the wrongs sustained at the hands of other, greedy nations.

In addition to the external threats Italy had faced in recent history, the Fascist regime proclaimed that the unified nation had also suffered domestic political neglect over the years. The ineffectual Liberal regime that ruled Italy from unification until the March on Rome had led to extreme economic, social, and military weaknesses within the country. One text argued that the incompetence of the Liberal government was responsible for the 1896 disaster at Adwa.[14] Another vignette, entitled "Shadows over the Fatherland," described the evils of Communism and Socialism in the period immediately after World War I. The authors described the nation as breaking apart as a result of "disorder and discord, strikes and revolts, misery and brutalization." Of course, the "socialists profited from the general disorder, mistrust, and exhaustion of the people to spread their venomous ideas. Men without God and without conscience, they worked to extinguish the joy of victory and the love of the fatherland in the hearts of all Italians."[15] With such chaos throughout the nation and little hope of the sitting government's ability to regain control, the piece concluded that Mussolini and the Fascist doctrine had been the only solution to the crises that engulfed the kingdom. As ten-year-old Elvira expressed in her school journal on the seventeenth anniversary of the March on Rome, "Today all of our gratitude and faith is dedicated to the Duce, who has returned Italy to primacy among the civilized nations of the world."[16] Such was the intended message of lessons on the aftermath of the war and Mussolini's great mission in Italy.

Between 1938 and 1940 the Italo-Ethiopian War served as a specific example of Mussolini's great efforts to "return Italy to primacy" in the world. The 1938 textbook for the third grade characterized the conquest of Ethiopia as a necessity; Italy had been "forced" to conduct the war in Africa until its "absolute victory," although the story did not elaborate on the specific causes. Instead, it simply related that the obstacles other nations placed in front of Italy had been inadequate and that Italian "faith, valor, and tenacity triumphs over all."[17] No powers, either European or African, would be able to defeat Italians when they worked together; utilized their greatest inherited gifts; and of course, trusted in the leadership of the Duce. Ten-year-old Elvira again shared in her journal the hoped-for response to the successful conquest of the new Italian Empire. On the fourth anniversary of its founding, she wrote, "our courageous soldiers know how to fight like heroes to bring civilization to these remote and uncivilized regions."[18]

The newly declared Italian Empire was the resurrection of an immortal reality, the 1939 third-grade literature textbook expressed in a vignette entitled "The Empire": "The imperial crown encircles the brow of the victorious King, descendent of the oldest and most illustrious stirpe of warriors, of the wisest dynasty of rulers." The piece continued with Mussolini's own words: "After fifteen centuries, the empire reemerges upon the fated hills of Rome. The Roman Empire has risen again? The strength of Rome has risen again. The integrity of Rome has risen again. Those who die and are resurrected are immortal. The empire has risen again because it is immortal." Italy's race of warriors—descendants of ancient Rome's magnificence—

had been responsible for the victory, but it was not enough simply to conquer those who were inferior to New Italians. As texts had stressed at least since 1934, racial superiority did not just bring military victories; Mussolini's words reminded third-grade readers that strength "will carry justice—that is love for those who deserve to be loved—where it has never before reached."[19] Mussolini's New Italians would continue to prove their inheritance of Rome's magnificence through military strength as well as by spreading their great civilization.

Emphasis on the duality of Fascist military might and racial superiority infiltrated all propaganda regarding the empire at the end of the 1930s. The authors of one third-grade text from 1939 addressed the subject of Italy's empire by voicing sympathy for Africans, while still adhering to fairly rigid racial stereotypes. The story featured a bird that flew over Ethiopia and described all that he saw to an Italian child. At one point, the child asked, "'And have you seen the Abyssinians? Is it true that they are ugly?' The bird replied, 'Ugly? Why so, child? They have clear and black skin, frizzy hair and red, swollen lips.... But they are tall and slender, strong and very fast. And, often, they have a light of pride in their eyes. Their children grow up fast. At one year they play among themselves and hit one another and make their mothers despair.'" The child responded to this last bit of information and exclaimed, "Then they are naughtier than we!" Further along in the same tale, the bird explained how much the land of Ethiopia had changed since it had become a colony. Italians had brought civilization to the area, improving both the land and the lives of the people.[20] Mirroring the lessons conveyed in this text, one elementary student articulated that his interest in visiting Addis Ababa lay in the fact that Ethiopians "were still barbarous and our soldiers conquered their lands not only for Italians to have fields to work, but also to civilize the people."[21] The idealization of Italian colonialism and the possibility of "civilizing" indigenous African populations continued to hold pride of place in the curriculum; and though many of the textbook lessons described the physical, infrastructural improvements Italians had made within the colonies, little to no mention was actually made of the promised moral "improvements" among the colonized populations.

Racial Purity through National Independence, Discipline, and Obedience

In the wake of the Italo-Ethiopian War, many textbook authors reminded students of the extreme importance autarky had in shedding Italian obligations to foreign powers, just as Miss D'Astore had in her address to the students on the first day of the 1938–39 school year. One book noted, "In seven months [Italy] conquered an Empire. The sanctions collapsed miserably. But the Duce still desired: he wanted to continue with the same passion to save, to work, to produce. Does it require sacrifice? Of course. But for the fatherland, any sacrifice is a source of joy and pride." And because of those national sacrifices, "Italy no longer needs to acquire essentials from other nations; it does not need to send its gold abroad. The Duce pronounced one word: autarky. And there is not a single person in Italy, not even a baby, who does not know the immense importance of this word."[22] National and racial superiority, in part, rested in shedding all types of foreign infiltration; introducing complete economic self-sufficiency would further strengthen the Fascist nation and the Italian race.

Such a mission unsurprisingly necessitated both the unity and obedience of the Italian population, each of which required years of preparation and training. And though some pedagogical texts still articulated the desire to have teachers and their students become independent in thought and action—remnants of Gentile's calls for active and organic teaching and learning—stress was overwhelmingly laid on uniform action and appearance.[23] The focus on discipline and conformity was intricately interwoven with lessons about the history and fundamentals of Fascism—all were assumed to garner a sense of personal discipline within the student body. The 1940 first-grade textbook was not subtle in its insinuation of Fascist imagery in its first pages, which were designed to help students learn to read: a *bandiera* (flag) represented the letter *b*, while the *fascio littorio* represented *f*. Most striking was the inclusion of a rifle on the page illustrating various children's toys.[24] Similarly, the passo romano and the Roman salute played important parts in training students in Fascist discipline. One selection articulated the great significance of the Roman salute as "a gesture of nobility," of soldiers, and of obedience. In an explicit equation of Fascism with italianità, the text concluded that the salute was "a Fascist gesture. Rapid, beautiful, strong. An Italian gesture."[25] Such practices ensured both discipline and submission to the hierarchy of the state while also suggesting the historic roots of such rituals.

Once discipline was established, the regime believed, the state could better demand uniformity of spirit and action among its students. In a piece written for second graders, the author metaphorically described the nation as having a "tricolor cloak": on November 11, King Vittorio Emanuele III's birthday, "in all of the cities, in all of the lands of Italy, thousands and thousands of flags display themselves, as if by magic, from the windows of homes and public buildings.... An airplane flies high above in the blue sky. From there, all of these flags seemed as one."[26] Individual Italians were only as important as their participation in the national collective—and that collective was to become one, in substance and in action.

To like ends, textbooks continued to underscore the value of uniforms, linking them to the general Fascist values of discipline, maturity, strength, and beauty. The text for first graders described the first outing of a young GIL *figlia di lupa* in her uniform on April 21—Rome's proclaimed birthday. As she passed, members of her community called out words of praise to her. Joining other young Fascists in their uniforms of the GIL, the author wrote of the girl's pride: "She was a young woman already, a soldier, in fact, as her mother had said. Her heart beat a little faster: it is wonderful to be an Italian soldier."[27] Though girls and women were never supposed to pick up the weapons of war, they were to guard the home front—fighting as a force against immorality and ill health—and instilling pride in appearance, discipline, and loyalty within all Italians was a building block to the formation of the new Italian race.

Of course, donning a uniform did not necessarily translate to perfect national or racial unity; the successful accomplishment of national uniformity depended heavily on the strict and continual adherence to the related Fascist values of obedience and obligation. The focus on personal discipline and the formation of a young, future-oriented ruling class were constant themes in the school texts and reflected the central tenets of Giuseppe Bottai's 1939 School Charter.

The first order of mandatory obedience for children remained the family, as the School Charter's request for familial involvement in education indicated. The first-grade textbook demanded of its readers, "If you need to help your mother, never say, 'later.'"[28] Again, family was not necessarily considered more important than the race or nation, but lessons extolling the significance of family acknowledged that family played a fundamental role in forming a child's personality. Family was the initial bond that united the race, as Carlo Curico emphasized in a 1938 article in *Motherhood and Childhood*: "Family is the transmission, from generation to generation, of emotions, of hereditary and moral materials, of accomplishment and character, of work and energy." And because the family unit was the building block of the nation, the fatherland could only be "as strong and young as the freshness of the elements that compose it. This is why childhood is a top priority of the state."[29] Instilling respect for one's family meant instilling the more general values of hierarchy and obedience that were so essential to the successful functioning of the Fascist state.

The second authority to which children and all Italians owed their deference was the church. In most cases, the MEN relegated religious lessons to specific religious texts and classes. Of course, there were always references to religious personalities who were central to Italian history, such as Saint Francis, or to religious holidays that dominated the national calendar, such as the Epiphany or Easter.[30] And while the sheer volume of these references declined in this period, the Catholic Church maintained an enduring cultural and political position in the empire that no Italian leader could ignore. Nazareno Padellaro's third-grade book began its text with a physical description of the classroom, and first among the objects that he described was the crucifix on the wall: "The divine arms spread out along the cross indicate the path of His love: from east to west," stretching to encompass all humanity. More important to the goals of the regime, however, the author later wrote to his readers, "You are the preferred ones because, if your heart is pure, it is more beautiful than the sky itself."[31] Italian children were proclaimed to be God's most favored children; and as long as they maintained pure hearts—presumably by meeting their religious and civic duties—they would maintain that privileged position.

The portraits of King Vittorio Emanuele III and Benito Mussolini on either side of the crucifix in every Italian classroom reflected the development of the Fascist state as an institution of civil religion and its position as the third authority to which children owed their obedience. The most relevant embodiment of the state authority for children was the school system. A 1940 textbook for first graders shared the story of one student's first day of school. He asked his mother, "What should I do to be especially good?" The mother replied simply, "Only one thing: obey."[32] Through the institution of the school, students were very clearly meant to recognize the Fascist state at large as the definitive authority. Coterelli Gaiba's first-grade textbook stated, "You are the future of the fatherland. The tricolor [flag] shines in the light of glory. Always advance! For Italy and for the king!"[33] Above all else, the texts stressed that Mussolini was always right, again implying the divine nature of the Duce and his reign. He was the father of all Italians, the savior of the empire; Italians served at his pleasure, and to question him meant to dishonor him.[34]

One story in a second-grade textbook further detailed some of the many ways in which students could respect the power of the state. It described a conversation among students about what they wanted to do when they grew up. One boy wanted to travel around the world, while another wished to fly airplanes. One girl wanted to become a physical education instructor, and another boy hoped to be viceroy of Ethiopia. The group praised all these goals. Each ambition represented a priority of the nation and required earnest intellectual and physical education: to be at the forefront of innovation, modernization, and political domination. Then the last girl spoke up, announcing that she wanted to become a mother: "I will put the house in order, I will attend to dinner, darn the linen, and, when I find a bit of time, I will read. Then I will have babies—many babies—and will dedicate all of my efforts to them so that they may grow beautiful, healthy, industrious, courageous, and worthy of our great fatherland."[35] This announcement received the most praise from the students and teacher. No other aspiration could be realized without maternal guidance. In this way, the students expressed their desires to serve the nation and race: boys imagined themselves as heroes and public officials, while the girls planned to become teachers and mothers to mold future generations of Italians. Above all else, he or she was to be a soldier, a fighter for success in his or her respective social role. The same second-grade textbook, in a vignette aptly titled "New Italy," described this Fascist ideal: "Every Italian is a soldier, and everyone works, in the noble name of the king and emperor, under the guidance of the Duce, to render [Italy] ever greater, more beautiful, more respected."[36]

The discussion of appropriate occupations for loyal New Italians also referred to the other critical factor in the regime's ongoing racial campaign—the successful protection of the race's physical and biological health through the promotion of both the quality and the quantity of Italians. And while textbooks continued to exalt the importance of physical education and motherhood, it was largely through the activities of the GIL and the ONMI that this aspect of Fascism's *bonifica umana* was advanced.

Promoting Both Quality and Quantity

Reclaiming the strength and numbers of the Italian race was not a simple task; as the regime's efforts over the previous sixteen years had shown, it required the active participation of numerous state institutions, particularly the ONMI and the GIL, in addition to the school system. Using language that was now quite familiar, one Fascist official noted that the "mind is not enough, the body, even if it is strong, does not stand alone; the harmony of all human elements is the true goal, and it is for that reason that the work of the youth organizations is integrative and parallels that of the school."[37] But while elementary lessons between 1938 and 1940 largely remained consistent with those from earlier years, the evolving demographic and public health campaigns of the period generally tackled their long-term projects with a more aggressive approach that clearly reflected the demands of the new racial legislation. After so many years of focus on the *quantitative* aspects of national population growth, Minister Bottai wrote in one article, Mussolini necessarily had to initiate more-intense demographic policies to address the *qualitative* aspects of the biopolitical problem.[38] It was not enough to read about the ideal Italian; children needed to embody the increasingly narrow model of italianità. And that would happen only through a multifaceted approach to lessons in physical education, hygiene, and public health.

Physical and health education could not be separated in the Fascist racial campaign. One 1938 guide to a course on Fascist culture described the two most significant ways in which the regime had consistently worked to protect and strengthen the Italian race:

> The razza, which serves to eternalize our stirpe, is protected from infancy to old age. ONMI has as its holy project to protect poor mothers, giving them and their newborns all possible assistance: medicine, food, clothing, money, often gathering them in refectories, asylums, etc. The GIL embraces all children between the ages of seven and twenty-one, integrating the work of the school system both physically and spiritually. At one time, children lived chaotically; now they have a center, they listen to a leader, they have a group; they know, in short, that they have obligations. They know they are the future soldiers of the fatherland and they know to embrace life with faith and responsibility.[39]

In the eyes of Fascist officials and educators, the project to defend and improve the Italian race had been a critical component of the ONMI and the GIL (or its predecessor, the ONB) since their establishment. Still, one sees the influence of the new phase of Fascist racism in the expanded demands for greater attention to the biological strength of young Italians. In the inaugural issue of *In Defense of the Race*, Lino Businco, one of the signers of the Manifesto of Race, declared that the physical health of Italian children was the most important component of the Fascist racial campaign: "They who grow up in the gymnasiums, in the fresh air of athletic competitions and the camps of the Party, have thereby been able to improve their bodies, making them ready for every activity; they can understand the necessity of defending the race, perpetuating this precious inheritance that is the biological substance of the Italian nation."[40] The underlying message of the article echoed calls for emphasis on physical health that had preceded the Fascist rise to power, but the source and the stress on biological objectives obviously cast long shadows of the new racial laws over the familiar idea.[41]

Per the mandate of the School Charter, even nursery schools were required to provide children with physical education. In the first years of schooling, manuals explained, children were to participate in "natural" exercises reflecting "habits and needs" that were ordinary to children everywhere, such as running, jumping, and skipping.[42] Harkening back to the relatively outmoded concept of organic learning, such an approach was meant to instill the basic habits of hygiene and health by building on recognizable and comfortable actions.

These natural exercises were also considered primarily imitative. They were natural actions to the young students, but they also inculcated the values and habits of discipline and obedience.[43] Obviously, such habits were essential to developing the minds of dutiful Fascists, but teaching manuals also warned readers to be careful about the nature of such imitative exercises and games. According to these texts, imitative activities had the potential, if they were not carried out appropriately, to turn children into Socialists rather than Fascists. A basic requirement of all games, then, was the inclusion of "nationalistic actions"; marching, for example, was suggested as an excellent exercise to teach children how to "place their feet."[44] With these exercises, the student "enlivens and strengthens the body." Between exercises, the author continued, it was equally important for teachers to remind their students of the purpose of such activities: "The word made alive from conviction impresses the essential principles upon the young minds and their still simple and pure souls."[45] In such a manner, individual activities designed for the mind and the body could be plainly connected to their shared goal.

Each school year's physical education curriculum, like all school curricula, was meant to build on previous years' work, increasing its rigor as well as its focus on agility and strength. By the third grade, marching, leading, and precision exercises were introduced into the curriculum. By the age of eleven, all Balilla had been given training rifles to use in their premilitary exercises. Such a gradual process was meant to put students at ease with behaviors that would become essential to their lives as healthy and disciplined Fascists. When they finished elementary education, young boys were well into their preliminary preparation for military service.

Physical education continued its role in the development of both boys and girls, despite the ever-increasing rigidity of gender roles in Fascist society. Just as for boys, girls received physical education in elementary school in order to "equip the body and spirit to guarantee the strengthening of their health, the harmonic and legitimate beauty of their development."[46] The ultimate goal of all women's organizations remained to create the "perfect female Fascist": wife and mother.[47] Consequently, physical exercises for girls needed to aid in developing strengths particular to motherhood. This take on girls' physical education persisted, according to one pedagogue, as a direct response to the apparent excesses of other, democratic nations that led to the degradation of their female populations. Italian women were banned from engaging in "all athletic excesses and any type of masculine pose characteristic of the American woman, and kept far from political activity in the British 'suffragist' sense, as well as from every frivolity and worldliness from the French origin." Instead, "the Italian woman is educated by the GIL, according to Italian traditions of femininity and gentleness, understanding that she is generally destined to be the queen of the domestic hearth, soul of the healthy Italian family, upon which the regime depends for the fortunes of the razza."[48]

The continued threat of the masculinization of the Italian female population required athletic trainers and teachers to vigilantly maintain the gender roles prescribed by the regime. The work of selecting suitable athletic trainers and teachers, therefore, was just as important as the job they were expected to fulfill. The requirements for acceptance into Orvieto's Fascist Academy of Physical and Youth Education for Women became more stringent in these last two years of the 1930s, reflecting these concerns as well as the increased focus on biological fitness. Students were required to "belong to the Aryan race as well as the PNF..., be no older than twenty-two, hold a junior high diploma," and possess physical and moral attributes necessary to uphold the "educational mission."[49] Interestingly enough, the administration in charge of the academy regarded many of these necessary moral and physical characteristics as being complementary aspects of virility; an appropriate physical education could only make these features of femininity more "harmonious and serene" in the students' bodies.[50] Once these characteristics were tempered and molded, these young women could adequately take charge of the training of Italy's youngest students.

In other words, young women were called on to do their part to protect the race just as young men were. This obligation included promoting the positive moral and physical strengths of italianità and also knowing how to keep from contaminating it.[51] Marriage and procreation were responsibilities of every Italian; as the last chapter explained, however, the new racial laws expanded marriage regulations to discriminate against all individuals who were potentially harmful to the race. Additionally, the state worked to make sure all those who were fit for marriage and procreation fulfilled their duties. These last years of the 1930s saw an increase in sanctions against those individuals who were unwilling to participate in the national project of marriage. Homosexuality, as a de facto rule, was not addressed in texts on public education and health.[52] More broadly, however, any Italians who chose to remain unmarried were viewed as dangerous to the future of Italian society. Just as Italian Jews lost their citizenship through the racial laws, Paolo Orano argued that the "celibate does not have a right to the honor of citizenship; he is inferior, lost, illegitimate. He has not given the evidence all must submit: that of being a husband and father, and for the woman, that of being a wife and mother." Ultimately, "there is nothing more just and sacrosanct than the exclusion of celibates from work, as if they were people of a foreign razza. The Fascist order is marriage and fertility."[53] Adults who did not actively participate in the national demographic campaign weakened the race.[54] Such a position echoed long-held beliefs of the Fascist regime, but the intensification of discriminatory laws in these last years proved advantageous for culling all undesirable elements from Italian society. Eugenicists would still not support negative measures such as abortion or sterilization; however, taxation, revocation of rights, and even internment of potential threats to the race were powerful translations of the regime's newest stance on the protection of the Italian race.[55]

Women and men were, therefore, not simply responsible for their own welfare; women in particular were responsible for the well-being of the race by pursuing the critical occupation of motherhood. As one writer for *Motherhood and Childhood* wrote, the Duce enacted measures for a racial campaign that "addressed the problem of defending the race above all in a positive, active, and organic way, creating institutes and laws particularly focused on favoring the fundamental and constitutional elements of the race: the mother and the child."[56] Further reflecting the increased focus on both the quantity and quality of New Italians, Nicola Pende explained there were two aspects of maternity—one spiritual and the other physiological—that were mutually dependent on one another and deserved equal respect and consideration by the state and its institutions.[57] For her part, Giuliana Sborgi wrote, "The Italian woman, from the peasant to the well-off, above all must cultivate the physical and moral health of her family and children." She admitted that "economic necessity, as well as modern cultural and social demands, can drive her also to work in the public sphere, but with the good sense and healthy instinct that is inherent to her, she must always maintain the balance between outside activities and her predominant function as a housewife."[58] Even amid economic necessity, the first priority of all Italian women was to protect the institution of motherhood. It was only with the diligent fulfillment of these duties that the ultimate mission of the Fascist state could be realized: to create and nurture the vanguard of the great Italian race.

In many ways, the great nationalist Paolo Orano summed up the entirety of the Fascist racial campaign—and the totalitarian project of the regime—when he wrote in 1938, "Land, motherhood and childhood, race. This is the trinomial of the defensive acts that, all at once, is an advocate for fertility, health, capacity for a greater and more prolific productivity of the superior power of the Italian stirpe and the Fascist state!"[59] The two-year period between July 1938 and June 1940 marked the apex of the state's struggle to clarify Italian racial identity. Discrimination and violence escalated in the following months and years as the nation became more entrenched in the war and less certain of its victory. The Manifesto of Race and the subsequent racial legislation devastated the Jewish and foreign populations of the Italian Empire, having established a pseudoscientific justification for a violent campaign that ultimately led to a very real national participation in the Holocaust. At the same time, historical, spiritual, and physical education remained key elements of the Italian racial campaign in this final phase as they did throughout the Fascist period. The increasingly aggressive racial policies of the Fascist regime, while creating an increasingly narrow definition of italianità, relied on a steady and persistent education in Fascist concepts of Italian identity that Mussolini established in his earliest days in power: by harnessing and improving their cultural, spiritual, and physical inheritance, Mussolini's children could control the future of the Italian race.

Conclusion

On the evening of June 10, 1940, Benito Mussolini emerged from his office in the Palazzo Venezia and announced Italy's march into World War II to the waiting audience below. Having declared war on Great Britain and France only hours earlier, Mussolini explained this decision as "a step in the logical development of our revolution." He continued, "It is a conflict between fertile, young peoples and sterile populations facing their decline."[1] Such an assertion echoed much of the rhetoric of the previous eighteen years; and as his son-in-law and minister of foreign affairs, Galeazzo Ciano, remembered the Duce remarking a few months earlier, it was "good for the Italian people to be put to tests that make them shake off their century-old mental laziness."[2]

Since 1922, Mussolini and his regime had worked to create generations of New Italians who would be the embodiment of Fascism's ideal Italian race and the driving force behind the resurrection of the Roman Empire. At the core of this project was the belief that all true Italians possessed an innate moral, spiritual, intellectual, and physical strength that fueled the greatest accomplishments in the peninsula's history: the rise of ancient Rome, the height of the Renaissance, the successful conclusion of the Risorgimento. Certainly, there had been periods of political and cultural crisis in the history of the Italians, but these episodes, according to Fascists, were caused by the submergence of the race's true character. The trauma of World War I and its subsequent economic and social turmoil constituted just such a period of crisis. However, the rise of Benito Mussolini's revolutionary movement in 1919 and its quick succession to power in 1922 heralded the reawakening of the eternal Italian spirit. It would be up to Mussolini and his growing state infrastructure not only to educate Italians about the inherited grandeur that flowed through their veins but also to promote the improvement of this glorious racial identity so that Italians could prove their collective superiority to the world. Consequently, over the course of eighteen years, the Fascist state developed a campaign of bonifica umana that spanned a complex network of educational institutions, extracurricular organizations, public health programs, and media platforms. The primary targets of these initiatives were Italy's children.

As the chapters of this book have shown, this multifaceted racial project evolved over the course of Mussolini's time in power, simultaneously expanding in terms of its control over Italians' lives and contracting in its definition of the Italian race. In other words, as the state increased its totalitarian reach, it narrowed its definition of the Italian racial ideal, demanding more of the race's members and tolerating less from its enemies. In the scope of this evolution, the 1920s served as a time of racial and Fascist identity formation and of power consolidation—within the education system and the state as a whole. Officials in the MPI fundamentally overhauled the Italian public education system in these years, relying primarily on Western trends in educational idealism to establish the regime's pedagogical ideals of organic and active learning. While the 1923 Gentile Reform resembled similar movements in other Western nations, its pedagogical principles emphasized the importance of the collective over the individual, the spiritual over the tangible, and action over passivity—all lessons that proved to be quite useful to the developing Fascist racial education program. Likewise, the institution of the ONMI in 1925 and the ONB in 1926 shared Western trends in physical and public health and yet became fundamental to the growing racial program through a focus on strengthening the bodies of Italy's children and training mothers to raise their babies according to Fascist principles of health. Lastly, the elementary lessons of the 1920s laid out for students the fundamental characteristics of italianità—

particularly the interconnected concepts of the Italian nation and race—that formed the foundation of Fascist racial ideology.

Between 1929 and 1934 the state seized on the relatively successful consolidation of Fascist power during Mussolini's first seven years in power and shifted its elementary education and youth culture from a largely Western-inspired system to a truly Fascist, totalitarian way of life. Such a transformation entailed the implementation of a single series of national textbooks and the renaming of the MPI to the MEN. It also required educators to establish the equation of the ideal Fascist with the ideal Italian. Thus, Fascism became the embodiment of italianità, and anyone who wished to represent the Italian race needed to represent the Fascist nation. The consequence of such an adjustment was an increased focus on both physical and military education and an awareness of Italians' birthright to a second Roman Empire.

Mussolini's regime followed this period of Fascistization with a concerted imperial campaign to realize the birth of a second Roman Empire. The 1936 declaration of the Italian Empire resulted from the long-term aims of the Fascist racial campaign as much as it augured the intensification of that campaign. Elementary lessons in the economic; political; and above all else, racial necessity of an expanded empire between 1934 and 1936 paralleled a successful propaganda campaign among Italians in general. Additionally, the colonial racial laws that the Fascist state implemented in 1937 and 1938 mirrored new messages to Italy's youth about the military and moral responsibilities of the New Italian in the new Roman Empire. They also coincided with a move in Fascism's biopolitical discourse, from a primary focus on the quantity of Italians to a greater concern for the quality of Italy's children.

The call for increased scrutiny of the quality of Italy's youngest members came in large part out of the fear that despite the success of the Italo-Ethiopian War, Italians were still not living up to the full potential of their race. The greatest evidence of this frustration was the 1938 Manifesto of Race and the state's subsequent racial legislation. Historians and laypeople alike have frequently cited the Manifesto of Race and the last years of Italy's interwar period as the beginning of a Fascist racial program. And yet evidence has demonstrated that while this period certainly marked the most discriminatory phase of Fascist racism, it by no means was the beginning of its tenure. Indeed, while the new racial laws politically, economically, socially, and physically destroyed hundreds of thousands, if not millions, of lives, much of the racial education program echoed lessons about the Italian race that had been in development at least since Mussolini's earliest days in power. The racial education campaign was not over; it was merely in its newest phase of maturity. In fact, Mussolini apparently exclaimed to his son-in-law in the early days of 1940 that the "Italian race is a race of sheep. Eighteen years is not enough to change them. It takes a hundred and eighty, or maybe a hundred and eighty centuries"; entering World War II was to be the next step along this path to racial rejuvenation.[3]

Despite these grand plans, involvement in the Second World War marked the beginning of the end of Mussolini's campaign to transform Italians into a powerful race that would repossess the title of ruling an eternal civilization. The determination with which the Duce finally threw his troops into the ongoing conflagration did not match Italy's military or economic preparedness.[4] For all of the regime's rhetoric of war and focus on military training, the armed forces had an astonishing lack of equipment and instruction.[5] Evidence of the military's deficiencies in organization and training gathered during the 1939 invasion of Albania had been promptly ignored, and the 1941 takeover of Greece—which Mussolini and his advisors had projected to be an easy victory—became only possible with the aid of German troops and munitions. Successes for the Italian armed forces were few and far between during World War II, and it was not long before it became clear that Italy would have little, if any, responsibility for an Axis victory.

Nevertheless, Mussolini continued to focus much of his attention on winning the war at home, devising literature and events that would convince Italians of the necessity of war, the bravery of their troops, and the glory of the race.[6] The regime published new educational materials that emphasized the glory of military life and the righteousness of Italy's cause.[7] The racial laws and rhetoric of the regime remained in force—and the hardships of wartime made life ever more difficult for Italians and especially non-Italians in and out of the Fascist concentration camps. At the same time, the principal concerns of the regime had adjusted, at least in theory, to accommodate the need for popular support of a war in which Italy was clearly struggling.

The propaganda efforts of Mussolini's totalitarian system were not successful; shortly after Allied forces landed on Sicily in July 1943, amid widespread popular unhappiness with the regime and the war effort, the Fascist Grand Council voted to depose the Duce. In the wake of this news, Italians and non-Italians alike anxiously awaited King Vittorio Emanuele III's decisions about a new government, though what followed represented little political, legal, diplomatic, or economic change. Fascism had supposedly fallen, but few administrators lost their jobs. Mussolini's military commander Marshal Pietro Badoglio stepped in as the country's prime minister; the government insisted that it would continue to fight alongside its allies; and no rollback of the racial laws was forthcoming.[8]

Forty-five days later, when Italy's highly secretive armistice with the Allies was announced on September 8, Adolf Hitler's soldiers were prepared to occupy the country as far as the advancing Allied troops would allow. In the following days, German forces took control of northern and central Italy; released the Duce from prison; and set up a new Nazi-Fascist government—called the Italian Social Republic (RSI), or the Republic of Salò—on the shores of Lake Garda, with Mussolini as the Italian mouthpiece for its German leadership. Mussolini resumed his rhetoric of racial entitlement, and educational materials from the RSI were explicitly anti-Semitic. They lamented the unfaithfulness of Italy's own king and the history of Mussolini's good deeds being repaid with betrayal.[9]

It was during the twenty months between September 1943 and April 1945 that the most gruesome racial violence since the years of Fascist *squadrismo* took place in Italy, and it was perpetrated by both Germans and Italians. Though Slavs, political enemies, and other social (and therefore racial) pariahs were similarly targeted, Italy's Jewish populations—both domestic and foreign—received the most attention. Somewhere between 6,746 and 7,495 Jewish Italians were deported to German-run labor and death camps and approximately 610 returned.[10] A large number of them were arrested because neighbors, coworkers, and rivals denounced them. Some citizens informed the Nazis and Fascists of the whereabouts and identities of Jews because they believed in the value of the anti-Semitic campaign. Many more, however, began informing the Nazis and Fascists after the government announced a reward for each Jew brought forward.[11] Tens of thousands of Jews and other undesirables were also deported from the territories in France, Greece, and Albania that Fascist Italy had previously controlled. And while Italians could proudly declare that no one had been deported from Italian-held territories as part of the German resettlement program before September 1943, they certainly could not and cannot deny that they were involved in the terrible events of that campaign between 1943 and 1945.[12]

After the Allies and Italian partisans drove the Nazis from Italy and left Mussolini's body swinging in a Milan piazza for everyone to view at the end of April 1945, Italians faced the unsavory task of de-Fascistization in order to prove their separation from the failures of both the Fascist state and the Italian military. Top-ranking Fascists were arrested (or summarily executed by members of the resistance), and some trials began taking place. The situation was complicated, however, by the fact that so many Italians had belonged to the National Fascist Party. If the Allies wanted to institute a national government that would be able to function effectively right away, they could not possibly rid the country of all former Fascists. Furthermore, many Italians believed themselves already to have been de-Fascistized; in the end, many argued, Italy had allied itself against Nazi Germany and had helped put an end to the war. Mussolini and his Nazi puppeteers of the RSI had been destroyed, and Italians simply wanted to return to their lives.[13] Of course, there were plenty of Italians and foreign observers—particularly those who had suffered from being enemies of the Fascist state and threats to the Italian race—who wanted Fascists to atone for their sins. In the end, however, full legal and political penitence was not forthcoming, and many former Fascists became members of the new government and leaders of the postwar economy.[14]

The de-Fascistization process was similarly complicated within the educational system. The Allies put the Progressive American pedagogue Carleton Washburne in charge of helping the Ministry of Public Instruction (as it was known again after the war) reform the system.[15] An intense effort was made to purge textbooks and curricula of the most overt references to Fascism and Fascist racism, though many second-generation Fascist textbooks remained in circulation well into the postwar period as a result of budgetary limitations and, quite simply, bureaucratic confusion. What Washburne and postwar Italian administrators worked for was a return to the idealist pedagogy of Gentile's 1923 reforms and a great number of pre- or early Fascist lessons. Thus, many of the lessons that glorified the Italian past and taught children to see the Italian people as one of inherited cultural and spiritual greatness underwent little reform. The lack of a so-called scientific basis for these concepts of Italian racial identity allowed them to remain in the curriculum and continue to influence the way students thought about Italy and italianità long after 1945. Only the most overtly racist—according to American and German standards—lessons and policies of the last years of Fascism were condemned; the more embedded ideas of inherited cultural and spiritual entitlement endured.

Despite these political and pedagogical continuities, there persists the popular argument that the Fascist attempts to indoctrinate Italians with racial ideals were unsuccessful—that a vast majority of Italians embraced post-Fascist society and despaired at the violence that had resulted from the totalitarian regime. Yet frankly, there appears to have been very little change between what were intellectually considered the fundamentals of Italian identity under Fascism and those under the first republic: Italians shared inherited, immutable characteristics that could be identified through history, culture, language, and (to a certain extent) physical health. In short, alongside the problems of purging Fascist racism from the education system were those of completely dismantling the intellectual (and legal) framework for the belief in an inherited Italian body and spirit. As Tommaso Dell'Era has recently pointed out, while many of the most vocal and aggressive racial theorists (and theories) were expelled from the Italian academy after 1945, Nicola Pende and his principles of bonifica umana largely remained in place within the Italian academy and the efforts of national institutions, such as the ONMI.[16] And while they did not demand the expulsion of racial "undesirables" from the Italian Republic, such ideas did maintain a conceptual basis on which such a project could be resurrected.

That there existed a thread of logic spanning the Fascist ventennio and, at least in part, connected ideas of Italian racial identity between Liberal and Republican Italy should not be a surprise. The fact that Fascists and non-Fascists alike used words such as *italianità, patria, stirpe*, and *razza* to create within the Italian population a sense of superiority over other populations while, at least until 1938, largely denying any connections between these ideas and the more popular "scientific" racism of Nazi Germany or the United States has allowed many Italians to believe that concepts of italianità prior to the Manifesto of Race were free of racial theory. Of course, the belief in the innate brilliance of the Italian race and its superiority over other peoples of the world witnessed a number of clarifications—additional layers of meaning—as the Fascist state strengthened both its political doctrine and cultural identity. International events and domestic developments, too, required the regime constantly to evaluate its policies geared toward protecting and fortifying the Italian race. However, these changes in no way negated the foundational belief in the inherited Italian superiority that would, by and large, continue in and after the war. Above all else, the Fascist educational system had popularized and standardized an elementary curriculum throughout the peninsula and islands that promoted a racial ideation of Italian identity. It developed a significant educational infrastructure and a vast network of pedagogical materials that reinforced such beliefs. Certainly, the Fascist efforts—or results—were not uniform throughout the nation; but for the first time in history, a majority of Italians were receiving a basic education, and one that supported an exclusionary definition of the Italian race and nation. These students and the most consistent ideas about Italian identity would play an active role in the foundation of a post-Fascist society.

It is for these reasons that we cannot say that Fascism definitively ended in 1945 and why the conclusion of this book, to borrow the concept from George L. Mosse, cannot really conclude.[17] There are certainly reasons to believe that the arguments of this book are becoming less revolutionary; the voices of scholars, activists, and politicians who echo them are multiplying and becoming louder.[18] At the same time, the arguments and theoretical framework presented in this study do not need to be limited to Fascist Italy and its legacy. The foundational assertions of this book—first, that concepts of race and racism played a fundamental role in Fascism and, second, that the interplay between education and politics is powerful in any nation-state—are clearly not germane simply to modern Italy. Race and racism continue to influence definitions of nationhood and, more generally, collective identity across the globe. Additionally, the practice of teaching students that textbooks are completely objective and that public schools always pursue the ideals of empirical learning does not limit itself to any specific nation-state. Combined, these beliefs impede the development of thoughtful students and self-aware global citizens. It is the hope of this author that readers will use the arguments and evidence of this work to reconsider popular ideas about Italy, italianità, and the legacy of Fascism and also to explore their own views of identity, difference, and the role of the state in developing the minds of students, who are indeed the future of any fatherland.

NOTES

Introduction

1. Anita Pensotti, *Rachele*, quoted in Bosworth, *Mussolini*, 42.

2. For details about Alessandro's political life, see Megaro, *Mussolini in the Making*, 21–38; Emiliani, *Il fabbro di Predappio*, 105–13; De Felice, *Mussolini, il rivoluzionario, 1883–1920*, 1, 15–16.

3. Bedeschi, *La giovinezza del duce*, 68.

4. Bedeschi, *La giovinezza del duce*, 69.

5. Bedeschi, *La giovinezza del duce*, 77.

6. Mussolini, *My Autobiography*, 12. Though titled an autobiography, the U.S. ambassador to Italy from 1921 to 1924, Richard Washburn Child, wrote the work. Megaro, *Mussolini in the Making*, 11–12.

7. A few years later Mussolini returned to the classroom in the northeastern region of Friuli, where the students "fondly" referred to him as "the tyrant." Margherita Sarfatti, *The Life of Benito Mussolini*, 136.

8. Liuzzi, "Fascismo, scuola, educazione nazionale," 6. For the idea of *bonificare* as a constituent of Fascist modernity, see Ben-Ghiat, *Fascist Modernities*.

9. Puccini, "Rieducazione del popolo."

10. Of fundamental importance to this work is a belief in Suzanne Stewart-Steinberg's assertion that culture and politics do not occupy separate spheres but rather are inextricably interwoven in any society. Stewart-Steinberg, *The Pinocchio Effect*, 2.

11. Here I use the term *identity* in its most generic and passive form. However, I take to heart Rogers Brubaker and Frederick Cooper's well-reasoned critiques of the concept and therefore will use the terms *identification* or *categorization* when referring to the active process of understanding oneself or others through markers of similarity or difference. Brubaker and Cooper, "Beyond 'Identity.'"

12. Isaac, *The Invention of Racism in Classical Antiquity*, 1.

13. Perhaps the most notable example of this scholarship is Snowden Jr., *Before Color Prejudice*. See also Goldberg, *Racist Culture*; Fredrickson, *Racism*; Hannaford, *Race*.

14. Isaac, *The Invention of Racism in Classical Antiquity*, 25–26; Eliav-Feldon, Isaac, and Ziegler, *The Origins of Racism in the West*; Blackburn, "Why Race Is Not a Biological Concept." My argument that racial identity and discrimination are not inherently modern is not meant to imply that they are a byproduct of "human nature" but merely expresses the deeper historicity of the concepts and practices. In other words, the modern usage of the terms *race* and *racism* did not in any way come out of the blue. Bethencourt, *Racisms*, 5; Fredrickson, *The Comparative Imagination*, 82; Boxill, *Race and Racism*, 63.

15. Wade, "From Eighteenth- to Nineteenth-Century Racial Science"; Fredrickson, *Racism*, 56–57; Jackson and Weidman, *Race, Racism, and Science*, 29.

16. Mosse, *Toward the Final Solution*; Poliakov, *The Aryan Myth*.

17. For the role of European imperialism in the development of modern European racial theory, see Ballantyne, *Orientalism and Race*.

18. Mosse, *Toward the Final Solution*, 2.

19. Even the "return of biology" to discussions of race, since the completion of the Human Genome Project in 2000, has not led to any fixed biological understanding of the idea. Brubaker, *Grounds for Difference*, 48–84.

20. Goldberg, *The Racial State*, 118–22.

21. Ballantyne, *Orientalism and Race*, especially 93–125; Nicholson, *Who Do We Think We Are?* For a discussion of the influence of nationalism on modern racism, see Bethencourt, *Racisms*, 307–34.

22. For more-insistent arguments for the relationship between nation and race, see Nicholson, *Who Do We Think We Are?*; Balibar, "Racism and Nationalism."

23. Bethencourt, *Racisms*, 2; Mosse, *Toward the Final Solution*, 68–69.

24. Blackburn, "Why Race Is Not a Biological Concept."

25. Goldberg, *Anatomy of Racism*, xiv.

26. Jacobson, *Whiteness of a Different Color*, 4.

27. The earliest efforts to understand the subject were largely satisfied with the explanation that the anti-Semitic legislation after 1938 was incongruent with the core of Fascist doctrine and that it was foreign pressure—principally from Nazi Germany—that led to its implementation. While Mussolini's evolving relationship with Adolf Hitler did influence Fascist policies in the 1930s, strong evidence indicates that Hitler never pressured the Fascist government to adopt stricter racial policies. In fact, on several occasions, the Fascist minister of foreign affairs (and Mussolini's son-in-law) Galeazzo Ciano insisted that the Nazis had never requested any racial laws from the Italians. Gillette, *Racial Theories in Fascist Italy*, 58; Ciano, *Diary*, 32. Renzo De Felice reopened the subject of Fascist anti-Semitism in the 1960s to argue that Hitler applied a more indirect diplomatic pressure on the Italian regime, compelling the Fascists to establish comprehensive racial laws to eliminate any major differences between the two governments. De Felice, *The Jews in Fascist Italy*. With little variation, this argument remains sufficient for some scholars and Italians. Gregor, *Giovanni Gentile*, 81–86; Michaelis, *Mussolini and the Jews*. It bears noting that Michaelis argues Mussolini was an anti-Semite long before 1938, but it was the pressure of international politics that led to the development of anti-Semitic laws.

28. For more on Jewish Italian participation in Fascism, see De Felice, *The Jews in Fascist Italy*, 63–67; Michele Sarfatti, *The Jews in Mussolini's Italy*, especially 15–16.

29. Renzo De Felice famously argued that there was no organic Italian racial theory before the twentieth century. De Felice, *The Jews in Fascist Italy*, 22–23, 178, 206.

30. Michele Sarfatti has argued that Mussolini had long been anti-Semitic and acted on its attendant beliefs (notably that there was a global Jewish conspiracy) in official and personal ways well before 1938. Michele Sarfatti, *The Jews in Mussolini's Italy*. See also Fabre, *Mussolini razzista*. Another article by Sarfatti analyzed characteristics of the Italian 1938 racial laws that differed in essence and scope from those implemented in the Third Reich. Michele Sarfatti, "Characteristics and Objectives of the Anti-Jewish Racial Laws in Fascist Italy, 1938–1943."

31. Kertzer, *The Popes against the Jews*; Kertzer, *The Pope and Mussolini*. See also part 1 of Zimmerman, *Jews in Italy under Fascist and Nazi Rule, 1922–1945*, 19–68.

32. The first scholars to discuss this argument were Preti, *Impero fascista, africani ed ebrei*; Goglia, "Note sul razzismo coloniale fascista." For a more recent example of this argument, see Ventura, *Il fascismo e gli ebrei*.

33. Ottolenghi, *Gli italiani e il colonialismo*; Lombardo, *Terre promesse*; Labanca, "Il razzismo coloniale italiano"; Sòrgoni, *Parole e corpi*. Regarding Italian racism in colonial education, see Matteo Pretelli, "Education in the Italian Colonies during the Interwar Period."

34. Some scholars have genuinely taken on the task of answering these questions. Galli della Loggia, *L'identità italiana*. More generally, however, scholars take for granted Italians' myriad cultural divisions and tendency toward self-deprecation. Emilio Gentile, *La Grande Italia*; Schiavone, *Italiani senza Italia*. A few even discuss the role of education in the resolution of these questions. Fiorelli, *La nazione tra i banchi*. Others undertake thematic analyses of Italian discourses regarding *italianità*. Ascoli and von Henneberg, *Making and Remaking Italy*; Bollati, *L'italiano*; Patriarca, *Italian Vices*; Stewart-Steinberg, *The Pinocchio Effect*.

35. While these regional languages are frequently termed dialects, I have chosen to characterize them as languages out of respect for the perspective of many of their speakers.

36. De Mauro, *Storia linguistica dell'Italia unita*, 43.

37. According to Renzo De Felice, the Jewish population numbered approximately forty-eight thousand in 1938—less than 1 percent of the population. De Felice, *Storia degli ebrei italiani*, 13. The numbers vary, however, depending on whether one includes the foreign Jews living in Italy at that date.

38. De Mauro, *Storia linguistica dell'Italia unita*, 43. On the nation as an imagined community, see Anderson, *Imagined Communities*, 44–45.

39. Istituto centrale di statistica, *Sommario di statistiche storiche dell'Italia, 1861–1975*, 14.

40. As many scholars have pointed out, d'Azeglio never actually uttered this aphorism. Soldani and Turi, *Fare gli italiani*, 1:17; Patriarca, *Italian Vices*, 51–52.

41. Emilio Gentile, *La Grande Italia*, 58–59.

42. On the Roman roots of the Italian nation, see Ascoli and von Henneberg, *Making and Remaking Italy*, 6–8. For an examination of post-Risorgimento economic policies and their consequences, see Bevilacqua, *Breve storia dell'Italia meridionale*, especially 38–58.

43. For a history of the early Italian eugenics movement, see Cassata, *Building the New Man*, 9–42. For an overview of Italian racial discourse, see Giuliani and Lombardi-Diop, *Bianco e nero*.

44. For an overview of Lombroso's career, see Gibson, *Born to Crime*. Lombroso would later use much of the research collected during his time in the South to earn an international reputation as the father of criminal anthropology. His work analyzing the anthropometric features of various criminals (including thieves, prostitutes, and general delinquents) also had broad, if not necessarily projected, implications for the future of biological racism. Lombroso, *Crime*.

45. Niceforo, *Il gergo nei normali, nei degenerati e nei criminali*.

46. Niceforo, *L'Italia barbara contemporanea*, 9–14. Nelson Moe argues that the characterization of the Italian South as a "liminal zone" between Europe and Africa developed (with the aid of foreigners and southerners themselves) in the second half of the eighteenth century. Moe, "'This Is Africa,'" 120–21.

Several studies of the so-called Southern Question were published in the late nineteenth and early twentieth centuries. The most famous account was the 1877 two-volume report by the politicians Leopoldo Franchetti and Sidney Sonnino. Franchetti and Sonnino, *Inchiesta in Sicilia*, especially vol. 1. In 1911 Senator Giustinio Fortunato published a report on the relationship between the Italian South and the central government. Fortunato, *Il mezzogiorno e lo stato italiano*. Francesco Saverio Nitti argued that malaria, before all else, was responsible for the South's difficulties. Snowden, *The Conquest of Malaria*, 3–4. For a small sampling of more-recent scholarship on the subject, see Mack Smith, "The Latifundia in Modern Sicilian History"; Dickie, *Darkest Italy*; Moe, *The View from Vesuvius*; Arlacchi, *Mafia, Peasants, and Great Estates*; Bevilacqua, *Breve storia dell'Italia meridionale*.

47. Sergi, *The Mediterranean Race*, 163–73.

48. Sergi, *The Mediterranean Race*, 31–34. For a discussion of Sergi's work in the broader field of Italian physical anthropology, see Sòrgoni, *Parole e corpi*, 33–52. On Sergi, Lombroso, and Niceforo and the Southern Question, see De Francesco, *The Antiquity of the Italian Nation*, 133–57.

49. Benedetto Croce's argument is described further in Bollati, *L'italiano*, 39.

50. For histories of the intellectual debates regarding theories and definitions of the Italian race under Fascism, see Gillette, *Racial Theories in Fascist Italy*; Raspanti, "I razzismi del fascismo"; Israel and Nastasi, *Scienza e razza nell'Italia fascista*; Israel, *Il fascismo e la razza*.

51. To highlight the presence of these terms in Fascist rhetoric, they remain untranslated in contemporary quotations.

52. Domenichelli, *L'adunata, quinta classe*, 174.

53. Casale, *A cuore aperto: Libro di lettura per la quinta classe*, 261–62.

54. Partito nazionale fascista, *Il cittadino soldato*, 24.

55. Mazower, *Dark Continent*, 71; Weindling, *Health, Race and German Politics between National Unification and Nazism, 1870–1945*, 241–48, 291–98.

56. Kallis, *Fascist Ideology*, 42.

57. French concern about falling birth rates began in the mid-nineteenth century. The 1891 census was the first to show concrete evidence of reduced population growth. Censuses in other European nations soon showed similar trends. Schneider, *Quality and Quantity*, 39; Ipsen, *Dictating Demography*, 13. A corresponding worry after World War I was that nonwhite populations were not declining; to the contrary, they were expanding. Benito Mussolini, "Prefazione di Benito Mussolini," in Korherr, *Regresso delle nascite*, 10. For a broader discussion of eugenic concerns in interwar Europe, see Burleigh and Wippermann, *The Racial State*, 33–34.

58. According to *European Historical Statistics*, Italy's births per thousand only fell from 33.3 to 32.2 between 1910 and 1920. By contrast, Germany's births per thousand had dropped from 29.8 to 25.9. Cited in Bock and Thane, *Maternity and Gender Policies*, 17. Also Dogliani, *Il fascismo degli italiani*, 103–4.

59. Bonetta, *Corpo e nazione*, 180, 245, 253. Similar concerns could be heard within many factions of the modernist movement between 1860 and 1960.

60. Foucault, *The History of Sexuality*, 26.

61. On the relationship between biopower and the law, see Foucault, *The History of Sexuality*, 82–84.

62. Foucault, *The History of Sexuality*, 92–93.

63. Several studies have considered the development of state and semiprivate institutions to regulate Italy's "national welfare." On the development of the public health system, see Snowden, *The Conquest of Malaria*; Snowden, *Naples in the Time of Cholera, 1884–1911*. On eugenic societies and demographic studies, see Cassata, *Building the New Man*; Horn, *Social Bodies*; Horn, "Constructing the Sterile City"; Horn, "Regarding the Modern Body"; Ipsen, *Dictating Demography*. Additional studies on the role of gender in the concepts of national welfare and the state also illuminate biopolitical discourses in Fascist Italy. On the role of masculinity in Italian Fascism, see Spackman, *Fascist Virilities*; Benadusi, *The Enemy of the New Man*. On the role of women in Fascist politics and policies, see De Grazia, *How Fascism Ruled Women*; Visani, *Genere, identità e razzismo nell'Italia fascista*.

64. Althusser, "Ideology and Ideological State Apparatuses," 104. As a good Marxist, Althusser was disinterested in the formal distinction between public and private institutions, claiming that they are all ultimately unified by a ruling ideology. Still, Italy's Fascist regime provides an ideal model of an Ideological State Apparatus insofar as Fascism's totalitarian ambition worked for the dissolution of any separation between public and private spheres.

65. Gramsci, *Prison Notebooks*, 12, 55–56n15, 170.

66. Gramsci also noted the power of an education system in the process of establishing political hegemony. Gramsci, *Prison Notebooks*, 10, 30–31, 242–43.

67. The classic study of the history of childhood in Europe remains Ariès, *Centuries of Childhood*. On childhood in the West during the nineteenth and twentieth centuries, see Gillis, *Youth and History*; Cunningham, *Children and Childhood in Western Society since 1500*; Zelizer, *Pricing the Priceless Child*. For a historiography of childhood in modern Italy, see Gibson, "Italy." On childhood under Fascism, see Gibelli, *Il popolo bambino*.

68. On the modern Italian educational system in Italy, see Genovesi, *Storia della scuola in Italia dal Settecento a oggi*; Cives, *La scuola italiana dall'Unità ai nostri giorni*; Bacigalupi and Fossati, *Da plebe al popolo*; Borghi, *Educazione e autorità nell'Italia moderna*; Di Luzio, *La scuola degli italiani*. On elementary education since the Risorgimento, see De Fort, *La scuola elementare dall'Unità alla caduta del fascismo*. On the political project of national education in Italy since the Risorgimento, see Di Luzio, *La scuola degli italiani*. On physical education in Liberal Italy, see Bonetta, *Corpo e nazione*. For a study of elementary school teachers in the first half of the twentieth century, see Dei, *Colletto bianco, grembiule nero*. For an overview of the Fascist education system, see Ricuperati, *La scuola italiana e il fascismo*; Charnitzky, *Die Schulpolitik des faschistischen Regimes in Italien (1922–1943)*; Ostenc, *La scuola italiana durante il fascismo*. On youth culture more generally, see Koon, *Believe, Obey, Fight*; Gibelli, *Il popolo bambino*. More recently, there has been some great work on the ideological form and uses of education under Fascism. Gabrielli and Guerrini, *I "problemi" del fascismo*; Gabrielli and Montino, *La scuola fascista*.

69. On the Hitlerjugend and Bund Deutscher Mädel in Nazi Germany, see Kater, *Hitler Youth*. In his recent book, Alessio Ponzio has clearly shown how much the Hitlerjugend adopted from the ONB (and GIL) and how, in the 1930s and 1940s, the two youth organizations influenced one another. Ponzio, *Shaping the New Man*. There is much less English-language literature on the Soviet Union's youth organization, the Komsomol. For a Soviet-supported explanation of the organization, see Andreyev et al., *The Komsomol*.

70. Linz, "Fascism, Breakdown of Democracy, Authoritarian and Totalitarian Regimes," 52.

71. On the difference between ideology and everyday life in Fascist Italy, see Corner, *The Fascist Party and Popular Opinion in Mussolini's Italy*; Ferris, *Everyday Life in Fascist Venice, 1929–1940*; Duggan, *Fascist Voices*; Emilio Gentile, *The Sacralization of Politics in Fascist Italy*.

72. Several prominent Fascist scientists, such as Giuseppe Sergi and Lidio Cipriani, were involved in the international scientific debates on eugenics and race; and some very public politicians, such as Giovanni Preziosi and Telesio Interlandi, were at the forefront of the movement to blame the "international Jewish community" for Europe's strained economic and social situation in the aftermath of the Great War.

1. Designing a Fascist Education

1. Grassini and Borella, *Per la patria di domani*, 32.

2. Grassini and Borella, *Per la patria di domani*, 28. In this translation, "the host" refers to the sacramental concept (*ostie*).

3. "Responsabilità."

4. Grassini and Borella, *Per la patria di domani*, 32; Puccini, "Rieducazione del popolo," 98.

5. Tomasi, *Idealismo e fascismo nella scuola italiana*, 2–4, 14.

6. Turi, *Giovanni Gentile*, 7.

7. Carlini, *Il pensiero pedagogico dell'idealismo*, xiv; Tomasi, *Idealismo e fascismo nella scuola italiana*, 14–15.

8. This is obviously a simplified explanataion of one part of Hegel's philosophy. For his most explicit articulation of *Geist* and historical dialectics, see Hegel, *Phenomenology of Spirit*.

9. Gregor, *Mussolini's Intellectuals*, 92–93.

10. Gregor, *Mussolini's Intellectuals*, 86–87.

11. For an English-language overview of Gentile's philosophy, see Gregor, *Giovanni Gentile*, 15–28. In Italian, see Sagramola, *Giovanni Gentile nella cultura e nella scuola italiana*, 11–21.

12. Giovanni Gentile, "Draft of 'L'educazione nazionale,'" 1919 (FGG, ser. 2 manoscritti gentiliani, box 57 dattiloscritti pubblicati).

13. Codignola, *Il problema dell'educazione nazionale in Italia*, 149.

14. Philippe Ariès famously argued that childhood was "discovered" among the middle and upper classes of Europe (primarily in France) in the seventeenth century. Ariès, *Centuries of Childhood*, 33–49, 412–13. More recently, historians Marcella Bacigalupi and Piero Fossati point out that as late as the early nineteenth century authors largely saw children as small men and women. Bacigalupi and Fossati, *Da plebe al popolo*, 112–14.

15. Gillis, *Youth and History*, 142–43.

16. For an overview of the international public health movement, see Fildes, Marks, and Marland, *Women and Children First*. For a comparison of the French and U.S. cases, see Klaus, *Every Child a Lion*. On the French case, see Schneider, *Quality and Quantity*. And on the United States, see Apple, *Perfect Motherhood*. Few Italian scholars have explored the international aspects of modern educational movements. One important exception is Bonetta, *Corpo e nazione*. Carl Ipsen, too, discusses issues of juvenile delinquency, abandonment, and public health during the Liberal era in Ipsen, *Italy in the Age of Pinocchio*.

17. The influence of Maria Montessori (1870–1952) and her pedagogy is particularly noteworthy, but not alone, in this regard.

18. Francesco Orestano, "Relazione a S. E. il Ministro dell'Istruzione intorno al III Congresso internazionale d'educazione morale," Rome, 1922 (ACS, MI, Opere pie, 1925–1927, box 5, folder "IV Congresso dell'Educazione Morale, Roma"); Raniero Paulucci de' Calboli, "Report on the Congresso generale del fanciullo,"

Rome, 1925 (ACS, MI, Opere pie, 1925–1927, box 5, folder "Ginevra, I Congresso internazionale per la protezione dell'infanzia, 'Esposizione del fanciullo'"). For a contemporary discussion of experimental schools that bridged the Liberal and Fascist periods, see Lombardo Radice, *Nursery Schools in Italy*.

19. Even early Fascists looked to the education systems of Germany and the United States for inspiration and comparison. Bertarelli, "Come si insegna al popolo a comprendere i valori della demografica," 84–85.

20. Lyttelton, *The Seizure of Power*, 406.

21. For more on this part of his philosophy, see Giovanni Gentile, *Fascismo e cultura*.

22. On the ethical state, see Giovanni Gentile, *I problemi della scolastica e il pensiero italiano*; Giovanni Gentile, "Draft of 'Per la futura scuola del popolo,'" Napoli, Italy, 1918 (FGG, ser. 2 manoscritti gentiliani, folder 56).

23. Gregor, *Giovanni Gentile*, 58; Giovanni Gentile, "Libertà d'insegnamento e scuola di Stato," 1919 (FGG, ser. 2 manoscritti gentiliani, folder 53 minuta di articolo).

24. The connections between Italian national and racial categories will be discussed in chapter 2.

25. Giovanni Gentile, *Origini e dottrina del fascismo*.

26. Giovanni Gentile, "Draft of 'Per la futura scuola del popolo,'" 1.

27. De Luca, "Fari d'italianità."

28. Bodrero, "Presentazione a S. E. il Ministro della pubblica istruzione," 5.

29. Pietro Fedele, "Note al bilancio per l'esercizio 1926–27," Rome, 1926 (ACS, Archivio personale Pietro Fedele, box 1, folder "Appunti sull'istruzione").

30. D'Ambrosio, *A scuola col duce*, 12; Ostenc, *La scuola italiana durante il fascismo*, 59–100.

31. Lombardo Radice has often been given primary credit for the reforms to elementary education. Tarquini, "The Anti-Gentilians during the Fascist Regime," 637; Borghi, *Educazione e autorità nell'Italia moderna*, 238; Tomasi, *Idealismo e fascismo nella scuola italiana*, 41–42.

32. Turi, *Giovanni Gentile*, 16. Colaci, *Gli anni della Riforma*, 17–31.

33. Catalfamo, *Giuseppe Lombardo-Radice*, 50–74; Tomasi, *Idealismo e fascismo nella scuola italiana*, 37–38.

34. Carlini, *Il pensiero pedagogico dell'idealismo*, xxix. Italics added for emphasis.

35. Catalfamo, *Giuseppe Lombardo-Radice*, 25, 29.

36. Turi, *Giovanni Gentile*, 305, 308; Giuseppe Lombardo Radice to Giovanni Gentile, October 31, 1922 (FGG, ser. 1, subseries 1, Lombardo Radice, Lombardo Radice a G. Gentile).

37. Borghi, *Educazione e autorità nell'Italia moderna*, 245–46.

38. Unfortunately, this obligation remained largely bound to paper, as many rural schools never expanded past the third grade. Cives, *La scuola italiana dall'Unità ai nostri giorni*, 83.

39. Ragazzini, "L'amministrazione della scuola," 294.

40. Such a system replaced the *corso popolare* that Minister Orlando established in 1904. Mencarelli, *Inquadrati e fedeli*, 21.

41. Giovanni Gentile, "Circolare n. 51. Esami di maturità nelle scuole elementari," 2101; Giovanni Gentile, "R. D. 1 ottobre 1923, n. 2185—Ordinamento dei gradi scolastici e dei programmi didattici dell'istruzione elementare," 4064–65. Nursery schools were not mandatory or free for children between the ages of three and six, and the vast majority of children in that age group remained at home. The number of children in nursery schools increased significantly over the next decade, but generally speaking, that demographic only became a real focus of educational efforts in the 1930s. Borghi, *Educazione e autorità nell'Italia moderna*, 253.

42. Steiner, *Coltura fascista*, 67.

43. D'Ambrosio, *A scuola col duce*, 12.

44. In 1921 Italy was one of the most densely populated nations in the world. While significant portions of the kingdom's land remained agricultural into the 1950s, most Italians lived in towns or cities with populations over one thousand. Even in Basilicata, the most rural of Italian regions, 414,816 of its 468,557 residents lived in such urban centers. For more statistics, see Istituto centrale di statistica, *Censimento della poplazione del Regno d'Italia al 1 dicembre 1921. XIX. Relazione generale*, vol. 19, especially pp. 97–99.

45. Marcucci, "Le scuole non classificate e l'opera degli enti delegati," 149.

46. Marcucci, "Ordinamento delle scuole rurali non classificate," 57–58. In 1928 most of these schools were placed under the governance of the ONB. Koon, *Believe, Obey, Fight*, 55.

47. Bellassai, "The Masculinity Mystique," 318–19.

48. Pietro Fedele, ". . . al R.D.L 20 Agosto 1926 . . . sulla istruzione delle scuole e sulla edilizia rurale," Rome, 1926 (ACS, Archivio personale Pietro Fedele, box 6); "Report on Rural Education," Rome, n.d. (ACS, Archivio personale Pietro Fedele, box 8, folder "Min. P. I. Balancio 1926–1927").

49. D'Ambrosio, *A scuola col duce*, 31. For more on the the modern history of Italy's literacy campaigns, see Vigo, "Gli italiani alla conquista dell'alfabeto"; Marchesini, "Città e campagna nello specchio dell'alfabetismo (1921–1951)."

50. "Report on Rural Education," Rome, n.d., 1–2.

51. Boccazzi, "Prefazione alla Terza Edizione."

52. Koon, *Believe, Obey, Fight*, 55–56.

53. Giovanni Gentile, "R. D. 1 ottobre 1923, n. 2185—Ordinamento dei gradi scolastici e dei programmi didattici dell'istruzione elementare," 4064.

54. Bellassai, "The Masculinity Mystique," 314. On the role of masculinity in Fascism more generally, see Mosse, *The Image of Man*, 155–66.

55. Covato, "Scuola e stereotipi di genere a Roma fra le due guerre," 117; Scarpa, "Mascolinizzare."

56. Brunialti and Douglas, "Di quella educazione che incomincia con la vita," 622–23.

57. Schumann, "Childhood and Youth in Nazi Germany," 454.

58. Ostenc, *La scuola italiana durante il fascismo*, 144, 165–66, 196–97; Lyttelton, *The Seizure of Power*, 408; Koon, *Believe, Obey, Fight*, 64–65.

59. Spirito, "Giovanni Gentile," 5; Carlini, *Il pensiero pedagogico dell'idealismo*, 38–56. See also Gentile's own writings, such as Giovanni Gentile, *The Reform of Education*, 36, 156, 175, 187; Giovanni Gentile, *Preliminari allo studio del fanciullo*.

60. On the Casati Law, see Cives, "La scuola elementare e popolare," 59–62.

61. Giovanni Gentile, "Libertà d'insegnamento e scuola di Stato."

62. Cives, *La scuola italiana dall'Unità ai nostri giorni*, 85; Sagramola, *Giovanni Gentile nella cultura e nella scuola italiana*, 37–38.

63. Still, the Vatican was not particularly pleased with the practice of lay teachers imparting religious instruction rather than priests. Wolff, "Catholicism, Fascism and Italian Education from the Riforma Gentile to the Carta Della Scuola 1922–1939," 6–7.

64. Giovanni Gentile, *The Reform of Education*, 9–10.

65. Tomasi, *Idealismo e fascismo nella scuola italiana*, 22.

66. Koon, *Believe, Obey, Fight*, 27–28; Emilio Gentile, *The Sacralization of Politics in Fascist Italy*; Falasca-Zamponi, *Fascist Spectacle*.

67. Lyttelton, *The Seizure of Power*, 380.

68. Gentile writes about this necessity for curricular freedom in articles prior to the development of his 1923 reform. Giovanni Gentile, "Libertà d'insegnamento e scuola di Stato." For an analysis of this theory, see Tomasi, *Idealismo e fascismo nella scuola italiana*, 15–16. There were precursors to this type of pedagogy in Italy, such as the Agazzi method, which based lessons on children's senses. Stewart-Steinberg, *The Pinocchio Effect*, 315.

69. Associazione nazionale per gli interessi del mezzogiorno d'Italia, *Esposizione sintetica dei programmi didattici*, 8; Giovanni Gentile, *Orari, programmi, e prescrizioni didattiche per le scuole elementari*, 4–5.

70. Codignola, *Il problema dell'educazione nazionale in Italia*, 276.

71. Giovanni Gentile, *The Reform of Education*, 156.

72. Musso, *Il "gioco" e il Fascismo*, 43–44.

73. Ministero dell'educazione nazionale, *Dalla riforma Gentile alla Carta della scuola*, 576; Giovanni Gentile, *The Reform of Education*, 85; Codignola, *Il problema dell'educazione nazionale in Italia*, 282–83; Carlini, *Il pensiero pedagogico dell'idealismo*, 35.

74. Musso, *Il "gioco" e il Fascismo*, 66.

75. Stewart-Steinberg, *The Pinocchio Effect*, 140–42; Bonetta, *Corpo e nazione*.

76. Ponzio, *Shaping the New Man*, 49.

77. Ente nazionale per l'educazione fisica, *Relazione sull'opera e sul funzionamento dell'ENEF nell'anno scolastico 1923–24*.

78. Historian John Gillis noted that in Great Britain and Germany at the turn of the century, many adults felt that schooling was insufficient to train future leaders. He argued that the establishment of extracurricular youth movements largely came out of the concern to continuously educate youth into adulthood. Gillis, *Youth and History*, 144–45.

79. "L'assistenza scolastica e il suo incremento," 10.

80. Vittorio Emanuele III, "Legge 3 aprile 1926, n. 2247," 293. However, there had been some organization of Italian youth within the Fascist Party since 1923.

For a broad history of the ONB, see Betti, *L'Opera nazionale Balilla e l'educazione fascista*; Ponzio, *Shaping the New Man*.

81. Vittorio Emanuele III, "Regio decreto-legge 9 gennaio 1927, n. 5," 371. For a short history of scouting in Great Britain and the United States, see Mechling, "Children in Scouting and Other Organizations." For a relatively recent history of the Hitler Youth (though one that argues children were not a central concern for Hitler), see Kater, *Hitler Youth*. For a longer history of youth movements in Germany, see Laqueur, *Young Germany*; Stachura, *The German Youth Movement 1900–1945*. In Italy, Carlo Colombo founded the Giovani esploratori and Giovani esploratrici in 1912. Pisa, *Crescere per la patria*. Mario Mazza founded the first groups of Italian scouts under the control of the Catholic Church. Trova, *Alle origini dello scoutismo cattolico in Italia*. For an overview of scouting in Italy, see Sica, *Storia dello scautismo in Italia*.

82. Rossi, *Diario di un balilla, 1932–1936*, 113.

83. Ciarlantini, *I miei amici di Villa Castelli*, 80.

84. Giurlanda, *A voi, bimbi d'Italia!*, 38.

85. Fiume (the Croatian town of Rijeka) was considered by many Italian nationalists to rightfully belong to Italy, and the rejection of Italy's bid for it at the 1919 Paris Peace Conference led Gabriele D'Annunzio (1863–1938) and his followers to occupy the city from September 1919 to December 1920. D'Annunzio and his defiance of the Liberal regime would become a popular image for the Fascist Party, and the regime mourned his death in 1938 as that of a national hero. See Tonini, *Gabriele D'Annunzio e l'impresa fiumana*; Ledeen, *D'Annunzio*. For biographies of D'Annunzio, see Woodhouse, *Gabriele D'Annunzio*; Hughes-Hallett, *Gabriele d'Annunzio*.

86. A contemporary biographical sketch of Ricci characterized him as "a young man of unquestionable faith, proven fascist passion, appropriate opinions, and a steadfast and organized temperament." Spina, "Figure del fascismo," 15.

87. For Ricci's own take on the goals of the ONB, see Ricci, "L'Opera nazionale balilla."

88. Cutrufelli et al., *Piccole Italiane*, 61.

89. Santini, "Le opere assistenziali dei Fasci femminili," 5–7.

90. Quercia Tanzarella, "La mirabile opera dei Fasci femminili," 7.

91. "L'attività dell'Opera nazionale Balilla nell'anno VIII," 10.

92. Gould, "The Komsomol and the Hitler Jugend," 311.

93. Morgagni, "La leva fascista, 'certezza del futuro,'" 5–6. For a brief discussion of the symbolism behind the *leva fascista* for Italian women, see De Grazia, *How Fascism Ruled Women*, 118–19. For its idea of Fascistizing the Italian youth, see Dogliani, *Il fascismo degli italiani*, 167–78.

94. For more on the role of the American Red Cross in the Italian public health community before and after World War I, see Irwin, *Making the World Safe*, 40–42, 113–35.

95. "La Croce rossa italiana giovanile," 130.

96. De Marinis, *Resurrezione eroica*, 58–59.

97. Ferlini, "Scuola nuova, metodi nuovi," 638.

98. "L'assistenza scolastica e il suo incremento," 14.

99. Ferlini, "Scuola nuova, metodi nuovi"; Lombardo Radice, "OGGETTO-Scuole all'aperto ed altre istituzioni sussidiarie della scuola con lo scopo dell'igiene del fanciullo," Rome, 1924 (ACS, PCM, 1924, folder 5.1.1006).

100. Belluzzo, *Le opere sussidiarie della scuola elementare in Italia*, 13. Patrizia Dogliani notes there were also some late nineteenth-century seaside hospitals with similar goals. Dogliani, *Il fascismo degli italiani*, 180.

101. Tona, "La funzione fondamentale del regime," 569. On the international movement to organize outdoor summer camps, see Mechling, "Children in Scouting and Other Organizations," 424–26. For the French experience, see Downs, *Childhood in the Promised Land*.

102. Fanelli, *Fascismo*, 144.

103. "L'assistenza scolastica e il suo incremento," 14.

104. Valagussa, "L'Opera nazionale per la protezione della maternità e dell'infanzia e le colonie estive," 18.

105. Valagussa, "Infanzia e colonizzazione interna," 9–17.

106. In particular, public health organizations expanded within rural Italy to defend the population from epidemic disease. The Istituto nazionale pel risanamento antimalarico della regione pontina, founded in 1923 and increasingly important in the following years, organized a vast antimalarial campaign among rural schools in Lazio. Istituto nazionale pel risanamento antimalarico della regione pontina, "Programma e funzionamento dell'istituto," Rome, 1927 (ACS, MI, DG sanità pubblica, 1896–1934, box 58BIS, folder "Instituto nazionale pel risanamento antimalarico della regione pontina: Bonifica dell'Agro Pontino"); Istituto nazionale pel risanamento antimalarico della regione pontina, "Organizzazione della lotta alla malaria e dei servizi igienici e demografici nell'Agro Pontino: Progetto di massima," Rome, 1927 (ACS, MI, DG sanità pubblica, box 58bis, folder "Instituto nazionale pel risanamento antimalarico della regione pontina: Bonifica dell'Agro Pontino").

107. Direttore generale dell'amministrazione civile, "Disegno di legge per la protezione e assistenza della maternità e dell'infanzia," Rome, 1924 (ACS, MI, Opere pie, ser. 10, 1928–1930, box 17, folder "Disegno di legge per la protezione e assistenza della maternità e della infanzia"), 1.

108. Blanc, *Il fascismo dinanzi al problema della razza*, 5–6.

109. Lo Monaco-Aprile, "L'assistenza igienico-sanitaria come elemento di politica demografica," 1043.

110. The conference was open to all Italian women, as well as foreign women who had lived in Italy for at least ten years, and illustrated the early efforts to expand Fascist ideas to the broadest audiences. Consiglio nazionale delle donne italiane, "Terzo congresso indetto dal Consiglio nazionale delle donne italiane: L'Educazione in famiglia," Rome, 1923 (ACS, CNDI, box 1, folder 2); "Memo regarding the conference 'L'educazione in famiglia,'" Rome, 1923 (ACS, CNDI, box 1, folder 1).

111. Palesa, "La cattedra ambulante di puericultura nell'Agro Romano," 599. The involvement of these auxiliary organizations was essential to the spread of

health education in rural communities, though progress was sometimes slower than the administration desired. Francesco Lepore, "Relazione dell'ispezione eseguita in Sardegna sulle condizioni sull'istruzione elementare e sullo incremento delle opere Fasciste per l'infanzia (Balilla e Piccole Italiane)," Cagliari, 1928 (ACS, Archivio personale Pietro Fedele, box 8).

112. D'Ormea, "Cattedre ambulanti di assistenza materna e di puericultura, elemento di ruralizzazione," 833–39.

113. Lo Monaco-Aprile, "Il programma totalitario dell'Opera nazionale per la protezione della maternità e dell'infazia," 375.

114. Generally speaking, separate elementary school textbooks were used for religion, math, and literature. In the *grado inferiore*, the literature books included texts on history, religion, and culture. In the *grado superiore*, additional books were used to teach science, geography, and second languages. For a discussion of elementary textbooks in the Liberal nation-building project, see Fujisawa, "I testi scolastici fanno il popolo."

115. Cives, *La scuola italiana dall'Unità ai nostri giorni*, 86. The commission was chosen on a biannual basis and was to meet twice a year. Giovanni Gentile, "R. D. 11 marzo 1923, n. 737, che detta norme per l'adozione dei libri di testo nelle scuole elementari e popolari pubbliche e private," 1404–7. No textbook would be honored unless the commission had selected it. Over the 1920s, however, the meetings did not adhere to this schedule. Over the course of the decade, there were five commissions to approve textbooks: 1923 (headed by director general Giuseppe Lombardo Radice), 1925 (under the pedagogue Giovanni Vidari), 1926 (with former minister Balbino Giuliano), 1927 (with undersecretary Michele Romano), and 1928 (with Alessandro Melchiori). Bacigalupi and Fossati, *Da plebe al popolo*, 163. For a discussion of the relationship between the publishing companies and the textbook commissions for this period, see Galfrè, *Il regime degli editori*, especially 14–17. For a compilation of all the books the commissions approved between 1923 and 1928, see Ascenzi and Sani, *Il libro per la scuola tra idealismo e fascismo*.

116. Fedele, "Decreto ministeriale 31 luglio 1926. Approvazione dei libri di testo per le scuole elementari e per i corsi integrativi d'avviamento professionale," 2009–47.

117. Giovanni Gentile, "Relazioni sui libri di testo per le scuole elementari e popolari ed elenco dei libri approvati. Supplemento 2 al n. 26 del 28 giugno 1923," 1–46; Fedele, "Decreto ministeriale 31 luglio 1926. Approvazione dei libri di testo per le scuole elementari e per i corsi integrativi d'avviamento professionale = rettifiche," 2441–42.

118. Viari, "Relazione della commissione ministeriale per l'esame dei libri di testo da adottarsi nelle scuole elementari."

119. Arrigo Solmi, "I libri e la scuola," 1926 (ACS, MPI, DG del personale e degli affari generali e amministrativi [1910–1964], box 206, folder 1129), 2.

120. Vittorio Emanuele III, "Regio decreto 18 marzo 1928, n. 780," 1569.

121. Michele Romano and Scarascia, "Relazione della Commissione ministeriale centrale per l'esame dei libri di testo da adottarsi nelle scuole elemtari e nei

corsi integrativi di avviamento professionale"; Belluzzo, "Decreto ministeriale 5 settembre 1928"; Belluzzo, "Decreto ministeriale 28 novembre 1928."

122. Michele Romano and Scarascia, "Relazione della Commissione ministeriale centrale per l'esame dei libri di testo da adottarsi nelle scuole elemtari e nei corsi integrativi di avviamento professionale"; Belluzzo, "Decreto ministeriale 5 settembre 1928."

123. Belluzzo, "Decreto ministeriale 28 novembre 1928"; Fedele, "Decreto ministeriale 7 luglio 1928."

124. Belluzzo, "Decreto ministeriale 20 novembre 1928."

125. Pietro Fedele, "Memo on Gentile Reform," Rome, 1928 (ACS, Archivio personale Pietro Fedele, box 4).

126. Colombu, "Aspetti della pedagogia di Giovanni Gentile," 17.

127. Giuseppe Lombardo Radice to Giovanni Gentile, June 30, 1924 (FGG, ser. 1, subseries 1, folder "Lombardo Radice a G. Gentile, 1922–1931"); Giuseppe Lombardo Radice to Giovanni Gentile, October 25, 1924 (FGG, ser. 1, subseries 1, folder "Lombardo Radice a G. Gentile, 1922–1931").

128. Tomasi, *Idealismo e fascismo nella scuola italiana*, 71–72.

129. Ostenc, *La scuola italiana durante il fascismo*, 100; Lyttelton, *The Seizure of Power*, 406; Koon, *Believe, Obey, Fight*, 60–61; Tomasi, *Idealismo e fascismo nella scuola italiana*, 181.

2. "Reawakening the Spirit"

1. Esposito, *Nei lieti riposi, classe quarta*, 69.

2. For other examples, see Casale, *A cuore aperto: Libro di lettura per la quinta classe*; Giromini, *Bontà, studio, lavoro, quarta classe*; Cuman Pertile, *Per le vie del mondo*, part 3, "Nel regno dei nani e dei giganti"; Cuman Pertile, *Fiori di campo*.

3. Tomaso Rinaldi, "La bella giovinezza italica," 29.

4. For a linguistic history of the idea of a nation, see Greenfeld, *Nationalism*, 3–9.

5. Renan, "What Is a Nation?," 18–19.

6. Gellner, *Nations and Nationalism*, 5.

7. Smith, *National Identity*, 82–83, 123–42.

8. Greenfeld, *Nationalism*, 12.

9. Gellner, *Nations and Nationalism*, 48–49. Adrian Lyttelton has appropriately qualified the invented nature of nationalist pasts by pointing out the importance of nationalists' building on existing tradition. Lyttelton, "Creating a National Past," 28–29. Of course, this definition of nationalism is only one aspect of the concept. For a nuanced discourse on the complexity of the terms *nation* and *nationalism*, as well as a literature review of the subjects, see Karolewski and Suszycki, *The Nation and Nationalism in Europe*.

10. On the need for the concurrent evolutions of market economies, bureaucratic infrastructures, and popular governments to promote nationalism, see Calhoun, *Nationalism*, 10–11. These features of Western modernity allowed for more-unified political and economic systems, through which authorities could

more easily control the information available to and behavior expected of a nation's population. In turn, this growth in political control and information access led to the greater ability of centralized bureaucracies to mold a common national character with which it could legitimize its own foundation according to the modern concept of the nation-state. Of course, not all scholars agree with this argument. Hastings, *The Construction of Nationhood*; Smith, *National Identity*, chap. 3.

11. Esposito, *Nei lieti riposi, classe quinta*, 56.

12. Pietro Romano, *Per una nuova coscienza pedagogica*, 42–43.

13. Esposito, *Nei lieti riposi, classe seconda*, 45.

14. Domenichelli, *L'adunata, quinta classe*, 23.

15. Anderson, *Imagined Communities*, 44, 145; Hastings, *The Construction of Nationhood*, 31.

16. Ostenc, *La scuola italiana durante il fascismo*, 77.

17. Ostenc, *La scuola italiana durante il fascismo*, 75.

18. Oreste Barbieri, "I nuovi orizzonti della scuola elementare italiana," *Il Veneto*, November 17, 1923, in Barbieri, *Direzione didattica italiana*; Calò, *Problemi vivi e orizzonti nuovi dell'educazione nazionale*, 183.

19. Crocioni, "La cultura regionale nella 'Riforma Gentile,'" 9.

20. Crocioni, "La cultura regionale nella 'Riforma Gentile,'" 10.

21. For an analysis of this part of Gentile's theory, see Dainotto, "'Tramonto' and 'Risorgimento,'" 249–50; Klein, *La politica linguistica del fascismo*, 27–57. This theory supported the ideas of pedagogue and folklorist Giovanni Crocioni (1870–1954). Cavazza, *Piccole patrie*, 44–54. Separate textbooks were published for the different provinces in order to facilitate the transition between local language and official Italian. See Gliozzi, *Su' calavrisi*; Tagliavini, *Esercizi di traduzione dai dialetti dell'Emilia*.

22. Cuman Pertile, *Primi voli*, 161.

23. The 1921 census reported that Venezia Tridentina (now known as Trentino-Alto Adige) contained 408,385 Italian speakers, 195,650 German speakers, and 18,253 Ladino speakers. Venezia Giulia (now known as Friuli Venezia Giulia) contained 479,591 Italian speakers, 50,589 Ladino speakers, 92,800 Serbo-Croatian speakers, 4,185 German speakers, 258,944 Slovene speakers, and 1,644 Romanian speakers. Istituto centrale di statistica, *Censimento della popolazione del Regno d'Italia al 1 dicembre 1921*, 19.

24. Giovanni Gentile, "R. D. 1 ottobre 1923, n. 2185—Ordinamento dei gradi scolastici e dei programmi didattici dell'istruzione elementare."

25. Scroccaro, *Dall'aquila bicipite alla croce uncinata*, 56–57, 83–84; De Fort, *La scuola elementare dall'Unità alla caduta del fascismo*, 372–77.

26. Di Michele, *L'italianizzazione imperfetta*, 218. For a contemporary discussion of Italianization measures in these areas, see Ministero della Pubblica Istruzione, "La ricostituzione della italianità nella zona di confine (1918–1928)," Rome Provveditorato Generale dello Stato Libreria, 1929 (ACS, PCM 1928–1930 3.2.6.8651).

27. Hagen, "The Most German of Towns," 209. On the modern Greek case, see Peckham, *National Histories, Natural States*. On the British and American cases, see Daniels, *Fields of Vision*.

28. Cuman Pertile, *Fiori di campo*, 258.

29. Giovanni Gentile, "Circolare n. 36. Pellegrinaggio alla tomba del milite ignoto," 1483–84; Giovanni Gentile, "Circolare n. 99. I Congresso nazionale di turismo educativo," 4334.

30. Agnew, "European Landscape and Identity," 216.

31. Aliotta, *La formazione dello spirito nello stato fascista*, 203.

32. Esposito, *Nei lieti riposi, classe quinta*, 7.

33. Meletti, *Il libro fascista del balilla*, 96. Also Casale, *A cuore aperto: Libro di lettura per la terza classe*, 85. For an analysis of Fascism's use of *romanità*—or Romanness—in its rhetoric, see Arthurs, *Excavating Modernity*. On Fascism's use of history more generally, see Fogu, *The Historic Imaginary*.

34. Marchetti, *Alle soglie della vita*, 13.

35. Tomaso Sillani, "Cultura fascista per l'Italia fascista: Commento alla lettera di Augusto Turati," 1926 (ACS, MPI, DG del personale e degli affari generali ed amministrativi [1910–1964], box 206, folder 1129). On Mussolini's project to redevelop Rome, see Painter, *Mussolini's Rome*. For an interesting discussion of Mussolini's modern goals for excavating Rome, see Arthurs, *Excavating Modernity*, chap. 3. More will be said about this project in chapter 3.

36. Agnew, "European Landscape and Identity," 219.

37. Liburdi, "L'insegnamento della storia del Risorgimento italiano nella scuola elementare," 1.

38. Gibelli, *Il popolo bambino*, 179–83.

39. *Balilla: Almanacco per i giovanetti italiani, anno scolastico 1926–1927*, 29.

40. Ostenc, *La scuola italiana durante il fascismo*, 86.

41. Giurlanda, *Il nuovo giorno per giorno*, 12.

42. For more on Italy at the Paris Peace Conference and the Treaty of London, see Macmillan, *Paris 1919*, 279–305.

43. Forges Davanzati, "Fascismo giovane," 12; Gabrielli, "La coscienza nazionale e la scuola," 193–94.

44. John R. Gillis, introduction to Gillis, *Commemorations*, 11.

45. Similar sites were erected in Britain, France, Belgium, and Portugal, as well as the United States, in the early 1920s. Winter, *Sites of Memory, Sites of Mourning*, 25–26.

46. Technically, the Vittoriano would not be completed until 1935. Koon, *Believe, Obey, Fight*, 27.

47. Marchetti, *Alle soglie della vita*, 37.

48. Domenichelli, *L'adunata, quarta classe*, 159.

49. Nicolò Giurlanda, *A voi, bimbi d'Italia!*, 45.

50. Cuman Pertile, *Primi voli*, 219.

51. Gaetano Salvemini, an Italian émigré during the Fascist regime, provides statistics that indicate the relative lack of success during the first years of the Battle for Wheat. Salvemini, "Mussolini's Battle of Wheat."

52. Fedele, "Circolare n. 25. Giornata coloniale italiana," 116.

53. For examples of Mussolini's earlier arguments against colonialism, see Mussolini, "Tripoli," 59; Mussolini, "Lo sciopero generale di protesta contro l'impresa di Tripoli," 61–73.

54. Curti, "L'esempio di Roma imperiale," 114–15. See also Giromini, *Bontà, studio, lavoro, quarta classe*, 119–20.

55. Bottai, *Mussolini costruttore d'impero*, 34.

56. Casale, *A cuore aperto: Libro di lettura per la terza classe*, 113.

57. Casale, *A cuore aperto: Libro di lettura per la quinta classe*, 261–62.

58. Codignola, *Il problema dell'educazione nazionale in Italia*, 150.

59. Giromini, *Bontà, studio, lavoro, terza classe*, 45–46.

60. Esposito, *Nei lieti riposi, classe prima*, 19.

61. Giromini, *Bontà, studio, lavoro, quarta classe*, 116; Casale, *A cuore aperto: Libro di lettura per la quarta classe*, 140–41.

62. Marchetti, *Alle soglie della vita*, 12.

63. Ciarlantini, *I miei amici di Villa Castelli*, 36.

64. Giovanni Gentile, "Il regime e l'istruzione," 1929 (FGG, ser. 2 manocritti gentiliani, box 112, articolo pubblicato), 3–4; Giovanni Gentile, "Libertà d'insegnamento e scuola di Stato," 5–6.

65. Giovanni Gentile, "Draft of 'L'educazione nazionale,'" 2–3.

66. Sagramola, *Giovanni Gentile nella cultura e nella scuola italiana*, 4. For a critique of this duality, see Borghi, *Educazione e autorità nell'Italia moderna*, 236–38.

67. Sagramola, *Giovanni Gentile nella cultura e nella scuola italiana*, 50.

68. Giovanni Gentile, *The Reform of Education*, 40, 190. Cambi, "Gentile pedagogista ed educatore nazionale," 113, 122–23.

69. Grassini and Borella, *Per la patria di domani*, 9. Also Bodrero, "Presentazione a S. E. il Ministro della pubblica istruzione," 5.

70. Esposito, *Il nostro paese*, 15.

71. Berezin, *Making the Fascist Self*, 41, 50–53.

72. Berezin, *Making the Fascist Self*, 55.

73. Chiarini, *Il giuoco dei balilla*, 8.

74. Consiglio nazionale delle donne italiane, "Terzo congresso indetto dal Consiglio nazionale delle donne italiane," 1.

75. De Marinis, *Resurrezione eroica*, 80.

76. Bertarelli, "Metodi educativi per le massaie e le madri."

77. Associazione nazionale per gli interessi del mezzogiorno d'Italia, *Esposizione sintetica dei programmi didattici*, 42. For Gentile's opinion of lessons in home economics, see Giovanni Gentile, "Lavori donneschi," n.d. (FGG, ser. 6 attività politica, AUI: riforma della scuola, folder 4, subfolder 52, programmi).

78. Bertarelli, "Metodi educativi per le massaie e le madri," 81.

79. Esposito, *Nei lieti riposi, classe quarta*, 7.

80. Benadusi, *The Enemy of the New Man*, 15.

81. Domenichelli, *L'adunata, terza classe*, 67.

82. Esposito, *Nei lieti riposi, classe terza*, 30.

83. For a discussion of the connections between virility and martial culture in the creation of the New Italian, see Benadusi, *The Enemy of the New Man*, chap. 1.

84. Casale, *A cuore aperto: Libro di lettura per la quarta classe*, 2–3; Marchetti, *Alle soglie della vita*; Ciarlantini, *I miei amici di Villa Castelli*, 64–65.

85. Fedele, "Tanti scolari, tanti balilla," 7.

86. Marchetti, *Alle soglie della vita*, 12.

87. As quoted in "L'O.N.B. nei primi dieci anni di vita," 267.

88. Grandi, *I giovani di Mussolini*, 44.

89. Grandi, *I giovani di Mussolini*, 132–33.

90. Ciarlantini, *I miei amici di Villa Castelli*, 83–84.

91. Augusto Carelli, "A proposito dei rapporti tra condizioni fisiche e qualità mentali nei fanciulli."

92. Chiarini, *Il giuoco dei balilla*, vi.

93. Chiarini, *Il giuoco dei balilla*, 7.

94. Marchetti, "I Balilla e la scuola," 274–75.

95. Morgagni, "Discipliniamo lo sport," 6.

96. Associazione nazionale per gli interessi del mezzogiorno d'Italia, *Esposizione sintetica dei programmi didattici*, 54.

97. Esposito, *Nei lieti riposi, classe prima*, 15.

98. Marchetti, "In margine al regolamento per l'Opera nazionale Balilla," 120–21; "Lo sport dei balilla," 69.

99. Augusto Carelli, "Fattori sociali nella vita morale della donna," 622.

100. Opera nazionale balilla, *Programma di educazione fisica*, 4.

101. Morgagni, "Le 'ferie' dei balilla e degli avanguardisti," 5.

102. Morgagni, "I boschi e l'Opera nazionale balilla," 5–6.

103. Morgagni, "Le 'ferie' dei balilla e degli avanguardisti," 6.

104. Casale, *A cuore aperto: Libro di lettura per la quarta classe*, 201. "Giovinezza," which translates to "Youth," was the official anthem of the PNF, its regime, and the Italian armed forces during the Fascist era. It became the official anthem of the Nazi-Fascist state, the Italian Social Republic (the RSI or the Republic of Salò) from 1943 to 1945.

105. Giromini, *Bontà, studio, lavoro, terza classe*, 76–77.

106. Cuman Pertile, *Fiori di campo*, 270.

107. Cuman Pertile, *Fiori di campo*, 14–15, 178.

108. Capodivacca, *La giovine aurora*, 33.

109. Dogliani, *Il fascismo degli italiani*, 102–3; Bellassai, "The Masculinity Mystique," 318–20; Ipsen, *Dictating Demography*, 117–19.

110. Marchetti, "Anti-urbanesimo"; Augusto Carelli, "Campi di gioco e delinquenza giovanile," 746.

111. D'Ormea, "Le cattedre ambulanti di assistenza materna e puericultura e la protezione del lattante," 704.

112. Santini, "Le opere assistenziali dei Fasci femminili," 6.

113. Dussin and Dossa, *Il libro del contadino*, inside cover.

114. Associazione nazionale per gli interessi del mezzogiorno d'Italia, *Esposizione sintetica dei programmi didattici*, 40.

115. Tomaso Rinaldi, "La bella giovinezza italica," 22. Quercia Tanzarella, "L'attività dell'Opera Nazionale Balilla." The government founded Istituto LUCE in 1924, primarily to combat the overwhelming number of foreign movies coming into the country. Ricci, "L'Opera nazionale balilla," 934–35. LV, "L'industria cinematografica e la difesa morale del fanciullo," 276–80.

116. Chiarini, *Il giuoco dei balilla*, 31.

117. Of course, in the rural schools, these concerns overlapped considerably. According to one source, many times physical education in rural schools entailed gardening or manual labor in addition to other exercises. Ltd. The Argus Press, "The Alto Adige: Articles Reprinted from *The Morning Post*, May, 1928," London, UK: Argus Press, 1928 (ACS, MCP, Reports, box 19, folder 13, subfolder 2 Alto Adige).

118. Marcucci, *Il programma didattico*, 68.

119. Lo Monaco-Aprile, "La protezione igienica della razza nella fabbrica e nella scuola," 48.

120. Associazione nazionale per gli interessi del mezzogiorno d'Italia, *Esposizione sintetica dei programmi didattici*, 37.

3. From Instruction to Education

1. The literature on the MRF, both contemporary and retrospective, is extensive. For collections of documents associated with the exhibition, see Schnapp, *Anno X*; Fioravanti, *Partito nazionale fascista*; Painter, *Mussolini's Rome*, 25–30; Golsan, *Fascism, Aesthetics, and Culture*, 30–37. For a walk-through of the exhibit in English, see Stone, *The Patron State*, chap. 4.

2. Di Marco, "La Mostra della Rivoluzione," 200.

3. Stone, *The Patron State*, 142.

4. For a description of each room, see Fioravanti, *Partito nazionale fascista*.

5. Mussolini moved his office from the Palazzo Chigi to the Palazzo Venezia in 1929. Painter, *Mussolini's Rome*, 2. For a discussion of "the nexus between Rome-as-idea . . . and Rome-as-place," see Arthurs, *Excavating Modernity*, 50–90.

6. Painter, *Mussolini's Rome*, 22–25; Arthurs, *Excavating Modernity*, 60.

7. Margherita Sarfatti, "Architettura, arte e simbolo alla Mostra del fascismo," *Architettura* 12 (1933), as quoted in Schnapp, *Anno X*, 69.

8. Di Marco, "La Mostra della Rivoluzione," 200. Italics added.

9. Ercole, "Circolare n. 3. Visita alla Mostra della Rivoluzione Fascista," 199.

10. A sample train ticket in the Mitchell Wolfson Jr. Collection at the Wolfsonian Museum in Miami Beach, Florida, shows that the fare was reduced as much as 70 percent, and that the ticket was accompanied not only by free entrance to the exhibition but also by coupons for various stores and services within Rome. Of course, some people likely used the reduced fares to take a vacation in the capital, only stopping at the exhibit briefly to validate their tickets. Even so, the scheme forced these opportunists into the galleries.

11. Mussolini, "Il discorso dell'Ascensione," 379.

12. Ludwig, *Talks with Mussolini*, 95. For a more theoretical discussion of Fascism's general need for a continued revolution once in power, see Paxton, *The Anatomy of Fascism*, 141–47. It is unclear what specific movements Mussolini had in mind in this context, but one can guess from a number of other, less successful attempts at Fascistic governments, such as General Primo de Rivera's military dictatorship in Spain, Antonio de Oliviera Salazar's rule in Portugal, and Leon Degrelle's Christus-Rex movement in Belgium. For an overview of many of these movements, see Weber, *Varieties of Fascism*; Payne, *Fascism*.

13. For the political maneuverings associated with these changes, see De Felice, *Mussolini il fascista*, bk. 2, most directly 161–63, 204–5.

14. On the long negotiations that led to the Lateran Accords, see Sale, *La Chiesa di Mussolini*, 205–44; De Felice, *Mussolini il fascista*, bk. 2, 383–486. For a copy of the official documents, see Pollard, *The Vatican and Italian Fascism, 1929–32*, 197–215. Of course, the presence of a parallel source of moral authority placed crucial limitations on the totalitarian potential of the Fascist regime. The church was allowed to maintain the extracurricular organizations of Catholic Action (Azione cattolica), whose existence established a critical distance between the overwhelmingly Catholic population and the Fascist government. Additionally, parochial schools continued to flourish into the 1930s, though they, too, were required to assign the state textbooks after 1930. Ricuperati, *La scuola italiana e il fascismo*, 14–16. In general, the policies of the church constrained Mussolini's projects, particularly in the realm of demographics. Ipsen, *Dictating Demography*, 75–78.

15. See the testimony of Miranda Miliotti, quoted in Grandi, *I giovani di Mussolini*, 323–24.

16. The idea of popular consensus in Fascist Italy is an intensely debated one. Most famously, Renzo De Felice termed the period 1929–1936 "the Years of Consensus." De Felice, *Mussolini il duce*, bk. 1, 3, 54–126. For an interesting discussion of the term's insufficiency in the context of a totalitarian state, see Corner, *The Fascist Party and Popular Opinion in Mussolini's Italy*, 7–8. It is my contention that although political and social tensions remained barely under the surface of Fascist control—both in the PNF and society at large—Mussolini managed to gain enough control and inspire enough fear that, at least superficially, there was the appearance of general support for the government and its policies.

17. Berardi, *Un balilla negli anni trenta*, 61.

18. Curico, "Nascere," 808.

19. Curico, "Un esempio per il mondo," 992.

20. Fabbri, *L'Opera nazionale per la protezione della maternità e dell'infanzia*, 20. These regulations mirrored similar policies enacted in France, particularly the 1920 ban on publicity about abortions and other contraceptive birth control. Schneider, *Quality and Quantity*, 41.

21. These taxes would increase again in 1936, when the government announced that they would also be applied to colonial residents. Ipsen, *Dictating Demog-*

raphy, 174–78. For a detailed, Fascist-era discussion of these measures, see Glass, *Population Policies and Movements in Europe*, 219–60.

22. Mussolini, "Il discorso dell'Ascensione," 364.

23. Gillette, *Racial Theories in Fascist Italy*, 41.

24. Benadusi, *The Enemy of the New Man*, see 87–110 for the legal debate.

25. Provinces, cities, and towns were also encouraged to establish local pro-natalist incentives for community members. "La giornata nazionale della madre e del fanciullo fissata dal duce per il 24 dicembre," 1.

26. "Anno dodicesimo," 1–2.

27. "Maternità e infanzia," 29.

28. Cutrufelli et al., *Piccole Italiane*, 93–95.

29. Alfieri, "La protezione della maternità di fronte al problema demografico," 281, 299.

30. "Mortalità infantile e mortinatalità."

31. Mussolini, "Il discorso dell'Ascensione," 361.

32. Lo Monaco-Aprile, *La protezione della maternità e dell'infanzia*, 5.

33. Fabbri, *L'Opera nazionale per la protezione della maternità e dell'infanzia*, 44–45.

34. Rodolfo Graziani, "Relazione sullo sviluppo della attività dell'Opera nazionale per la protezione della maternità e infanzia (1926–1930)," Rome, Stabilimento Tipografico R. Garroni, 1931 (ACS, MI, Opere pie, 1931–1933, box 35, folder "Circolari").

35. Caldwell, "Reproducers of the Nation."

36. Among the social illnesses Mussolini included were yellow fever, tuberculosis, cancer, alcoholism, pellagra, malaria, and Bolshevism. Mussolini, "Il discorso dell'Ascensione," 362–64.

37. Mussolini, "Il discorso dell'Ascensione," 367.

38. "Vicende della natività in Italia." For a discussion of this field and Pende's later work on endocrinology, orthogenesis, and racial theory, see Gillette, *Racial Theories in Fascist Italy*, 95–99. These beliefs followed in the footsteps of neo-Lamarckian theories stating that acquired attributes could be passed to one's offspring. On the other hand, Giuseppe Tallarico (a scholar who later became a member of Giacomo Acerbo's High Council on Demography and Race) directly questioned the ability to affect the quality and quantity of children through altered environments and firmly argued that all people were clearly not created equal. Tallarico, "Saggi di eugenica ambientale."

39. Lacchè, "Bonifica umana," 382–83.

40. "Le finalità scientifiche e i mezzi di indagine dell'Istituto biotipologico di Genova." By *ethnic*, it appears Pende referred to Italy's varied regional identities.

41. Fabbri, "La tutela morale dei minorenni," 6.

42. Lo Monaco-Aprile, *La protezione della maternità e dell'infanzia*, 40.

43. Tarlazzi, *Ripetenti d'eccezione, classe terza, 1936–1937*.

44. Bascone, "Ordiamento didattico della scuola elementare, grado preparatorio," 20–21; Belluzzo, *Le opere sussidiarie della scuola elementare in Italia*, 8.

45. Cammarata, *Pedagogia di Mussolini*, 13.

46. Giovanni Gentile to Ernesto Codignola, 1925 (FGG, ser. 1, subseries 1, folder "Gentile a Codignola, 1916–1943").

47. Minesso, *Giuseppe Belluzzo*, 208–11.

48. Belluzzo, *Le opere sussidiarie della scuola elementare in Italia*, 7.

49. Isnenghi, "Introduzione alla ristampa anastatica," 1–2.

50. Regarding the importance of a single national textbook in the forging of an imperial mindset, see Pes, "Becoming Imperialist."

51. Bacigalupi and Fossati, *Da plebe al popolo*, 161.

52. Bacigalupi and Fossati, *Da plebe al popolo*, 164.

53. Quoted in Grifone, *Primavera italica*, 9.

54. "L'adozione del 'testo unico' di stato per le scuole elementari," 1.

55. Belluzzo, "Legge 7 gennaio 1929, n. 5," 226–27.

56. "Il libro di stato nel prossimo anno scolastico," 255–56.

57. "Il libro di stato per le scuole elementari," 6.

58. It seems that a prominent children's author from the Liberal period, Oronzina Quercia Tanzarella (Ornella), was the primary author of the first- and second-grade textbooks, as well as those written for the colonies. Other textbook authors included Dina Belardinelli-Bucciarelli, Alessandro Marcucci, Grazia Deledda, Angiolo Silvio Novaro, and Roberto Forges Davanzati. For a full list of state textbooks in this period, see Bacigalupi and Fossati, *Da plebe al popolo*, 181, 196–97. This new approach to textbook adoption did not make publishing houses very happy; ultimately, the regime compromised by releasing a few different versions of each textbook (published by different companies). Galfrè, *Il regime degli editori*, 100–2.

59. "Il libro di stato per le scuole elementari," 15.

60. It was during Belluzzo's string of restructurings that Giuseppe Lombardo Radice proclaimed in a letter to Gentile, "Currently, your reform of elementary school is crumbling." Giuseppe Lombardo Radice to Giovanni Gentile, November 15, 1928 (FGG, ser. 1, subseries 1, folder "Lombardo Radice a G. Gentile, 1922–1931").

61. Dean of the R. Liceo Ginnasio G. B. Niccolini e F. D. Guerrazzi, "Memo to Benito Mussolini, Presidente del Consiglio dei Ministri," Livorno, October 9, 1929 (ACS, PCM 1928–1930 folder 1.1.2.8617).

62. Partito nazionale fascista, *Il cittadino soldato*, 39.

63. Cammarata, *Pedagogia di Mussolini*, 17.

64. Di Carlo, "Il passaggio di tutte le scuole elementari allo stato," 12.

65. Gini, "Scuola, eugenica, e Opera balilla," 5.

66. La Redazione, "Frequenza alla scuola e criminalità giovanile."

67. Gini, "Scuola, eugenica, e Opera balilla," 1.

68. Mario, "La collaborazione dei giovani," 99–100.

69. De Fort, *La scuola elementare dall'Unità alla caduta del fascismo*, 376.

70. Giovanni Battista Marziali to Benito Mussolini, September 29, 1932, (ACS, SPD [CO], folder 541.261/3).

71. Mario, "La collaborazione dei giovani," 99–100.

72. Ercole, "Circolare n. 59. (Gabinetto del Ministro). Compiti domestici nei giorni di vacanza," 2395–96.

73. Belluzzo, "Circolare n. 35. (Ufficio centrale del personale.) Sul vestire delle signore insegnanti e delle alunne nelle scuole," 807.

74. Covato, "Scuola e stereotipi di genere a Roma fra le due guerre," 121. See also Dogliani, *Il fascismo degli italiani*, 103.

75. Bonanni, "I giovanissimi e lo sport," 40–41.

76. "L'assistenza scolastica e il suo incremento," 35.

77. Renato Ricci, as quoted in Painter, *Mussolini's Rome*, 46, 40. For more on the academy, see Ponzio, *Shaping the New Man*, 59–71.

78. Opera nazionale balilla, *Il foro Mussolini*, 5.

79. "L'accademia femminile dell'O. N. B. a Orvieto," 56–57.

80. Renato Ricci, "Accademia femminile fascista di educazione fisica e giovanile," 1932 (ACS, PCM 1928–1930, folder 1.1.15.2104/56).

81. For an interesting comparison of ONB and Hitlerjugend teacher training, see Ponzio, *Shaping the New Man*, 108–9.

82. Cutrufelli et al., *Piccole Italiane*, 85.

83. Isola, *Abbassa la tua radio, per favore*, 122.

84. The ERR was run by a commission of nine members nominated by the Ministry of Communications, with representatives from the Ministries of Education, Finance, Communications, and Agriculture and Forestry, as well as from the General Fascist Confederation of Industries, the National Fascist Confederation of Commerce, the General Fascist Confederation of Agriculture, and the Confederation of Fascist Agricultural Inspectors. Mencarelli, *Inquadrati e fedeli*, 48.

85. Arcamone, "La radio rurale nelle scuole," 149.

86. Campanile, "La radio e i rurali," 14.

87. Foreign words were banned from film and print media between 1930 and 1934. Dogliani, *Il fascismo degli italiani*, 261.

88. According to a bulletin published by the MEN, between January and June 1934, 472 radios were put in schools in Piedmont, 110 in Liguria, 409 in Lombardy, 326 in the Venezie, 120 in Emilia and Romagna, 126 in Tuscany, 59 in Marche, 55 in Umbria, 89 in Lazio, 35 in Abruzzo and Molise, 83 in Campania, 45 in Apulia, 69 in Lucania, 34 in Calabria, 120 in Sicily, and 45 in Sardinia, for a grand total of 2,196 radios for an estimated 557,594 students and 12,539 teachers. Of those radios, 587 were placed in areas where there were not any others. Ercole, "Circolare n. 49. (Gabinetto). Radiotrasmissioni scolastiche dell'anno 1934–35," 2314–2315.

89. Vittorio Emanuele III, "Legge 15 giugno 1933, n. 791," 1647–48.

90. Ricci, "L'Opera nazionale balilla," 935. This compromise experienced some significant growing pains in 1931 when the regime argued that the church was using Catholic Action to reintroduce an Italian Catholic political party and consequently attempted to shut it down. The regime was not successful. Pollard, *The Vatican and Italian Fascism, 1929–32*, 133–66; Wolff, "Catholicism, Fascism and Italian Education from the Riforma Gentile to the Carta Della Scuola 1922–1939."

91. "La 'Casa del Balilla,'" 30–37.

92. "L'attività dell'Opera nazionale Balilla nell'anno VIII," 30.

93. Grassini, "Per un'azione totalitaria," 27.

94. Opera nazionale balilla, *Le vacanze dei balilla, classe prima*, 5.

95. "L'attività dell'Opera nazionale Balilla nell'anno VIII," 30.

96. Renato Ricci, "ONB: Relazione anno VIII," Rome, November 10, 1930 (ACS, PCM 1928–1930, box. 1.1.15.2104/56, folder "ONB: Relazione anno VIII"); "L'attività dell'Opera nazionale Balilla nell'anno VIII," 5. Emphasis original to source.

97. Ricci, "ONB: Relazione anno VIII," 84.

98. Renato Ricci, "ONB: Relazione anno IX," Rome, January 1932 (ACS, PCM 1928–1930, box 1.1.15.2104/56, folder "ONB: Relazione anno IX").

99. Ricci, "ONB: Relazione anno IX," 5.

100. Barbieri, *La scuola del littorio*, 33; Barbieri, *Direzione didattica italiana*.

4. From Fit to Fascist

1. Quoted in Genovesi, "Scuola e fascismo nel pistoiese," 30–31. Interestingly, this young student does remark that she wished there were also a portrait of the queen alongside the others. Gabriele D'Annunzio originally coined the exclamation "Eia! Eia! Alalà!" in the First World War and later appropriated it for his 1919 takeover of Fiume. Fascists subsequently adopted it as a cry of exaltation.

2. Genovesi, "Scuola e fascismo nel pistoiese," 30–31.

3. Bianca Lusena, *La fanciullezza*, 86.

4. Idir, "Scuola e Opera Balilla," 3.

5. Ferretti, *Esempi e idee per l'italiano nuovo*, 8–9.

6. Quercia Tanzarella, "L'Opera Balilla."

7. Opera nazionale balilla, *Giovinezza eroica*, 4.

8. Opera Balilla di Milano, *Manuale per il capo squadra balilla*, 31.

9. Cammarosano, "Concetto fascista dello stato," 19.

10. Cammarosano, "Concetto fascista dello stato," 19.

11. Fabbri, *L'Opera nazionale per la protezione della maternità e dell'infanzia*, 51–52.

12. Lastrucci, "La necessità della nuova Italia," 666–67.

13. Ilvento, "La salute della stirpe e la sua difesa," 927–28. On the academic tradition of this argument, see De Francesco, *The Antiquity of the Italian Nation*, 51–112.

14. Steiner, *Coltura fascista*, 1–2.

15. According to Aaron Gillette, the Mediterraneanist school dominated Italian academic circles of racial theorists in this period, with only a few Nordicists advocating the predominant German racial theories. Gillette, *Racial Theories in Fascist Italy*, 41–49.

16. Ludwig, *Talks with Mussolini*, 69–70.

17. Steiner, *Coltura fascista*, 4; Di Michele, *L'italianizzazione imperfetta*; Ministero dell'educazione nazionale, "Schema per l'albo di coltura regionale," Rome, July 27, 1932 (ACS, SPD [CO], box 809, folder 500.009).

18. De Fort, *La scuola elementare dall'Unità alla caduta del fascismo*, 376. This was a job for which Minister Giuliano nominated a commission of educational

experts headed by Professor Michele Romano. Ministero dell'educazione nazionale, "Schema per l'albo di coltura regionale," 1–2.

19. *Il libro della quarta classe elementare*; Adami and Domenichelli, *Il mio libro*.

20. *Il libro della terza classe elementare*, 322.

21. Quercia Tanzarella, *Il libro della seconda classe*, 23.

22. Opera nazionale balilla, *Le vacanze dei balilla, classe terza*, 14; Casale, *L'indispensabile*, 5–6; Opera nazionale balilla, *Le vacanze dei balilla, classe prima*, 31; *Il libro della quinta classe elementare*, 130.

23. Casale, *L'indispensabile*, 5–6.

24. Quercia Tanzarella, *Il libro della seconda classe*, 35.

25. Quercia Tanzarella, *Il libro della seconda classe*, 34–35.

26. Quercia Tanzarella, *Il libro della seconda classe*, 100; Opera nazionale balilla, *Le vacanze dei balilla, classe terza*, 20. For more on Mussolini's declaration, see Falasca-Zamponi, *Fascist Spectacle*, 91–92.

27. Longo, "Romanità della Rivoluzione fascista," 18.

28. Mabel Berezin, *Making the Fascist Self*, 67.

29. Quercia Tanzarella, *Il libro della seconda classe*, 100.

30. Emilio Gentile, *The Sacralization of Politics in Fascist Italy*, 65.

31. Benito Mussolini, *Scritti e discorsi dal 1927 al 1928*, 156.

32. Perroni, *Il Duce ai Balilla*, 66.

33. Fanelli, *Fascismo*, 6.

34. Meletti, *Civiltà fascista*, 96.

35. Adami and Domenichelli, *Il mio libro*, 22–23.

36. For an overview of topics, see Pes, "Becoming Imperialist," 605.

37. *Il libro della terza classe*, 212. Also Dogliani, *Il fascismo degli italiani*, 252.

38. *Il libro della terza classe*, 279. The general exception was the inclusion of highlights from the Italian Renaissance in fifth-grade textbooks. *Il libro della quinta classe elementare*, 41–45.

39. *Il libro della terza classe*, 327.

40. For a lengthier discussion of the importance of World War I in Fascist lessons about sacrifice and manliness, see Mosse, *The Image of Man*, 156–58.

41. *Il libro della terza classe*, 327.

42. Roberto Paribeni, "Gli ebrei," in *Il libro della quarta classe elementare*, 74.

43. *Il libro della quarta classe elementare*, 98.

44. *Il libro della quarta classe elementare*, 98.

45. *Il libro della quarta classe elementare*, 142–43. For more on the Fascist understanding of Roman imperialism, see Pes, "Becoming Imperialist," 610.

46. Perroni, *Il Duce ai Balilla*, 51–52.

47. Perroni, *Il Duce ai Balilla*, 89.

48. Opera Balilla di Milano, *Manuale per il capo squadra balilla*, 15.

49. *Il libro della quinta classe elementare*, 28.

50. *Il libro della quinta classe elementare*, 35.

51. *Il libro della quinta classe elementare*, 124–25.

52. *Il libro della quinta classe elementare*, 99–101.

53. *Il libro della quarta classe elementare*, 180.

54. Fanciulli, *I grandi navigatori italiani*, 1.

55. *Il libro della quarta classe elementare*, 258–59.

56. Steiner, *Coltura fascista*, 25.

57. Meletti, *Civiltà fascista*, 107.

58. Meletti, *Civiltà fascista*, 103.

59. Pretelli, "Education in the Italian Colonies during the Interwar Period," 284.

60. Fanelli, *Amore di terra lontana*, 11.

61. Fanelli, *Amore di terra lontana*, 55, 61–62.

62. *Il libro della terza classe*, 283–84.

63. Casale, *L'indispensabile*, 88.

64. Quercia Tanzarella, "L'Opera Balilla," 26.

65. Lusena, *La fanciullezza*.

66. La redazione, "La funzione del gioco nell'infanzia," 1236.

67. Opera nazionale balilla, *Metodo per l'educazione fisica dei balilla*, 120.

68. Opera nazionale balilla, "Norme programmatiche e regolamentari per l'organzzazione delle piccole e giovani italiane," x.

69. "L'attività dell'Opera nazionale Balilla nell'anno VIII," 26.

70. Quercia Tanzarella, "L'Opera Balilla," 17.

71. Quercia Tanzarella, "L'Opera Balilla," 17.

72. Augusto Carelli, "La salute degli scolari e il profitto scolastico," 1025.

73. Opera nazionale balilla, *Le vacanze dei balilla, classe prima*, 9.

74. Sinisi, "La propaganda e le gare d'igiene nelle scuole elementari," 44.

75. La Patriottica, *La Patriottica, Bari*. Members were responsible for purchasing these uniforms from private companies, which meant that families incurred a significant financial burden with their children's participation. Gibelli, *Il popolo bambino*, 326–27.

76. Opera nazionale balilla, *Le vacanze dei balilla, classe prima*, 14.

77. Ministero della educazione nazionale, "Report Card for Franca Rizzi, 1931–1932," Foggia scuole elementari pubbliche a Foggia, 1932 (Wolfsonian Library, XC2005.01.3.1 [.2, .3, .4, and .5]).

78. Grifone, *Primavera italica*, 291.

79. Lanzalone, "Il dovere di essere belle?," 1–2.

80. Opera nazionale balilla, *La capo squadra Piccola italiana*, 9–10.

81. Opera nazionale balilla, *La capo squadra Piccola italiana*, 13.

5. Libro e moschetto

1. De Vecchi, "La politica scolastica del governo fascista," 108–9.

2. De Vecchi, "La politica scolastica del governo fascista," 113.

3. De Vecchi, "La politica scolastica del governo fascista," 115.

4. Roughly one hundred individuals were at the original meeting in Milan's Piazza San Sepulcro on March 23, 1919, when Mussolini declared the founding

of the *fasci di combattimento*. Those who were present—and remained Fascist—earned acclaim throughout the Fascist period for their early support.

5. For a brief biography of Cesare Maria De Vecchi di Val Cismon, see Setta, *Tra papa, Duce e re*, especially 12.

6. Ostenc, *La scuola italiana durante il fascismo*, 214. Of course, the idea of what constitutes "true" or "authentic" Fascism is vague and controversial at best.

7. De Felice, *Mussolini il duce*, bk. 1, chap. 4, see especially 323. Aristotle Kallis pushes back against the characterization of the period 1925–35 as the "decade of good behavior," convincingly arguing that international affairs was consistently a concern of the regime, despite international perception. Kallis, *Fascist Ideology*, 69–72.

8. Gillette, *Racial Theories in Fascist Italy*, 44. We also see this conversation between the two dictatorships—both agreements and conflicts—in the form of an active relationship between the ONB (and later the GIL) and the Hitlerjugend from 1933 until 1945. Ponzio, *Shaping the New Man*, 118–37, 171–98.

9. The literature on Nazi racism and racial policies is rich and deep. For a study of German racial science before and during the Nazi regime, see Weindling, *Health, Race and German Politics between National Unification and Nazism, 1870–1945*. For an outline of Hitler's racial theories, see Burleigh and Wippermann, *The Racial State*, 37–43. To place Nazi racism in the larger context, see Turda and Weindling, "*Blood and Homeland*."

10. Loffredo, "Dalla politica demografica alla politica della famiglia," 163.

11. For an interesting analysis of Fascism's efforts to raise "imperial consciousness" through commercial advertisements, see Pinkus, "Shades of Black in Advertising and Popular Culture"; Pinkus, *Bodily Regimes*, 22–81.

12. Ebner, *Ordinary Violence in Mussolini's Italy*, 95, 132, 181–84; Bellassai, "The Masculinity Mystique," 322–25.

13. Tauro, "La missione del maestro," 100.

14. Montanari, *I programmi per le scuole rurali dell'Opera Balilla*, 46.

15. Orioli, "Il partito e i bimbi," 6.

16. Marzolo, "La scuola rurale dell'Opera Balilla," 17.

17. Marzolo, "La scuola rurale dell'Opera Balilla," 20.

18. Ercole, "Circolare n. 49. (Gabinetto). Radiotrasmissioni scolastiche dell'anno 1934–35," 2314–15.

19. According to the average exchange rates given for 1936 ($.072916/lire) and 1940 ($.050407/lire), such spending translates to an approximate increase from $50,826 to $67,027. Board of Governors of the Federal Reserve System (U.S.), *Banking and Monetary Statistics, 1914–1941*, 673.

20. Istituto centrale di statistica, *Sommario di statistiche storiche dell'Italia, 1861–1975*, 59.

21. Arcamone, "La radio rurale nelle scuole," 148.

22. Fanelli, *Il mio tesoretto*, 38; Ercole, "La scuola elementare in regime fascista," 375. On the dual roles of "modernity" and "tradition" in twentieth-century ide-

ologies, see Kiernan, *Blood and Soil*, 393–570. For the role of landscape and peasant life in Nazi ideology, see Mosse, *The Crisis of German Ideology*, 16–25. For a case study of Nazi idealization of small town life, see Hagen, "The Most German of Towns," 207–27.

23. Direzione e amministrazione di "Italia maestra," *La scuola rurale nell'Opera balilla*, 40–41.

24. Campanile, "La radio e i rurali."

25. Toscano, *L'educazione dei Balilla e delle Piccole Italiane*, 18. This modification of Gentile's 1923 reforms appears to have distressed the philosopher. A letter from the national schoolbook commission charged with overseeing modifications to the state elementary textbook delimit a number of his concerns about the decrease in emphasis on learning Italian organically through the mastery of local dialects. The commission responded delicately, explaining that the changes had attempted to ensure the proper understanding of Italian grammar and composition while still supporting the relative "spontaneity" of the teachers and students. La commissione, "La opportunità di rinnovare il Libro di Stato per le scuole elementari," Rome, April 24, 1934 (FGG, ser. 6: Attività politica, AUI: Riforma della scuola. SF.4, 52. Programmi).

26. Bargellini, "Del libro unico," 214. Piero Bargellini was also a signatory of the *Manifesto of Racial Scientists* in 1938 and remained in public office until his death in 1980.

27. Bargellini, "Del libro unico," 214.

28. Ercole, "Circolare n. 5. (Direzione generale per l'istruzione elementare). Settimanale 'Il Balilla,'" 163–64.

29. Ercole, "Circolare n. 5. (Direzione generale per l'istruzione elementare). Settimanale 'Il Balilla'"; Ercole, "Circolare n. 14. (Direzione generale per l'istruzione elementare). Settimanale 'Il Balilla,'" 551.

30. Anderson, *Imagined Communities*, 44.

31. De Grazia, *The Culture of Consent*, 57–58.

32. Antonietta Ferrari to Benito Mussolini, 1934 (MPI, DG istruzione elementare, Div. I, box 164, folder "Fascicoli personali").

33. Costanzo Ciarla, "Rapporto informativo annuale (da spedire al R. Ispettore scolastico) di Condiglioti Giuseppe," 1934 (ACS, MPI, DG istruzione elemenatere, Div. I, box 32, folder "Fascicoli personali").

34. Marrella, *I diari della gioventù italianissima*, 231.

35. De Vecchi, "Il discorso del ministro De Vecchi ai fanciulli d'Italia," 198.

36. Again, the letter to Giovanni Gentile from the national schoolbook commission reveals that the regime was increasingly interested in limiting the pieces of history and geography to those that emphasized Italy's grandeur. Books were to include less information on ancient history that was not Roman and more on events since 1918. La commissione, "La opportunità di rinnovare il Libro di Stato per le scuole elementari." On the roles of imperialism and *romanità* in the definition of the New Italian during the mid-1930s, see Pes, "Becoming Imperialist," 608.

37. Strata, *La patria fascista*, 20.

38. Strata, *La patria fascista*, 9.

39. Kallis, *Fascist Ideology*, 35–38.

40. Pretelli, "Education in the Italian Colonies during the Interwar Period," 284.

41. The majority of scholarship on early Italian colonialism has focused on this embarrassment. Conti Rossini, *Italia ed Etiopia dal trattato d'Uccialli alla Battaglia di Adua*; Crispi, *La prima guerra d'Africa*. On the role Adwa played in Italian national consciousness in the Liberal period, see Finaldi, *Italian National Identity in the Scramble for Africa*, 13–21.

42. Vittorio Pisani, "Il soldato d'Italia temprato al clima del fascismo . . . ," notebook cover, 1930–39, Wolfsonian–Florida International University, Miami Beach, Florida, Mitchell Wolfson Jr. Collection.

43. For Mussolini's own words, see Partito nazionale fascista, "Foglio d'ordini: Gran Consiglio del Fascismo, Riunione dell'11 marzo XVI-E.F.," Gran consiglio del Fascismo, 1938 (ACS, MCP, Gabinetto, box 85, folder "Varie"). On the use of children's literature to fulfill this need, see Giorgi, "Forging the New Man."

44. Meletti, *Il libro fascista del balilla*, 96.

45. Quercia Tanzarella, "Un prezioso documentario (lettere di bimbi e di combattenti)," 97.

46. Pes, *La costruzione dell'impero fascista*, especially 101–4.

47. Gregorio, "Generazione dell'impero," 9.

48. Benedetti, "Civiltà e barbarie," 4.

49. G. E. P., "Le nostre colonie," 6.

50. Fanelli, *I fiori più belli*, 5.

51. Bottai, *Mussolini costruttore d'impero*, 26.

52. Benedetti, "L'Italia e la schiavitù in Abissinia," 12; Opera nazionale balilla, *La capo squadra Piccola italiana*, 104–9; Benedetti, "La giustizia in Abissinia," 4. For the official Italian analysis of the Ethiopian system of slavery, see League of Nations, *Dispute between Ethiopia and Italy*, 41–42, 46–58. Italians were not the only ones to remark on Ethiopia's system of slavery. Min. Murray, "English (British) Evidence against Ethiopia," (ACS, MCP, NUPIE, box 32, folder 119, subfolder "Documenti inglesi contro l'Europa"). For English-language scholarship on the Ethiopian slave economy, see Edwards, "Slavery, the Slave Trade, and the Economic Reorganization of Ethiopia 1916–1935"; Ahmad, "Trading in Slaves in Bela-Shangul and Gumuz, Ethiopia"; Fernyhough, "Slavery and the Slave Trade in Southern Ethiopia."

53. Benedetti, "L'Italia e la schiavitù in Abissinia"; Oreste Gasperini, *Ente radio rurale radioprogramma scolastico n. 93 del 17 maggio 1937-XV: L'impero fascista*, Wolfsonian–Florida International University, Miami Beach, Florida, Mitchell Wolfson Jr. Collection; Benedetti, "La giustizia in Abissinia."

54. "Quaderno di ____ [civiltà]," notebook cover, c. 1938, Wolfsonian–Florida International University, Miami Beach, Florida, Wolfsonian FIU Library Collection (ITA2).

55. Ahmad, "Trading in Slaves in Bela-Shangul and Gumuz, Ethiopia," 445.

56. For a discussion of the international politics surrounding the war, see Mack Smith, *Mussolini's Roman Empire*, chap. 5. For a discussion of the "popular" opinion of the war, see Corner, "L'opinione popolare italiana di fronte alla guerra d'Etiopia."

57. Mack Smith, *Mussolini's Roman Empire*, 71; Hoyt, *Mussolini's Empire*, 151.

58. De Felice, *Mussolini il duce*, bk. 1, specifically 642. De Grazia, *The Culture of Consent*, 58.

59. "Cronaca," 15.

60. Terhoeven, *Oro alla patria*, 9–10.

61. Berardi, *Un balilla negli anni trenta*, 63; De Grazia, *How Fascism Ruled Women*, 77–78.

62. Opera nazionale balilla, *Il capo squadra Balilla*; Scifoni, "Oro e braccia di italiani all'estero."

63. Comitato Comunale Vipiteno ONB, "Attività svolte nell'anno XIII dai ricordi gioiosi delle Organizzate di 3a classe," Vipiteno (ACS, Renato Ricci, archivio fotografica, box 2, folder 282–87).

64. Scifoni, "Oro e braccia di italiani all'estero," 7.

65. Pignatari, "La Gioventù italiana del littorio."

66. Mussolini, "Intervista al 'Matin,'" 1.

67. "Le leggi della nazione guerriera," 10.

68. *Balilla: Giovinezza*, 4.

69. Quoted in Rossi, *Diario di un balilla, 1932–1936*, 42.

70. Faudella, "Nazione preparata," 17–18.

71. Strata, *La patria fascista*, 40.

72. Vittorio Emanuele III, "Legge 31 dicembre 1934-XIII, n. 2150"; Vittorio Emanuele III, "Legge 31 dicembre 1934-XIII, n. 2152." For an analysis of this decision, see Bottoni, "La 'marcia da Roma' a scuola," 325–29.

73. Rapisarda, "La cultura militare nelle scuole," 8.

74. "Le leggi della nazione guerriera."

75. Resta, "Educazione guerriera ed eroica," 417–18.

76. Toscano, *L'educazione dei Balilla e delle Piccole Italiane*, 12.

77. Cuesta, "Combattere," 17.

78. Orano, "Regime di stato," 57–58.

79. Opera nazionale balilla, *La capo squadra Piccola italiana*, 9–10; Opera nazionale balilla, *Il capo squadra Balilla*, 9; *Balilla: Giovinezza*, 1.

80. De Vecchi, "La politica scolastica del governo fascista," 113.

81. "Le leggi della nazione guerriera."

82. Direzione e amministrazione di "Italia maestra," *La scuola rurale nell'Opera balilla*, 11.

83. Direzione e amministrazione di "Italia maestra," *La scuola rurale nell'Opera balilla*, 10.

84. Opera nazionale balilla, *La capo squadra Piccola italiana*, 9–10.

85. Opera nazionale balilla, *La capo squadra Piccola italiana*, 84.

86. Piccoli, *The Youth Movement in Italy*, 19.

87. On the image of the woman in Nazi Germany, see Rupp, "Mother of the 'Volk," 375–76.

88. "L'accademia femminile dell'O. N. B. a Orvieto," 56.

89. "L'accademia femminile dell'O. N. B. a Orvieto," 56–57.

90. Mack Smith, *Mussolini's Roman Empire*, 57–58; Gillette, *Racial Theories in Fascist Italy*, 44; Pende, "Biologia delle razze ed unità spirituale mediterranea."

91. An exception to this generalization is an article that explored the benefits of state involvement in selecting the parents of Italy's children. Lancellotti, "L'eugenica." Nicola Pende, who would become a significant player in official state racism in the late 1930s, had also been peddling his vision of "biological" racism for quite some time. Pende, "Biologia delle razze ed unità spirituale mediterranea."

92. De Leva, "Demografia," 5; Lojacono, "La politica sociale del Fascismo."

93. Mauro Carelli, *Frammenti di lirica didattica*; Lacchè, "Bonifica umana," 382–83.

94. Opera nazionale per la protezione della maternità e dell'infanzia, *Origine e sviluppi dell'Opera nazionale per la protezione della maternità e dell'infanzia*, 31. See also Opera nazionale maternità e infanzia, "Protection of Maternity and Child Welfare in Italy."

95. Opera nazionale per la protezione della maternità e dell'infanzia, *Origine e sviluppi dell'Opera nazionale per la protezione della maternità e dell'infanzia*, 6.

6. Educating Rulers

1. It is unclear whether these five postcards present a complete series from a particular moment. Bertiglia did produce other postcards and illustrations regarding the conflict, but there is no complete inventory of his work on the subject.

2. Row, "Mobilizing the Nation."

3. Perhaps the most popular example of this phenomenon can be seen in Herge's 1931 graphic novel *Tintin in the Congo*. For a brief, scholarly analysis of this tendency in the British context, see McClintock, *Imperial Leather*, 49–51. On the development of Western ideas of children's innocence, see Bernstein, *Racial Innocence*, 4–8. Also see Bernstein, *Racial Innocence*, 30–36, for representations of "Black" (primarily American) "pickaninnies" and innocence.

4. Domenichelli, *L'adunata, terza classe*, 3; Fanelli, *Il mio tesoretto*, 46.

5. On the initial campaign, see Del Boca, *Italiani, brava gente?*, 185–203. Despite the declaration of the Italian Empire in May 1936, Italian troops continued to combat resistance until they were forced out of Ethiopia in 1941. Rochat, *Le guerre italiane in Libia e in Etiopia dal 1896 al 1939*, 48–61; Rochat, "The Italian Air Force in the Ethiopian War (1935–1936)," 43–44.

6. Del Boca, *The Ethiopian War, 1935–1941*, 14–15. For more on the WelWel incident, see Mockler, *Haile Selassie's War*, 37–43.

7. Mack Smith, *Mussolini's Roman Empire*, 72.

8. The violence of Italy's 1911–12 takeover of Libya was only surpassed by Graziani's bloody and repressive "pacification" campaign in the late 1920s and early 1930s. Ottolenghi, *Gli italiani e il colonialismo*, 25. During his tenure, Graziani con-

structed several concentration and labor camps for Libya's "problematic" nomadic peoples. Thousands of men, women, and children died in these camps, and Graziani earned the name the Butcher of Fezzan among Libya's Arabs. Ottolenghi, *Gli italiani e il colonialismo*; Di Sante and Hasan Sury, *Mostra foto-documentaria*; Del Boca, *Italiani, brava gente?*, 165–84; Rochat, *Le guerre italiane in Libia e in Etiopia dal 1896 al 1939*, 88–136; Labanca, "L'internamento coloniale italiana." He would use a similar approach in Ethiopia.

9. Badoglio, *The War in Abyssinia*, v.

10. Quoted in Del Boca, *The Ethiopian War, 1935–1941*, 21.

11. Mack Smith, *Mussolini's Roman Empire*, 67. According to Mack Smith, Mussolini did not consult the Fascist Grand Council before ordering the invasion of Ethiopia, "because he intended the victory to be very much his own personal success." Mack Smith, *Mussolini's Roman Empire*, 70. Alessandro Pes further argues that the participation of Fascist Party troops (from the MSVN) in the conflict proved Mussolini's determination that it be a *Fascist* victory for the nation. Pes, *La costruzione dell'impero fascista*, 106, 114.

12. Sources vary in the number of Italian troops involved. The cited number comes from Rochat, "La guerra italiana in Etiopia," 105.

13. Mack Smith, *Mussolini's Roman Empire*, 73. For copies of the original telegrams authorizing the use of chemical warfare, see Del Boca, *I gas di Mussolini*, 148–62.

14. Haile Selassie's requests for the League of Nations to investigate Italian acts of aggression before the war were collected in a 1935 volume. League of Nations, *Dispute between Abyssinia and Italy*.

15. For Ethiopian accounts of the chemical campaign, see Del Boca, *I gas di Mussolini*, 117–31. For more on Italy's use of aerial bombing and chemical warfare, see Baudendistel, *Between Bombs and Good Intentions*; Rochat, *Le guerre italiane in Libia e in Etiopia dal 1896 al 1939*, 163–93; Sbacchi, "Poison Gas and Atrocities in the Italo-Ethiopian War (1935–1936)."

16. Del Boca, *Italiani, brava gente?*, 205–27; Rochat, *Le guerre italiane in Libia e in Etiopia dal 1896 al 1939*, 194–230. On the attempted assassination of Graziani and his subsequent retributions, see Mockler, *Haile Selassie's War*, 174–82.

17. Sòrgoni, *Parole e corpi*.

18. Pretelli, "Education in the Italian Colonies during the Interwar Period," 276–77. On some of the difficulties in maintaining this segregation, see Fuller, "Wherever You Go, There You Are," 402–6; Larebo, "Empire Building and Its Limitations." Interestingly, Libya—which was declared an Italian territory (as opposed to colony) in 1937 and some of its inhabitants, citizens of the nation—faced looser policies of racial discrimination in this period. This distinction does not mean, however, they were not subjected to continued violence.

19. Barrera, "Mussolini's Colonial Race Laws and State-Settler Relations in Africa Orientale Italiana (1935–1941)," 426.

20. On the legal changes in Eritrea, see Sòrgoni, *Parole e corpi*, 141–70. On the legal oversight of sexual relations and citizenship, see Barrera, "Patrilinearity, Race, and Identity."

21. Sbacchi, *Ethiopia under Mussolini*, 167–68.

22. See Pretelli, "Education in the Italian Colonies during the Interwar Period." On the situation in Eritrea, see Negash, "The Ideology of Colonialism."

23. Barrera, "Mussolini's Colonial Race Laws and State-Settler Relations in Africa Orientale Italiana (1935–1941)," 427. See also Larebo, "Empire Building and Its Limitations." For more of Barrera's research on the origins and evolution of Italian colonial relationships and Fascist racial policies in Italian East Africa, see Barrera, "The Construction of Racial Hierarchies in Colonial Eritrea"; Barrera, "Patrilinearity, Race, and Identity."

24. Sbacchi, *Ethiopia under Mussolini*, 167.

25. Cipriani, "Su alcuni criteri antropologici per la colonizzazione in Africa," 859.

26. Ugolini, *Sono balilla!*, 61.

27. Lacchè, "Bonifica umana"; G. E. P., "Le nostre colonie"; Oreste Gasperini, *Ente radio rurale radioprogrammi scolastici n. 91–92 del 13–14 maggio 1938-xvi: Radioviaggio nell'impero, la bonifica della terra e degli uomini*, Wolfsonian–Florida International University, Miami Beach, Florida, Mitchell Wolfson Jr. Collection.

28. "L'istruzione degli indigeni dell'A. O.," 407. Padellaro, "Coscienza imperiale nella scuola"; Pankhurst, "Education in Ethiopia during the Italian Fascist Occupation (1936–1941)"; Pretelli, "Education in the Italian Colonies during the Interwar Period," 278.

29. On the importance of colonial relationships to the development of European racism, see Labanca, "Il razzismo coloniale italiano," 146–59.

30. Pes, "Becoming Imperialist," 606.

31. Giuseppe Bottai would remain the minister of education until July 1943, when he and nineteen other members of the Gran consiglio del fascismo voted to depose Mussolini. For more on Bottai and his intellectual role in the regime, see Galfrè, *Giuseppe Bottai*. On his role in the reformation of the education system, see Gentili, *Giuseppe Bottai e la riforma fascista della scuola*.

32. On Hitler's early ability to delegate authority, see Fischer, *The Rise of the Nazis*, 80.

33. Bottai, "Scuola politica," 71.

34. Bottai, "Circolare n. 23. Direttive alle autorità scolastiche: 'Tutta la vita italiana deve essere portata sul piano dell'Impero,'" 1364–65.

35. Tauro, "La missione del maestro."

36. However, there continued to be writings protesting this pedagogical shift, such as Pucci, *Nuovo metodo d'insegnamento per le scuole elementari*.

37. Strata, *La patria fascista*, 60.

38. Meletti, *Il libro fascista del balilla*, 72.

39. Dogliani, *Il fascismo degli italiani*, 294; Choate, *Emigrant Nation*.

40. For Liberal-era colonial theories and policies, see Finaldi, *Italian National Identity in the Scramble for Africa*.

41. Nani, "L'impero," 163.

42. *La gazettino dei ragazzi* was full of comics that made fun of Ethiopia's "backward" culture and politics in contrast to Italy's strength and courage. A

1936 board game, succinctly titled *The Conquest of Abyssinia*, had its players conquer Ethiopia city by city until the first player reached Addis Ababa. *La conquista dell'Abissinia*, Wolfsonian–Florida International University, Miami Beach, Florida, Mitchell Wolfson Jr. Collection.

43. Ciarlantini, "Necessità di una pedagogia imperiale," 203.

44. Padellaro, "Coscienza imperiale nella scuola," 288.

45. Fanelli, *Balilla: A sole!*

46. Fanelli, *Balilla: A sole!*, 9, 15–18.

47. Padellaro, "Coscienza imperiale nella scuola," 287.

48. Said, *Orientalism*, 5–7.

49. La Direzione, "Vittoria e pace romana," 82. For the full speech, see Mussolini, "L'Etiopia è italiana."

50. La Direzione, "Vittoria e pace romana," 90.

51. Ciarlantini, "Disciplina interiore," 2–3.

52. Arthurs, *Excavating Modernity*, 90–124.

53. Dogliani, *Il fascismo degli italiani*, 250. The ERR presented a detailed description of the exhibit and its aims. Oreste Gasperini, *Ente radio rurale radioprogramma scolastico n. 80 del 20 aprile 1938-xvi : La mostra augustea della romanità*, Wolfsonian–Florida International University, Miami Beach, Florida, Mitchell Wolfson Jr. Collection.

54. Ruberti, "L'istruzione e le associazioni giovanili alla mostra della romanità," 150.

55. Ruberti, "L'istruzione e le associazioni giovanili alla mostra della romanità," 151.

56. Ruberti, "L'istruzione e le associazioni giovanili alla mostra della romanità," 159.

57. Ruberti, "L'istruzione e le associazioni giovanili alla mostra della romanità," 160.

58. Oreste Gasperini, *Ente radio rurale radioprogramma scolastico n. 69 del 3 aprile 1937-xv: Il Risorgimento e la monarchia Sabauda*, Wolfsonian–Florida International University, Miami Beach, Florida, Mitchell Wolfson Jr. Collection. Toscano, *L'educazione dei Balilla e delle Piccole Italiane*, 18–19.

59. Bargellini, "L'insegnamento della storia," 133.

60. Fanelli, *Il mio tesoretto*, especially 230–60; Forges Davanzati, *Il balilla Vittorio*.

61. Vittorio Emanuele III, "Regio decreto-legge 21 agosto 1937-XV, n. 1542."

62. Marcucci, "Il 'bello' come elemento di educazione," 317.

63. Lidio Cipriani to DG demorazza, December 5, 1937 (ACS, MI, DG demorazza, Divisione razza, box 4, folder 4.6).

64. Vittorio Emanuele III, "Regio decreto-legge 12 maggio 1938-XVI, n. 1123," 1915–16.

65. On Nazi views on women, families, and the role of sterilization, see Bock, "Racism and Sexism in Nazi Germany." See also David, Fleischhacker, and Hohn, "Abortion and Eugenics in Nazi Germany." For a broader discussion of the role of women in the Nazi regime, see Koonz, *Mothers in the Fatherland*.

66. However, a number of scholars started to show concern for the apparent lack of effectiveness of the pronatalist campaign. Armando Lovato, "Per un'associazione delle famiglie numerose e per la propaganda demografica: Estratto di un proprio studio sui problemi della popolazione," Bologna, May 1936 (ACS, MCP, Gabinetto, II Versamento, box 7, folder 1); Silus, "Commentario," 164–65.

67. De Grazia, *How Fascism Ruled Women*, 43.

68. La Direzione, "Mostra nazionale delle colonie estive e dell'assistenza all'infanzia"; Arcamone, "Aspetti e visioni della mostra." See also Dogliani, *Il fascismo degli italiani*, 181–83.

69. Valori, *Alle soglie della vita*, 6.

70. Scaligero, "Giornata della madre e del fanciullo," 13.

71. Opera nazionale per la protezione della maternità e dell'infanzia, *Origine e sviluppi dell'Opera nazionale per la protezione della maternità e dell'infanzia*, 98.

72. Meletti, *Il libro fascista del balilla*, 64.

73. Direzione e amministrazione di "Italia maestra," *La scuola rurale nell'Opera balilla*, 62–63.

74. Direzione e amministrazione di "Italia maestra," *La scuola rurale nell'Opera balilla*, 64.

75. Silvio Petrucci, "Il libretto del cittadino-soldato," 19; Gioventù italiana del littorio, *Libretto personale di valutazione dello stato fisico e della preparazione militare di Pelleschi Bruno*, Wolfsonian–Florida International University, Miami Beach, Florida, Mitchell Wolfson Jr. Collection.

76. Partito nazionale fascista, *Il cittadino soldato*.

77. Partito nazionale fascista, *Il cittadino soldato*, 23.

78. "Il decennale dell'O.N.B."

79. Marzolo, "L'Opera balilla all'alba del secondo decennio," 12.

80. Puccini, "Giovinezza d'Italia," 273.

81. *Balilla: Giovinezza*, 4.

82. "L'O.N.B. nei primi dieci anni di vita," 268.

83. Cammarata, "L'Opera Balilla nel suo decennale, 3 aprile 1926–3 aprile 1936," 19–20.

84. Resta, "Educazione guerriera ed eroica," 417–18.

85. Toscano, *L'educazione dei Balilla e delle Piccole Italiane*, 10.

86. Meletti, *Il libro fascista della piccola italiana*, such as 63–64.

87. Vittorio Emanuele III, "Regio decreto-legge 27 ottobre 1937-XV, n. 1839." For an in-depth analysis of this institutional shift, see Ponzio, *Shaping the New Man*, 152–62.

88. Morgagni, "Gioventù italiana del littorio," 5.

89. Vittorio Emanuele III, "Regio decreto-legge 27 ottobre 1937-XV, n. 1839."

90. Curico, "Caratteri della politica fascista per l'infanzia," 8.

91. Ugolini, *Sono balilla!*, 54–55.

7. Enforcing the Racial Ideal

1. Mussolini, "Proclamazione dell'impero," 268–69.

2. Duggan, *Fascist Voices*, 292.

3. For similar arguments, see Duggan, *Fascist Voices*, 302–4; Gillette, *Racial Theories in Fascist Italy*, 52–53.

4. For the entire document, see Camera dei deputati, *La persecuzione degli ebrei durante il fascismo*, 111–13. Aaron Gillette has carefully outlined how Mussolini

recruited several young—and fairly unknown—racial theorists, led by Guido Landra, to act as signatories of the document. Gillette, *Racial Theories in Fascist Italy*, 59, 69–70. For more on these academics, see Cuomo, *I dieci*.

5. It has alternately been called the "Manifesto of Racial Scientists," "Racial Manifesto," and "Manifesto of Race." I will use the "Manifesto of Race" throughout this text.

6. In some circles, this aspect of Italian racism was emphasized in order to differentiate it further from its German counterpart. Duggan, *Fascist Voices*, 312.

7. Curico, "Caratteri della politica demografica fascista," 15. After the manifesto's publication, the regime encouraged publications arguing for this concept of accretion in Fascist racial doctrine, particularly in an effort to prove the Fascist state was not simply copying the Nazi model. Ufficio razza Ministero della cultura popolare, "Appunto per S. E. il Ministro: La razza nei discorsi del Duce," Rome, February 24, 1939 (ACS, MCP, Gabinetto, Ufficio razza, box 12, folder 130: "Razzismo-'Appunti Vari'"); Landra, "Gli studi della razza in Italia prima del razzismo," 20–23; Cipriani, "Il razzismo in Italia," 545; Acerbo, *I fondamenti della dottrina fascista della razza*, 11–12.

8. The rise of European Aryanism found its roots in the mid-nineteenth century, when linguists began to argue for the Sanskrit roots of European languages. Language was considered an integral part of race (as it was for Fascists), and racial theorists posited that elite Aryans of northern India had migrated to central and northern Europe, ultimately composing the continent's dominant racial group. Mosse, *Toward the Final Solution*, 39–45; Poliakov, *The Aryan Myth*.

9. For more on this shift, see Raspanti, "I razzismi del fascismo," 73.

10. "Rassegna della stampa," 311.

11. Gran consiglio del fascismo, "La dichiarazione del Gran consiglio," 7.

12. Landra, "Difendiamo nella maternità le qualità della razza," 6.

13. Orano, "Bonifica della razza," 337.

14. For more on the laws resulting from the Manifesto of Race, see Pavan, *Tra indifferenza e oblio*, 69–87; Michele Sarfatti, "La legislazione antiebraica fascista," 68–82. Emilio Gentile argues that discrimination was perpetrated much more in terms of a Fascist versus non-Fascist binary than an Italian versus non-Italian one. It is my contention that those two frames of reference were supposed to be identical. Emilio Gentile, *La Grande Italia*, 165.

15. Duggan, *Fascist Voices*, 300.

16. Gillette, *Racial Theories in Fascist Italy*, 53. Patrizia Dogliani, on the other hand, explains that *Lei* was considered a "Spanish-ism" left over from the years of Spanish occupation. Dogliani, *Il fascismo degli italiani*, 260.

17. These concerns are evident in the text of press summaries from the director general of Italian press to the director general of demographics and race in the late 1930s, particularly in terms of film and radio. Direttore generale per il Servizio della stampa italiana, "Relazione delle principali discussioni in corso nei quotidiani e nei periodici italiani, dal 26 marzo al 1 aprile XVII," Rome, April 2, 1939 (ACS, MI, DG demorazza, Affari diversi, box 12, folder 29).

18. Gran consiglio del fascismo, "Deliberazioni del Gran consiglio del fascismo sulla razza," Rome, 1938 (ACS, M I, DG demorazza, Affari diversi, box I, folder 2), 2299.

19. For the creation and functions of domestic internment camps under Fascism, see Ebner, *Ordinary Violence in Mussolini's Italy*, 15–39; Di Sante, *I campi di concentramento in Italia*.

20. For a full list of Fascist anti-Semitic laws, see Camera dei deputati, *La persecuzione degli ebrei durante il fascismo*.

21. For the initial legislation allowing for certain exemptions, see Vittorio Emanuele III, "Regio decreto-legge 5 settembre 1938-XVI, n. 1390," 2257–58.

22. Gran consiglio del fascismo, "Deliberazioni del Gran consiglio del fascismo sulla razza," Rome, 1938, 2298.

23. Direttore generale per il Servizio della stampa italiana, "Relazione delle principali discussioni in corso nei quotidiani e nei periodici italiani, dal 6 al 12 agosto XVII."

24. Quoted in "Rassegna della stampa," 311.

25. For a Fascist discussion of the origins of razza, see Callari, "Fortuna del vocabolo razza nella nostra lingua," 39.

26. Acerbo, *I fondamenti della dottrina fascista della razza*, 15–16.

27. Acerbo, *I fondamenti della dottrina fascista della razza*, 23.

28. Masselli, "Razze e razzismo," 5–6.

29. As quoted in "Rassegna della stampa," 312. Emphasis original to source.

30. As Joshua Arthurs notes, this evocation of the Roman Empire and its heterogeneous population in the service of racism is problematic if you consider (ancient) imperial Rome's emphasis on universalism. The freedom for (some) members of all ethnicities within the classical empire to gain citizenship meant that there was no single race that defined the Romans of the Roman Empire. Arthurs, *Excavating Modernity*, 125–50. Of course, Fascist racism, like all racism, was not particularly logical; as they had throughout the Fascist regime, references to Italians' inherent *romanità* still argued for its contribution to the development of a single, superior race. Even at this late date, these messages flourished, both among pedagogues and within educational texts.

31. Pino, "Il pensiero dei giovani," 50.

32. Fraddosio, "Il nucleo familiare in relazione alla politica razzista," 88.

33. Curico, "Caratteri della politica demografica fascista," 17.

34. "Razza e costume," 596.

35. Interlandi, "Confini razziali," 7.

36. On the role of the Italian scientific community in this discussion, see Israel and Nastasi, *Scienza e razza nell'Italia fascista*.

37. Partito nazionale fascista, *Manuale di educazione fascista*, 159.

38. Partito nazionale fascista, *Manuale di educazione fascista*, 159.

39. Partito nazionale fascista, *Manuale di educazione fascista*, 162.

40. Partito nazionale fascista, *Manuale di educazione fascista*, 165.

41. Gioventù italiana del littorio di Torino, *Primi elementi di cultura fascista per la Gioventù italiana del littorio*, 6.

42. Giovanazzi, *La scuola del balilla*, 2–3.

43. Giovanazzi, *La scuola del balilla*, 6. Emphasis original to source.

44. Giovanazzi, *La scuola del balilla*, 9.

45. Padellaro, "Coltivare nell'infanzia l'orgoglio di razza," 14.

46. Bottai, "Rivista 'La difesa della razza'-diffusione," Rome, August 6, 1938 (ACS, MI, DG demorazza, Affari diversi, box 11, folder 26: "Comunicazioni provvedimenti sulla razza").

47. Bottai, "Istruzioni per la partecipazione degli studiosi italiani a Congressi e a manifestazioni culturali all'estero," August 3, 1938 (ACS, MI, DG demorazza, Affari diversi, box 11, folder 26: "Comunicazioni provvedimenti sulla razza").

48. Vittorio Emanuele III, "Regio decreto-legge 5 settembre 1938-XVI, n. 1390"; Vittorio Emanuele III, "Regio decreto-legge 23 settembre 1938-XVI, n. 1630," 2619.

49. Vittorio Emanuele III, "Regio decreto-legge 15 novembre 1938-XVII, n. 1779"; Bottai, "Circolare n. 33. (Gabinetto). Divieto di adozione nelle scuole di libri di testo di autori di razza ebraica."

50. Vittorio Emanuele III, "Regio decreto-legge 5 settembre 1938-XVI, n. 1390." On the exclusion of Jewish academics, see Capristo, "The Exclusion of Jews form Italian Academies"; Finzi, "The Damage to Italian Culture."

51. Bottai, "Circolare n. 39. (Gabinetto). Stile facista nella scuola."

52. Bottai, *Diario, 1935–1944*, 140.

53. Bottai, "Relazione al Duce del Fascismo sulla 'Carta della Scuola,'" February 4, 1939 (SPD [CR], box 38, folder "Gran consiglio"). Emphasis original to source.

54. Bottai, "Formazione mussoliniana della Carta della scuola," 5.

55. Pagliaro, *La scuola fascist*, 70–71.

56. Partito nazionale fascista, "Il Gran consiglio approva la Carta della scuola," 132.

57. Bottai, *Diario, 1935–1944*, 140.

58. Partito nazionale fascista, "Il Gran consiglio approva la Carta della scuola," 131.

59. Pagliaro, "Una fucina di 'italiani nuovi,'" 94.

60. Ministero dell'educazione nazionale, *Scuole rurali*, 18.

61. Ministero dell'educazione nazionale, *Scuole rurali*, 15.

62. Bottai, "Ordinanza 24 giugno 1939-XVII," 1842.

63. Triz, "Tutela fascista del rurale," 39. Studies continued to show that rural populations were more prolific, reinforcing the Fascist belief that the Italian peasant population carried the key to Italy's future. Gasteiner, "Un pericolo per la razza."

64. Nieddu, "Aspetti spirituali della difesa della razza," 7.

65. Partito nazionale fascista, *Manuale di educazione fascista*, 84; Pignatari, "La Gioventù italiana del littorio"; Pignatari, "Le colonie climatiche della Gioventù italiana del littorio," 381.

66. Curico, "Caratteri della politica fascista per l'infanzia," 8; Pignatari, "Le colonie climatiche della Gioventù italiana del littorio," 383.

67. Gabrielli, *Principi, fini, e metodi della scuola fascista seconda la Carta della scuola*, 32.

68. Giovanazzi, *La scuola del balilla*, 14.

69. Partito nazionale fascista, "Il Gran consiglio approva la Carta della scuola," 129–33.

70. Bottai, "Relazione al Duce del Fascismo sulla 'Carta della Scuola,'" 3.

71. Partito nazionale fascista, "Il Gran consiglio approva la Carta della scuola," 130.

72. Bottai, "Relazione al Duce del Fascismo sulla 'Carta della Scuola,'" 3.

73. Partito nazionale fascista, "Definizione dei rapporti fra scuola e G.I.L."

74. Giovanazzi, *La scuola del balilla*, 26.

75. Bottai, "Relazione al Duce del Fascismo sulla 'Carta della Scuola,'" 3.

76. Ente radio rurale, *Trasmissioni radiofoniche per le scuole elementari*, 10.

77. The EIAR was founded in 1927, replacing the previous state organization, the Unione radiofonica italiana (URI). It remained the state radio service until 1944, when it assumed the new name Radio audizioni italiani (RAI). In 1954 RAI also assumed responsibility for state television broadcasting. Forgacs and Stephen, *Mass Culture and Italian Society*, 169–73.

78. EIAR, *Anno XVII*, no page numbers included.

79. EIAR, *Anno XVII*.

80. EIAR, *Anno XVII*.

81. While radio subscriptions were consistently lower in Italy during this period than in Great Britain or Germany, David Forgacs and Stephen Gundle argue that it would be unfair to describe the Fascist regime as "slow" to understand the propagandistic potential of radio transmissions, as no other regime used radio programming politically until the 1930s. Forgacs and Gundle, *Mass Culture and Italian Society*, 174.

8. Enduring Principles

1. Marrella, *I diari della gioventù italianissima*, 215.

2. Isnenghi, "Introduzione alla ristampa anastatica," 1.

3. Bottai, "Circolare n. 33. (Gabinetto). Divieto di adozione nelle scuole di libri di testo di autori di razza ebraica," 2396.

4. Rieppi, "La scuola per la difesa della razza," 48.

5. Rieppi, "La scuola per la difesa della razza"; "Il Partito e il razzismo italiano," 2.

6. Padellaro, *Il libro della terza classe elementare*, 183–84.

7. Bertone, *I figli d'Italia si chiaman Balilla*, 105–6.

8. Ente radio rurale, *Trasmissioni radiofoniche per le scuole elementari*, 85.

9. Italy's blatant disregard for the demands of the League of Nations in regards to Ethiopia's sovereignty in 1935 did not bolster much good will between the Fascist foreign office and its counterparts in Great Britain and France. At the same time, the lack of support from these former allies for Italy's imperial ambitions appeared hypocritical to Italians. Mussolini's aid to General Francisco

Franco's Nationalists in the Spanish Civil War (1936–39) and withdrawal from the League of Nations (1937) ran alongside his initially cautious alliance with Germany's Adolf Hitler in 1937. After Germany's annexation of Austria (March 1938), Italian officials began to sense that Hitler did not consider Mussolini an equal partner in international affairs. Still, Mussolini continued to support the German-Italian alliance diplomatically. On Fascist foreign policy in these years, see Kallis, *Fascist Ideology*; Bosworth, *Italy, the Least of the Great Powers*; Mack Smith, *Mussolini's Roman Empire*.

10. Zanetti and Zanetti, *Il libro di lettura per la terza classe dei centri urbani*, 41.

11. Bargellini, "L'insegnamento della storia," 133.

12. Gioventù italiana del littorio di Torino, *Primi elementi di cultura fascista per la Gioventù italiana del littorio*, 2.

13. Zanetti and Zanetti, *Il libro di lettura per la terza classe dei centri urbani*, 39.

14. Sammartano, *Corso di cultura fascista*, 7.

15. Sammartano, *Corso di cultura fascista*, 7.

16. Marrella, *I diari della gioventù italianissima*, 171.

17. Zanetti and Zanetti, *Il libro di lettura per la terza classe dei centri urbani*, 109.

18. Marrella, *I diari della gioventù italianissima*, 174.

19. Padellaro, *Il libro della terza classe elementare*, 207.

20. Zanetti and Zanetti, *Il libro di lettura per la terza classe dei centri urbani*, 186–88.

21. Bertone, *I figli d'Italia si chiaman Balilla*, 108.

22. Zanetti and Zanetti, *Il libro di lettura per la terza classe dei centri urbani*, 41.

23. Catalano and Goad, *Education in Italy*, 24.

24. Cotterelli Gaiba, *Il libro della prima classe*, 42.

25. Padellaro, *Il libro della terza classe elementare*, 13–14.

26. Alfredo Petrucci, *L'Italiano nuovo*, 41–42.

27. Cotterelli Gaiba, *Il libro della prima classe*, 113.

28. Cotterelli Gaiba, *Il libro della prima classe*, 42.

29. Curico, "Caratteri della politica fascista per l'infanzia," 6.

30. For example, Zanetti and Zanetti, *Il libro di lettura per la terza classe dei centri urbani*; Alfredo Petrucci, *L'Italiano nuovo*; Cotterelli Gaiba, *Il libro della prima classe*.

31. Padellaro, *Il libro della terza classe elementare*, 3.

32. Cotterelli Gaiba, *Il libro della prima classe*, 91.

33. Cotterelli Gaiba, *Il libro della prima classe*, 96.

34. Gioventù italiana del littorio di Torino, *Primi elementi di cultura fascista per la Gioventù italiana del littorio*, 2.

35. Alfredo Petrucci, *L'Italiano nuovo*, 151.

36. Alfredo Petrucci, *L'Italiano nuovo*, 117–18.

37. Gabrielli, *Principi, fini, e metodi della scuola fascista seconda la Carta della scuola*, 108.

38. Bottai, "Rivista 'La difesa della razza'-diffusione."

39. Sammartano, *Corso di cultura fascista*, 38.

40. Businco, "I giovani e la razza italiana."

41. Other contributors to the journal were more skeptical of the ultimate benefits of physical education. Gasteiner, "Un pericolo per la razza," 26.

42. Ferrauto, *Esercizi imitativi*, 11.

43. Ferrauto, *Esercizi imitativi*, 21.

44. Ferrauto, *Esercizi imitativi*, 21.

45. Ferrauto, *Esercizi imitativi*, 73.

46. Ferrauto, *Esercizi imitativi*, 10.

47. Partito nazionale fascista, "La gioventù italiana del littorio nell'anno XVII," 5.

48. Marzolo, "La gioventù italiana del littorio," 214.

49. Comando generale della GIL, *L'accademia femminile di Orvieto*, 7.

50. Comando generale della GIL, *L'accademia femminile di Orvieto*, 13–15.

51. Partito nazionale fascista, "Foglio di disposizioni, n. 1149," Rome, 1938 (ACS, MPI, DG del personale e degli affari generali ed amministrativi [1910–1964], box 195, folder "1938–1939").

52. Benadusi, *The Enemy of the New Man*, 87–110.

53. Orano, "Bonifica della razza," 334.

54. Curico, "Caratteri della politica fascista per l'infanzia," 6.

55. Dino Alfieri to Carlo Cosimo Borromeo, November 16, 1938 (ACS, MCP, Gabinetto, box 151, folder "Fascicoli Vari-Carlo Cosimo Borromeo").

56. Bergamaschi, "La difesa della razza e l'O.N.M.I.," 245.

57. Pende, "Maternità fisiologica e maternità spirituale," 63–64.

58. Sborgi, "La donna nello stato fascista," 284. Victoria De Grazia has termed this contradiction of ideals and necessity as "oppositional familism." De Grazia, *How Fascism Ruled Women*, 112–15. See also Ipsen, *Dictating Demography*, 145–46. For a comparative look at similar policies regarding female labor in Nazi Germany, see Burleigh and Wippermann, *The Racial State*, 258–66.

59. Orano, "Bonifica della razza," 338.

Conclusion

1. Mussolini, "Popolo italiano! Corri alle armi . . . ," 404.

2. Ciano, *Diary*, 318.

3. Ciano, *Diary*, 316.

4. For more on the events leading up to and the historiography on Mussolini's decision to enter the war, see Kallis, *Fascist Ideology*, 168–74.

5. Numerous scholars have written on Italy's military weakness on the eve of its involvement with World War II. See Kennedy, *The Rise and Fall of the Great Powers*, 292–93; Bosworth, *Mussolini's Italy*, 443–48; Mack Smith, *Mussolini's Roman Empire*, 169–89.

6. Ben-Ghiat, *Fascist Modernities*, 174–80.

7. On the youth experience of the war between 1940 and 1943, see Gibelli, *Il popolo bambino*, 341–65.

8. On the situation for Jews in Italy during the forty-five days between July 25 and September 8, 1943, see Zuccotti, *Under His Very Windows*, 137–149; De Felice, *The Jews in Fascist Italy*, 427–32.

9. See, for example, Dante Coscia, *Storia del bene e del male*. For analysis of this practice, see Gibelli, *Il popolo bambino*, 366–93.

10. Numbers are necessarily imprecise. The former number is from Fargion, *Il libro della memoria*, 26. The latter is from De Felice, *Storia degli ebrei italiani*, 465.

11. Mayda, *Storia della deportazione dall'Italia, 1943–1945*, 134. On anti-Semitism between 1943 and 1945, see Michele Sarfatti, *The Jews in Mussolini's Italy*, 178–211.

12. Picciotto, "The Shoah in Italy."

13. Duggan, *Fascist Voices*, 418–25.

14. Duggan, *Fascist Voices*, 422.

15. On the transition from Fascist to post-Fascist education, see White, *Progressive Renaissance*.

16. Dell'Era, "Scienza, razza e politica tra fascismo e repubblica."

17. Mosse, *Toward the Final Solution*, 232.

18. Academics and activists are increasingly bringing to popular attention the problems of postcolonialism, immigration, homophobia, and sexism in contemporary Italy. In addition to scholars mentioned elsewhere in this book, see the variety of work in Parati, *New Perspectives in Italian Cultural Studies*, vol. 1, *Definitions, Theory, and Accented Practices*; Parati, *New Perspectives in Italian Cultural Studies*, vol. 2, *The Arts and History*; Deplano, *Costruire una nazione*.

Archival Sources

Archivio centrale dello stato, Rome (ACS)
    Archivio personale Pietro Fedele
    Archivio personale Renato Ricci
    Consiglio nazionale delle donne italiane (CNDI)
    Ministero della cultura popolare (MCP)
        Gabinetto
        Ufficio nuclei per la propaganda in Italia e all'estero (NUPIE)
        Reports
    Ministero di pubblica istruzione (MPI)
        Direttore generale (DG) del personale e degli affari generali ed amminis-
            trativi (1910–1964)
        Direttore generale (DG) istruzione elementare
    Ministero interiore (MI)
        Direttore generale demografia e razza (DG demorazza)
        Direttore generale sanità pubblica (DG sanità pubblica)
        Opere pie
    Partito nazionale fascista (PNF)
        Servizi vari
    Presidenza consiglio dei ministri (PCM)
    Segretaria particolare del Duce (SPD)
        Autografi del Duce
        Carteggio ordinario (CO)
        Carteggio riservato (CR)
Fondazione Giovanni Gentile, Rome (FGG)
    Attività politici
    Lettere
    Manoscritti gentiliani
Museo storico della didattica, Rome (MSD)
Wolfsonian Object Collection, Miami Beach, Florida

Contemporary Periodicals

Annali dell'istruzione elementare
Bollettino del comando generale della GIL
La difesa della razza
I diritti della scuola
Il gazzettino dei ragazzi
Gerarchia
Giovanissima
Gioventù fascista
L'impero
Maternità ed infanzia
La rivista illustrata del Popolo d'Italia

Published Primary Sources

"L'accademia femminile dell'O. N. B. a Orvieto." *La rivista illustrata del Popolo d'Italia*, August 1935, 56–57.

Acerbo, Giacomo. *I fondamenti della dottrina fascista della razza*. Rome: Ministero della cultura populare–Ufficio studi e propaganda sulla razza, 1940.

Adami, Luigi, and Piero Domenichelli. *Il mio libro di preparazione agli esami di ammissione alla prima classe delle scuole medie*. Florence: Vallecchi Editore, 1933.

"L'adozione del 'testo unico' di stato per le scuole elementari." *L'impero* 6 (1928): 1.

Alfieri, Emilio. "La protezione della maternità di fronte al problema demografico." *Maternità ed infanzia* 5, no. 3 (1930): 281–90.

Aliotta, Antonio. *La formazione dello spirito nello stato fascista*. Rome: Francesco Perrella, 1938.

"Anno dodicesimo." *Maternità ed infanzia* 8, no. 11 (1933): 1–2.

Arcamone, Guido. "Aspetti e visioni della mostra." *Annali dell'istruzione elementare* 12, nos. 3–4 (1937): 220–59.

———. "La radio rurale nelle scuole." *Annali dell'istruzione elementare* 10, no. 2 (1935): 145–57.

"L'assistenza scolastica e il suo incremento." *Annali dell'istruzione elementare* 3, no. 4 (1928): 8–56.

Associazione nazionale per gli interessi del mezzogiorno d'Italia. *Esposizione sintetica dei programmi didattici per le scuole elementari uniche miste rurali*. Rome: Editrice Laziale, A. Marchesi, 1924.

"L'attività dell'Opera nazionale Balilla nell'anno VIII." *Annali dell'istruzione elementare* 5, no. 6 (1930): 5–33.

Badoglio, Pietro. *The War in Abyssinia*. New York: G. P. Putnam's Sons, 1937.

Balilla: Almanacco per i giovanetti italiani, anno scolastico 1926–1927. Milan: Casa Editrice del "Piccolo Corriere," 1926.

Balilla: Giovinezza. Florence: Deposito Edizioni, 1934.

Barbieri, Oreste. *Direzione didattica italiana: 30 pubblicazioni (1922–1932)*. Venice: privately printed, 1932.

————. *La scuola del littorio: Saggio di educazione italiana con dedica a S. E. Benito Mussolini*. Milan: Vallardi, 1931.

Bargellini, Piero. "Del libro unico." *Annali dell'istruzione elementare* 10, no. 3 (1935): 208–16.

————. "L'insegnamento della storia." *Annali dell'istruzione elementare* 13, no. 2 (1938): 123–33.

Bascone, Francesco. "Ordiamento didattico della scuola elementare, grado preparatorio." *I diritti della scuola* 36, no. 2 (1934): 20–21.

Bedeschi, Edoardo. *La giovinezza del duce: Libro per la gioventù italiana*. Turin: Società Editrice Internazionale di Torino, 1939.

Belluzzo, Giuseppe. "Circolare n. 35. (Ufficio centrale del personale.) Sul vestire delle signore insegnanti e delle alunne nelle scuole." *Bollettino ufficiale: Parte 1. Leggi, regolamenti e altre disposizioni generali* 56, no. 8 (1929): 806–7.

————. "Decreto ministeriale 5 settembre 1928. Approvazione dei libri di testo per le scuole elemtentari e per i corsi integrativi di avviamento professionale." *Bollettino ufficiale: Parte 1. Leggi, regolamenti e altre disposizioni generali* 55, no. 38 (1928): 3160–70.

————. "Decreto ministeriale 20 novembre 1928. Approvazione di libri di testo di lettura per le scuole elementari e per i corsi integrativi di avviamento professionale." *Bollettino ufficiale: Parte 1. Leggi, regolamenti e altre disposizioni generali* 56, no. 4 (1929): 286–303.

————. "Decreto ministeriale 28 novembre 1928. Approvazione di libri di testo per le scuole elementari e per i corsi integrativi di avviamento professionale." *Bollettino ufficiale: Parte 1. Leggi, regolamenti e altre disposizioni generali* 55, no. 49 (1928): 3825–54.

————. "Legge 7 gennaio 1929, n. 5. Norme per la compilazione e l'adozione del testo unico di stato per le singole classi elementari." *Bollettino ufficiale: Parte 1. Leggi, regolamenti e altre disposizioni generali* 46, no. 4 (1929): 226–27.

————. *Le opere sussidiarie della scuola elementare in Italia*. Rome: Libreria del Littorio, 1928.

Benedetti, Dante. "Civiltà e barbarie." *Gioventù fascista*, November 30, 1935, 4.

————. "La giustizia in Abissinia." *Gioventù fascista*, February 15, 1936, 4.

————. "L'Italia e la schiavitù in Abissinia." *Gioventù fascista*, January 15, 1936, 12.

Bergamaschi, Carlo. "La difesa della razza e l'O.N.M.I." *Maternità ed infanzia* 13, nos. 4–5 (1938): 243–51.

Bertarelli, E. "Come si insegna al popolo a comprendere i valori della demografica." *La rivista illustrata del Popolo d'Italia*, June 1928, 84–85.

————. "Metodi educativi per le massaie e le madri." *La rivista illustrata del Popolo d'Italia*, July 1928, 81.

Blanc, Gian Alberto. *Il fascismo dinanzi al problema della razza*. Rome: Stabilimento Tipografico Riccardo Garroni, 1927.

Boccazzi, Isotto. "Prefazione alla terza edizione." In Dussin and Dossa, *Il libro del contadino*, v–vi.

Bodrero, Emilio. "Presentazione a S. E. il Ministro della pubblica istruzione." *Annali dell'istruzione elementare* 3, no. 1 (1928): 5–6.

Bonanni, Pietro. "I giovanissimi e lo sport." *Giovanissima*, January 1931, 40–41.

Bottai, Giuseppe. "Circolare n. 23. Direttive alle autorità scolastiche: 'Tutta la vita italiana deve essere portata sul piano dell'Impero." *Bollettino ufficiale: Parte 1. Leggi, regolamenti e altre disposizioni generali* 63, no. 48 (1936): 1364–65.

———. "Circolare n. 33. (Gabinetto). Divieto di adozione nelle scuole di libri di testo di autori di razza ebraica." *Bollettino ufficiale: Parte 1. Leggi, regolamenti e altre disposizioni generali* 65, no. 41 (1938): 2396–99.

———. "Circolare n. 39. (Gabinetto). Stile facista nella scuola." *Bollettino ufficiale: Parte 1. Leggi, regolamenti e altre disposizioni generali* 65, no. 52 (1938): 3122–24.

———. *Diario, 1935–1944*. Milan: Rizzoli Editore, 1982.

———. "Formazione mussoliniana della Carta della scuola." *La rivista illustrata del Popolo d'Italia*, March 1939, 5–6.

———. *Mussolini costruttore d'impero*. Mantova: Edizioni Paladino, 1928.

———. "Ordinanza 24 giugno 1939-XVII. Corsi di cultura per le maestre di scuole rurali." *Bollettino ufficiale: Parte 1. Leggi, regolamenti e altre disposizioni generali* 66, no. 27 (1939): 1842–43.

———. "Scuola politica." *Annali dell'istruzione elementare* 12, no. 2 (1937): 71–75.

Brunialti, Scotti, and Maria Douglas. "Di quella educazione che incomincia con la vita." *Maternità ed infanzia* 4, no. 6 (1929), 617–24.

Businco, Lino. "I giovani e la razza italiana." *La difesa della razza* 1, no. 1 (1938): 35.

Callari, Francesco. "Fortuna del vocabolo razza nella nostra lingua." *La difesa della razza* 1, no. 2 (1938): 39–40.

Calò, Giovanni. *Problemi vivi e orizzonti nuovi dell'educazione nazionale*. Florence: S. A. G. Barbera Editore, 1935.

Cammarata, Angelo. "L'Opera Balilla nel suo decennale, 3 aprile 1926–3 aprile 1936." *Annali dell'istruzione elementare* 11, no. 1 (1936): 15–32.

———. *Pedagogia di Mussolini: I corsi per i capi-centuria e i campi Dux*. Palermo: Buttafuoco, 1932.

Cammarosano, Angelo. "Concetto fascista dello stato." *Annali dell'istruzione elementare* 5, no. 5 (1930): 17–31.

Campanile, Aristide. "La radio e i rurali." *Gioventù fascista*, June 15, 1935, 14.

Capodivacca, Giovanni. *La giovine aurora: Libro di lettura per la prima classe elementare rurale maschile e femminile*. 4th ed. Florence: R. Bemporad e Figlio, 1927.

Carelli, Augusto. "Campi di gioco e delinquenza giovanile." *Maternità ed infanzia* 4, no. 7 (1929): 745–50.

———. "Fattori sociali nella vita morale della donna." *Maternità ed infanzia* 3, no. 8 (1928): 617–22.

———. "A proposito dei rapporti tra condizioni fisiche e qualità mentali nei fanciulli." *Maternità ed infanzia* 4, no. 10 (1929): 1070–74.

———. "La salute degli scolari e il profitto scolastico." *Maternità ed infanzia* 5, no. 10 (1930): 1022–27.

Carelli, Mauro, ed. *Frammenti di lirica didattica*. Bari: Canosa di Bari, 1934.

"La 'Casa del Balilla.'" *Annali dell'istruzione elementare* 8, no. 1 (1933): 30–37.

Casale, Felice. *A cuore aperto: Libro di lettura per la quarta classe elementare maschile e femminile*. Florence: G. B. Paravia, 1929.

———. *A cuore aperto: Libro di lettura per la quinta classe elementare maschile e femminile*. Florence: G. B. Paravia, 1929.

———. *A cuore aperto: Libro di lettura per la terza classe elementare maschile e femminile*. Turin: G. B. Paravia, 1929.

———. *L'indispensabile: Italiano scritto, nozioni grammaticali, aritmetica e geometria, coltura generale; Appunti, temi e problemi per i candidati all'esame di ammissione alle scuole medie*. Florence: G. B. Paravia, 1932.

Chiarini, Alfredo. *Il giuoco dei balilla: Nuovo ed italianissimo e cose utili a sapersi nel campo dell'educazione fisica*. Florence: Felice Le Monnier, 1927.

Ciano, Galeazzo. *Diary, 1937–1943*. Translated by Robert L. Miller and V. Umberto Coletti-Perucca. New York: Enigma Books, 2002. First published 1946.

Ciarlantini, Franco. "Disciplina interiore." *I diritti della scuola* 36, no. 1 (1934): 2–3.

———. *I miei amici di Villa Castelli: Letture per le scuole elementari rurali, classe seconda*. Florence: R. Bemporad e Figlio, 1929.

———. "Necessità di una pedagogia imperiale." *I diritti della scuola* 37, no. 14 (1936): 200–203.

Cipriani, Lidio. "Il razzismo in Italia." *Gerarchia* 18, no. 8 (1938): 544–47.

———. "Su alcuni criteri antropologici per la colonizzazione in Africa." *Gerarchia* 16, no. 12 (1936): 856–60.

Codignola, Ernesto. *Il problema dell'educazione nazionale in Italia*. Florence: Vallecchi Editore, 1925.

Comando generale della GIL, ed. *L'accademia femminile di Orvieto*. Rome: Comando generale della GIL, 1938.

Conti Rossini, Carlo. *Italia ed Etiopia dal trattato d'Uccialli alla Battaglia di Adua*. Rome: Istituto per l'Oriente, 1935.

Coscia, Dante. *Storia del bene e del male. Fiaba per grandi e per piccini*. Venice and Milan: Edizioni "Erre," 1944.

Cotterelli Gaiba, Vera. *Il libro della prima classe*. Rome: Libreria dello Stato, 1940.

Crispi, Francesco. *La prima guerra d'Africa: Documenti e memorie dell'archivio Crispi ordinati da T. Palamenghi-Crispi*. Milan: Fratelli Treves, 1914.

"La Croce rossa italiana giovanile." *Annali dell'istruzione elementare* 3, no. 6 (1928): 130–35.

Crocioni, Giovanni. "La cultura regionale nella 'Riforma Gentile.'" *Annali dell'istruzione elementare* 5, no. 5 (1930): 8–16.

"Cronaca." *Gioventù fascista*, January 15, 1936, 15.

Cuesta, Ugo. "Combattere: La prima necessità di un popolo." *Gioventù fascista*, July 30–August 15, 1935, 17.

Cuman Pertile, Arpalice. *Fiori di campo: Letture per le scuole rurali; Libro per la quarta classe*. 3rd ed. Florence: R. Bemporad e Figlio, 1928.

———. *Per le vie del mondo: Libro per la terza classe elementare maschile e femminile*. 10th ed. Florence: R. Bemporad e Figlio, 1928.

———. *Primi voli: Libro di lettura per la quarta classe elementare*. Florence: R. Bemporad e Figlio, 1928.

Curico, Carlo. "Caratteri della politica demografica fascista." *Maternità ed infanzia* 14, no. 1 (1939): 15–18.

———. "Caratteri della politica fascista per l'infanzia." *Maternità ed infanzia* 13, no. 1 (1938): 5–10.

———. "Un esempio per il mondo." *Maternità ed infanzia* 7, no. 10 (1932): 992–96.

———. "Nascere." *Maternità ed infanzia* 7, no. 9 (1932): 805–8.

Curti, Cesare. "L'esempio di Roma imperiale." *I diritti della scuola* 29, no. 8 (1927): 114–15.

"Il decennale dell'O.N.B." *Gioventù fascista*, April 15, 1936, 12.

De Leva, Raffaele. "Demografia: Problema morale." *Gioventù fascista*, April 30–May 15, 1935, 5.

De Luca, Carmelo. "Fari d'italianità." *I diritti della scuola* 36, no. 5 (1934): 77.

De Marinis, Giuseppe Maria. *Resurrezione eroica: L'italiano nuovo*. Naples: Tommaso Pironti, 1929.

De Vecchi, Cesare Maria. "Il discorso del ministro De Vecchi ai fanciulli d'Italia." *Annali dell'istruzione elementare* 10, no. 3 (1935): 197–99.

———. "La politica scolastica del governo fascista: Discorso di S. E. il quadrumviro De Vecchi di Val Cismon al senato." *Annali dell'istruzione elementare* 10, no. 2 (1935): 105–16.

Di Carlo, Salvatore. "Il passaggio di tutte le scuole elementari allo stato." *Annali dell'istruzione elementare* 9, no. 1 (1934): 6–16.

Di Marco, Ercole. "La Mostra della Rivoluzione." *Annali dell'istruzione elementare* 8, no. 3 (1933): 189–209.

La Direzione. "Mostra nazionale delle colonie estive e dell'assistenza all'infanzia: Sguardo d'insieme." *Annali dell'istruzione elementare* 12, nos. 3–4 (1937): 151–74.

———. "Vittoria e pace romana." *Annali dell'istruzione elementare* 11, nos. 2–3 (1936): 81–91.

Direzione e amministrazione di "Italia maestra," ed. *La scuola rurale nell'Opera balilla*. Rome: Italia Maestra, 1936.

Domenichelli, Piero. *L'adunata: Nuovo corso di letture per le scuole elementari, libro per la quarta classe maschile e femminile*. Florence: R. Bemporad e Figlio, 1929.

———. *L'adunata: Nuovo corso di letture per le scuole elementari, libro per la quinta classe maschile e femminile*. Florence: R. Bemporad e Figlio, 1929.

———. *L'adunata: Nuovo corso di letture per le scuole elementari, libro per la terza classe maschile e femminile*. Florence: R. Bemporad e Figlio, 1929.

D'Ormea, Guido. "Cattedre ambulanti di assistenza materna e di puericultura, elemento di ruralizzazione." *Maternità ed infanzia* 4, no. 8 (1929): 833–39.

———. "Le cattedre ambulanti di assistenza materna e puericultura e la protezione del lattante." *Maternità ed infanzia* 5, no. 7 (1930): 702–11.

Dussin, Roberto, and Giovanni Dossa. *Il libro del contadino: Racconti di vita campestre*. 3rd ed. Florence: R. Bemporad e Figlio, 1928.

EIAR. *Anno XVII*. Florence: Casa Editrice Ballerini e Fratini, 1938.

Ente nazionale per l'educazione fisica. *Relazione sull'opera e sul funzionamento dell'ENEF nell'anno scolastico 1923–24.* Milan: Stucchi Ceretti, 1924.

Ente radio rurale. *Trasmissioni radiofoniche per le scuole elementari: Fascicolo I, anno XVII.* Florence: A. Vallecchi, 1938.

Ercole, Francesco. "Circolare n. 3. Visita alla Mostra della Rivoluzione fascista." *Bollettino ufficiale: Parte 1. Leggi, regolamenti e altre disposizioni generali* 60, no. 4 (1933): 199.

———. "Circolare n. 5. (Direzione generale per l'istruzione elementare). Settimanale 'Il Balilla.'" *Bollettino ufficiale: Parte 1. Leggi, regolamenti e altre disposizioni generali* 61, no. 6 (1934): 163–64.

———. "Circolare n. 14. (Direzione generale per l'istruzione elementare). Settimanale 'Il Balilla.'" *Bollettino ufficiale: Parte 1. Leggi, regolamenti e altre disposizioni generali* 61, no. 14 (1934): 551.

———. "Circolare n. 49. (Gabinetto). Radiotrasmissioni scolastiche dell'anno 1934–35." *Bollettino ufficiale: Parte 1. Leggi, regolamenti e altre disposizioni generali* 61, no. 41 (1934): 2314–15.

———. "Circolare n. 59. (Gabinetto del Ministro). Compiti domestici nei giorni di vacanza." *Bollettino ufficiale: Parte 1. Leggi, regolamenti e altre disposizioni generali* 60, no. 48 (1933): 2395–96.

———. "La scuola elementare in regime fascista." *Annali dell'istruzione elementare* 9, no. 5–6 (1934): 361–77.

Esposito, Armando. *Nei lieti riposi: Corso euristico di esercizi per gli alunni delle scuole elementari nelle vacanze, classe prima.* Palermo: Remo Sandron Editore, 1927.

———. *Nei lieti riposi: Corso euristico di esercizi per gli alunni delle scuole elementari nelle vacanze, classe quarta.* Palermo: Remo Sandron Editore, 1927.

———. *Nei lieti riposi: Corso euristico di esercizi per gli alunni delle scuole elementari nelle vacanze, classe quinta.* Palermo: Remo Sandron Editore, 1927.

———. *Nei lieti riposi: Corso euristico di esercizi per gli alunni delle scuole elementari nelle vacanze, classe seconda.* Palermo: Remo Sandron Editore, 1927.

———. *Nei lieti riposi: Corso euristico di esercizi pr gli alunni delle scuole elementari nelle vacanze, classe terza.* Palermo: Remo Sandron Editore, 1927.

———. *Il nostro paese: Nozioni di diritto e di economia per la quinta classe elementare.* Palermo: Remo Sandron Editore, 1926.

Fabbri, Sileno. *L'Opera nazionale per la protezione della maternità e dell'infanzia.* Verona: A. Mondadori, 1933.

———. "La tutela morale dei minorenni." *Maternità ed infanzia* 8, no. 6 (1933): 5–8.

Fanciulli, Giuseppe. *I grandi navigatori italiani.* Rome: Libreria dello Stato, 1931.

Fanelli, Giuseppe. *Amore di terra lontana: Esplorazioni, avventure e scoperte di pionieri italiani in Africa.* Florence: Vallecchi Editore, 1931.

———. *Balilla: A sole! Lezioni e letture per le vacanze, classe prima.* Venice: Mutua Magistrale Assicurativa, 1937.

———. *Fascismo: Scuola di potenza.* Edizioni del popolo. Venice: Veneta, 1932.

———. *I fiori più belli: Scelta graduata di 40 racconti facili e piacevoli con dizionarietto delle parole spiegate ed un'appendice di prose e poesie per esercizi di reci-

tazione ad uso dei candidati agli esami di ammissione alla prima classe di scuole medie. Venice: Edizioni del Popolo, 1935.

———. *Il mio tesoretto: Lezioni esercizi e letture per i candidati agli esami di ammissione alla prima classe di scuole medie.* 6th ed. Venice: Libreria Emiliana Editrice, 1937.

Faudella, Pietro. "Nazione preparata." *I diritti della scuola* 36, no. 2 (1934): 17–18.

Fedele, Pietro. "Circolare n. 25. Giornata coloniale italiana." *Bollettino ufficiale: Parte 1. Leggi, regolamenti e altre disposizioni generali* 53, no. 14 (1926): 116–17.

———. "Decreto ministeriale 31 luglio 1926. Approvazione dei libri di testo per le scuole elementari e per i corsi integrativi d'avviamento professionale." *Bollettino ufficiale: Parte 1. Leggi, regolamenti e altre disposizioni generali* 53, no. 33 (1926): 2009–47.

———. "Decreto ministeriale 31 luglio 1926. Approvazione dei libri di testo per le scuole elementari e per i corsi integrativi d'avviamento professionale = rettifiche." *Bollettino ufficiale: Parte 1. Leggi, regolamenti e altre disposizioni generali* 53, no. 39 (1926): 2441–42.

———. "Decreto ministeriale 7 luglio 1928. Modelli, programmi, norme e prescrizioni didattiche per le scuole elementari." *Bollettino ufficiale: Parte 1. Leggi, regolamenti e altre disposizioni generali* 55, no. 34 (1928): 2811–931.

———. "Tanti scolari, tanti balilla." *Annali dell'istruzione elementare* 3, no. 1 (1928): 7–10.

Ferlini, Aldo. "Scuola nuova, metodi nuovi." *Maternità ed infanzia* 4, no. 6 (1929): 636–40.

Ferrauto, Eugenio. *Esercizi imitativi.* Turin: G. B. Paravia, 1940.

Ferretti, Lando. *Esempi e idee per l'italiano nuovo.* Rome: Libreria del Littorio, 1930.

"Le finalità scientifiche e i mezzi di indagine dell'Istituto biotipologico di Genova." *Annali dell'istruzione elementare* 5, nos. 3–4 (1930): 18–54.

Forges Davanzati, Roberto. *Il balilla Vittorio: Racconto; Il libro della quinta classe elementare.* Rome: Libreria dello Stato, 1937. First published 1930.

———. "Fascismo giovane." *I diritti della scuola* 28, no. 4 (1926): 12.

Fortunato, Giustinio. *Il mezzogiorno e lo stato italiano.* 2 vols. Florence: Vallecchi, 1973. First published 1911.

Fraddosio, Oberdan. "Il nucleo familiare in relazione alla politica razzista." *Maternità ed infanzia* 14, no. 2 (1939): 87–114.

Franchetti, Leopoldo, and Sidney Sonnino. *Inchiesta in Sicilia.* 2 vols. Florence: Vallechi, 1974. First published 1877.

Gabrielli, Giorgio. "La coscienza nazionale e la scuola." *I diritti della scuola* 27, no. 13 (1926): 193–94.

———. *Principi, fini, e metodi della scuola fascista seconda la Carta della scuola.* Florence: La "Nuova Italia" Editrice, 1940.

Gasteiner, Elio. "Un pericolo per la razza: La decadenza dei ceti superiori." *La difesa della razza* 1, no. 2 (1938): 26–28.

Gentile, Giovanni. "Circolare n. 36. Pellegrinaggio alla tomba del milite ignoto." *Bollettino ufficiale del Ministero dell'istruzione pubblica: 1. Parte ufficiale,* no. 19 (1923): 1483–84.

———. "Circolare n. 51. Esami di maturità nelle scuole elementari." *Bollettino ufficiale del Ministero dell'istruzione pubblica: 1. Parte ufficiale*, no. 26 (1923): 2101.

———. "Circolare n. 99. 1 Congresso nazionale di turismo educativo." *Bollettino ufficiale del Ministero dell'istruzione pubblica: 2. Parte non ufficiale*, no. 49 (1923): 4334.

———. *Fascismo e cultura*. Milan: Fratelli Treves Editori, 1928.

———. *Orari, programmi, e prescrizioni didattiche per le scuole elementari*. Palermo, Milan, Naples, Bologna, Genoa, Turin, Florence: Remo Sandron Editore, 1924.

———. *Origini e dottrina del fascismo*. Rome: Libreria del Littorio, 1929.

———. *Origins and Doctrine of Fascism*. Translated and edited by A. James Gregor. New Brunswick NJ: Transaction Publishers, 2002.

———. *Preliminari allo studio del fanciullo*. Rome: C. De Alberti, Editore, 1924.

———. *I problemi della scolastica e il pensiero italiano*. Bari: Giuseppe Laterza e Figli, 1923.

———. "R. D. 11 marzo 1923, n. 737, che detta norme per l'adozione dei libri di testo nelle scuole elementari e popolari pubbliche e private." *Bollettino ufficiale del Ministero dell'istruzione pubblica: 1. Parte ufficiale*, no. 18 (1923): 1404–7.

———. "R. D. 1 ottobre 1923, n. 2185—Ordinamento dei gradi scolastici e dei programmi didattici dell'istruzione elementare." *Bollettino ufficiale del Ministero dell'istruzione pubblica: 2. Parte non ufficiale*, no. 47 (1923): 4061–68.

———. *The Reform of Education*. Translated by Dino Bigongiari. New York: Harcourt, Brace, 1922.

———. "Relazioni sui libri di testo per le scuole elementari e popolari ed elenco dei libri approvati. Supplemento 2 al n. 26 del 28 giugno 1923." *Bollettino ufficiale del Ministero dell'istruzione pubblica: 1. Parte ufficiale*, no. 26 (1923): 1–46.

G. E. P. "Le nostre colonie." *Gioventù fascista*, January 15, 1935, 6.

Gini, Gino. "Scuola, eugenica, e Opera balilla." In *Il secondo convegno provinciale dei medici dell'Opera balilla*. Perugia: G. Benucci, 1933.

"La giornata nazionale della madre e del fanciullo fissata dal duce per il 24 dicembre." *Maternità ed infanzia* 8, no. 5 (1933): 1.

Giovanazzi, Giuseppe. *La scuola del balilla: Commento ai programmi per le scuole elementari*. 3rd ed. Turin: G. B. Paravia, 1940.

Gioventù italiana del littorio di Torino. *Primi elementi di cultura fascista per la Gioventù italiana del littorio*. Turin: GIL Comando federale di Torino, 1939.

Giromini, Dante. *Bontà, studio, lavoro: Libro di lettura per la quarta classe elementare maschile e femminile*. Florence: R. Bemporad e Figlio, 1927.

———. *Bontà, studio, lavoro: Libro di lettura per la terza classe elementare maschile e femminile*. Florence R. Bemporad e Figlio, 1927.

Giurlanda, Nicolò. *A voi, bimbi d'Italia! Letture di educazione patriottica e di cultura fascista*. Palermo: Francesco Lao, 1927.

———. *Il nuovo giorno per giorno: Esercizi di lingua e di aritmetica per tutto l'anno scolastico; Classi quarta e quinta*. Palermo: Francesco Lao, 1927.

Glass, David V. *Population Policies and Movements in Europe*. Oxford: Clarendon Press, 1940.

Gliozzi, Ettore. *Su' calavrisi: Libro per gli esercizi di traduzione dal dialetto nelle scuole elementari della Calabria. Parte prima—per la terza classe. Proverbi, indovinelli, novelline.* Torino: Società Editrice Internazionale, 1924.

Goad, Harold, and Michele Catalano. *Education in Italy.* Rome: Laboremus, 1939.

Gran consiglio del fascismo. "La dichiarazione del Gran consiglio." *La difesa della razza* 1, no. 6 (1938): 7.

Grassini, Luigi. "Per un'azione totalitaria: Le case dell'Opera nazionale balilla." *La rivista illustrata del Popolo d'Italia,* November 1931, 26–27.

Grassini, Luigi, and Gino Borella. *Per la patria di domani: Lo stato fascista e i giovani.* Milan: Casa Editrice "Alba," 1928.

Gregorio, Giovanni. "Generazione dell'impero." *Gioventù fascista,* February 15, 1935, 9.

Grifone, Domenico. *Primavera italica: Libro di lettura amena e ricreativa (quinta classe).* Lanciano: Giuseppe Carabba, 1932.

Guida della Mostra della Rivoluzione Fascista. Florence: Stabilimenti Grafici di A. Vallecchi, 1933.

Hegel, G. W. F. *Phenomenology of Spirit.* Translated by A. V. Miller. Oxford: Clarendon Press, 1977.

Idir. "Scuola e Opera Balilla." *I diritti della scuola* 32, no. 1 (1930): 3.

Ilvento, Arcangelo. "La salute della stirpe e la sua difesa." *Maternità ed infanzia* 7, no. 10 (1932): 926–45.

Interlandi, Telesio. "Confini razziali." *La difesa della razza* 2, no. 6 (1940): 7.

Isnenghi, Mario. "Introduzione alla ristampa anastatica." In Rinaldi, *Il libro della quinta classe: Letture,* 1–4.

Istituto centrale di statistica. *Censimento della poplazione del Regno d'Italia al 1 dicembre 1921. XIX. Relazione generale.* 19 vols. Rome: Stabilimento poligrafico per l'amministrazione dello stato, 1928.

———. *Sommario di statistiche storiche dell'Italia, 1861–1975.* Rome: Istituto centrale di statistica, 1976.

"L'istruzione degli indigeni dell'A. O." *I diritti della scuola* 38, no. 26 (1937): 407.

Lacchè, Augusto. "Bonifica umana." *I diritti della scuola* 35, no. 25 (1934): 382–83.

Lancellotti, Arturo. "L'eugenica." *I diritti della scuola* 36, no. 27 (1935): 85–86.

Landra, Guido. "Difendiamo nella maternità le qualità della razza." *La difesa della razza* 2, no. 4 (1939): 6–8.

———. "Gli studi della razza in Italia prima del razzismo." *La difesa della razza* 2, no. 8 (1940): 20–23.

Lanzalone, Giovanni. "Il dovere di essere belle?" *I diritti della scuola* 32, no. 1 (1930): 1–2.

Lastrucci, Gustavo. "La necessità della nuova Italia." *Maternità ed infanzia* 7, no. 7 (1932): 666–68.

League of Nations. *Dispute between Ethiopia and Italy. Request by the Ethiopian Government. Memorandum by the Italian Government on the Situation in Ethiopia.* League of Nations Publications 7, Political, 1–63. Geneva: League of Nations, 1935.

"Le leggi della nazione guerriera." *Gioventù fascista,* January 15, 1935, 10.

Il libro della quarta classe elementare: Religione, storia, geografia, aritmetica, scienze. Rome: Libreria dello Stato, 1931.

Il libro della quinta classe elementare: Storia e geografia. Scuole italiane all'estero. Verona: A. Mondadori, 1933.

Il libro della terza classe elementare: Letture, religione, storia, geografia, aritmetica. Rome: Libreria dello Stato, 1931.

"Il libro di stato nel prossimo anno scolastico." *Annali dell'istruzione elementare* 8, no. 3 (1933): 255–56.

"Il libro di stato per le scuole elementari." *Annali dell'istruzione elementare* 5, no. 2 (1930): 5–15.

Liburdi, Enrico. "L'insegnamento della storia del Risorgimento italiano nella scuola elementare." In *XVI congresso dell'Associazione nazionale per lo studio della storia del Risorgimento italiano.* Bologna: Società nazionale per la storia del Risorgimento italiana, 1928.

Liuzzi, Cristoforo. "Fascismo, scuola, educazione nazionale." In *Fascismo, scuola, educazione nazionale.* Rome: Avsonia, 1926.

Loffredo, Ferdinando. "Dalla politica demografica alla politica della famiglia." *Maternità ed infanzia* 13, no. 3 (1938): 163–75.

Lojacono, Luigi. "La politica sociale del Fascismo." *Gerarchia* 15, no. 1 (1935): 18–27.

Lombardo Radice, Giuseppe. *Nursery Schools in Italy: The Problem of Infant Education.* Translated by M. C. Glasgow. London: George Allen and Unwin, 1934. First published 1928.

Lombroso, Cesare. *L'antisemitismo e le scienze moderne.* Turin and Rome: L. Roux, 1894.

———. *Crime: Its Causes and Remedies.* Translated by Henry P. Horton. Boston: Little, Brown, 1912.

Lo Monaco-Aprile, Attilio. "L'assistenza igienico-sanitaria come elemento di politica demografica." *Maternità ed infanzia* 3, no. 12 (1928): 1043–54.

———. "Il programma totalitario dell'Opera nazionale per la protezione della maternità e dell'infazia." *Maternità ed infanzia* 4, no. 4 (1929): 375–87.

———. *La protezione della maternità e dell'infanzia.* Rome: Istituto nazionale fascista di cultura, 1934.

———. "La protezione igienica della razza nella fabbrica e nella scuola." *Maternità ed infanzia* 4, no. 1 (1929): 40–50.

Longo, Franco. "Romanità della Rivoluzione fascista." *Gioventù fascista,* May 10, 1930, 18.

Ludwig, Emil. *Talks with Mussolini.* Translated by Eden Paul and Cedar Paul. Boston: Little, Brown, 1933. First published 1932.

Lusena, Bianca. *La fanciullezza: Note pratiche di igiene fisica e intellettuale.* Florence: "Nuova Italia" Editrice, 1934.

LV. "L'industria cinematografica e la difesa morale del fanciullo." *Maternità ed infanzia* 4, no. 3 (1929): 276–80.

Marchetti, Italiano. *Alle soglie della vita: Letture per la formazione dell'italiano nuovo, classe quinta elementare.* 7th ed. Florence: R. Bemporad e Figlio, 1929.

————. "Anti-urbanesimo." *I diritti della scuola* 28, no. 10 (1926): 145.

————. "I Balilla e la scuola." *I diritti della scuola* 27, no. 19 (1926): 274–75.

————. "In margine al regolamento per l'Opera nazionale Balilla." *I diritti della scuola* 28, no. 16 (1927): 120–21.

Marcucci, Alessandro. "Il 'bello' come elemento di educazione." *Annali dell'istruzione elementare* 10, nos. 4–6 (1935): 313–28.

————. *La casa della scuola; dalla relazione sulle scuole per i contadini dell'Agro Romano e delle paludi pontine di Alessandro Marcucci*. Rome: Le scuole per i contadini dell'Agro Romano, 1925.

————. "Ordinamento delle scuole rurali non classificate." *Annali dell'istruzione elementare* 4, no. 6 (1929): 47–80.

————. *Il programma didattico*. Rome: Le scuole per i contadini dell'Agro Romano, 1925.

————. "Le scuole non classificate e l'opera degli enti delegati." *Annali dell'istruzione elementare* 7, nos. 4–5 (1932): 145–68.

Mario, Ezio. "La collaborazione dei giovani: Il maestro e il problema demografico." *I diritti della scuola* 35, no. 7 (1933): 99–100.

Marzolo, Renato. "La Gioventù italiana del littorio." *Annali dell'istruzione elementare* 13, nos. 3–4 (1938): 204–19.

————. "L'Opera balilla all'alba del secondo decennio." *Annali dell'istruzione elementare* 12, no. 1 (1937): 10–19.

————. "La scuola rurale dell'Opera Balilla." *Annali dell'istruzione elementare* 10, no. 1 (1935): 17–25.

Masselli, Vittorio. "Razze e razzismo." *I diritti della scuola* 40, no. 2 (1938): 5–6.

"Maternità e infanzia." *La rivista illustrata del Popolo d'Italia*, December 1934, 28–29.

Megaro, Gaudens. *Mussolini in the Making*. Boston: Houghton Mifflin, 1938.

Meletti, Vincenzo. *Civiltà fascista per la gioventù, per gl'insegnanti, per il popolo*. 3rd ed. Florence: La "Nuova Italia" Editrice, 1933.

————. *Il libro fascista del balilla*. Florence: La "Nuova Italia" Editrice, 1936.

————. *Il libro fascista della piccola italiana*. Florence: La "Nuova Italia" Editrice, 1936.

Ministero dell'educazione nazionale. *Dalla riforma Gentile alla Carta della scuola*. Rome: Vallecchi Editore, 1941.

————, ed. *Scuole rurali*. Rome: Ministero dell'educazione nazionale, 1940.

Montanari, Pietro. *I programmi per le scuole rurali dell'Opera balilla*. Rome: Opera nazionale balilla, 1936.

Morgagni, Manlio. "I boschi e l'Opera nazionale balilla." *La rivista illustrata del Popolo d'Italia*, July 1927, 5–6.

————. "Discipliniamo lo sport." *La rivista illustrata del Popolo d'Italia*, December 1928, 5–6.

————. "Le 'ferie' dei balilla e degli avanguardisti." *La rivista illustrata del Popolo d'Italia*, September 1927, 5–6.

————. "Gioventù italiana del littorio." *La rivista illustrata del Popolo d'Italia*, October 1937, 5.

———. "La leva fascista, 'certezza del futuro.'" *La rivista illustrata del Popolo d'Italia*, April 1927, 5–6.

"Mortalità infantile e mortinatalità." *Maternità ed infanzia* 2, no. 3 (1927): 17–27.

Mussolini, Benito. "Il discorso dell'Ascensione (26 maggio 1927)." In *Opera omnia di Benito Mussolini*, vol. 22, *Dall'attentato Zaniboni al discoso dell'Ascensione (5 novembre 1925 – 26 maggio 1927)*, edited by Edoardo Susmel and Duilio Susmel, 360–90. Florence: La Fenice, 1964.

———. "L'Etiopia è italiana." In *Opera omnia di Benito Mussolini*, vol. 27, *Dall'inaugurazione della Provincia di Littoria alla proclamazione dell'impero*, edited by Edoardo Susmel and Duilio Susmel, 265–66. Florence: La Fenice, 1959.

———. "Intervista al 'Matin' (13? Maggio 1936)." In *Opera omnia di Benito Mussolini*, vol. 28, *Dalla proclamazione dell'impero al viaggio in Germania (10 maggio 1936–30 settembre 1937)*, edited by Edoardo Susmel and Duilio Susmel, 1. Florence: La Fenice, 1959.

———. *My Autobiography*. Translated by Richard Washburn Child. New York: Charles Scribner's Sons, 1938. First published 1928.

———. "Popolo italiano! Corri alle armi . . ." In *Opera omnia di Benito Mussolini*, vol. 29, *Dal viaggio in Germania all'intervento dell'Italia nella Seconda guerra mondiale (1 ottobre 1937–10 giugno 1940)*, edited by Edoardo Susmel and Duilio Susmel, 403–5. Florence: La Fenice, 1959.

———. "Proclamazione dell'impero." In *Opera omnia di Benito Mussolini*, vol. 27, *Dall'inaugurazione della Provincia di Littoria alla proclamazione dell'impero*, edited by Edoardo Susmel and Duilio Susmel, 268–69. Florence: La Fenice, 1959.

———. "Lo sciopero generale di protesta contro l'impresa di Tripoli." In *Opera omnia di Benito Mussolini*, vol. 4, *Dal primo complotto contro Mussolini alla sua nomina a direttore dell'Avanti! (7 maggio 1911–30 novembre 1912)*, edited by Edoardo Susmel and Duilio Susmel. 61–73. Firenze: La Fenice, 1952.

———. *Scritti e discorsi dal 1927 al 1928*. Milan: Ulrico Hoepli Editore, 1934.

———. "Tripoli." In *Opera omnia di Benito Mussolini*, vol. 4, *Dal primo complotto contro Mussolini alla sua nomina a direttore dell'Avanti! (7 maggio 1911–30 novembre 1912)*, edited by Edoardo Susmel and Duilio Susmel, 59. Firenze: La Fenice, 1952.

Nani, Umberto. "L'impero." *Gioventù fascista*, May 31, 1936, 162–63.

Niceforo, Alfredo. *Il gergo nei normali, nei degenerati e nei criminali*. Palermo, Messina, Catania: Fratelli Bocca Editori, 1897.

———. *L'Italia barbara contemporanea*. Milan, Palermo: Remo Sandron, 1898.

Nieddu, Ubaldo. "Aspetti spirituali della difesa della razza." *La difesa della razza* 2, no. 10 (1940): 6–7.

"L'O.N.B. nei primi dieci anni di vita." *I diritti della scuola* 37, no. 18 (1936): 266–72.

Opera balilla di Milano. *Manuale per il capo squadra balilla*. Milan: Quaderni dell'Opera balilla di Milano, 1933.

Opera nazionale balilla. *Il capo squadra Balilla*. 4th ed. Rome: Presidenza centrale dell'Opera balilla, 1935.

———. *La capo squadra Piccola italiana*. Rome: Presidenza centrale dell'Opera balilla, 1934–35.

———. *La capo squadra Piccola italiana*. 2nd ed. Rome: Presidenza centrale dell'Opera balilla, 1935.

———. *Il foro Mussolini*. Milan: Valentino Bompiani Editore, 1937.

———. *Giovinezza eroica*. Rome: A. Vallecchi, 1932.

———. *Metodo per l'educazione fisica dei balilla*. Rome: Tipografia Moyne e Alessandroni, 1932.

———. *Programma di educazione fisica. Quaderno 1. femminile. Età 8–11 anni*. Rome: Opera nazionale balilla, n.d.

———. *Le vacanze dei balilla, classe prima*. Rome: Ente nazionale per forniture scolastiche, 1931.

———. *Le vacanze dei balilla, classe terza*. Rome: Ente nazionale per forniture scolastiche, 1931.

Opera nazionale per la protezione della maternità e dell'infanzia. *Origine e sviluppi dell'Opera nazionale per la protezione della maternità e dell'infanzia*. Rome: Stabilimento Tipografico Ditta Carlo Colombo, 1935.

———. "Protection of Maternity and Child Welfare in Italy." Rome: Società Editrice di Novissima, 1935.

Orano, Paolo. "Bonifica della razza." *Maternità ed infanzia* 13, no. 6 (1938): 329–39.

———. "Regime di stato." *I diritti della scuola* 36, no. 4 (1934): 57–58.

Orioli, Giuseppe. "Il partito e i bimbi." *Gioventù fascista*, July 15, 1935, 6.

Padellaro, Nazareno. "Coltivare nell'infanzia l'orgoglio di razza." *La difesa della razza* 2, no. 7 (1940): 14–17.

———. "Coscienza imperiale nella scuola." *Annali dell'istruzione elementare* 12, nos. 5–6 (1937): 279–89.

———. *Il libro della terza classe elementare: Letture*. Rome: Libreria dello Stato, 1939.

Pagliaro, Antonino. "Una fucina di 'italiani nuovi.'" *Giovanissima*, January 1931, 18–19.

———. *La scuola fascista*. Milan: A. Mondadori, 1939.

Palesa, Oscar. "La cattedra ambulante di puericultura nell'Agro Romano." *Maternità ed infanzia* 3, no. 8 (1928): 598–614.

"Il partito e il razzismo italiano." *La difesa della razza* 1, no. 1 (1938): 1–2.

Partito nazionale fascista. *Il cittadino soldato*. Rome: Libreria dello Stato, 1936.

———. "Definizione dei rapporti fra scuola e G.I.L." *Bollettino del comando generale della GIL* 14, no. 8 (1940): III–12.

———. "La Gioventù italiana del littorio nell'anno XVII." *Bollettino del comando generale della GIL* 13, no. S24 (1939): 1–12.

———. "Il Gran consiglio approva la Carta della scuola." *Bollettino del comando generale della GIL* 13, no. 9 (1939): 129–33.

———. *Manuale di educazione fascista: Autoritarismo e razzismo nei due libri fondamentali dell'educazione politica elementare e media durante il regime fascista*. Rome: Savelli, 1977.

La Patriottica, ed. *La Patriottica, Bari: Catalogo quadrimestrale anno XIII n. 4 bis (1 novembre 1935 a. XIV)*. Bari: La Patriottica, 1935.

Pende, Nicola. "Biologia delle razze ed unità spirituale mediterranea." Paper presented at Centro Universitrio Mediterraneo di Nizza, Nice, France, January 5, 1934.

———. "Maternità fisiologica e maternità spirituale." *Maternità ed infanzia* 15, no. 2 (1940): 63–66.

Perroni, Vito. *Il Duce ai Balilla: Brani e pensieri dei discorsi di Mussolini, ordinati e illustrati per i bimbi d'Italia.* Rome: Libreria del Littorio, 1930.

Petrucci, Alfredo. *L'italiano nuovo: Letture della seconda classe elementare.* Rome: Libreria dello Stato, 1938.

Petrucci, Silvio. "Il libretto del cittadino-soldato." *Gioventù fascista*, May 31, 1936, 19.

Piccoli, D. S. *The Youth Movement in Italy.* Rome: Società Editrice di "Novissima," 1936.

Pignatari, Marziola. "Le colonie climatiche della Gioventù italiana del littorio." *Maternità ed infanzia* 14, no. 6 (1939): 379–83.

———. "La Gioventù italiana del littorio." *Maternità ed infanzia* 13, no. 3 (1938): 177–87.

Pino, Carlo. "Il pensiero dei giovani: Razza e nazione." *Gerarchia* 19, no. 1 (1939): 48–50.

Pucci, Argia. *Nuovo metodo d'insegnamento per le scuole elementari: Guida didattico-pratica per insegnare divertendo.* Florence: La "Nuova Italia" Editrice, 1936.

Puccini, Mario. "Giovinezza d'Italia." In "L'O.N.B. nei primi dieci anni di vita," *I diritti della scuola* 37, no. 18 (1936): 266–72.

———. "Rieducazione del popolo." *I diritti della scuola* 29, no. 7 (1927): 97–98.

Quercia Tanzarella, Ornella. "L'attività dell'Opera nazionale Balilla." *Annali dell'istruzione elementare* 3, no. 2 (1928): 11–20.

———. *Il libro della seconda classe.* Rome: Libreria dello Stato, 1932.

———. "La mirabile opera dei Fasci femminili." *Annali dell'istruzione elementare* 4, no. 1 (1929): 5–17.

———. "L'Opera Balilla." *Annali dell'istruzione elementare* 5, no. 2 (1930): 16–34.

———. "Un prezioso documentario (lettere di bimbi e di combattenti)." *Annali dell'istruzione elementare* 12, no. 2 (1937): 89–108.

Rapisarda, Andrea. "La cultura militare nelle scuole." *Gioventù fascista*, February 15, 1935, 8.

"Rassegna della stampa." *Maternità ed infanzia* 13, nos. 4–5 (1938): 311–19.

"Razza e costume." *Gerarchia* 18, no. 9 (1938): 596.

La Redazione. "Frequenza alla scuola e criminalità giovanile." *Maternità ed infanzia* 5, no. 10 (1930): 1012–15.

———. "La funzione del gioco nell'infanzia." *Maternità ed infanzia* 5, no. 12 (1930): 1232–36.

"Responsabilità." *La rivista illustrata del Popolo d'Italia*, February 15, 1925, 1.

Resta, Raffaele. "Educazione guerriera ed eroica." *I diritti della scuola* 38, no. 27 (1937): 417–18.

Ricci, Renato. "L'Opera nazionale balilla." *Maternità ed infanzia* 3, no. 11 (1928): 934–38.

Rieppi, Antonio. "La scuola per la difesa della razza." *I diritti della scuola* 40, no. 3 (1938): 48.

Rinaldi, Luigi. *Il libro della quinta classe: Letture*. Milan: Editore Mondadori, 1985. First published 1940.

Rinaldi, Tomaso. "La bella giovinezza italica." Paper presented at La bella giovinezza italica, Salerno, May 20, 1928.

Romano, Michele, and Giuseppe Scarascia. "Relazione della Commissione ministeriale centrale per l'esame dei libri di testo da adottarsi nelle scuole elemtari e nei corsi integrativi di avviamento professionale." *Bollettino ufficiale: Parte I. Leggi, regolamenti e altre disposizioni generali* 54, no. 40 (1927): 3333–72.

Romano, Pietro. *Per una nuova coscienza pedagogica*. Turin: G. B. Paravia, 1923.

Ruberti, Guido. "L'istruzione e le associazioni giovanili alla mostra della romanità." *Annali dell'istruzione elementare* 13, no. 2 (1938): 149–63.

Salvemini, Gaetano. "Mussolini's Battle of Wheat." *Political Science Quarterly* 46, no. 1 (March 1931): 25–40.

Sammartano, Nino. *Corso di cultura fascista*. Florence: Felice Le Monnier, 1938.

Santini, Giulio. "Le opere assistenziali dei Fasci femminili." *Annali dell'istruzione elementare* 3, nos. 5–6 (1928): 5–7.

Sarfatti, Margherita G. *The Life of Benito Mussolini*. Translated by Frederic Whyte. New York: Frederick A. Stokes, 1925.

Sborgi, Giuliana. "La donna nello stato fascista." *Maternità ed infanzia* 14, nos. 4–5 (1939): 272–84.

Scaligero, Massimo. "Giornata della madre e del fanciullo." *Gioventù fascista*, December 30, 1936, 13.

Scarpa, Attilio. "Mascolinizzare." *I diritti della scuola* 29, no. 15 (1928): 217–18.

Scifoni, Domenico. "Oro e braccia di italiani all'estero." *Gioventù fascista*, January 15, 1936, 1–7.

Sergi, Giuseppe. *The Mediterranean Race: A Study of the Origin of European Peoples*. London: Charles Scribner's Sons, 1901. First published 1895.

Silus. "Commentario: La demoltiplica demografica." *Gerarchia* 17, no. 3 (1937): 164–65.

Sinisi, Donato. "La propaganda e le gare d'igiene nelle scuole elementari." *Annali dell'istruzione elementare* 6, no. 1 (1932): 38–50.

Spina, Giuseppe. *Figure del fascismo: Renato Ricci, destinato agli Avanguardisti e Balilla d'Italia*. Rome: Casa Editrice "Avanguardia," 1929.

"Lo sport dei balilla." *La rivista illustrata del Popolo d'Italia*, September 1924, 69.

Steiner, Giuseppe. *Coltura fascista: Brevi nozioni intorno all'opera e alla dottrina fascista*. Turin: G. B. Paravia, 1931.

Strata, Guglielmo. *La patria fascista: Elementi di coltura fascista e nozioni sullo stato corporativo fascista per i Balilla e le Piccole Italiane*. Milan: Casa Editrice A. Milesi e Figli, 1935.

Tagliavini, Carlo. *Esercizi di traduzione dai dialetti dell'Emilia: Bolognese. Parte seconda per la quarta classe elementare*. Turin and Florence: B. Paravia e R. Bemporad e Figlio, 1924.

Tallarico, Giuseppe. "Saggi di eugenica ambientale." *Maternità ed infanzia* 5, no. 8 (1930): 779–93.

Tarlazzi, Mario. *Ripetenti d'eccezione, classe terza, 1936–1937.* Imola: R. Direzione Didattica di Imola, 1937.

Tauro, Giacomo. "La missione del maestro." *Annali dell'istruzione elementare* 11, nos. 2–3 (1936): 92–102.

Tona, Annibale. "La funzione fondamentale del regime." *I diritti della scuola* 28, no. 36 (1927): 569.

Toscano, Carmela. *L'educazione dei Balilla e delle Piccole Italiane.* Messina: Tipografia Ditta D'Amico, 1935.

Triz, Paolo. "Tutela fascista del rurale." *La difesa della razza* 2, no. 12 (1940): 39–40.

Ugolini, Gherardo. *Sono balilla!* Brescia: Società Editrice "La Scuola," 1936.

Valagussa, Francesco. "Infanzia e colonizzazione interna." *Maternità ed infanzia* 2, no. 12 (1927): 9–17.

———. "L'Opera nazionale per la protezione della maternità e dell'infanzia e le colonie estive." *Maternità ed infanzia* 2, no. 9 (1927): 17–30.

Valori, Etre Maria. *Alle soglie della vita: Conferenze per "La giornata della madre."* Rome: Unione fra le donne cattoliche d'Italia, n.d.

Viari, Giovanni. "Relazione della commissione ministeriale per l'esame dei libri di testo da adottarsi nelle scuole elementari." *Bollettino ufficiale: Parte 1. Leggi, regolamenti e altre disposizioni generali* 53, no. 8 (1926): 616–759.

"Vicende della natività in Italia." *Maternità ed infanzia* 2, no. 2 (1927): 33–39.

Vittorio Emanuele III. "Legge 3 aprile 1926, n. 2247. Istituzione dell'Opera nazionale 'Balilla' per l'assistenza e l'educazione fisica e morale della gioventù." *Bollettino ufficiale: Parte 1. Leggi, regolamenti e altre disposizioni generali* 54, no. 3 (1927): 293–99.

———. "Legge 15 giugno 1933, n. 791. Costituzione dell'Ente Radio Rurale." *Bollettino ufficiale: Parte 1. Leggi, regolamenti e altre disposizioni generali* 60, no. 30 (1933): 1647–48.

———. "Legge 31 dicembre 1934-XIII, n. 2150. Norme sull'istruzione pre-militare." *Bollettino ufficiale: Parte 1. Leggi, regolamenti e altre disposizioni generali* 62, no. 6 (1935): 347–352.

———. "Legge 31 dicembre 1934-XIII, n. 2152. Istituzione di corsi di cultura militare nelle Scuole medie superiori del Regno." *Bollettino ufficiale: Parte 1. Leggi, regolamenti e altre disposizioni generali* 62, no. 6 (1935): 352–55.

———. "Regio decreto 18 marzo 1928, n. 780. Disposizione relative ai libri di testo per le scuole elementari." *Bollettino ufficiale: Parte 1. Leggi, regolamenti e altre disposizioni generali* 55, no. 18 (1928): 1569–71.

———. "Regio decreto—legge 9 gennaio 1927, n. 5. Modificazioni alla legge 3 aprile 1926, n. 2247, concernente la istituzione dell'Opera nazionale Balilla per l'assistenza e l'educazione fisica e morale della gioventù." *Bollettino ufficiale: Parte 1. Leggi, regolamenti e altre disposizioni generali* 54, no. 4 (1927): 344–87.

———. "Regio decreto—legge 21 agosto 1937-XV, n. 1542. Provvedimenti per l'incremento demografico della Nazione." *Bollettino ufficiale: Parte 1. Leggi, regolamenti e altre disposizioni generali* 64, no. 39 (1937): 2524–41.

————. "Regio decreto—legge 27 ottobre 1937-XV, n. 1839. Istituzione della Gioventù italiana del Littorio." *Bollettino ufficiale: Parte I. Leggi, regolamenti e altre disposizioni generali* 64, no. 47 (1937), 2903–9.

————. "Regio decreto—legge 12 maggio 1938-XVI, n. 1123. Autorizzazione alla costruzione in Roma della sede dell'Istituto per la bonifica umana e la ortogenesi della razza." *Bollettino ufficiale: Parte I. Leggi, regolamenti e altre disposizioni generali* 65, no. 33 (1938): 1915–1916.

————. "Regio decreto—legge 5 settembre 1938-XVI, n. 1390. Provvedimenti per la difesa della razza nella scuola fascista." *Bollettino ufficiale: Parte I. Leggi, regolamenti e altre disposizioni generali* 65, no. 39 (1938): 2257–58.

————. "Regio decreto—legge 23 settembre 1938-XVI, n. 1630. Istituzione di scuole elementari per fanciulli di razza ebraica." *Bollettino ufficiale: Parte I. Leggi, regolamenti e altre disposizioni generali* 65, no. 45 (1938): 2619–2620.

————. "Regio decreto—legge 15 novembre 1938-XVII, n. 1779. Integrazione e coordinamento in unico testo delle norme già emanate per la difesa della razza nella Scuola italiana." *Bollettino ufficiale: Parte I. Leggi, regolamenti e altre disposizioni generali* 65, no. 50 (1938): 2915–18.

Zanetti, Maria, and Adele Zanetti. *Il libro di lettura per la terza classe dei centri urbani*. Rome: Libreria dello Stato, 1939.

Secondary Sources

Agnew, John. "European Landscape and Identity." In Graham, *Modern Europe*, 213–31.

Ahmad, Abdussamad H. "Trading in Slaves in Bela-Shangul and Gumuz, Ethiopia: Border Enclaves in History, 1897–1938." *Journal of African History* 40, no. 3 (1999): 433–46.

Allen, Beverly, and Mary Russo, eds. *Revisioning Italy: National Identity and Global Culture*. Minneapolis: University of Minnesota Press, 1997.

Althusser, Louis. "Ideology and Ideological State Apparatuses (Notes towards an Investigation)." In *Mapping Ideology*, edited by Slavoj Žižek, 100–140. London: Verso, 1994.

Andall, Jacqueline, and Derek Duncan, eds. *National Belongings: Hybridity in Italian Colonial and Postcolonial Cultures*. Bern, Switzerland: Peter Lang, 2010.

Anderson, Benedict. *Imagined Communities: Reflections on the Origin and Spread of Nationalism*. Rev. ed. London: Verso, 1991. First published 1983.

Andreyev, Andrei, Vladimir Krivoruchenko, Victor Moshnyaga, Dolores Polyakova, and Stanislav Chibiryayev. *The Komsomol: Questions and Answers*. Translated by Alex Timofeyev. Moscow: Progress Publishers, 1980.

Apple, Rima D. *Perfect Motherhood: Science and Childrearing in America*. New Brunswick NJ: Rutgers University Press, 2006.

Ariès, Philippe. *Centuries of Childhood: A Social History of Family Life*. Translated by Robert Baldick. New York: Alfred A. Knopf, 1962.

Arlacchi, Pino. *Mafia, Peasants, and Great Estates: Society in Traditional Calabria*. Translated by Jonathan Steinberg. Cambridge: Cambridge University Press, 1983.

Arthurs, Joshua. *Excavating Modernity: The Roman Past in Fascist Italy.* Ithaca NY: Cornell University Press, 2012.

Ascenzi, Anna, and Roberto Sani, eds. *Il libro per la scuola tra idealismo e fascismo: L'opera della Commissione centrale per l'esame dei libri di testo da Giuseppe Lombardo Radice ad Alessandro Melchiori (1923–1928).* Milan: Vita e Pensiero, 2005.

Ascoli, Albert Russell, and Krystyna von Henneberg, eds. *Making and Remaking Italy: The Cultivation of National Identity around the Risorgimento.* Oxford, UK: Berg, 2001.

Bacigalupi, Marcella, and Piero Fossati. *Da plebe a popolo: L'educazione popolare nei libri di scuola dall'Unità d'Italia alla Repubblica.* Florence: La Nuova Italia, 1986.

Balibar, Etienne. "Racism and Nationalism." In *Nations and Nationalism: A Reader,* edited by Philip Spencer and Howard Wollman, 163–72. Edinburgh, UK: Edinburgh University Press, 2005.

Ballantyne, Tony. *Orientalism and Race: Aryanism in the British Empire.* New York: Palgrave Macmillan, 2006.

Barrera, Giulia. "The Construction of Racial Hierarchies in Colonial Eritrea: The Liberal and Early Fascist Period (1897–1934)." In Palumbo, *A Place in the Sun,* 81–115.

———. "Mussolini's Colonial Race Laws and State-Settler Relations in Africa Orientale Italiana (1935–1941)." *Journal of Modern Italian Studies* 8, no. 3 (2003): 425–45.

———. "Patrilineary, Race, and Identity: The Upbringing of Italo-Eritreans during Italian Colonialism." In Ben-Ghiat and Fuller, *Italian Colonialism,* 97–108.

Baudendistel, Rainer. *Between Bombs and Good Intentions: The Red Cross and the Italo-Ethiopian War, 1935–1936.* New York: Berghahn Books, 2006.

Bellassai, Sandro. "The Masculinity Mystique: Antimodernism and Virility in Fascist Italy." *Journal of Modern Italian Studies* 10, no. 3 (2005): 314–35.

Benadusi, Lorenzo. *The Enemy of the New Man: Homosexuality in Fascist Italy.* Translated by Suzanne Dingee and Jennifer Pudney. Madison: University of Wisconsin Press, 2005.

Ben-Ghiat, Ruth. *Fascist Modernities: Italy, 1922–1945.* Berkeley: University of California Press, 2001.

Ben-Ghiat, Ruth, and Mia Fuller, eds. *Italian Colonialism.* New York: Palgrave Macmillan, 2005.

Berardi, Roberto. *Un balilla negli anni trenta: Vita di provincia dalla Grande depressione alla guerra.* Cuneo: L'arciere, 1994.

Berezin, Mabel. *Making the Fascist Self: The Political Culture of Interwar Italy.* Ithaca NY: Cornell University Press, 1997.

Bernstein, Robin. *Racial Innocence: Performing American Childhood from Slavery to Civil Rights.* New York: New York University Press, 2011.

Bertone, Gianni. *I figli d'Italia si chiaman Balilla: Come e cosa insegnava la scuola fascista.* Rimini and Florence: Guaraldi Editore, 1975.

Bethencourt, Francisco. *Racisms: From the Crusades to the Twentieth Century.* Princeton NJ: Princeton University Press, 2013.

Betti, Carmen. *L'Opera nazionale Balilla e l'educazione fascista*. Perugia: La Nuova Italia, 1984.

Bevilacqua, Piero. *Breve storia dell'Italia meridionale dall'ottocento a oggi*. Rome: Donzelli Editore, 1993.

Blackburn, Daniel G. "Why Race Is Not a Biological Concept." In Lang, *Race and Racism in Theory and Practice*, 3–26.

Board of Governors of the Federal Reserve System (U.S.). *Banking and Monetary Statistics, 1914–1941*. Washington DC: Board of Governors of the Federal Reserve System, 1943.

Bock, Gisela. "Racism and Sexism in Nazi Germany: Motherhood, Compulsory Sterilization, and the State." In Bridenthal, Grossmann, and Kaplan, *When Biology Became Destiny*, 271–96.

Bock, Gisela, and Pat Thane, eds. *Maternity and Gender Policies: Women and the Rise of the European Welfare States, 1880s–1950s*. London: Routledge, 1991.

Bollati, Giulio. *L'italiano: Il carattere nazionale come storia e come invenzione*. Turin: Einaudi, 1983.

Bonetta, Gaetano. *Corpo e nazione: L'educazione ginnastica, igienica e sessuale nell'Italia liberale*. Milan: FrancoAngeli, 1990.

Borghi, Lamberto. *Educazione e autorità nell'Italia moderna*. Florence: La Nuova Italia, 1951.

Bosworth, R. J. B. *The Italian Dictatorship: Problems and Perspectives in the Interpretation of Mussolini and Fascism*. London: Arnold, 1998.

———. *Italy, the Least of the Great Powers: Italian Foreign Policy before the First World War*. Cambridge: Cambridge University Press, 1979.

———. *Mussolini*. London: Arnold, 2002.

———. *Mussolini's Italy: Life under the Fascist Dictatorship, 1915–1945*. New York: Penguin Books, 2005.

Bottoni, Riccardo, ed. *L'impero fascista: Italia ed Etiopia (1935–1941)*. Bologna: Società Editrice il Mulino, 2008.

———. "La 'marcia da Roma' a scuola. Fascisti e cattolici per la 'civiltà' e l'Impero." In Bottoni, *L'impero fascista*, 321–67.

Boxill, Bernard, ed. *Race and Racism*. Oxford: Oxford University Press, 2001.

Bridenthal, Renate, Atina Grossmann, and Marion Kaplan, eds. *When Biology Became Destiny: Women in Weimar and Nazi Germany*. New York: Monthly Review Press, 1984.

Brubaker, Rogers. *Grounds for Difference*. Cambridge MA: Harvard University Press, 2015.

Brubaker, Rogers, and Frederick Cooper. "Beyond 'Identity.'" *Theory and Society* 29, no. 1 (February 2000): 1–47.

Burgwyn, H. James. *The Legend of the Mutilated Victory: Italy, the Great War, and the Paris Peace Conference, 1915–1919*. Westport CT: Greenwood Press, 1993.

Burleigh, Michael, and Wolfgang Wippermann. *The Racial State: Germany, 1933–1945*. Cambridge: Cambridge University Press, 1991.

Caldwell, Lesley. "Reproducers of the Nation: Women and the Family in Fascist Policy." In Forgacs, *Rethinking Italian Fascism*, 110–41.

Calhoun, Craig. *Nationalism*. Minneapolis: University of Minnesota Press, 1998.

Cambi, Franco. "Gentile pedagogista ed educatore nazionale." In Coli, *Giovanni Gentile filosofo e pedagogista*, 113–30.

Camera dei deputati. *La persecuzione degli ebrei durante il fascismo: Le leggi del 1938*. Rome: Camera dei deputati, 1998.

Capristo, Annalisa. "The Exclusion of Jews from Italian Academies." In Zimmerman, *Jews in Italy under Fascist and Nazi Rule, 1922–1945*, 81–95.

Carlini, Armando, ed. *Il pensiero pedagogico dell'idealismo*. 3rd ed. Brescia: "La Scuola" Editrice, 1968.

Cassata, Francesco. *Building the New Man: Eugenics, Racial Science and Genetics in Twentieth-Century Italy*. Translated by Erin O'Loughlin. Budapest: Central European University Press, 2011.

Catalfamo, Giuseppe. *Giuseppe Lombardo-Radice*. Brescia: "La Scuola" Editrice, 1958.

Cavazza, Stefano. *Piccole patrie: Feste popolari tra regione e nazione durante il fascismo*. Bologna: Società Editrice il Mulino, 1997.

Charnitzky, Jürgen. *Die Schulpolitik des faschistischen Regimes in Italien (1922–1943)*. Tübingen, Germany: Max Niemeyer Verlag, 1994.

Choate, Mark I. *Emigrant Nation: The Making of Italy Abroad*. Cambridge MA: Harvard University Press, 2008.

Cives, Giacomo. "La scuola elementare e popolare." In Cives, *La scuola italiana dall'Unità ai nostri giorni*, 55–103.

———, ed. *La scuola italiana dall'Unità ai nostri giorni*. Florence: La Nuova Italia Editrice, 1990.

Colaci, Anna Maria. *Gli anni della Riforma: Giuseppe Lombardo-Radice e "L'educazione nazionale."* Lecce: Pensa Multimedia, 2000.

Coli, Daniela, ed. *Giovanni Gentile filosofo e pedagogista*. Florence: Casa Editrice Le Lettere, 2007.

Colombu, Mario. "Aspetti della pedagogia di Giovanni Gentile." *Nuova rivista pedagogica* 14, no. 2 (April 1964): 11–23.

Corner, Paul. *The Fascist Party and Popular Opinion in Mussolini's Italy*. Oxford: Oxford University Press, 2012.

———. "L'opinione popolare italiana di fronte alla guerra d'Etiopia." In Bottoni, *L'impero fascista*, 167–85.

Covato, Carmela. "Scuola e stereotipi di genere a Roma fra le due guerre." In Museo di Roma in Trastevere, *A passo di marcia*, 115–22.

Cunningham, Hugh. *Children and Childhood in Western Society since 1500*. Harlow, UK: Pearson Education Limited, 2005.

Cuomo, Franco. *I dieci: Chi erano gli scienziati italiani che firmarono il Manifesto della razza*. Milan: Baldini Castoldi Dalai, 2005.

Cutrufelli, Maria Rosa, Elena Doni, Elena Gianini Belotti, Laura Lilli, Dacia Maraini, Cristiana di San Marzano, Mirella Serri, and Chiara Valentini, eds. *Piccole Italiane: Un raggiro durato vent'anni*. Milan: Anabasi, 1994.

Dainotto, Roberto. "'Tramonto' and 'Risorgimento': Gentile's Dialectics and the Prophecy of Nationhood." In Ascoli and von Henneberg, *Making and Remaking Italy*, 241–56.

D'Ambrosio, Elena. *A scuola col duce: L'istruzione primaria nel ventennio fascista*. Como: Istituto di storia contemporanea di Como, 2001.

Daniels, Stephen. *Fields of Vision: Landscape Imagery and National Identity in England and the United States*. Cambridge, UK: Polity Press, 1993.

David, Henry P., Jochen Fleischhacker, and Charlotte Hohn. "Abortion and Eugenics in Nazi Germany." *Population and Development Review* 14, no. 1 (March 1988): 81–112.

De Felice, Renzo. *The Jews in Fascist Italy: A History*. Translated by Robert L. Miller. New York: Enigma Books, 2001. First published 1961.

———. *Mussolini, il rivoluzionario, 1883–1920*. Turin: Giulio Einaudi Editore, 1965.

———. *Mussolini il duce: 1. Gli anni del consenso, 1929–1936*. Turin: Giulio Einaudi Editore, 1974.

———. *Mussolini il fascista: 2. L'organizzazione dello Stato fascista, 1925–1929*. Turin: Giulio Einaudi Editore, 1968.

———. *Storia degli ebrei italiani sotto il fascismo*. 4th ed. Turin: Giulio Einaudi Editore, 1988. First published 1961.

De Fort, Ester. *La scuola elementare dall'Unità alla caduta del fascismo*. Bologna: Società editrice il Mulino, 1996.

De Francesco, Antonino. *The Antiquity of the Italian Nation: The Cultural Origins of a Political Myth in Modern Italy, 1796–1943*. Oxford: Oxford University Press, 2013.

De Grazia, Victoria. *The Culture of Consent: Mass Organization of Leisure in Fascist Italy*. Cambridge: University of Cambridge Press, 1981.

———. *How Fascism Ruled Women: Italy, 1922–1945*. Berkeley: University of California Press, 1992.

Dei, Marcello. *Colletto bianco, grembiule nero: Gli insegnanti elementari italiani tra l'inizio del secolo e il secondo dopoguerra*. Bologna: Società editrice il Mulino, 1994.

Del Boca, Angelo. *The Ethiopian War, 1935–1941*. Translated by P. D. Cummins. Chicago: University of Chicago Press, 1969.

———. *I gas di Mussolini: Il fascismo e la guerra d'Etiopia*. Rome: Editori Riuniti, 1996.

———. *Italiani, brava gente? Un mito duro a morire*. Vicenza: Neri Pozza Editore, 2005.

Dell'Era, Tommaso. "Scienza, razza e politica tra fascismo e repubblica: Il caso Pende-Terracini." In Menozzi and Mariuzzo, *A settant'anni dalle leggi razziali*, 334–43.

De Mauro, Tullio. *Storia linguistica dell'Italia unita*. 4th ed. Rome and Bari: Editori Laterza, 1974.

Deplano, Valeria, ed. *Costruire una nazione: Politiche, discorsi e rappresentazioni che hanno fatto l'Italia*. Verona: Ombre Corte, 2013.

Dickie, John. *Darkest Italy: The Nation and Stereotypes of the Mezzogiorno, 1860–1900*. New York: St. Martin's Press, 1999.

Di Luzio, Adolfo Scotto. *La scuola degli italiani*. Bologna: Società editrice il Mulino, 2007.

Di Michele, Andrea. *L'italianizzazione imperfetta: L'amministrazione pubblica dell'Alto Adige tra Italia liberale e fascismo*. Alessandria: Edizioni dell'Orso, 2003.

Di Sante, Costantino, ed. *I campi di concentramento in Italia: Dall'internamento alla deporazione (1940–1945)*. Milan: FrancoAngeli, 2001.

Di Sante, Costantino, and Salaheddin Hasan Sury. *Mostra foto-documentaria: L'occupazione italiana della Libia; Violenza e colonialismo, 1911–1943*. Maltignano, Ascoli Piceno: Arti Grafiche Picene Srl, 2009.

Dogliani, Patrizia. *Il fascismo degli italiani: Una storia sociale*. Turin: UTET Libreria, 2008.

Downs, Laura Lee. *Childhood in the Promised Land: Working-Class Movements and the Colonies de Vacances in France, 1880–1960*. Durham NC: Duke University Press, 2002.

Duggan, Christopher. *Fascist Voices: An Intimate History of Mussolini's Italy*. Oxford: Oxford University Press, 2013.

Ebner, Michael R. *Ordinary Violence in Mussolini's Italy*. Cambridge: Cambridge University Press, 2011.

Edwards, Jon R. "Slavery, the Slave Trade, and the Economic Reorganization of Ethiopia 1916–1935." *African Economic History*, no. 11 (1982): 3–14.

Eliav-Feldon, Miriam, Benjamin Isaac, and Joseph Ziegler, eds. *The Origins of Racism in the West*. Cambridge: Cambridge University Press, 2009.

Emiliani, Vittorio. *Il fabbro di Predappio: Vita di Alessandro Mussolini*. Bologna: Società editrice il Mulino, 2010.

Fabre, Giorgio. *Mussolini razzista: Dal socialismo al fascismo; La formazione di un antisemita*. Milan: Garzanti Libri, 2005.

Falasca-Zamponi, Simonetta. *Fascist Spectacle: The Aesthetics of Power in Mussolini's Italy*. Berkeley: University of California Press, 1997.

Fargion, Liliana Picciotto. *Il libro della memoria. Gli ebrei deportati dall'Italia (1943–1945)*. Milan: Ugo Mursia Editore, 1991.

Fernyhough, Timothy. "Slavery and the Slave Trade in Southern Ethiopia: A Historical Overview, ca. 1800–1935." In *New Trends in Ethiopian Studies: Papers of the 12th International Conference of Ethiopian Studies*, edited by Harold G. Marcus, 680–708. Trenton NJ: Red Sea Press, 1994.

Ferris, Kate. *Everyday Life in Fascist Venice, 1929–1940*. Houndmills, Basingstoke, UK: Palgrave Macmillan, 2012.

Fildes, Valerie, Lara Marks, and Hilary Marland, eds. *Women and Children First: International Maternal and Infant Welfare, 1870–1945*. London: Routledge, 1992.

Finaldi, Giuseppe Maria. *Italian National Identity in the Scramble for Africa: Italy's African Wars in the Era of Nation-Building, 1870–1900*. Bern, Switzerland: Peter Lang, 2009.

Finzi, Roberto. "The Damage to Italian Culture: The Fate of Jewish University Professors in Fascist Italy and After, 1938–1946." In Zimmerman, *Jews in Italy under Fascist and Nazi Rule, 1922–1945*, 96–113.

Fioravanti, Gigliola. *Partito nazionale fascista: Mostra della Rivoluzione fascista*. Rome: Ministero per i beni culturali e ambientali, Pubblicazioni degli archivi di stato, 1990.

Fiorelli, Vittoria, ed. *La nazione tra i banchi. Il contributo della scuola alla formazione degli Italiani tra otto e novecento*. Soveria Mannelli: Rubbettino Editore, 2012.

Fischer, Conan. *The Rise of the Nazis*. 2nd ed. Manchester: Manchester University Press, 2002.

Fogu, Claudio. *The Historic Imaginary: Politics of History in Fascist Italy*. Toronto: University of Toronto Press, 2003.

Forgacs, David, ed. *Rethinking Italian Fascism: Capitalism, Populism and Culture*. London: Lawrence and Wishart, 1986.

Forgacs, David, and Stephen Gundle. *Mass Culture and Italian Society from Fascism to the Cold War*. Bloomington: Indiana University Press, 2007.

Foucault, Michel. *The History of Sexuality*. Vol. 1, *An Introduction*. New York: Vintage Books, 1990. First published 1978.

Fredrickson, George M. *The Comparative Imagination: On the History of Racism, Nationalism, and Social Movements*. Berkeley: University of California Press, 1997.

———. *Racism: A Short History*. Princeton NJ: Princeton University Press, 2002.

Fujisawa, Fusatoshi. "I testi scolastici fanno il popolo." *Rassegna storica del Risorgimento* 95, no. 4 (2008): 495–527.

Fuller, Mia. "Wherever You Go, There You Are: Fascist Plans for the Colonial City of Addis Ababa and the Colonizing Suburb of EUR '42." *Journal of Contemporary History* 31, no. 2 (April 1996): 397–418.

Gabrielli, Gianluca, and Davide Montino, eds. *La scuola fascista: Istituzioni, parole d'ordine e luoghi dell'immaginario*. Verona: Ombre Corte, 2009.

Gabrielli, Gianluca, and Maria Guerrini, eds. *I "problemi" del fascismo: Può la matematica essere veicolo di ideologie? Immagini e documenti sulla matematica nel periodo fascista*. Bologna: VIII Circolo Didattico, 2000.

Galfrè, Monica. *Giuseppe Bottai: Un intellectuale fascista*. Prato: Giunti, 2000.

———. *Il regime degli editori: Libri, scuola e fascismo*. Rome and Bari: Gius. Laterza e Figli Spa, 2005.

Galli della Loggia, Ernesto. *L'identità italiana*. Bologna: Società editrice il Mulino, 1998.

Gellner, Ernest. *Nations and Nationalism*. Ithaca NY: Cornell University Press, 1983.

Genovesi, Giovanni, ed. *Il quaderno umile segno di scuola*. Milano: FrancoAngeli, 2008.

———. "Scuola e fascismo nel pistoiese. Il problema della fascistizzazione attraverso i diari di classe (1928–1929)." In Genovesi, *Il quaderno umile segno di scuola*, 10–34.

———. *Storia della scuola in Italia dal Settecento a oggi*. Rome: Editori Laterza, 1998.

Gentile, Emilio. *La Grande Italia: The Myth of the Nation in the Twentieth Century*. Translated by Suzanne Dingee and Jennifer Pudney. Madison: University of Wisconsin Press, 2009.

———. *The Sacralization of Politics in Fascist Italy*. Translated by Keith Botsford. Cambridge MA: Harvard University Press, 1996.

Gentili, Rino. *Giuseppe Bottai e la riforma fascista della scuola*. Florence: La Nuova Italia Editrice, 1979.

Gibelli, Antonio. *Il popolo bambino: Infanzia e nazione dalla Grande Guerra a Salò*. Turin: Giulio Einaudi editore, 2005.

Gibson, Mary. *Born to Crime: Cesare Lombroso and the Origins of Biological Criminology*. Westport CT: Praeger, 2002.

———. "Italy." In *Children in Historical and Comparative Perspective: An International Handbook and Research Guide*, edited by Joseph M. Hawes and N. Ray Hiner, 361–88. Westport CT: Greenwood Press, 1991.

Gillette, Aaron. *Racial Theories in Fascist Italy*. Routledge Studies in Modern European History. New York: Routledge, 2002.

Gillis, John R., ed. *Commemorations: The Politics of National Identity*. Princeton NJ: Princeton University Press, 1994.

———. *Youth and History: Tradition and Change in European Age Relations 1770–Present*. New York: Academic Press, 1974.

Giorgi, Marisa. "Forging the New Man: World War I Narratives for Children." *gender / sexuality / italy*, 2014, 1–11.

Giuliani, Gaia, and Cristina Lombardi Diop. *Bianco e nero: Storia dell'identità razziale degli italiani*. Milan: Le Monnier, 2013.

Goglia, Luigi. "Note sul razzismo coloniale fascista." *Storia contemporanea* 19, no. 6 (June 1988): 1223–66.

Goldberg, David Theo, ed. *Anatomy of Racism*. Minneapolis: University of Minnesota Press, 1990.

———. *The Racial State*. Malden MA: Blackwell, 2002.

———. *Racist Culture: Philsophy and the Politics of Meaning*. Cambridge MA: Blackwell, 1993.

Golsan, Richard J., ed. *Fascism, Aesthetics, and Culture*. Hanover NH: University Press of New England, 1992.

Gould, Julius. "The Komsomol and the Hitler Jugend." *The British Journal of Sociology* 2, no. 4 (December 1951): 305–14.

Graham, Brian, ed. *Modern Europe: Place, Culture and Identity*. London: Arnold, 1998.

Gramsci, Antonio. *Selections from the Prison Notebooks of Antonio Gramsci*. Translated by Quintin Hoare and Geoffery Nowell Smith. New York: International Publisher, 1977. First published 1971.

Grandi, Aldo. *I giovani di Mussolini: Fascisti convinti, fascisti pentiti, antifascisti*. Milano: Baldini e Castoldi, 2001.

Greenfeld, Liah. *Nationalism: Five Roads to Modernity*. Cambridge MA: Harvard University Press, 1992.

Gregor, A. James. *Giovanni Gentile: Philosopher of Fascism*. New Brunswick NJ: Transaction Publishers, 2001.

———. *Mussolini's Intellectuals: Fascist Social and Political Thought*. Princeton NJ: Princeton University Press, 2005.

Hagen, Joshua. "The Most German of Towns: Creating an Ideal Nazi Community in Rothenburg ob der Tauber." *Annals of the Association of American Geographers* 94, no. 1 (March 2004): 207–27.

Hannaford, Ivan. *Race: The History of an Idea in the West*. Baltimore MD: Johns Hopkins University Press, 1996.

Hastings, Adrian. *The Construction of Nationhood: Ethnicity, Religion and Nationalism*. Cambridge: Cambridge University Press, 1997.

Horn, David G. "Constructing the Sterile City: Pronatalism and Social Sciences in Interwar Italy." *American Ethnologist* 18, no. 3 (August 1991): 581–601.

———. "Regarding the Modern Body: Science, the Social and the Construction of Italian Identities." In *Language and Revolution: Making Modern Political Identities*, edited by Igal Halfin, 249–68. Portland OR: Frank Cass, 2002.

———. *Social Bodies: Science, Reproduction, and Italian Modernity*. Princeton NJ: Princeton University Press, 1994.

Hoyt, Edwin P. *Mussolini's Empire: The Rise and Fall of the Fascist Vision*. New York: John Wiley and Sons, 1994.

Hughes-Hallett, Lucy. *Gabriele d'Annunzio: Poet, Seducer, and Preacher of War*. New York: Knopf, 2013.

Ipsen, Carl. *Dictating Demography: The Problem of Population in Fascist Italy*. Cambridge: Cambridge University Press, 1996.

———. *Italy in the Age of Pinocchio: Children and Danger in the Liberal Era*. Houndmills, Basingstoke, UK: Palgrave Macmillan, 2006.

Irwin, Julia F. *Making the World Safe: The American Red Cross and a Nation's Humanitarian Awakening*. Oxford: Oxford University Press, 2013.

Isaac, Benjamin. *The Invention of Racism in Classical Antiquity*. Princeton NJ: Princeton University Press, 2004.

Isola, Gianni. *Abbassa la tua radio, per favore . . . Storia dell'ascolto radiofonico nell'Italia fascista*. Florence: La Nuova Italia, 1990.

Israel, Giorgio. *Il fascismo e la razza: La scienza italiana e le politiche razziali del regime*. Bologna: Società editrice il Mulino, 2010.

Israel, Giorgio, and Pietro Nastasi. *Scienza e razza nell'Italia fascista*. Bologna: Società editrice il Mulino, 1998.

Jackson, John P., Jr., and Nadine M. Weidman. *Race, Racism, and Science: Social Impact and Interaction*. Santa Barbara CA: ABC-CLIO, 2004.

Jacobson, Matthew Frye. *Whiteness of a Different Color: European Immigrants and the Alchemy of Race*. Cambridge MA: Harvard University Press, 1998.

Jonas, Raymond Anthony. *The Battle of Adwa: African Victory in the Age of Empire*. Cambridge MA: Belknap Press, 2011.

Kallis, Aristotle. *Fascist Ideology: Territory and Expansionism in Italy and Germany, 1922–1945*. Abingdon, UK: Routledge, 2000.

Karolewski, Ireneusz Pawel, and Andrzej Marcin Suszycki. *The Nation and Nationalism in Europe: An Introduction.* Edinburgh: Edinburgh University Press, 2011.

Kater, Michael H. *Hitler Youth.* Cambridge MA: Harvard University Press, 2004.

Kennedy, Paul. *The Rise and Fall of the Great Powers.* New York: Vintage Books, 1987.

Kertzer, David I. *The Pope and Mussolini: The Secret History of Pius XI and the Rise of Fascism in Europe.* New York: Random House, 2014.

——. *The Popes against the Jews: The Vatican's Role in the Rise of Modern Anti-Semitism.* New York: Alfred A. Knopf, 2001.

Kiernan, Benedict. *Blood and Soil: A World History of Genocide and Extermination from Sparta to Darfur.* New Haven CT: Yale University Press, 2007.

Klaus, Alisa. *Every Child a Lion: The Origins of Maternal and Infant Health Policy in the United States and France, 1890–1920.* Ithaca NY: Cornell University Press, 1993.

Klein, Gabriella. *La politica linguistica del fascismo.* Bologna: il Mulino, 1986.

Koon, Tracy H. *Believe, Obey, Fight: Political Socialization of Youth in Fascist Italy, 1922–1943.* Chapel Hill: University of North Carolina Press, 1985.

Koonz, Claudia. *Mothers in the Fatherland: Women, the Family, and Nazi Politics.* New York: St. Martin's Press, 1987.

Korherr, Richard. *Regresso delle nascite: Morte dei popoli; Prefazioni di Spengler e Mussolini.* Rome: Littorio, 1928.

Labanca, Nicola. "L'internamento coloniale italiana." In Di Sante, *I campi di concentramento in Italia*, 40–67.

——. "Il razzismo coloniale italiano." In *Nel nome della razza: Il razzismo nella storia d'Italia, 1870–1945*, edited by Alberto Burgio, 145–63. Bologna: Società editrice il Mulino, 1999.

Lang, Berel, ed. *Race and Racism in Theory and Practice.* Lanham MD: Rowman and Littlefield, 2000.

Laqueur, Walter Z. *Young Germany: A History of the German Youth Movement.* New York: Basic Books, 1962.

Larebo, Haile. "Empire Building and Its Limitations: Ethiopia (1935–1941)." In Ben-Ghiat and Fuller, *Italian Colonialism*, 83–94.

Ledeen, Michael A. *D'Annunzio: The First Duce.* New Brunswick NJ: Transaction Publishers, 2002. First published 1977.

Linz, Juan J. "Fascism, Breakdown of Democracy, Authoritarian and Totalitarian Regimes: Coincidences and Distinctions." Working paper. Madrid: Instituto Juan March de Estudios e Investigaciones, 2002.

Lombardo, Mario. *Terre promesse: Le colonie e l'impero dall'archivio fotografico Tci.* Milan: Touring Editore, 2004.

Lyttelton, Adrian. "Creating a National Past: History, Myth and Image in the Risorgimento." In Ascoli and von Henneberg, *Making and Remaking Italy*, 27–74.

——. *The Seizure of Power: Fascism in Italy, 1919–1929.* 3rd ed. London: Routledge, 2004. First published 1973.

Mack Smith, Denis. "The Latifundia in Modern Sicilian History." In *Proceedings of the British Academy*, 85–124. Oxford: Oxford University Press, 1965.

———. *Mussolini's Roman Empire*. New York: Viking Press, 1976.

Macmillan, Margaret. *Paris 1919: Six Months that Changed the World*. New York: Random House, 2003.

Marchesini, Daniele. "Città e campagna nello specchio dell'alfabetismo (1921–1951)." In *Fare gli italiani: Scuola e cultura nell'Italia contemporanea*, edited by Simonetta Soldani and Gabriele Turi, 2:9–40. Bologna: Società editrice il Mulino, 1993.

Marrella, Luigi. *I diari della gioventù italianissima*. Manduria: Barbieri Editore, 2006.

Mayda, Giuseppe. *Storia della deportazione dall'Italia, 1943–1945: Militari, ebrei e politici nei lager del Terzo Reich*. Turin: Bollati Boringhieri, 2002.

Mazower, Mark. *Dark Continent: Europe's Twentieth Century*. New York: Vintage Books, 1998.

McClintock, Anne. *Imperial Leather: Race, Gender and Sexuality in the Colonial Contest*. New York: Routledge, 1995.

Mechling, Jay. "Children in Scouting and Other Organizations." In *The Routledge History of Childhood in the Western World*, edited by Paula S. Fass, 419–33. London: Routledge, 2013.

Mencarelli, Antonio. *Inquadrati e fedeli: Educazione e fascismo in Umbria nei documenti scolastici*. Perugia: Università degli studi di Perugia, 1996.

Menozzi, Daniele, and Andrea Mariuzzo, eds. *A settant'anni dalle leggi razziali: Profili culturali, giuridici e istituzionali dell'antisemitismo*. Rome: Carocci editore, 2010.

Michaelis, Meir. *Mussolini and the Jews: German-Italian Relations and the Jewish Question in Italy, 1922–1945*. Oxford: Oxford University Press, 1978.

Minesso, Michela. *Giuseppe Belluzzo: Tecnico e politico nella storia d'Italia, 1876–1952*. Milano: FrancoAngeli, 2012.

Mockler, Anthony. *Haile Selassie's War*. Oxford: Oxford University Press, 1984.

Moe, Nelson. "'This Is Africa': Ruling and Representing Southern Italy, 1860–61." In Ascoli and von Henneberg, *Making and Remaking Italy*, 119–54.

———. *The View from Vesuvius: Italian Culture and the Southern Question*. Berkeley: University of California Press, 2002.

Mosse, George L. *The Crisis of German Ideology: Intellectual Origins of the Third Reich*. New York: Grosset and Dunlap, 1964.

———. *The Image of Man: The Creation of Modern Masculinity*. Oxford: Oxford University Press, 1996.

———. *Toward the Final Solution: A History of European Racism*. New York: Howard Fertig, 1978.

Museo di Roma in Trastevere, ed. *A passo di marcia: L'infanzia a Roma tra le due guerre*. Rome: Palombi Editori, 2004.

Musso, Maria Pia. *Il "gioco" e il Fascismo: Il ruolo dell'ideologia nelle esperienze del ludico durante il Ventennio*. Rome: Aracne, 2005.

Negash, Tekeste. "The Ideology of Colonialism: Educational Policy and Praxis in Eritrea." In Ben-Ghiat and Fuller, *Italian Colonialism*, 109–19.

Nicholson, Philip Yale. *Who Do We Think We Are? Race and Nation in the Modern World*. Armonk NY: M. E. Sharpe, 1999.

Ostenc, Michel. *La scuola italiana durante il fascismo*. Translated by Luciana Libutti. Rome and Bari: Editori Laterza, 1981.

Ottolenghi, Gustavo. *Gli italiani e il colonialismo: I campi di detenzione italiani in Africa*. Milan: Sugarco Edizioni, 1997.

Painter, Borden W., Jr. *Mussolini's Rome: Rebuilding the Eternal City*. New York: Palgrave Macmillan, 2005.

Palumbo, Patrizia, ed. *A Place in the Sun: Africa in Italian Colonial Culture from Post-Unification to the Present*. Berkeley: University of California Press, 2003.

Pankhurst, Richard. "Education in Ethiopia during the Italian Fascist Occupation (1936–1941)." *International Journal of African Historical Studies* 5, no. 3 (1972): 361–96.

Parati, Graziella, ed. *New Perspectives in Italian Cultural Studies*. Vol. 1, *Definitions, Theory, and Accented Practices*. Madison NJ: Fairleigh Dickinson University Press; Lanham NJ: Rowman and Littlefield, 2012.

———, ed. *New Perspectives in Italian Cultural Studies*. Vol. 2, *The Arts and History*. Madison NJ: Fairleigh Dickinson University Press; Lanham NJ: Rowman and Littlefield, 2013.

Passerini, Luisa. *Mussolini immaginario: Storia di una biografia, 1915–1939*. Bari: Gius. Laterza e Figli Spa, 1991.

Patriarca, Silvana. *Italian Vices: Nation and Character from the Risorgimento to the Republic*. Cambridge: Cambridge University Press, 2010.

Pavan, Ilaria. *Tra indifferenza e oblio: Le conseguenze economiche delle leggi razziali in Italia, 1938–1970*. Florence: Le Monnier, 2004.

Paxton, Robert O. *The Anatomy of Fascism*. New York: Vintage Books, 2005.

Payne, Stanley G. *Fascism: Comparison and Definition*. Madison: University of Wisconsin Press, 1980.

Peckham, Robert Shannan. *National Histories, Natural States: Nationalism and the Politics of Place in Greece*. London: I. B. Tauris, 2001.

Pes, Alessandro. "Becoming Imperialist: Italian Colonies in Fascist Textbooks for Primary Schools." *Journal of Modern Italian Studies* 18, no. 5 (December 2013): 599–614.

———. *La costruzione dell'impero fascista: Politiche di regime per una società coloniale*. Rome: Aracne, 2010.

Picciotto, Liliana. "The Shoah in Italy: Its History and Characteristics." In Zimmerman, *Jews in Italy under Fascist and Nazi Rule, 1922–1945*, 209–23.

Pinkus, Karen. *Bodily Regimes: Italian Advertising under Fascism*. Minneapolis: University of Minnesota Press, 1995.

———. "Shades of Black in Advertising and Popular Culture." In Allen and Russo, *Revisioning Italy*, 134–55.

Pisa, Beatrice. *Crescere per la patria: I Giovani Esploratori e le Giovani Esploratrici di Carlo Colombo (1912–1927)*. Milan: Edizioni Unicopli, 2000.

Poliakov, Léon. *The Aryan Myth: A History of Racist and Nationalist Ideas in Europe*. London: Chatto Heinemann for Sussex University Press, 1974.

Pollard, John F. *The Vatican and Italian Fascism, 1929–32: A Study in Conflict*. Cambridge: Cambridge University Press, 1985.

Ponzio, Alessio. *Shaping the New Man: Youth Training Regimes in Fascist Italy and Nazi Germany*. Madison: University of Wisconsin Press, 2015.

Pretelli, Matteo. "Education in the Italian Colonies during the Interwar Period." *Modern Italy* 16, no. 3 (August 2011): 275–93.

Preti, Luigi. *Impero fascista, africani ed ebrei*. Milan: U. Mursia, 1968.

Procacci, Giovanna. "The Disaster of Caporetto." In *Disastro! Disasters in Italy since 1860: Culture, Politics, Society*, edited by John Dickie, John Foot, and Frank M. Snowden, 141–61. New York: Palgrave, 2002.

Ragazzini, Dario. "L'amministrazione della scuola." In Cives, *La scuola italiana dall'Unità ai nostri giorni*, 263–322. Florence: La Nuova Italia Editrice, 1990.

Raspanti, Mauro. "I razzismi del fascismo." In *La menzogna della razza: Documenti e immagini del razzismo e dell'antisemitismo fascista*, 73–89. Bologna: Grafis Edizioni, 1994.

Renan, Ernest. "What Is a Nation?" In *Nation and Narration*, edited by Homi K. Bhabha, 8–22. London: Routledge, 1990.

Ricuperati, Giuseppe. *La scuola italiana e il fascismo*. Bologna: Consorzio provinciale pubblica lettura, 1977.

Rochat, Giorgio. "La guerra italiana in Etiopia: Modernità e limiti." In Bottoni, *L'impero fascista*, 105–16.

———. *Le guerre italiane in Libia e in Etiopia dal 1896 al 1939*. Udine: Gaspari editore, 2009.

———. "The Italian Air Force in the Ethiopian War (1935–1936)." In Ben-Ghiat and Fuller, *Italian Colonialism*, 37–46.

Rossi, Pietro. *Diario di un balilla, 1932–1936: Conoscere i fatti per scoprire qualche verità*. Collegno: R. Chiaramonte Editore, 2003.

Row, Thomas. "Mobilizing the Nation: Italian Propaganda in the Great War." In "Design, Culture, Identity: The Wolfsonian Collection," *Journal of Decorative and Propaganda Arts* 24 (2002): 141–69.

Rupp, Leila J. "Mother of the 'Volk': The Image of Women in Nazi Ideology." *Signs* 3, no. 2 (Winter 1977): 362–79.

Sagramola, Oreste. *Giovanni Gentile nella cultura e nella scuola italiana: Rivisitazione storico-critica del filosofo a 60 anni dalla morte*. Rome: Vacchiarelli Editore, 2004.

Said, Edward W. *Orientalism*. New York: Vintage Books, 2003. First published 1979.

Sale, Giovanni. *La Chiesa di Mussolini: I rapporti tra fascismo e religione*. Milano: Rizzoli, 2011.

Salvemini, Gaetano. *Il ministro della mala vita: Notizie e documenti sulle elezioni giolittiane nell'Italia meridionale*. Turin: Bollati Boringhieri, 2000.

Sarfatti, Michele. "Characteristics and Objectives of the Anti-Jewish Racial Laws in Fascist Italy, 1938–1943." In Zimmerman, *Jews in Italy under Fascist and Nazi Rule, 1922–1945*, 71–80.

———. *The Jews in Mussolini's Italy: From Equality to Persecution*. Translated by John and Anne C. Tedeschi. Madison: University of Wisconsin Press, 2006.

———. "La legislazione antiebraica fascista." In Di Sante, *I campi di concentramento in Italia*, 68–82.

———. *La Shoah in Italia: La persecuzione degli ebrei sotto il fascismo*. Turin: Einaudi, 2005.

Sbacchi, Alberto. *Ethiopia under Mussolini: Fascism and the Colonial Experience*. London: Zed Books, 1985.

———. "Poison Gas and Atrocities in the Italo-Ethiopian War (1935–1936)." In Ben-Ghiat and Fuller, *Italian Colonialism*, 47–56.

Schiavone, Aldo. *Italiani senza Italia: Storia e identità*. Turin: Giulio Einaudi editore, 1998.

Schnapp, Jeffrey T. *Anno X: La Mostra della Rivoluzione fascista del 1932*. Pisa and Rome: Istituti editoriali e poligrafici internazionali, 2003.

Schneider, William H. *Quality and Quantity: The Quest for Biological Regeneration in Twentieth-Century France*. Cambridge: Cambridge University Press, 1990.

Schumann, Dirk. "Childhood and Youth in Nazi Germany." In *The Routledge History of Childhood in the Western World*, edited by Paula S. Fass, 451–68. London: Routledge, 2013.

Scotto di Luzio, Adolfo. *La scuola degli italiani*. Bologna: Società editrice il Mulino, 2007.

Scroccaro, Mauro. *Dall'aquila bicipite alla croce uncinata: L'Italia e le opzioni nelle nuove provincie Trentino, Sudtirolo, Val Canale (1919–1939)*. Trento: Nuove Arti Grafiche "Artigianelli," 2000.

Setta, Sandro, ed. *Tra papa, Duce e re: Il conflitto tra chiesa cattolica e stato fascista nel diario 1930–1931 del primo ambasciatore del Regno d'Italia presso la Santa Sede*. Rome: Jouvence, 1998.

Sica, Marlo. *Storia dello scautismo in Italia*. Florence: La "Nuova Italia" Editrice, 1973.

Smith, Anthony D. *National Identity*. Reno: University of Nevada Press, 1991.

Snowden, Frank M. *The Conquest of Malaria: Italy, 1900–1962*. New Haven CT: Yale University Press, 2006.

———. *Naples in the Time of Cholera, 1884–1911*. Cambridge: Cambridge University Press, 1995.

Snowden, Frank M., Jr. *Before Color Prejudice: The Ancient View of Blacks*. Cambridge MA: Harvard University Press, 1991.

Soldani, Simonetta, and Gabriele Turi, eds. *Fare gli italiani: Scuola e cultura nell'Italia contemporanea*. Vol. 1, *La nascita dello stato nazionale*. Bologna: Società editrice il Mulino, 1993.

———, eds. *Fare gli italiani: Scuola e cultura nell'Italia contemporanea*. Vol. 2, *Una società di massa*. Bologna: Società editrice il Mulino, 1993.

Sòrgoni, Barbara. *Parole e corpi: Antropologia, discorso giuridico e politiche sessuali interrazziali nella colonia Eritrea (1890–1941)*. Naples: Liguori Editore, 1998.

Spackman, Barbara. *Fascist Virilities: Rhetoric, Ideology, and Social Fantasy in Italy*. Minneapolis: University of Minnesota Press, 1996.

Spirito, Ugo. "Giovanni Gentile." *Nuova rivista pedagogica* 14, no. 2 (April 1964): 3–10.

Stachura, Peter D. *The German Youth Movement 1900–1945*. London: Macmillan Press, 1981.

Stewart-Steinberg, Suzanne. *The Pinocchio Effect: On Making Italians, 1860–1920*. Chicago: University of Chicago Press, 2007.

Stone, Marla Susan. *The Patron State: Culture and Politics in Fascist Italy*. Princeton NJ: Princeton University Press, 1998.

Tarquini, Alessandra. "The Anti-Gentilians during the Fascist Regime." *Journal of Contemporary History* 40, no. 4 (2005): 637–62.

Terhoeven, Petra. *Oro alla patria: Donne, guerra e propaganda nella giornata della Fede fascista*. Translated by Marco Cupellaro. Bologna: Società editrice il Mulino, 2006.

Thompson, Mark. *The White War: Life and Death on the Italian Front, 1915–1919*. New York: Basic Books, 2008.

Tomasi, Tina. *Idealismo e fascismo nella scuola italiana*. Florence: La "Nuova Italia" Editrice, 1969.

Tonini, Paolo. *Gabriele D'Annunzio e l'impresa fiumana: Una collezione di libri, documenti e cimeli*. Gussago: L'Arengario Studio Bibliografico, 2005.

Traina, Augusto, and Patrizia Veroli. *Gabriele D'Annunzio: Le immagini di un mito*. Palermo: L'EPOS Società Editrice, 2003.

Trova, Assunta. *Alle origini dello scoutismo cattolico in Italia: Promessa scout ed educazione religiosa (1905–1928)*. Milan: FrancoAngeli, 1986.

Turda, Marius, and Paul J. Weindling, eds. *"Blood and Homeland": Eugenics and Racial Nationalism in Central and Southeast Europe, 1900–1940*. Budapest: Central European University Press, 2007.

Turi, Gabriele. *Giovanni Gentile: Una biografia*. Florence: Giunti Gruoppo Editoriale, 1995.

Ventura, Angelo. *Il fascismo e gli ebrei: Il razzismo antisemita nell'ideologia e nella politica del regime*. Rome: Donzelli editore, 2013.

Vigo, Giovanni. "Gli italiani alla conquista dell'alfabeto." In Soldani and Turi, *Fare gli italiani: Scuola e cultura nell'Italia contemporanea*, 1:37–66.

Visani, Alessandro. *Genere, identità e razzismo nell'Italia fascista*. Rome: Aracne Editrice, 2012.

Wade, Maurice L. "From Eighteenth- to Nineteenth-Century Racial Science: Continuity and Change." In Lang, *Race and Racism in Theory and Practice*, 27–43.

Weber, Eugen. *Varieties of Fascism: Doctrines of Revolution in the Twentieth Century*. Malabar FL: Robert E. Kriegger, 1982. First published 1964.

Weindling, Paul. *Health, Race and German Politics between National Unification and Nazism, 1870–1945*. Cambridge: Cambridge University Press, 1989.

White, Steven F. *Progressive Renaissance: America and the Reconstruction of Italian Education, 1943–1962*. New York: Garland, 1991.

Winter, Jay. *Sites of Memory, Sites of Mourning: The Great War in European Cultural History*. Cambridge: Cambridge University Press, 1995.

Wolff, Richard J. "Catholicism, Fascism and Italian Education from the Riforma Gentile to the Carta della Scuola 1922–1939." *History of Education Quarterly* 20, no. 1 (Spring 1980): 3–26.

Woodhouse, John. *Gabriele D'Annunzio: Defiant Archangel*. Oxford: Clarendon Press, 1998.

Zelizer, Viviana A. *Pricing the Priceless Child: The Changing Social Value of Children*. New York: Basic Books, 1985.

Zimmerman, Joshua D., ed. *Jews in Italy under Fascist and Nazi Rule, 1922–1945*. New York: Cambridge University Press, 2005.

Zuccotti, Susan. *The Italians and the Holocaust: Persecution, Rescue, and Survival*. Lincoln: University of Nebraska Press, 1996. First published 1987.

———. *Under His Very Windows: The Vatican and the Holocaust in Italy*. New Haven CT: Yale University Press, 2000.

CPSIA information can be obtained
at www.ICGtesting.com
Printed in the USA
LVOW12*1923170518

577561LV00006B/203/P